THE GODLESS CRUSADE

This book postulates that the rise of right-wing populism in the West and its references to religion are less driven by a resurgence of religious fervour, than by the emergence of a new secular identity politics. Based on exclusive interviews with 116 populist leaders, key policy makers and faith leaders in the USA, Germany, and France, it shows how right-wing populists use Christianity as a cultural identity marker of the 'pure people' against external 'others', while often remaining disconnected from Christian values, beliefs, and institutions. However, right-wing populists' willingness and ability to employ religion in this way critically depends on the actions of mainstream party politicians and faith leaders. They can either legitimise right-wing populists' identitarian use of religion or challenge it, thereby cultivating 'religious immunity' against populist appeals. As the populist wave breaks across the West, a new debate about the role of religion in society has begun.

TOBIAS CREMER is a Junior Research Fellow at Pembroke College, and an Associate Member of the Department of Politics and International Relations at the University of Oxford. His research focuses on the relationship between religion, secularisation and the rise of right-wing identity politics. He is the co-author of *Faith, Nationalism and the Future of Liberal Democracy* (2021).

T0371527

THE GODLESS CRUSADE

Religion, Populism and Right-Wing
Identity Politics in the West

TOBIAS CREMER

University of Oxford

Shaftesbury Road, Cambridge CB2 8EA, United Kingdom

One Liberty Plaza, 20th Floor, New York, NY 10006, USA

477 Williamstown Road, Port Melbourne, VIC 3207, Australia

314–321, 3rd Floor, Plot 3, Splendor Forum, Jasola District Centre, New Delhi – 110025, India

103 Penang Road, #05–06/07, Visioncrest Commercial, Singapore 238467

Cambridge University Press is part of Cambridge University Press & Assessment, a department of the University of Cambridge.

We share the University's mission to contribute to society through the pursuit of education, learning and research at the highest international levels of excellence.

www.cambridge.org
Information on this title: www.cambridge.org/9781009262163

DOI: 10.1017/9781009262125

A catalogue record for this publication is available from the British Library

A Cataloging-in-Publication data record for this book is available from the Library of Congress

ISBN 978-1-009-26216-3 Hardback
ISBN 978-1-009-26214-9 Paperback

Contents

Figures

vii

Acknowledgements

The initial idea for this book dates back to 9 November 2016, the day after the election of Donald Trump. At that time a graduate student at the Harvard Kennedy School I, like many of my colleagues, had to acknowledge that our old frameworks of analysis were insufficient to understand the deeper causes that had led to this development. Over the following six years I had hundreds of conversations with interviewees and colleagues in a host of different countries, but also with mentors, friends and family in an effort to better understand the sources of the remaking of our political and religious landscapes. Each one of these conversations has shaped my way of thinking and moulded the outlook of this book. Each one of my conservation partners deserves credit and gratitude for their ideas and their patience with me over the years.

Above all, however, I am indebted to the subjects of this study. This book is built on the insights of the 114 religious, political and civil society leaders who gracefully agreed to be interviewed for this research. For this and for the many gestures of kindness they showed me I am immensely grateful. Without their contributions I would have nothing to say, and although some of them may not agree with all of my conclusions, I hope that they can sense the respect, gratitude and careful attention with which I have sought to represent each one of their perspectives in this book.

Special thanks also goes to Pembroke College, Oxford, and in particular to the Religion and Frontier Challenges Programme. Justin Jones, and the whole programme team as well as the Pembroke College's fellows and staff have been an incredible support, without which this project would not have been possible. I also want to thank John Hallam and his team at Cambridge University Press for their invaluable support, their patience and their expertise during the publication and production process. This book would not have been possible without them. Since the findings and arguments presented in this book are to a large extent base on research and ideas that I developed during my PhD at the University of Cambridge I equally want to express my profound gratitude to my former PhD Supervisor Julie Smith, for her vital support and advice during my time at Cambridge as well as my two secondary advisors: Aaron Rapport, whose premature passing was a bitter loss for Cambridge and each one of his students, as well as to Andrew Preston, for his steadfast kindness, continuous encouragement and thoughtful comments. My two PhD examiners, Phil Gorski and Chris Bickerton, are also due an enormous amount of credit and gratitude for their insightful feedback, invaluable guidance and continued support.

During the fieldwork for this book, I had the privilege of spending several months as a visiting researcher at the Berlin Social Sciences Center, at the Sciences Po Paris School of International Affairs and at the Berkley Center at Georgetown University. I want to thank the amazing staff and colleagues, who made each of these stays a stimulating, enriching and enjoyable experience. In particular, I want to thank Shaun Casey, Claudia Winkler, José Casanova, Jocelyne Cesari and Ruth Gopin at Georgetown; Pascal Perrineau, Nadia Marzouki and Cristobal Kaltwasser in Paris; and Wolfgang Merkel, Ruud Koopmans and Jan-Werner Müller in Berlin. I am also deeply indebted to all the mentors, colleagues and friends from other universities and organisations who have helped, guided and encouraged me along the way; in particular David Elcott, Judd Birdsall, Brendan Simms, Stephan Hampton, Stephan Steinlein, Pete Wehner, Jim Walters, Mark Tooley, Bryan Hehir, Jonathan Rauch, Anne Snyder, David Brooks, Rob Schenck, Josh Dickson, Andrew Whitehead, Katherine Stewart, Tom Simpson, Joshua Holdern, Paul Martin, Matthias Dilling, Marietta van der Tol, Tariq Modood, Meghan O'Sullivan, Matthieu Rougé, Richard Parker, Jeff Haynes, Anne Guillard, Niall Ferguson and Jonathan Walton. Their input and support have helped to make this book what it is.

Just as important as this invaluable intellectual input was, however, the unwavering love and support of my friends and family who made the years I spent researching for this book not only a productive but also a highly enjoyable experience for me. In particular, Daniel McKay, William and Johnny Aslet, Thomas Langley, Léonie de Jonge, Alexander Abdel-Gawad, Alexander Schauer, Romain Cherrier, Benoît Chaya-Rinnert, Thomas Mumford, Charlotte Wright, Alastair Feeney, Eloise Davies, Alicia Mavor, Harry Spillane, Jenny Ward, Mathilda Gillis, Harry Begg, Gehan Gunatilleke, Shamara Wettimuny, Barnabas Asprey, Emily Qureshi-Hurst, Phillipp-Maximilian Jacob, James Walsh, Jan-Jonathan Bock, David Talbott and Christopher Martens have been great sources of companionship and wisdom.

Lastly, I want to thank my family for their constant love and encourage-ment. My grandparents, cousins, aunts, uncles and especially my siblings, Mirjam and John, have always provided me with support, advice and per-spective. My deepest gratitude goes to my mother for her unconditional love and support throughout my whole life; and of course, to Jessica, who not only spent innumerable hours of her life proofreading every word of this book several times, but also accompanied me on this often-bumpy journey with all its ups and downs, travels and months of physical separa-tion, showing nothing but love and support. Without her this book would not exist.

I dedicate this book to my late father, Wolfgang Hahn-Cremer, who once ignited my interest in politics and religion, whose own path has been an inspiration for my life, and whose presence and advice I have missed most throughout this project.

Abbreviations

AEI	American Enterprise Institute
AF	Action Française (French Action)
AfD	Alternative für Deutschland (Alternative for Germany)
BLM	Black Lives Matter
BPB	Bundeszentrale für Politische Bildung (Federal Agency for Civic Education)
CDU	Christdemokratische Union (Christian Democratic Union)
ChrAfD	Christen in der AfD (Christians in the AfD)
COMECE	Commission des Épiscopats de la Communauté Européenne (Commission of the Bishops' Conferences of the European Union)
CSU	Christsoziale Union (Christian Social Union)
CT	*Christianity Today*
DEA	Deutsche Evangelische Allianz (German Evangelical Alliance)
DNC	Democratic National Committee
EKD	Evangelische Kirche Deutschlands (Protestant Church in Germany)
ENL	Europe of Nations and Freedom
EPPC	Ethics and Public Policy Center
ERLC	Ethics and Religious Liberty Commission of the Southern Baptist Convention
EU	European Union
EVS	European Values Survey
FDP	Freie Demokratische Partei (Free Democratic Party)
FES	Friedrich-Ebert-Stiftung (Friedrich Ebert Foundation)
FN	Front National (National Front)
FPF	Fédération Protestante de France (Protestant Federation of France)

GOP	Grand Old Party (Republican Party)
GPA	Gestation Pour Autrui (Surrogacy)
GRECE	Groupement de Recherche et d'Études pour la Civilisation Européenne (Research and Study Group for European Civilisation)
GSS	General Social Survey
IFOP	Institut Français d'Opinion Publique (French Institute of Public Opinion)
IRD	Institute on Religion and Democracy
ISSEP	Institut des Sciences sociales, Économiques et Politiques (Institute for Social, Economic and Political Sciences)
KAS	Konrad-Adenauer-Stiftung (Konrad Adenauer Foundation)
LGBT	Lesbian, Gay, Bisexual and Transgender
LR	Les Républicains (The Republicans)
LREM	La République en Marche (The Republic on the Move)
MP	Member of Parliament
MRP	Mouvement Républicain Populaire (Popular Republican Movement)
NAE	National Association of Evangelicals
NCC	National Council of Churches
NSDAP	Nationalsozialistische Deutsche Arbeiterpartei (National Socialist German Workers' Party)
PCD	Parti Chrétien-Démocrate (Christian Democratic Party)
PdV	Partij voor de Vrijheid (Dutch Freedom Party)
PEGIDA	Patriotische Europäer Gegen die Islamisierung des Abendlandes (Patriotic Europeans against the Islamisation of the Occident)
PMA	Procréation médicalement assistée (Assisted reproductive technology)
PRRI	Public Religion Research Institute
PS	Parti Socialist (Socialist Party)
RN	Rassemblement National (National Rally)
RNC	Republican National Committee
SC	Sens commun (Common Sense)
SPD	Socialdemokratische Partei Deutschlands (Social Democratic Party of Germany)
UMP	Union pour un Movement Populaire (Union for a Popular Movement)

USCCB	United States Conference of Catholic Bishops
WVS	World Values Study
WWII	World War II
WZB	Wissenschaftszentrum Berlin (Berlin Social Sciences Centre)

CHAPTER I

Introduction
The New Crusaders

In front of Dresden's baroque Frauenkirche, a large crowd had gathered. Many were carrying oversized crosses, others candles. A few hundred kilometres to the west, in Paris, thousands of people rallied in veneration of a Catholic saint. Meanwhile, across the Atlantic, several thousand activists gathered in the centre of the nation's capital in support of a leader who had made headlines by posing with the Bible in front of a prominent church in the city. They too, were carrying crosses, waving 'Jesus saves' flags and blaring Christian music from their speakers.

What is remarkable about these events is that none of them occurred during religious services, processions or any other form of religious gathering. Nor were any of the speakers or leaders in question clergy or representatives of a church. Instead, each event was instigated by a right-wing populist movement: the first was a demonstration by Germany's anti-immigrant 'Patriotic Europeans against the Islamisation of the Occident' movement (PEGIDA), the second, an annual march of the French far-right Rassemblement National party (RN, formerly the Front National, FN) to honour France's national saint Joan of Arc, and the third were scenes from the pro-Trump protests, which ended in the deadly storming of the US Capitol on 6 January 2021. Donald Trump was also the leader who had held up a Bible in front of the cameras at St John's Church in Washington, DC in the summer of 2020.[1] But he did so only after instructing the National Guard to use tear gas and rubber bullets to forcibly clear a path through peaceful protesters who had gathered between the White House and the church to protest against racism and white nationalism after the killing of George Floyd, an unarmed black man, by a white police officer.[2]

---

[1] Appenzeller 2015; Albertini 2015; Green 2021.
[2] Bennett et al. 2020.

Although these events took place hundreds and thousands of miles apart, in different nations and for varied causes, they are all emblematic of two monumental developments in contemporary Western democracies. First, the astonishing rise of right-wing populism, a political movement that prioritises national identity and culture and that claims that the 'pure and homogenous' people are threatened by a neglectful, contemptuous and corrupt liberal elite on the one hand, and by the mass immigration of culturally different, external 'others' on the other.[3] Having steadily grown in importance across many Western countries for decades, right-wing populist parties and movements firmly established themselves at the centre of the public imagination in the mid-2010s through the successful Brexit Referendum in the UK, the election of Donald Trump to the US presidency and the rise of the RN and the Alternative für Deutschland (AfD, Alternative for Germany) as the largest opposition parties in France and Germany at the time.[4] What unifies right-wing populist movements across Germany, France and the United States – alongside parties like Geert Wilders' Freedom Party in the Netherlands, Giorgia Meloni's Brothers of Italy and the Austrian Freedom Party (FPÖ) – is not their positions on traditional left–right divides such as taxation, abortion, free trade, gay marriage or church–state relations (questions on which these movements, in fact, often diverge), but that they all prioritise national culture and group identities over universalist multiculturalism and individualism and that they all claim to defend the 'group rights' of the majority through their own brand of right-wing identity politics.[5]

As the episodes in Dresden, Paris and Washington DC suggest, references to religion in general, and to Christianity in particular, feature prominently in this new brand of right-wing identity politics, leading us to a second major trend in the West: the dramatic resurgence of religious rhetoric and symbolism in the political arena. From Washington to Warsaw and from Reykjavik to Rome, far-right politicians are evoking their countries' Christian identity, displaying Christian symbols, debating the role of religion in public and presenting themselves as defenders of the Christian West. This is remarkable since most of these countries were previously perceived as secularised, or at least on the path towards further secularisation.[6]

---

[3] Roy, McDonnell and Marzouki 2016; Mudde 2017; Eatwell and Goodwin 2018.
[4] Eatwell and Goodwin 2018; Kaufmann 2018; Roy, McDonnell and Marzouki 2016; Mudde 2017.
[5] Like the identity politics of the left, this identity politics of the radical right emphasises racial, ethnocultural and sexual identity as drivers of political action over ideological, confessional or class divides. However, unlike left-wing identity politics, it does not claim to defend the group rights and identities of minorities but rather those of the ethnic majority, which often includes claims to cultural hegemony within the national community. Jardina 2019.
[6] Roy, McDonnell and Marzouki 2016; Elcott et al. 2021.

This book offers a fresh perspective on the complex links between religion, populism and the rise of right-wing identity politics on both sides of the Atlantic. Based on the analysis of survey data and of exclusive in-depth interviews with 114 populist leaders, key policymakers and faith leaders in the United States, Germany and France, it draws a picture showing a rise of right-wing populism and references to religion in the West less driven by a resurgence of conservative religiosity than by the emergence of a new social cleavage centred on secular identity politics. In this context, right-wing populists are using Christian symbols and language as insignia of a culturalised 'Christianism' – a symbol of whiteness and Western civilisation directed against Islam and immigration that is interchangeable with Viking-veneer, neo-pagan symbols and even secularism, but often increasingly dissociated from Christian beliefs, values and institutions.

With these insights, this book challenges widespread assumptions and narratives about how right-wing populism and Christianity relate to one another. Various scholars, politicians and commentators have previously suggested that the rise of the populist right and their use of Christian symbols are emblematic of a resurgence of religious fervour across the West, and of religiously inspired 'cultural backlashes' against the liberalisation of cultural norms and the influx of new waves of (Muslim) immigration.[7] In the United States for instance, many observers took Trump's and his supporters' religious-laden rhetoric at face value and interpreted Trumpism as a continuation of the old religious culture wars driven by Christian nationalism and the Christian right.[8] Meanwhile, in Europe, commentators have warned of the Americanisation of European politics through the expansion of an identitarian Christian right that opposes globalisation, liberal values and immigration.[9]

Yet, as straightforward as such interpretations may seem in the light of right-wing populists parading oversized crosses, holding up Bibles and posing as the saviours of the Christian West, several indicators complicate this picture. For instance, although in the United States over 80 per cent of white Evangelicals voted for Donald Trump both in 2016 and 2020, surveys revealed that during the 2016 Republican primaries, Trump initially did best among those GOP voters who never attend church, whereas he underperformed amongst the most frequent

---

[7] Norris and Inglehart 2019.
[8] Jones 2016; Norris and Inglehart 2019; Whitehead and Perry 2020.
[9] Becher 2016; Bednarz 2018; Du Cleuziou 2018; Fourquet 2018a; Weiss 2017; Brockschmidt 2021.

churchgoers.[10] Meanwhile, although white Christian nationalist attitudes have been rightly identified as a key driver for Trump's success, the studies that did so also revealed that religious *practice* often correlates with *greater* openness towards immigrants, *more positive* attitudes towards racial minorities and *higher* levels of tolerance towards religious minorities.[11] Moreover, the public focus on Trump's faith advisory board of loyal Evangelical leaders has often overshadowed the fact that many prominent American faith leaders have loudly criticised the former president's use of religious symbols.[12] For example, after Trump's photo stunt at St John's Church, Mariann Budde, the bishop who oversees the church, decried the fact that Trump 'used our symbols and our sacred space as a way to reinforce a message that is antithetical to everything that the person of Jesus and the Gospel texts represent'.[13] The Catholic Archbishop of Washington DC called a similar visit by Trump to the shrine of Pope John Paul II 'baffling' and 'reprehensible', emphasising that the then president 'egregiously misused and manipulated [the shrine] in a fashion that violates our religious principles'.[14] Even staunch leaders of the Christian right such as Pat Robertson publicly lamented Trump's behaviours, saying 'You just don't do that, Mr President. It isn't cool!'[15]

In Europe, the situation is more ambiguous still. Despite the ostentatious use of religious symbols by Western European right-wing populist movements, their supporters are often shown to be disproportionately irreligious. Surveys among the cross-carrying PEGIDA demonstrators in Dresden revealed, for example, that three-quarters of participants self-identified as atheist or irreligious (compared with about a third of Germany's overall population at the time).[16] Scholars have found that in this they were representative of far-right supporters in many Western European countries, where church attendance turns out to be a powerful empirical predictor for *not* voting for a right-wing populist party, causing some to speak of a 'religious vaccination effect' or 'religious immunity' against the populist right.[17] Meanwhile, European church leaders and institutions, including

[10] Carney 2019; Pew 2016b; Smith and Martinez 2016.
[11] Whitehead and Perry 2020, 143.
[12] Alexander 2016; Crouch 2016; Galli 2019; Moore 2015.
[13] Chappell 2020.
[14] Gregory 2020.
[15] Teague 2020.
[16] Appenzeller 2015.
[17] Arzheimer 2009; Dargent 2016; Immerzeel, Jaspers and Lubbers 2013; Lubbers and Scheepers 2001; Perrineau 2014; Siegers and Jedinger 2021; Cremer 2021a.

Pope Francis, most national Catholic Bishop Conferences and the leadership of most of Europe's Protestant churches, have been united in their public condemnation of right-wing populist movements, with some going as far as the former president of the Lutheran World Federation Bishop, Christian Krause, who called their use of religious symbols 'perverted'.[18]

Such paradoxical expressions of the relationship between right-wing populism, identity politics and Christianity in Western societies raise fundamental questions: What are the social and demographic roots behind the rise of right populist movements and their new brand of identity politics in Western democracies? How and why does religion feature in right-wing populist rhetoric and strategies? How do Christian communities react to national populists' religious-laden rhetoric? And what is the role of mainstream parties and religious leaders in shaping the relationship between religion and right-wing populism?

By addressing these questions, this book sets out to unravel the origins behind a social and political phenomenon that is reshaping the very fabric of Western democracies. It does so based on an in-depth analysis of the contemporary relationship between right-wing populism, religion and identity politics in three major Western democracies: Germany, France and the United States. All three countries have experienced the rise of powerful national populist movements throughout the 2010s, and a resurgence of religious references by these movements. Yet, the way in which the relationship between religion and national populism has played out in each country has differed profoundly. Whereas in America, white Christians – Evangelicals in particular, but also Catholics and Mainline Protestants – have emerged as some of Donald Trump's most loyal supporters,[19] their French and German brethren have proven themselves comparatively 'immune' to right-wing populists' appeals, often voting for these parties at much lower rates than their secular compatriots.[20] Similarly, church leaders and prominent Christian politicians have reacted very differently to the far right's co-optation of religious symbols, ranging from consistent and outspoken condemnation of the far right in Germany, to quieter opposition in France and to an amalgamation of more muted criticism, ambiguous silence and outright support in the United States.

---

[18] Die Welt 2015.
[19] Schwadel and Smith 2019; Smith and Martinez 2016.
[20] Dargent 2016; Immerzeel, Jaspers and Lubbers 2013; Siegers and Jedinger 2021; Cremer 2021a; Montgomery and Winter 2015.

To understand these diverging dynamics between right-wing populist movements and Christian communities' reactions, this volume explores how the historical relationship between church and state has shaped the role of religion in politics in each country. It investigates the socio-demographic origins behind the rise of national populist politics and puts their references to Christianity under greater scrutiny. It examines the responses of Christian voters, mainstream politicians and church leaders in each country and addresses the question of what role faith can still play in the politics of increasingly multicultural and fragmented democracies. This book thereby distinguishes between 'demand-side variables', such as socio-demographic, cultural and political shifts that determine the demand for national populist politics among the electorate, and political and religious 'supply-side factors', such as the structure of church–state relations, a country's voting system or the behaviour of political and religious elites and institutions, which enable national populists to harness this demand. To study these phenomena, it relies on new survey data, speeches, party manifestos and other documents. But most importantly it draws on the insights from the 114 exclusive in-depth elite interviews with top-level leaders of national populist movements, mainstream parties, civil society and the institutional churches in Germany, France and the United States.[21]

Based on these conversations, this book finds that rather than embracing Christianity as a faith, right-wing populists in the United States, Germany and France are politicising Christianity as a secularised identity marker to mobilise voters in the context of a new social cleavage, centred around the question of identity and around a new wave of right-wing identity politics. In this context, national populists often paint themselves as staunch defenders of the Christian West, while remaining distanced from Christian beliefs, values and institutions. In fact, national populist movements seem to have capitalised on the accelerating secularisation of the white working class, by openly combining ethnocultural references to Christian heritage and symbols (rather than Christian beliefs) with secular policy stances on issues like immigration, church–state relations and religious freedom. These developments suggest a significant political shift in Western societies, where the old faith-driven religious right is gradually being replaced by a new identitarian and populist right that is much more secular in nature and may – through its culturalised uses of

---

[21] For a complete list of individuals interviewed for this book see Appendix A.

Christian symbols – be not just a symptom but also a harbinger of secularisation. This is not to say that Christian conservatives and Christian nationalists have disappeared from the scene, nor that religious fundamentalists may not still pose formidable threats to liberal democracy. In fact, this book shows that there is nothing in principle to prevent the old religious right from entering an alliance with the new secular identitarian right. However, what this book has found is a transformative shift in the balance of power in Western right-wing movements. Rather than being dominated by religiously defined culture wars, the new right is increasingly driven by a more secular but no less radical identitarian struggle for Western Civilisation: a godless crusade in which Christianity is turned into a secularised 'Christianism', an ethno-cultural identifier of the nation and a symbol of whiteness that is increasingly independent of Christian practice, beliefs and the institution of the church.

However, this book also shows that the battle over Christianity's role in liberal democracy is far from over. It reveals that right-wing populists' ability to successfully instrumentalise religion critically depends on factors on the political and religious supply-side, such as the institutional settlement of church–state relations, the electoral and party system, and perhaps most importantly, the actions of mainstream political party politicians and faith leaders. Christian leaders play a particularly critical role by either legitimising right-wing populist appeals to Christian identity or by erecting powerful social taboos against these movements among Christian voters. For instance, in countries such as Germany or France, where faith leaders have vehemently spoken out against right-wing populism, we can observe a powerful religious 'vaccination effect' among Christians, which prevents many of them from voting for right-wing populist parties. By contrast, in countries such as the United States, where faith leaders have largely remained silent, Christian communities appear more amenable to entering what some interviewees called 'Faustian bargains' with the post-religious populist right.

All this suggests that as the populist crusade for identity is gathering strength in the West, a new debate about the future role of religion in society has just begun, not only amongst scholars and practitioners but across political parties, churches and the public writ large. One key takeaway of this book is that far from being helpless bystanders, faith leaders and policymakers have a tremendous influence in this context. Their actions will shape whether, in our increasingly diverse and polarised democracies, religion will become a source of unity or division, of tolerance or exclusion, of faith or identity politics.

1.1   Overview

This book is divided into four parts. Part I lays out the book's intellectual, theoretical and methodological foundations as well as its overall argument. Specifically, Chapter 2 outlines in more detail the working definitions of contested concepts such as 'right-wing populism' and 'religion' used in this study and frames them within the academic literature. It briefly explains the book's demand- and supply-side framework, the sources this research is based on, the methods employed to analyse these sources, and the rationale of selecting Germany, France and the United States as the case studies for this book. Chapter 2 contains essential details about the mechanics underlying this research and is primarily written with a scholarly audience in mind.

Those who are satisfied with the briefer descriptions given above may skip straight to Chapter 3, which presents the book's overall argument in the context of the existing literature. Specifically, Chapter 3 lays out four main arguments in response to the research questions formulated above. First, that far from being the result of reignited religious culture wars, the dramatic surge of right-wing populism and white identity politics in Western democracies has been driven by the emergence of a new identity cleavage between cosmopolitans and communitarians that is rooted in the rapid advance of secularisation and the erosion of traditional sources of belonging and identity on the demand side. Second, that to capitalise on this new divide, right-wing populists employ references to Christianity in the context of a new brand of white identity politics as a secularised cultural identity marker, but often remain distanced from Christian values, beliefs and institutions. Third, that this strategy tends to be most successful amongst irreligious voters or non-practising 'cultural Christians', whereas practising Christians often remain comparatively 'immune' to right-wing populist appeals. And fourth, that the existence and strength of this 'religious vaccination effect' against the populist right critically depends on two supply-side factors: one, on the availability of a 'Christian alternative' in the political landscape and two, on churches' and faith leaders' willingness and ability to publicly denounce the populist right and create a social taboo around them. These four claims constitute the theoretical cornerstones of this book's overall argument and will serve as an underlying structure for each empirical case study.

After establishing in Part I a theoretical framework showing how right-wing populism, religion and identity politics interact in principle, Parts II–IV show empirically how these factors have shaped the landscapes of three different Western societies. Part II explores how religion and national

populism interact in Germany, focusing on the dynamics between the AfD
and Germany's churches. The German case study captures the paradoxical
expression of this relationship particularly well. While the AfD has been
vocal in positioning itself as the defender of Germany's 'Judeo-Christian
heritage',[22] the churches' reactions have been strongly negative, with many
church leaders openly declaring that the AfD's platform is in direct 'contradiction to the Christian faith'.[23] Spanning Chapters 4–7, Part II begins
by exploring the historical background of Germany's church-friendly
institutional settlement of 'benevolent neutrality' and its implications for
modern-day politics, before examining the re-politicisation of religion and
the rise and transformation of the AfD in the context of a new identity
cleavage. Following a close analysis of the AfD's references to religion, we
find that their identitarian references to Christianity are not representative
of an embrace of Christian beliefs, values and institutions but rather an
attempt by a disproportionately secular party to employ Christianity as a
secularised national identity marker against Islam. Part II concludes with
an examination of Christian communities' reactions to the AfD's religious
rhetoric, and the ways in which these reactions have been shaped by
mainstream parties and religious leaders. Overall, the German case study
emerges as a key example of how the existence of a credible Christian
electoral alternative in the form of the CDU/CSU, as well as a powerful
social taboo erected by a broad coalition of faith leaders can undermine
national populists' willingness and ability to co-opt religion as an ethno-
national identity marker.

Part III (Chapters 8–11) of this book moves on to the case of France.
As the nation with the oldest major right-wing populist party in Europe,
a well-established electoral constituency of political Catholicism, and one
of the strictest models of church–state separation, the French case study
provides a unique opportunity to trace the historical development of the
relationship between religion and right-wing populism. To study these
phenomena, Part III begins by showing how the historical antagonism
between *la France Catholique* and *la Republique laïque* still shapes the relationship between politics and religion today, and how the hard-fought
compromise between the two has recently been challenged by a return
of political tensions surrounding religion and *laïcité*. Next, it investigates how this re-politicisation of religion may be less linked to a revival
of Catholicism than to the emergence of a new identity cleavage, which

---

[22] AfD 2017.
[23] Bedford Strohm 2018.

is rooted in Catholicism's demise, but which has led to a new bipolarity between a liberal-cosmopolitan camp around Emmanuel Macron and populist-communitarian camp around Marine Le Pen and – more recently – Éric Zemmour. The section then examines the French far right's approach to religion and *laïcité* in particular, exploring how these two political wedge-issues and cultural identity markers can be used against Islam. Part III concludes by exploring how the resurgence of a new conservative (though initially not necessarily populist and identitarian) Catholic grassroots movement around the *Manif-pour-Tous*, and the restructuring of the French political landscape have changed the ways in which French Catholics and church officials approach the far right's ambiguous co-optation attempts of both Catholicism and *laïcité*. Overall, Part III posits that a recent narrowing of the historical 'vaccination effect' of religiosity against the RN and Zemmour in France might be less a result of the latter's embracing religion or Catholics moving towards national populist attitudes, than of a perceived lack of political alternatives and a gradual retreat of the French episcopate from political debates.

The final part of this book (Chapters 12–15) explores the relationship between right-wing populism and religion in the USA. The unexpected election of Donald Trump to the most powerful office in the world in 2016 was one of the most momentous impacts of the right-wing populist tide to date, and the fact that his election occurred in the most religious country in the West makes the USA a highly relevant case study for this book. Yet, while many commentators seek to explain the Trump phenomenon as a continuation of America's religiously laden culture wars and a victory of the religious right, Part IV explores a different possibility. It begins by discussing the historical background of the First Amendment, American civil religion, and America's culture wars in the twentieth century. It then moves on to explore how the emergence of a new identity cleavage, itself partly linked to the rapid decline of American Christianity in recent years, has shifted America's right away from the old faith-driven culture wars, towards a new more secular and race-driven white identity politics. Through a detailed exploration of this new identity cleavage, it becomes clear that Trump's national populist approach to religion has not only been at odds with America's civil religious tradition but also represents a marked radicalisation and secularisation of America's tradition of white Christian nationalism. Having established this fact, Part IV concludes by discussing the varied reactions of America's Christian communities, noting the apparent absence (or even the reversal) of the 'religious vaccination effect', as well as the choice of many Christian leaders to remain silent vis-à-vis their criticism of Trump. Overall, Part IV explores the possibility that rather than being a victory for the Christian right, Trump's ascent to power may be indicative of the former's crisis and decline, and of the rise of a post-religious right in its stead. However, it also posits that due to structural factors undermining American faith leaders' willingness and ability to challenge national populism, many American Christians have chosen to strike what some observers have called a 'Faustian bargain' and support right-wing populist politics at much higher rates than their European brethren. The subsequent embracing of Trump's ethno-populist agenda by many American evangelicals may be more indicative of the politicisation of the evangelical label, rather than of a return of religious fervour within US politics.

Having taken the reader through the rapidly evolving political and religious landscape of three major Western democracies, in its conclusion this book returns to the fundamental challenges that right-wing populists' religiously flavoured identity politics poses for the social, political and religious fabric of our societies. Namely, that instead of being just the latest iteration of a reactionary religious opposition to the advent of a progressive and secular brave new world, these developments point to an uncomfortable but unavoidable question of post-religious politics itself: what can still unite us in a society in which traditional sources of social connectedness and integration such as class, shared understandings of history, national culture and religion have lost most of their appeal and in which large swathes of the population are left in a profound crisis of identity? Who are 'we'? Who is the 'other'? As these questions drive a fundamental split within Western societies, between cosmopolitans and communitarians, right-wing populists have recognised a gap of representation on the communitarian end of the divide and offered their own remedy: an ethno-cultural identity politics based on nationality and sweeping ideas of Western civilisation. In this struggle for identity Christian symbols play a major role, but not as an insignia of the living, vibrant, universal and increasingly diverse faith in Jesus Christ that is practiced in most Christian churches around the world today. Instead, in this crusade without God, Christianity has become a secularised idea of 'Christendom': a cultural identity marker and symbol of whiteness. Many Christians may be dismayed over such a use of their faith by right-wing populist leaders. Some may even be tempted to join them. However, this book's findings show that faith leaders and mainstream party politicians still have a tremendous influence over right-wing populists' ability to politicise Christianity. While the godless crusade may be well under way, its destination and success are yet to be determined.

Foundations

When dealing with 'contested concepts' such as 'religion', 'right-wing populism' or 'identity politics', one enters what political scientist Cas Mudde has referred to as a 'War of Words'.[1] Generations of scholars have built doctrinal fortresses, drawn methodological trenches, engaged in battle-like conceptual debates and led campaigns for theoretical hegemony. Establishing firm intellectual foundations on which to build empirical research is therefore all the more essential when venturing into this field of study. Part I seeks to do precisely that. Chapter 2 begins by clearly outlining accessible working definitions of contested concepts such as 'right-wing populism' or 'religion' and situating them in the academic literature. Chapter 2 also provides an overview over the book's theoretical framework of demand- and supply sides, its sources, the methods used to analyse them, as well as why Germany, France and the United States have been chosen as empirical case studies for this volume. As Chapter 2 is primarily written with a scholarly audience in mind, those who are satisfied with the briefer descriptions provided in the Introduction may also skip straight to Chapter 3, which lays out the book's main four arguments about how and why right-wing populists reference religion in their rhetoric, how Christian communities across the West have responded to this development, and what this means for the future of faith and politics in liberal democracy.

---

[1] Mudde 1996.

CHAPTER 2

Definitions, Methods, Cases and Sources

2.1 Definitions: 'Right-Wing Populism' and 'Religion'

This book does not claim to hold the 'Holy Grail' of universally applicable definitions and concepts.[1] Rather it seeks to establish epistemological 'truces' in the 'War of Words', by providing working definitions of 'right-wing populism' and 'religion' that clarify and demarcate the aspects of these concepts most relevant to the questions this book seeks to address.

Populism, in particular, has become one of the most hotly debated topics in politics, the media and academia. Cas Mudde noted, for instance, already in 2014 that 'a search for the term returned over five million hits on Google'.[2] This number has since surged to over 152 million by the beginning of 2022. A similar surge of interest is observable when looking at the number of scholarly contributions on the topic, which cover subjects ranging from historical and country-specific studies,[3] through the role of gender,[4] economics,[5] immigration,[6] the media[7] or individual leaders,[8] to name but a few examples. This increased interest in populism is not surprising given the growing influence of populist politics on both sides of the Atlantic since the beginning of the twenty-first century. However, given the high level of geographical, historical, cultural and political diversity among populist movements (as well as among those studying them), some scholars have lamented that, as a result, 'both the concept and the word have lost most of their heuristic utility'.[9] This is not

---

[1] Taggart 2006, 66.
[2] Mudde 2015, 431.
[3] Abromeit et al. 2015; Berezin 2017; Finchelstein 2017; Shields 2004.
[4] Kampwirth 2010; Mudde and Kaltwasser 2015; Spierings, Lubbers and Zaslove 2017.
[5] Acemoglu, Georgy and Konstantin 2013; Judis 2016; Piketty 2015; Rodrik 2018.
[6] Kaufmann 2018; Art 2011; Eatwell and Goodwin 2018.
[7] Bale, van Kessel and Taggart 2011; de Jonge 2019; Moffitt and Tormey 2014.
[8] McDonnell 2016; Mudde 2014a; Torre 2013.
[9] Mény and Surel 2002, 2.

helped by the tendency in politics and the media to use 'populism' as a *Kampfbegriff*, where it is largely used synonymously with opportunism or demagogy and 'reserved for the political "enemy"'.[10]

Nevertheless, there is an emerging consensus among scholars of populism that at the core of these movements is the juxtaposition of 'the people' and 'the elite'.[11] One of the most-cited definitions of populism, that of Cas Mudde, views populism, for instance, as 'a thin-centred ideology[12] that considers society to be ultimately separated into two homogeneous and antagonistic camps, "the pure people" versus "the corrupt elite", and argues that politics should be an expression of the *volonté générale* (general will) of the people'.[13] This definition encapsulates the ideological core of right-wing populism around the concepts of 'the pure people', 'the corrupt elite' and 'the general will' and thus allows us to systematically relate populism to other ideologies and systems of beliefs such as liberalism, nationalism and religion.[14] Moreover, this definition identifies populism as a 'pathological normalcy' in Western democracies, meaning that while populism might be illiberal it is not necessarily anti-democratic.[15] Rather it is a radicalisation of mainstream democratic values, embracing a more direct, identitarian and radical concept of democracy while rejecting liberal tenets such as individualism, minority rights and checks-and-balances, because they are seen as illegitimate constraints on the 'true' democratic rule of the people.[16]

In the case of 'right-wing' or 'national' populism, this binary relationship of 'the pure people' and 'the corrupted elite' is further expanded by a third component: the external other. Indeed, what distinguishes national or right-wing populism from other populisms is its tendency towards 'nativism'; that is, the view that 'states should be inhabited exclusively by members of the native group ("the nation") and that non-native

---

[10] Bale, van Kessel and Taggart 2011, 127; Albertazzi and McDonnell 2008; Mudde 2004; Stanley 2016.
[11] Torre 2018; Heinisch 2017; Kaltwasser et al. 2017a.
[12] Compared to 'thick ideologies' such as liberalism or communism, a 'thin ideology' lacks a common genealogy, key texts or philosophers, and usually appears in combination with a 'host ideology' (Aslanidis 2015; Freeden 2003; Moffitt and Tormey 2014; Pauwels 2014; Stanley 2008; Taggart 2000).
[13] Mudde 2004, 543.
[14] Hawkins et al. 2018; Mudde 2017.
[15] Mudde 2010.
[16] Populists' identitarian ideal of democracy is closely related to the conception put forward by German legal scholar Carl Schmitt, who became (in)famous as the crown jurist of the Third Reich for developing Rousseau's theory of the General Will into a conception of identitarian democracy, in which the General Will of the (homogeneous) people is directly discernible, absolute in its authority and can readily be incarnated by a single person or party. See Espejo 2015; Mudde and Kaltwasser 2017; Schmitt 1929.

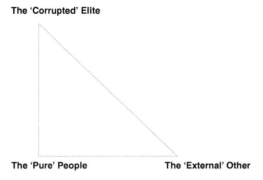

Figure 2.1   The triangular national populist worldview
Note: all figures are the author's own work unless otherwise stated.

elements are fundamentally threatening the homogenous nation-state'.[17] As a result, in national populism the 'pure and homogenous people' (the 'us') are often defined, *ex negativo*, in a triangular relationship with two 'evil other(s)': the 'internal other', that is, 'the corrupt liberal elite', and the 'external other', which is defined through their racial, ethnic, national and increasingly religious and civilisational 'otherness' (see Figure 2.1). This volume, therefore, adopts Albertazzi and McDonnell's triangular definition of right-wing populism as 'a thin-centred ideology, which pits a virtuous and homogenous people against a set of elites and dangerous "others" who are together depicted as depriving (or attempting to deprive) the sovereign people of their rights and values, prosperity, identity and voice'.[18]

As a result of this focus on the identity of the pure and homogenous 'us' versus the internal and external 'others', right-wing populist movements often define themselves less with regards to traditional left-right divides about security, economics or personal morality than in relation to a new social cleavage centred around the question of identity; of who may belong to the 'us' and who may not. This 'identity cleavage', whose social and political origins this book will explore in depth, pits two visions of how to define the 'I', the 'us' and the 'other' against one another. On the one end of the divide stands a globalist vision of cosmopolitanism, multiculturalism and diversity that is perceived to embrace group identities only for minorities, while transcending traditional collective ties and identities for majority populations and replacing them with individualist

---

[17] Mudde 2007, 19; Betz 2018a; Casanova 2012a.
[18] Albertazzi and McDonnell 2015, 5.

forms of identity.[19] Opposed, on the communitarian end of the divide,
stand those who favour clearly defined collective identities based on inherited group identity markers such as ethnicity, culture, history, institutions
and language.[20] In recent years, immigration, race relations and Islam have
emerged as the core issues in this divide and it is by prioritising national
culture, majority group identities and opposition to immigration over universalist multiculturalism and individualism that national populists seek
to politicise and capitalise on this new divide. Specifically, this book will
show how national populists seek to appeal to the communitarian end of
the new identity divide through their own brand of right-wing or white
identity politics.[21] The key common denominator which makes the AfD
in Germany, the RN in France and Trumpism in the USA identifiable
as right-wing populist movements is in fact less their views on national
security, abortion, economics or the welfare state, but their prioritising of
national culture and group identities over universalism, multiculturalism
and individualism. This centrality of the identitarian question is expressed
in the name of the European parliamentary group that since 2019 unifies
RN and AfD MEPs with those of the Italian Lega or the Austrian FPÖ on
the European level: 'Identity and Democracy'.[22]

  The second key concept this book grapples with is religion. As the episodes
described at the outset of Chapter 1 suggest, references to religious identity
play a key part in the rhetoric of right-wing populist movements in the West
and in the three case studies under investigation in particular. In Germany
the PEGIDA demonstrators' parading of crosses through Dresden were mirrored by AfD politicians stylising themselves as the defenders of Germany's
Christian heritage and as the 'only Christian party left in Germany'.[23]
Meanwhile in France, RN leaders claimed to defend France's status as the
'first-born daughter of the church' and pushed for the public display of
nativity scenes in city halls while Éric Zemmour declared that he wanted to
'reaffirm what I call the cultural pre-eminence of Catholicism in France'.[24]
And even in the USA, where after decades of religious culture wars, public
debates about America's 'Christian identity' had been much more common-
place, scholars have observed that the politicisation of Christian symbols has
achieved a new quality in recent years, as oversized memorials of the Ten

---

[19] Fukuyama 2018; De Wilde et al. 2019.
[20] Kaufmann 2018; De Wilde et al. 2019; Eatwell and Goodwin 2018; Sobolewska and Ford 2020.
[21] Eatwell and Goodwin 2018; Kaufmann 2018; Jardina 2019.
[22] Identity & Democracy Parliamentary Group 2019.
[23] Focus 2017.
[24] Roy 2019; Zemmour 2016.

Commandments were erected in front of several state capitols and demonstrators displayed giant crosses and 'Jesus saves' flags during the violent storming of the US capitol by pro-Trump supporters in January 2021.[25]

To systematically study the dynamics behind the connections between religion and right-wing populism it is necessary to define 'religion' and 'Christianity' in concrete and measurable terms. Both are, however, contested concepts par excellence.[26] So to avoid going down century-old rabbit holes of theological, philosophical and historical debates about the essence of Christianity and its role in politics, this book builds on Jonathan Z. Smith's famous insight that 'religion is not a native category' but always 'a term created by scholars for their intellectual purposes and therefore is theirs to define'.[27] In this book religion and Christianity are therefore conceptualised in two dimensions that are of particular relevance to this study. On the one hand, this book adopts a minimalistic substantive definition of Christianity as a universal monotheistic religion based on the teachings and life of Jesus Christ. This minimalist definition is then expanded in each case study based on the official doctrine of each country's main religious institutions, to compare 'Christian doctrine' with right-wing populist policies in specific national settings. In this context, this book will mainly speak of Christian 'doctrine', 'values' or 'beliefs'. On the other hand, the term 'religion' will be primarily reserved for Christianity's empirical expression in society in terms of political behaviour, social orders, group identities and the institution of the church. These expressions can be concretely measured through the impact of factors like religious affiliation, church attendance, private religious practice and self-stated religiosity on voting behaviour or political attitudes, as well as through the study of religious elite actors and institutions and their involvement in politics.[28]

To identify the key religious supply-side actors for each case study (i.e., church authorities and Christian faith leaders), it is necessary to determine which churches, denominations or institutions most authoritatively 'speak for Christianity' in each country. In Germany and France, this is comparatively

---

[25] E. Green 2021; Whitehead and Perry 2020.

[26] Over the last two centuries it has for instance been defined as 'the feeling of absolute dependence on God' (Schleiermacher), as 'the Divine Spirit becoming conscious of Himself through the finite spirit' (Hegel), as 'the opium of the people' (Marx) or as a 'unified system of beliefs and practices relative to sacred things' (Durkheim). Until recently most social scientists agreed, however, that it was becoming less relevant to political or sociological studies due to the process of secularisation (Brown 2009; Kuru 2007; Mills 1959; Norris and Inglehart 2011; Taylor 2007).

[27] Smith 1998, 281.

[28] This volume follows Arzheimer and Carter's approach of conceptualising religiosity in four dimensions: religious affiliation, church attendance, private religious practice and self-stated religiosity (Arzheimer 2009, 988).

straightforward, as the official Protestant and Catholic churches are centrally organised within clear institutional hierarchies and remain relatively uncontested in their representation of Christianity in society.[29] In the USA, by contrast, the question is more fluid, with over 200 different denominations, around 35,000 non-denominational churches and strong divides along race-lines and theological traditions.[30] This makes it much more complicated to define 'who speaks for Christianity' in the USA than it is in Europe. We will see in later chapters that this structural difference on the religious supply side also plays an important factor in accounting for divergences in Christian communities' reactions to right-wing populism between European countries and the USA on the demand side. However, even in the USA, the growing relevance of the Catholic Church, the ecumenical efforts of the Mainline Protestant denominations in the National Council of Churches (NCC) and the representation of many Evangelical churches through the National Association of Evangelicals (NAE) has led to a consolidation of Christian representation within the USA, around these three pillars thereby enabling us to identify key religious supply-side actors.[31]

Having thus established working definitions of 'right-wing populism' and 'religion' and having identified the key populist and religious actors in Germany, France and the USA, the next step is to have a closer look at this book's case studies, as well as the methods and sources used to analyse them.

2.2   Cases, Sources and Methods

This book is problem-driven, rather than method-driven. That means that it begins by translating the core problem of religion's relationship with populism and right-wing identity politics into a number of key research questions: What are the social and demographic roots behind the rise of right populist movements and their new brand of identity politics in Western democracies? How and why does religion feature prominently in national populist rhetoric and strategies? How do Christian communities react to national-populists' religious-laden rhetoric? What is the role of mainstream parties and religious leaders in shaping these responses?

---

[29] Pollack and Rosta 2017.
[30] 'National Council of the Churches of Christ in the U.S.A.' 2016
[31] Given the high level of denominational fragmentation in American Protestantism, and to facilitate discussions of survey data, this book adopts the terminology used by the Pew Research Center, which divides American Protestants into three traditions: 'Evangelical Protestantism' (e.g. Southern Baptists or Pentecostals), 'Mainline Protestantism' (e.g. Episcopal Church, United Church of Christ) and 'historically Black Protestantism' (e.g. National Baptist convention, African Methodist Episcopal) Cooperman, Smith and Ritchey 2015, 100.

What do these trends mean for the role of faith and religious institutions in Western democracies going forward? The aim of the book is then to explore the existing literature and to identify the most promising research tools, methods and sources that should be used to address these questions.

Given this volume's ambition to investigate how socio-demographic trends such as individualisation, secularisation or rapid ethnic change shape the demand for right-wing populism and identity politics in the electorate, and how different settlements of church–state relations, party systems and elite behaviours impact right-wing populist leaders' ability to realise this potential, a comparative case study approach that distinguishes between demand- and supply-side factors emerged as most suitable. This book thereby relies on the demand- and supply-side approach to populism as advanced and developed by scholars like Kitschelt, Eatwell, Mudde, Kaltwasser and van Kessel.[32] In this context, demand-side factors refer to socio-economic, cultural, demographic or political trends such as individualisation, secularisation, immigration or rapid ethnic change that can shape social cleavages and create fertile grounds in the electorate for national populist movements to succeed. Supply-side factors denote the institutional factors, as well as the strategies and actions of political and religious elites that determine right-wing populists' ability to harness this demand. Importantly, this book makes a further distinction between the *political* supply-side (national populist parties and leaders, decision-makers in mainstream parties, journalists, political institutions etc.) and the *religious* supply-side (institutional churches, individual faith leaders, religious orders and organisations).[33]

With this distinction in mind, this research then uses a comparative case study approach to draw out which specific demand or supply factors may explain different outcomes across countries. This approach rests on a well-established research technique used in social sciences, first codified by John Stuart Mill in 1868, in which, 'in inquiring into the potential cause of an effect', the researcher can resort to two approaches: 'Either the researcher compares cases as similar as possible or as different as possible, except for the dimensions in which he or she is interested.'[34] Both approaches consist of systematically assessing similarities and differences between different case subjects, in order to disentangle the explanatory variables of variation.

---

[32] Kitschelt 1995; Eatwell 2003; Mudde 2007; Kaltwasser et al. 2017b; Van Kessel 2015.

[33] The demand- and supply-side approach is particularly well suited for this study, as it allows for the coherent integration of auxiliary theories, specifically social cleavage theory as advanced by Lipset and Rokkan (1990), Kriesi (2008) and Bornschier (2010), updated forms of secularisation theory, and theories of belonging and belief. Berger 1999; Berger 1990; Casanova 1994; G. Davie 2000; Norris and Inglehart 2011; Roy 2008.

[34] Vannoni 2014, 3.

For this book I have selected cases that are 'comparable' in that they are 'similar in a large number of important characteristics (variables) which one wants to treat as constants, but dissimilar as far as those variables are concerned which one wants to relate to each other'.[35]

In other words, this book's three case studies – the USA, Germany, and France – were chosen because they are largely comparable in that they are all advanced Western democracies with a Judeo-Christian heritage and a largely shared history – especially in the twentieth century, as they have all been subject to similar social upheavals such as industrialisation, two World Wars, the cultural and social upheaval of the 1960s, and processes of individualisation and globalisation. Geopolitically they were all part of the Western alliance during the Cold War and continue to be institutionally connected through organisations such as NATO. They also exhibit comparable levels of development, education, religious freedom, and commitment to capitalism and liberal democracy.[36] Crucially, all three countries have also been confronted with similar demand-side developments such as a recent surge in immigration, rapid ethnic change, accelerated levels of secularisation and globalisation, and subsequent debates about national identity and the role of Islam in society, which make them particularly relevant for this study.[37] For instance, America's population is projected to be 'majority-minority' before the middle of the century, with a majority of Americans expected to identify with a race other than 'white', while Germany and France have experienced similar trends of ethnic and racial diversification over the last couple of decades.[38] In Europe this process has been further accelerated by the 'refugee crisis' of 2016, which saw over one million Syrian refugees migrate to Germany alone and which further intensified debates about Islam.[39]

In each of the three case studies, such new debates, and demographic shifts on the demand side, have been mirrored by a fundamental upheaval in their political landscape on the political supply side and, more specifically, by the rise of powerful national populist movements. This is remarkable, as for most of the twentieth century, party systems in the three countries had been comparatively 'frozen', with politics being largely dominated on the one hand by a mainstream conservative party, typically representing business and free-trade interests on the economic plane and social conservatism on cultural issues; and on the other hand by a progressive or left-wing party

---

[35] Lijphart 1971, 687.

[36] 'Human Development Index' 2017; Economist Intelligence Unit 2017; GESIS Leibniz 2017

[37] Betz and Meret 2009; De Wilde et al. 2019; Eatwell and Goodwin 2018; Kaufmann 2018; Mandaville and Silvestri 2015; Mudde and Kaltwasser 2017; Pollack and Rosta 2017.

[38] Kaufmann 2018.

[39] Casanova 2012a; Modood, London and Bleich 2019.

representing the interests of the secular state and the working class.[40] In recent years, however, scholars have observed a 'thawing' and transformation of Western party systems, with right-wing populist movements being some of the key agents and main beneficiaries of this development. As a result, by the early 2020s the French RN had risen to become France's largest opposition party with its leader Marine Le Pen entering the run-off for the presidential elections in 2017 and 2022, Germany's AfD was the biggest opposition party in the German parliament, and the Trump campaign had taken over the Republican Party and then the US presidency from 2016 to 2020. Importantly, the Trump campaign, the RN and the AfD have also all ostentatiously used Christian symbols and language in their rhetoric.[41]

Yet, despite these similarities, Germany, France and the USA were also chosen as case studies because they differ in key variables under consideration. For one, German, French and American Christian communities profoundly diverge in their reactions to the populist right. In the USA, Christians – and white Evangelicals in particular – were among Donald Trump's most loyal supporters: 81 per cent of white Evangelicals and strong majorities of white Catholics (64 per cent) and other Protestants (58 per cent) voted for Trump in 2016 and continued to support him throughout his presidency.[42] By contrast, in Western Europe scholars have identified a 'religion gap' or 'religious vaccination effect' among Christian voters against voting for right-wing populists.[43]

In addition to these discrepancies in Christians' reactions to the populist right, the three case studies also differ in important ways on the political and religious supply side, which may help us study the roots of these differences. For example, Germany, France and the USA sharply diverge in their historical institutional settlement of church–state relations. While Germany possesses a church-friendly system of 'benevolent neutrality' that endows churches with a quasi-official public status and legal benefits, both the French and American constitutions prescribe a strict legal separation of state and church.[44] However, whereas French *laïcité* was designed to protect the Republic from the influence of religion, the First Amendment in the US Constitution sought to guarantee the free flourishing of religion without state interference.

On the political plane, the three countries not only vary in their electoral systems (First Past the Post in the USA, Proportionate Representation in

---

[40] Kriesi 2008; Lipset and Rokkan 1990.
[41] Focus 2017; Roy 2019; Whitehead and Perry 2020.
[42] Schwadel and Smith 2019; Smith and Martinez 2016.
[43] Dargent 2016; Immerzeel, Jaspers and Lubbers 2013; Siegers and Jedinger 2021; Cremer 2021a; Montgomery and Winter 2015.
[44] Cremer 2021b.

Germany, and a two-round system in France) and the party landscapes they produce, but also in the ways in which political entrepreneurs in these systems have reacted to the rise of the new identity divide between globalists and communitarians. These institutional differences in each country's political and religious setups shape the opportunity structures for national populist movements to emerge, act and reference religion, as well as the ways in which mainstream parties and religious leaders respond to them. Comparing the relationship between religion and right-wing populism in these three countries therefore allows us to identify some of the key factors that allow populists to successfully deploy religion.

To study factors such as socio-demographic trends on the one hand and institutions, elite actors, and complex contextual and historical factors on the other, this book relies on mixed methods, with a focus on the qualitative analysis of in-depth elite interviews for the supply side. This approach has the advantage of taking context into account more effectively and of exploring causal complexity in greater depth, which is particularly important when dealing with contested concepts such as religion and populism, and their role in elite actors' considerations. Thereby, this book relies on a combination of primary and secondary sources. It builds on a growing body of pre-existing qualitative and quantitative studies in the secondary literature[45] while adding its own analysis of new survey data from sources such as the European Values Survey (EVS), the World Values Survey (WVS), the General Social Survey (GSS), the Eurobarometer, IPSOS, the Allensbach Institute, Forsa, Pew and PRRI, as well as from other primary sources including archival records of speeches and party manifestos. However, the core primary source are the 114 interviews conducted with German, French and American elite actors over a number of years (for a full list of interviewees see Appendix A). Of the 114 interviews, 26 were conducted in Germany, 37 in France and 51 in the USA.[46] They include interviews with the leaders of national populist parties and movements like the AfD, the RN and the Trump campaign (N = 30), government officials, civil society leaders and representatives from the political mainstream parties (N = 31), as well as religious leaders from each country's most prominent churches and denominations (N = 43).[47]

---

[45] Bornschier 2010; Dargent 2016; De Wilde et al. 2019; Fourquet 2019; Fourquet 2018b; Kaufmann 2018; Norris and Inglehart 2019; Rebenstorf 2018; Whitehead and Perry 2020.

[46] The variation in interview numbers between the countries is largely due to the more decentralised structure of America's religious landscape.

[47] My conversation partners were recruited through the 'snowballing system'. This means that each case study began with me emailing or calling politicians or religious leaders whom I had identified through earlier research. This outreach would usually result in a handful of initial interviews at the

The interviews were conducted in a semi-structured fashion, with similar questions being asked of all interviewees (see Appendix B for a sample questionnaire). The advantage of semi-structured interviews is that they ensure a certain level of comparability while enabling both the interviewer and the interviewee to explore unanticipated topics or go into greater detail in certain areas, according to the interviewee's expertise and experiences.[48] Most interviews were conducted face to face and locations included parliamentary offices, cafes and restaurants and interviewees' own homes.[49] Whenever possible the interviews were conducted and transcribed in the interviewee's native language (French, German or English).[50]

To conduct these interviews, I spent several months in Berlin, Paris and Washington, DC as a visiting research fellow at a number of academic institutions.[51] These associations provided me with an institutional base from which to travel to each country to conduct my interviews. They also enabled me to engage with leading academic specialists and country experts, as well as to immerse myself in the current political and religious debates of each society. This immersion into the national context facilitated a more targeted identification of relevant interviewees and allowed me to triangulate my findings in the context of current events and their broader cultural and historical background (for a list of consulted experts see Appendix A). Taken together, these methods and sources enabled me to distil the four key arguments about the relationship between religion and populism and right-wing identity politics in the West, which will be expounded in the next chapter.

---

end of which I would then ask each interview partner for further recommendations or additional contacts. Thanks to my interviewees' interest and generosity, this often resulted in interviewees making several further suggestions or even personal introductions to additional interview partners, allowing the research to proceed from one interviewee to the next, until a natural 'saturation point' was reached, at which point additional interviews ceased to provide new relevant data.

[48] With permission from the interviewees, the interviews were digitally recorded to ensure detailed and accurate transcription. All interviewees were fully informed about the research project and verbally provided consent to the use of the material. In addition, each interviewee was sent a list of direct quotes to be used in this volume, providing them with an opportunity to review and provide feedback prior to publication of the material. Whenever an interviewee requested a quote be taken 'off-the record', the quote appears anonymised in this book. Interviewees have, however, graciously agreed for the majority of quotes to be cited with name attributions.

[49] If a face-to-face interview was not possible, phone or video calls were conducted.

[50] All translations within the book have been made by the author.

[51] Berlin Social Sciences Center in Germany, July–October 2018, Sciences Po Paris in France, March–June 2019, and Georgetown University's Berkley Center in the USA, October 2019–March 2020.

CHAPTER 3

A Fourfold Argument
The Identity Cleavage, the Secular Right, Religious Immunity and Christian Leadership

This book lays out four main arguments in response to the key questions formulated above. These four arguments, each building on the preceding argument, confirm some findings in the existing literature, challenge others and collectively serve as cornerstones for a new and more comprehensive understanding of the relationship between religion, right-wing populism and identity politics in Western democracies.

3.1 What Are the Social and Demographic Roots behind the Rise of National Populist Politics in Western Democracies?

The first key argument of this book is that the rise of right-wing populist movements and their references to religion are less the result of traditional social divides about economics and moral or religious issues, and rather a consequence of a new identity cleavage between cosmopolitans and communitarians in Western societies. This divide has emerged in response to demand-side developments such as secularisation, globalisation, individualisation and rapid ethnic change and has subsequently been politicised by right-wing populists through their new brand of identity politics.

Social cleavages refer to the main social divides within a society that shape and define the political system and the parties that populate it.[1] Historically, Western democracies have been divided by four critical cleavage lines: the centre versus the periphery; the state versus the church; the land versus industry; and owners versus workers.[2] More recently, scholars have argued that in modern-day politics this system 'essentially boils down to two dimensions: a cultural (religion) and a social-economic one (class)'.[3] As a result, throughout the twentieth century, politics in Western societies

---

[1] Bornschier 2010; Lipset and Rokkan 1990; Marks and Wilson 2000.
[2] Lipset and Rokkan 1990, 101.
[3] Kriesi 2008, 11.

was dominated by economic questions about economic redistribution, taxation and class relations, alongside social issues such as abortion, church–state relations and sexual freedom.[4] The traditional party systems of most Western democracies, which have 'instrumental and representative functions' in mirroring, prioritising and bridging social cleavages, are largely ordered according to these fault lines.[5] Mainstream conservative parties, for instance, typically represented capitalists on the economic cleavage and the church or social conservatism on the moral cleavage, whereas progressive or left-wing parties represented the interests of the secular state and the working class. Throughout the twentieth century, these party systems have proven remarkably resilient, thanks to the organisational advantages of established parties, and their strategic alliances, which have prevented split-offs and narrowed new parties' mobilisation potential.[6]

In recent years, however, this organisational advantage seems to have reached its limit. Since the 1990s scholars have observed a 'thawing' of the Western European party system, with new parties emerging both on the left and right margins of the political spectrum, and a shrinking of the old mainstream parties.[7] Some of the main beneficiaries of this fragmentation were national populist movements, which between 2006 and 2016 doubled their share of parliamentary seats and tripled their absolute share of votes.[8] In many places, supply-side factors such as national electoral systems can significantly impact the speed and extent of this transformation process.[9] For instance, while electoral systems based on Proportionate Representation (PR) allow for a more direct translation of shifting demand-side patterns into new parties, majoritarian or First Past the Post (FPF) voting systems disproportionately favour established two-party systems and disadvantage new party formations.[10] As a result, populist movements are more likely to express themselves early in PR-voting systems through the rise of separate and new populist parties, as seen in countries like the

---

[4] Although social cleavage theory was first conceptualised for the Western European context and remains less prevalent in the study of American politics (Franklin 2010), studies have shown that it can also be fruitfully applied to the American context (Manza and Brooks 1999; Gary Marks et al. 2017; Goldberg 2020).

[5] Lipset and Rokkan 1990, 93.

[6] In the second half of the twentieth century Western party systems still reflected the cleavage structure of the 1920s with most 'party alternatives [being] older than the majorities of national electorates' (Lipset and Rokkan 1990, 133).

[7] Taggart 1996.

[8] Eatwell and Goodwin 2018; Norris and Inglehart 2016.

[9] Kriesi 2008; Bornschier 2010; Ezrow 2010.

[10] Cox 1997.

Netherlands, Denmark, Germany or Austria.[11] By contrast in majoritarian systems, like those in the UK or the USA, which favour established parties and party consolidation, right-wing populist movements are more likely to change the party system by operating from within an established party. However, the fact that right-wing populist movements have successfully transformed party systems in both PR and majoritarian systems (albeit through different strategies, as this book will explore) suggests that shifts on the demand side are the main precondition for right-wing populists' success.

Indeed, although these parties are often referred to as 'right-wing' populist, closer analysis shows that the new movements no longer fit neatly into the conventional two-by-two matrix of the traditional economic and moral cleavage system. Certainly, scholars have repeatedly sought to interpret the rise of right-wing populism in terms of the traditional economic cleavage between free-trade capitalists on the one hand and planned-economy socialists on the other; so much so that the identification of right-wing populists politics and neoliberal economics had become a 'conventional wisdom' in much of the populism literature in the early 2000s.[12] However, there has been little empirical evidence that a focus on neoliberal economics is a widespread feature of contemporary national populist parties.[13] On the contrary, in its latest wave, right-wing populist proponents like Donald Trump, Marine Le Pen or the 'Vote Leave' Brexit movement campaigned on a platform of anti-globalism, protectionism, big-state social welfare and infrastructure programmes – policies that were traditionally put forward by the left.[14]

In response, some scholars have placed right-wing populists on the anti-free trade side of the economic cleavage arguing that contemporary right-wing populist movements reflect an economic backlash against rising levels of inequality.[15] The 'rust-belt revolt' of former blue-collar Democrats in the 2016 US presidential election, and the abandonment of many centre-left parties in Europe by their traditional working-class electorate are often cited as symptoms of this development.[16] Yet, this account too seems insufficient. Not only does it fail to account for the rising role of

---

[11] Kaltwasser et al. 2017b.
[12] Mudde 2007, 120; Burghard 2010; Friedrich 2015; Höbelt 2003; Jungerstam-Mulders 2003; Thompson 2000; Burghard 2010; Formisano 2012; Guardino and Snyder 2012.
[13] Arzheimer and Badinter 2006; Mudde 2007; Norris and Inglehart 2019.
[14] Amann 2017; Goodwin, Olsen and Good 2019; Olsen 2017; Perrineau 2017.
[15] Perrineau 2017; Rodrik 2018.
[16] Fourquet 2018b; Lilla 2018.

religion and civilisational references in right-wing populist rhetoric, but its claims about the centrality of the economic cleavage seem inadequate given recent election data. For instance, Rothwell and Diego-Rosell have shown that most Trump supporters were relatively unconcerned about their personal economic situation.[17] Similarly, during the 2017 German federal election, 'unemployment', the traditional key voting issue in Germany, was relegated to a much lower spot in voters' motivations, a trend that was mirrored in other Western European countries where the populist right achieved electoral success.[18] Cas Mudde, therefore, concluded that 'economics is not a primary issue to the party family' but has been subordinated by other, more crucial parts of right-wing populists' agendas.[19]

Given this lack of evidence for the centrality of the economic cleavage to the rise of national populism, other scholars have reverted to the West's second traditional political cleavage: the culture–religion cleavage. Pippa Norris and Ronald Inglehart for instance interpret right-wing populism as a 'cultural backlash' against a progressive value change on social issues.[20] This implicitly places phenomena like Trumpism, Brexit and the rise of the populist right in continental Europe in the context of traditional 'culture wars' that have raged in the USA for decades, mainly between Christian conservatives and secular liberals.[21] This view appears substantiated by well-researched studies, such as Andrew Whitehead and Samuel Perry's suggesting a strong relationship between 'White Christian Nationalism' and far-right politics in the USA,[22] as well as a large number of scholars agreeing that 'socio-cultural' rather than 'socio-economic' questions dominate right-wing populists' priorities.[23] Moreover, right-wing populists' own rhetoric seems to push towards the same conclusion.

However, as the analysis of this book will show, taking right-wing populists' religiously laden rhetoric at face value and equating the new identity politics of the present with America's religious 'culture wars' of the past, risks overlooking important shifts on the political right by

---

[17] Rothwell and Diego-Rosell 2016.
[18] The very fact that right-wing populists often do best in some of 'the most egalitarian European societies, with cradle-to-grave welfare states, containing some of the best-educated and most secure populations in the world' (Norris and Inglehart 2019; Norris and Inglehart 2016, 16) casts further doubt on the centrality of the economic insecurity thesis.
[19] Mudde 2007, 136.
[20] Norris and Inglehart 2019.
[21] Gorski 2019a; Whitehead and Perry 2020.
[22] Whitehead and Perry 2020.
[23] Kaufmann 2018; Kriesi 2008.

conflating religious traditionalism and secular authoritarianism. Daenekindt, De Koster and Van der Waal have shown that whilst across most
of the literature these 'cultural issues are considered interchangeable', in
reality, these two components of 'right-wing' positions are quite distinct.[24]
This seems underlined by one essential (but often overlooked) finding
of Whitehead and Perry that while Christian cultural identity correlates
with Christian nationalist attitudes, religious practice does not.[25] The
analysis of this book supports this observation and furthermore reveals
that national populist movements in many Western countries have often
non-traditionalist attitudes with respect to social issues and religion. In
many European countries they, for instance, combine authoritarianism and
anti-immigration policies with culturally liberal stances on gay marriage,
gender equality or church–state separation.[26] The Dutch Freedom Party
(PdV) claims to be the party for gay rights and gender equality,[27] while the
RN in France presents itself as the chief guardian of *laïcité* (see Part III).
Germany's PEGIDA has clearly stated its support for sexual
self-determination (meaning support for LGBT rights)[28] and even during
the 2016 presidential election, the Trump campaign spent less time on
traditional social issues like abortion or gay marriage and focused more on
questions surrounding immigration and race relations (see Part IV).

In addition, neither populist leaders nor their supporters appear to be
ideal incarnations of 'cultural warriors' in the defence of Christianity.
Geert Wilders in the Netherlands identifies as irreligious, as do Alexander
Gauland in Germany and Nigel Farage in the UK. Italy's Matteo Salvini,
who in 2018 invoked the Holy Ghost in campaign speeches, had for many
years publicly embraced neo-paganism, and Donald Trump famously
declared during the 2016 campaign that he has never asked God for forgiveness and would not want to bring Him into the picture.[29] Combined
with the negative correlation between religiosity and support for right-wing
populists observed in many Western European countries (the 'religious
vaccination effect') and further studies showing that right-wing populist
voters in Western Europe tend to be disproportionally irreligious and to
care comparatively little about religious or moral issues when making their

---

[24] Daenekindt, De Koster and Van Der Waal 2017, 792.
[25] Whitehead and Perry 2020, 87.
[26] Akkerman 2005; Betz and Meret 2009, 322; De Koster et al. 2014; Elcott et al. 2021; Mudde 2016; Spierings, Lubbers and Zaslove 2017.
[27] De Koster et al. 2014.
[28] Coury 2016, 60.
[29] Betz and Meret 2009, 12; F.A.Z. 2016a; Kešić and Duyvendak 2019; Mudde 2016, 317; Scott 2015.

electoral decisions,[30] there appears to be insufficient empirical evidence for the extrapolation of the American culture war to Europe. Instead, as this book will show in Part IV, there is reason to believe that the latter may well be in decline in the USA itself.[31]

As the recent surge of national populist movements and their use of religion does not appear to be primarily an expression of an economic 'class struggle' nor of religiously motivated 'culture wars', this book explores a third possibility: that demand for right-wing populist politics is driven by a new social cleavage centred around identity politics, which drives demand for national populist politics, and in whose context religion can be politically used as a cultural identity marker.

Polls and empirical studies suggest that in many Western countries concerns about immigration, national culture and ethnic identity increasingly trump economic, social or moral issues. Maria Sobolewska and Robert Ford Clarke have shown that immigration and a new 'identity conflict' between 'identity liberals' and 'identity conservatives' were the key drivers for 'Leave' voters in the Brexit referendum and the subsequent transformation of Britain's political landscape.[32] Similarly, 'refugees and foreigners' were the chief concern for voters in the 2017 German federal election.[33] This trend is even more evident when looking at right-wing populist voters. In the 2017 French presidential election, 80 per cent of FN voters ranked 'immigration' as the most important electoral issue, placing it above economic concerns such as unemployment or social questions such as gay marriage.[34] Similar trends could be observed amongst Trump voters who rated identitarian issues like immigration, Islam and race relations particularly high in their voting motivation.[35]

There is a growing body of literature describing the rise of right-wing identity politics on both sides of the Atlantic, suggesting that many voters are beginning to think less in terms of class struggles, or culture wars, and more in terms of a new contest over the status of ethno-cultural, racial and civilisational identities of majority populations in the West.[36] At the same time, there

---

[30] Dargent 2016; Immerzeel, Jaspers and Lubbers 2013; Konrad Adenauer Stiftung 2021; Perrineau 2014; Siegers and Jedinger 2021; Cremer 2021a; Montgomery and Winter 2015; Arzheimer 2009.
[31] Goodhart 2017; Jones 2016; Jung 2016; Moreton 2015, 150.
[32] Sobolewska and Ford 2020; Clarke, Goodwin and Whiteley 2017.
[33] Dostal 2017; Allensbach Institut 2016.
[34] Harris Interactive 2017; Mayer 2017; Perrineau 2017; Perrineau 2014.
[35] Sides, Tesler and Vavreck 2019.
[36] Betz and Meret 2009; Rogers Brubaker 2017; De Wilde et al. 2019; Eatwell and Goodwin 2018; Fukuyama 2018; Haynes 2017; Jardina 2019; Kaufmann 2018; Kešić and Duyvendak 2019; Sides, Tesler and Vavreck 2019.

is a sizeable and outspoken part of the population – including much of the economic and political 'elite' – that fundamentally opposes the prioritisation of the majority culture. Instead, these parts of the population define identity in much more cosmopolitan and individualistic terms, fervently defending globalist ideals of equality and diversity, while also advocating for the group rights of minority populations.[37] As a result, observers speak of a new divide between 'Somewheres' and 'Anywheres',[38] 'Sedentaries' and 'Nomads',[39] 'Nativists' and 'Globalists',[40] 'Communitarians' and 'Cosmopolitans',[41] or 'Identity Conservatives' and 'Identity Liberals'.[42] These terms are certainly varied and focus on different aspects of this divide. It is also important to acknowledge the normative assumptions and in some cases to problematise potential antisemitic overtones implicit in certain terminologies.[43] Yet, each of these distinctions still points to the same question: how to define the 'us' and the 'other' in times of rapid social and demographic change. Who may belong and who may not? This is the core of the new identity cleavage, which is reshaping the old cleavage system (see Figure 3.1).

When looking for the roots of this divide, we can detect both international and domestic factors. At an international level, factors such as immigration, the rise of Islamist terrorism and the erosion of traditional forms of sovereignty appear critical as they have moved questions about how to define national identity into the centre of political debate. Specifically, scholars have emphasised that immigration and rapid ethnic change pose challenges to concepts of citizenship, sovereignty and national identity.[44] Meanwhile, authors like Casanova, Hamid, Betz and Meret point to a link between Muslim immigration and the resurgence of religion as a cultural identifier in Western political discourse, often in the form of Islamophobia.[45] Moreover, international integration and

[37] De Wilde et al. 2019; Eatwell and Goodwin 2018; Fourquet 2019; Goodhart 2017.
[38] Goodhart 2017.
[39] Fourquet 2018a.
[40] Piketty 2020.
[41] De Wilde et al. 2019.
[42] Sobolewska and Ford 2020.
[43] See Rensmann 2011. In order to avoid such normative pitfalls this book primarily uses the comparatively value-neutral terminology put forward by De Wilde et al. 2019.
[44] Betz 1994; Joppke 1999; Karapin 2002; Kaufmann 2018; Mudde 2017; Norris and Inglehart 2019; Schain, Zolberg and Hossay 2002.
[45] Acts of Islamic terrorism have further exacerbated this tendency, as they are often portrayed as an outside attack of a civilisational 'other' on 'us' (Sunar 2017). Moreover, 'the intrusion of fear into everyday life' (Walzer 2019, 51) has driven a wedge between parts of the population that already felt threatened by foreign migrants, and an allegedly globalist elite that has failed to protect the people by curbing immigration.

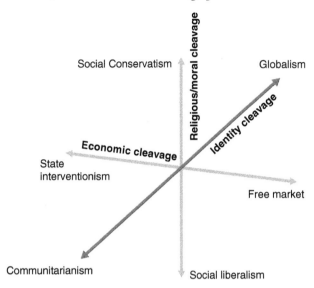

Figure 3.1   The new cleavage system

supranational institutions have pushed the public debate towards a focus on questions of national identity by appearing to threaten national sovereignty from above, and pitting national forms of identity against new globalist ones.[46] Such international developments have confronted many Western societies with the question of how to define 'us' and 'them'. However, the reasons as to why Western societies seem so divided in answering these questions appear to lie in the erosion of traditional group identities on the national level.

For example, if in 1960 one had asked the average white European about their identity, they would likely have responded with a reference to a group identity such as their nationality or region, their religion, their social class, their commitment to an ideology, or their membership in a political party or union. In 2022, many of these group identities have been weakened or have entirely disappeared. Instead, a person would most likely point to acquired individual identities such as their specific profession, education and maybe the sport they practise. While this may be a simplified example,

---

[46] De Cleen 2017; Fligstein 2008; Halikiopoulou, Nanou and Vasilopoulou 2012; Hooghe and Marks 2018; Kaltwasser 2014; Silvestri 2009.

it reflects the tendency observed by scholars in most Western societies that inherited group identities and associated social structures have been eroded and replaced by individualist acquired identities among cosmopolitans, while communitarians have been left with regret for the erosion of inherited collective identities.[47]

This book discusses how in Germany, France and the USA, the surge of ethno-nationalism can be linked specifically to increasing levels of individualisation, secularisation and social atomisation, and the subsequent decline of the two key group identity markers of the traditional economic and cultural cleavages: class and religion.[48] The decline of class identity is primarily due to processes of technological modernisation, digitalisation, the spread of secondary education and the rise of meritocracy.[49] Although generally seen as positive developments, some authors have highlighted the associated social costs in terms of lost group identities and social structures. The decline of class identities is extensively discussed in politics as it is widely seen as the cause for the end of working-class voting, and for the defection of blue-collar voters from left-wing parties to right-wing populist groups.[50] Yet, the loss or transformation of religious identity through the process of secularisation could be even more momentous in understanding the emergence of the new cleavage.

Although religion has far from disappeared from world politics, studies show that individual faith and religious practice are in rapid and continuous decline in the West.[51] For instance, Chapter 13 shows that secularisation has accelerated in the USA since the 2000s, with those professing to have no faith at all outnumbering any single religious group in 2016 for the first time.[52] In other traditionally Christian societies such as Britain, Germany or France, Christians are projected to become a minority within a matter of years rather than decades.[53]

---

[47] Arendt 1973; Fukuyama 2018; Holmes 1995; Huntington 2004; Reckwitz 2018.

[48] Sociologists have observed for several decades that growing levels of individualisation coincide with a lower identification with collective institutions, as well as a decreasing willingness to commit to groups (Beck 2016; Beck and Beck-Gernsheim 2001; Blokland 1997; Levin 2020; Putnam 2000; Putnam and Campbell 2012; Wilcox et al. 2012). This phenomenon has impacted labour unions, political parties, social clubs, youth associations and even marriage (Beaumont 1987; Bock 2019; Denver 2008; Haute 2011; Wattenberg 1998).

[49] Pakulski and Waters 1996; Atkinson 2007; Heath, Curtice and Elgenius 2009; Sandel 2020.

[50] Evans 1999; Frank 2005; Olsen 2017; Rydgren 2010.

[51] Carney 2019; Chaves 2011; Fourquet 2019; Norris and Inglehart 2011; Pollack and Rosta 2017; Turner 2011.

[52] Pew 2019a; Pew 2016a.

[53] Pollack and Rosta 2017; Pew 2016a.

Though scholars are divided as to whether individual spirituality will take the place of formal religiosity, Putnam and Campbell predict a significant loss of social capital associated with this decline of institutionalised religion.[54] Zúquete and Fourquet even speak of the collapse of the social matrix of society and the subsequent emergence of a social and spiritual identity vacuum that can readily be exploited by political actors such as national populists.[55]

However, for this study, even more important than religious identity's potential disappearance is its transformation into a cultural rather than religious concept as a result of secularisation. Roy, McDonnell and Marzouki have emphasised that in many societies the decline of individual religiosity has paradoxically coincided with an increased emphasis on 'Christian culture' in public discourse.[56] Scholars have sought to understand such developments by drawing a distinction between religious belief and belonging, which appear as increasingly separate phenomena.[57] 'Believers without belonging' are individuals who self-identify as 'spiritual but not religious' and subscribe to much of the general Christian doctrine, without committing to the social institution of a church.[58] Conversely, 'belongers without belief' are individuals who may identify with the cultural heritage of a particular faith, its symbols, language and derived rules in society (belonging), but do so without identifying with its values, beliefs and institutions (believing).[59]

Phenomena such as 'belonging without believing' suggest that although commitment to religion or class may be waning on the political demand side, the yearning for group identity is not. While the cosmopolitan part of the population embraces new individualist forms of acquired identities, international developments such as immigration, Islamic terrorism, and international integration, seem to have incited the communitarians to search for new group identities, creating a new demand for political entrepreneurs to harness.[60]

---

[54] Putnam (1993 p. 35) defines social capital as 'features of social organizations, such as networks, norms and trust that facilitate action and cooperation for mutual benefit'.

[55] Fourquet 2019; Zúquete 2017.

[56] Roy, McDonnell and Marzouki 2016.

[57] Brubaker 2017; Casanova 2012a; Davie 2015; Davie 2000; Roy 2019.

[58] Campbell and Layman 2015; Davie 2000; Nicolet and Tresch 2009.

[59] This phenomenon is well articulated by the German term *Kulturchrist* ('cultural Christian') and epitomised by a quote from an Estonian scholar who described the difference between Estonians and Russians, explaining, 'We are all atheists; but I am a Lutheran atheist, and they are Orthodox atheists' (Norris and Inglehart 2011, 17).

[60] Eatwell and Goodwin 2018; Fourquet 2018b; Fukuyama 2018; Goodhart 2017; Kaufmann 2018.

3.2   How and Why Does Religion Feature in
Right-Wing Populists' New Brand of Identity Politics?

The second argument of this book is that right-wing populists seek to capitalise on the new identity cleavage through their own brand of right-wing identity politics, in the context of which they use Christian symbols and language as cultural identity markers, while often remaining distanced from Christian doctrine, ethics and institutions.

Scholars have noted that national populists respond to voters' concerns about national identity and immigration by using a new form of white identity politics, which emphasises ethno-national identities over traditional class or religious identities.[61] To better understand the role of religion in this context, we need to explore the nature and origins of right-wing identity politics on the supply side. Right-wing identity politics is not simply to be equated with traditional racism based on a biological racial hierarchy. Rather, it is built on the 'ethno-pluralist' doctrine of 'equal but different', which holds that particular nations, cultures or ethnic groups have the right to defend their cultural differences.[62] Thus, whilst – like left-wing identity politics – white identity politics emphasises racial, cultural or sexual identity as drivers of political action, it reverses the roles by claiming to defend the rights of the ethnic majority, rather than those of minorities.[63] It thereby abandons the predominant view that whites 'have a moral obligation to eschew group partiality', and instead claims, as Eric Kaufmann put it, that the ethnic majority has the right to identify as a group and act in their collective self-interest.[64] One critical distinction between left-wing and right-wing identity politics, in this context, is the claim that the ethnic majority's cultural norms and identity should enjoy a pre-eminent or even hegemonic position within society. Within the boundaries of national community there is, hence, an expectation for minorities to assimilate themselves into the majority's *Leitkultur* ('lead-culture').

Appealing in such ways to the majority's ethno-cultural group identity is of strategic value for national populists for two reasons. First, the concept is sufficiently vague to appeal to large parts of an increasingly

---

[61] Fukuyama 2018; Hochschild 2018; Jardina 2019; Kaufmann 2018; Kaufmann 2017a; Kaufmann 2017b; Rydgren 2018; Sides 2017.
[62] Kaufmann 2018; McCulloch 2006; Rydgren 2005; Zúquete 2018.
[63] Fukuyama 2018; Heyes 2002; Kaufmann 2018.
[64] Kaufmann 2017a.

fragmented populace. Reflecting Hannah Arendt's insight that it is only natural that 'the masses of a highly atomized society … have tended toward an especially violent nationalism',[65] ethno-cultural group identity can serve as the smallest common denominator in an otherwise highly individualised and fragmented society. The second advantage is that formulating this appeal in terms of identity politics resonates with the mainstream rhetoric about the importance of (minority) group rights, common perceptions of (in)justice and victimhood narratives.[66] In this context, many members of the majority population feel 'left out' by the identity politics of the left, which is perceived as defending the group rights of minorities but undermining those of the majority.[67] They are therefore often susceptible to rhetoric and policies that appeal to feelings of victimhood and decline.[68]

Scholars have pointed out that national or ethno-cultural group identities often compete with other group identities, such as those defined by religion (especially if the latter is universalist or internationalist in nature).[69] Right-wing populist appeals to religion are therefore often different from traditional religious appeals of conservative or Christian-Democratic movements.[70] Whereas Christian-Democrats' focus has been to translate Christian values into democratic politics, promote Christian virtues in public life, and establish the Christian churches as an important partner and critic of the state, national populists appeal to other aspects of religion that do not clash with, but might advance, their own ethno-national identity politics.[71]

One such way to use religion is through the sacralisation of politics and the nation. Arato and Zúquete, for instance, show that secular concepts such as territory, the population, immigrants and political elites are systematically 'theologised' in right-wing populist rhetoric into 'the sacred homeland', 'the pure people', 'the dangerous others' and 'the corrupted elite'.[72] Similarly, populists' Manichean distinction between the 'pure people' and the 'corrupted elite' or the 'dangerous other', reflects religious concepts of good and evil.[73] Scholars have emphasised that Western

---

[65] Arendt 1973, 15.
[66] Fukuyama 2018; Jardina 2019.
[67] Gaston and Hilhorst 2018; Hochschild 2018; Jones 2016; Kaufmann 2018; Sides, Tesler and Vavreck 2019.
[68] Jardina 2019.
[69] Brubaker 2017; Brubaker 2012; Roy 2019.
[70] Casanova 2012b; Cremer 2019; Geisser 2018; Heredia 2011; Roy 2019; Wolfgang Thielmann 2017.
[71] Barber and Pope 2019a; Gerson and Wehner 2010; Kalyvas and Van Kersbergen 2010; Müller 2018a; Müller 2013.
[72] Arato 2013; Zúquete 2017.
[73] Hawkins 2009; Hermet 2007, 81; Samuel 2009, 1142; Torre and Arato 2015, 9.

Europe, with its unusually high level of secularisation, is a particularly fertile breeding ground for such strategies;[74] and as the USA continues to secularise further, this approach may also become increasingly attractive on the other side of the Atlantic.

However, this book will show that another use of religion in right-wing populists' identity politics is of even greater relevance: the employment of religious language and symbols as secularised cultural and civilisational identity markers of the 'us' against the 'external other'. To better understand this dynamic, let us recall our definition of the right-wing populist worldview in terms of a triangular relationship. On the one side we have the pure and homogenous people ('the us'), and on the other we have a set of two 'others' who threaten the people's identity. The first is the internal other, that is, the corrupted liberal and cosmopolitan elite, who erode the people's identity and cohesion from the inside. And second is the external other who threaten the people's homogeneity through their cultural 'otherness' from the outside. What has happened over the last few decades is that whereas historically the differentiation between the 'pure people' and the 'the external other' in right-wing populist rhetoric had been made based on race, ethnicity and nationality, since the 2000s there has been a shift to where this distinction has increasingly been made on the basis of religious and civilisational characteristics.[75] José Casanova for instance emphasised that

> Only a few decades ago immigrants from Turkey in Germany were viewed as Turks and not as Muslims, immigrants from Pakistan in the UK were viewed as Pakistani and not as Muslims, and immigrants from the Maghreb in France were viewed as Moroccans, Algerians or Tunisians, or generally as Maghrebis, and not as Muslims. But today throughout Europe immigrants from Muslim countries are not only primarily classified as Muslims, but they have come to represent 'Islam' with all the baggage.[76]

In right-wing populists' worldview, in which the 'us' is largely defined *ex negativo* in relation to internal and external others, this shift from

---

[74] Lecoeur 2003, 173.

[75] Betz and Meret 2009; Brubaker 2017; Haynes 2019; Huntington 1996; Kešić and Duyvendak 2019. Traditionally, such classifications have been less prominent in the USA, where, throughout the second half of the twentieth century, there was near consensus (even on the right) that any form of religious identity had an 'important role in the process of immigrant incorporation' (Casanova 2012a, 493; Cesari 2007; Hamid 2019; Kaufmann 2018). However, as we shall see in Part IV, since 9/11, and in particular since the rise of Trump, Islamophobia has become an ever-more important tenet in American populism.

[76] Casanova 2012a, 489.

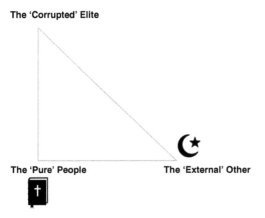

Figure 3.2 The role of religion in national populist identity politics

biological racism to cultural 'civilisations' and the consequent definition of 'the other' in terms of religion and culture as 'Islamic', appears to also have allowed Christianity to become an analogous identity marker of the 'us', even in highly secularised societies (see Figure 3.2).[77]

However, such a use of Islam and Christianity as markers of identity does not necessarily amount to a resurgence of religiosity in Western societies. Rather, the three case studies explore the extent to which right-wing populist movements use Christian traditions, symbols and language as markers to bolster a nativist ethno-cultural identity, without committing to Christian doctrine, ethics or institutions. In other words, they show explores how the populist right's identitarian use of Christian symbols in Germany France and the US represents a culturalisation – or perhaps even a secularisation – of the concept of Christianity itself, whereby belonging is further dissociated from believing and religion becomes a cultural identifier delinked from theological faith or church institutions. As we will see, the findings from the empirical case studies show that the policies of the AfD, the RN and the Trump administration often clash with church doctrine (in particular on signature issues such as immigration), that their leadership largely defies Christian ideals of public ethics, and that they often exhibit deeply fraught relations with institutional churches, with a growing

---

[77] Scholars like Rosenberg or Schwörer and Garcia have shown for instance that one key difference between Christian Democratic and right-wing populist parties' references to religion is that the former primarily focuses on positive references to the Christian 'in-group' whereas the latter focuses on negative references to the Muslim 'out-group' (Rosenberg 2021; Schwörer and Fernández-García 2021).

number of national populist movements actually embracing radical forms
of secularism. Moreover, the elite interviews of right-wing populist leaders,
faith leaders and mainstream party politicians reveal fundamentally different
conceptions of Christianity between the three groups. For instance, whereas
interviewed church officials and mainstream party politicians, when asked
how they define 'Christian identity', primarily referenced aspects of Christian
believing (such as Christian values, anthropology or theological concepts
about sinfulness, the trinity or the resurrection), interviewed right-wing populist leaders focused overwhelmingly on what we could call 'Christendom',
that is, Christianity primarily as a form of national and cultural belonging
(referencing history, architecture, music, traditions and territory) and as a
contrast point against the Islamic 'other'. Éric Zemmour, the rising star of the
French populist right, recently epitomised this dynamic when confirming in
an interview that he is for Catholicism but 'against Christ'.[78]

Perhaps even more strikingly, under the surface of such identitarian
references to religion the elite interviews often revealed powerful anti-
Christian currents within many right-wing populist movements. This
is particularly true for Europe, where some right-wing populist insiders
described an internal marginalisation of Christians within these parties,
due to the growing influence of secularist or neo-pagan groups. And, even
in the USA, where few Republicans would ever openly embrace secularist
or anti-Christian stances, several Trump campaign officials reported growing infighting between a new secular nationalist wing around individuals
like Steve Bannon and Stephen Miller on the one hand and Christian conservative voices on the other. This gradual rise of a populist 'post-Christian
right' in the USA was also exemplified during the Capitol riots where neo-
pagan symbolism, confederate flags, and shamans in Viking veneer where
just as present as Jesus saves flags and oversized crosses.[79]

Such a 'culturalisation of religion' as an identity marker has two strategic advantages for right-wing populists in secularising Western societies. For one, a 'culturalised' form of Christian identity devoid of religious
beliefs does not compete with ethno-cultural or national identities. On
the contrary, it can endow the latter with the appearance of greater historical, cultural and civilisational substance, making the narrative of a 'clash
of civilisations' more credible.[80] Second, the dissociation of Christian

[78] Neuville 2021.
[79] Cremer 2021e.
[80] Huntington 1996; Kriesi 2008.

identity from Christian beliefs makes the former more malleable. This makes religious references accessible and convenient for increasingly irreligious voters, who may be yearning for a strong group identity, without wanting to commit to Christian doctrine, as well as for right-wing populist leaders who can more easily 'mix and match' references to Christianity with other markers of 'Western identity' such as secularism, sexual freedom, ethnicity or concepts of whiteness.[81]

3.3   How Do Christian Communities React to National Populists' Religious-Laden Rhetoric?

The third argument of this book looks at how Christian communities react to right-wing populists' uses of Christian references in their new identity politics. The key claim here is that national populists' identitarian rhetoric is often most successful amongst irreligious voters and non-practising 'cultural Christians', whereas practising Christians remain comparatively 'immune' to such appeals.

At first glance this claim may appear counter-intuitive given Donald Trump's record levels of support among white Christians in America, as well the high levels of support for right-wing populist movements among Christian voters in other parts of the world. In Brazil, for instance, Jair Bolsonaro could count on Evangelical voters as a solid support base, while in Eastern Europe Poland's Peace and Justice Party or Victor Orban in Hungary are closely associated with national churches.[82] A closer look at the situation in Western Europe, however, paints a very different picture. Here right-wing populists consistently underperform among Christian voters in general, and churchgoers in particular. In Germany for instance, the AfD regularly scored almost twice as high amongst irreligious voters than amongst Protestants or Catholics in regional, federal and European elections between 2014 and 2021.[83] Similarly, in countries like the Netherlands, Italy or France, scholars have identified religious practice and church attendance as powerful empirical predictors for not voting for right-wing populist parties. Pascal Perrineau, for example, concluded that 'the nationalist drive that feeds the far right in France always stumbled against the block of practising Catholics who yield far less to

[81] Roy 2019; Roy 2008; Wohlrab-Sahr 2003.
[82] Bozóki and Ádám 2016; Alvis 2012; Freston 2020.
[83] Cremer 2021a; Siegers and Jedinger 2021.

the temptation of the FN than most other parts of the population'.[84] As a result, there is a growing academic exploration of the 'religion gap' or 'religious vaccination effect' against voting for right-wing populists among Christian voters in Western Europe.[85]

What is more, in spite of the high level of variation between the situation in the USA and Western Europe on the surface of electoral outcomes, a closer inspection of Christians' attitudes and sociodemographic backgrounds in the three case studies shows a more uniform development underneath: namely a growing schism between the traditional religious right and a new secular right. In the USA for instance, the 2016 GOP primary results showed that Donald Trump's earliest and most solid supporters were not the most pious Republicans, but religiously unaffiliated voters. Throughout the primaries Trump performed twice as well among those Republicans who never attended church (57 per cent) compared to frequent churchgoers (29 per cent).[86] Moreover, studies found a growing attitudinal divergence between the Trumpist electoral core and conservative Christians, with Ruth Melkonian-Hoover and Lyman Kellstedt stressing that between 2011 and 2018, just as anti-immigrant sentiment surged among Trump's base of secular conservatives, American Evangelicals 'increased their support [for immigration] over time'.[87] The German and French case studies seem to substantiate such claims. Thus, while in Germany, the AfD's core constituency shifted from disproportionately well-educated, upper-middle-class, socially conservative and often church-affiliated voters, to a new electorate of less-educated, working-class voters who held more secular attitudes,[88] in France, practising Catholics were often diametrically opposed to the RN's electorate in terms of attitudes and sociodemographic background. Although socially more conservative, they tend, for example, to be more sympathetic towards migrants and Islam than the French in general, and whereas the RN primarily draws support from young, rural, male and working-class voters, the pews of France's churches are increasingly filled by elderly, female, well-off city dwellers as well as by a growing number of immigrants.[89]

---

[84] Perrineau 2014, 39.
[85] Arzheimer and Carter 2009; Dargent 2016; Siegers and Jedinger 2021; Montgomery and Winter 2015; Cremer 2021a.
[86] Carney 2019, 121.
[87] Ekins 2018; McAlister 2018a; Melkonian-Hoover and Kellstedt 2019, 58.
[88] Arzheimer and Berning 2019.
[89] Fourquet 2019.

Such observations appear representative of a broader socio-demographic and attitudinal chasm within the right-wing core electorate, between the traditional religious right and a new secular right.[90] Broadly speaking, the former is composed of the churchgoing and more educated middle classes, committed to socially conservative church teachings but also to openness on immigration, and attached to conservative parties. By contrast, the latter typically consists of disenchanted working-class voters, who combine secular values with cultural nativism and populist tendencies, have less allegiance to church teachings, and look more favourably on right-wing populist policies.

These developments are in line with demographic trends like the rapid secularisation of the white working class in Western countries and might help us understand the observation of 'religious immunity' to the populist right in Germany, France and even in the 2016 GOP primaries in the USA. However, socio-demographic and attitudinal factors alone fail to explain why after the GOP primaries American Christians diverged so strongly from their German and French brethren in their support for the populist right, or why French Christians' religious immunity appeared to wane in the 2017 and 2022 presidential elections after decades of consistent opposition to the far right. To understand why religious immunity persisted in some countries while in other countries Christian voters seemed to enter an alliance with the new populist right, this book examines several potential explanations on the religious and political supply side ranging from historical and institutional factors, through the availability of political alternatives and the behaviour of religious elites.

3.4   What Is the Role of Mainstream Parties and Religious Leaders in Shaping the Relationship between Religion and Right-Wing Populism?

The fourth and final cornerstone of this book's argument is that right-wing populists' ability to successfully employ religion as part of their ethno-nationalist identity politics and to overcome the religious vaccination effect critically depends on two supply-side factors: the availability of a Christian alternative in the party system, and the willingness and ability of faith leaders to either challenge or legitimise national populists' use of

---

[90] Daenekindt, De Koster and Van Der Waal 2017; De Koster and Van der Waal 2007; Achterberg 2009; Ribberink, Achterberg and Houtman 2017.

religion. Both factors are in turn importantly shaped by a nation's institutional settlement of church–state relations.

The behaviour of mainstream parties is a commonly discussed factor when examining right-wing populists' electoral success. Bornschier for example has demonstrated 'the importance of the strategic response of the established parties to new political potentials' in hampering the ability of national populist parties to capitalise on new cleavages.[91] For instance, Germany's long-standing lack of a right-wing populist party has been partly explained by the fact that 'Christian democrats have retained ownership of the issues related to traditionalism and immigration'.[92] However, most traditional party systems in Western democracies appear increasingly ill-equipped to deal with the new identity cleavage. Thus, although in later years individual politicians have attempted to tap into the communitarian potential, for example by attacking the 'global elite' as 'citizens of nowhere' as former UK Prime Minister Theresa May did, or by designing a new *Heimatministerium* (Homeland Security Department) as the German CSU did, most mainstream parties had converged on the cosmopolitan side of the new cleavage throughout the 2000s and early 2010s.[93] On the left, the economic 'third way', an increasing focus on minority rights, meritocracy and the prioritisation of progressive cultural issues had largely substituted the communitarian instincts of old working-class parties with what Thomas Frank provocatively called the 'liberalism of the rich'.[94] Meanwhile, on the right, a traditional emphasis on patriotism and national identity had been replaced by a cosmopolitan and socially liberal conservatism.[95] Right populists have been able to tap into the new market niche with their own brand of right-wing identity politics.

However, the extent to which Christian rhetoric is a prominent feature of national populists' identity politics seems to depend on a second factor in the party system: the existence of a credible electoral alternative for Christians.[96] Arzheimer and Carter argue that a party that maintains ownership over the political expression of Christian values and identity

---

[91] Bornschier 2010, 13.
[92] For instance, Germany's long-standing immunity to right-wing populist parties has been partly explained by the fact that 'Christian democrats have retained ownership of the issues related to traditionalism and immigration' – at least through the Chancellorship of Angela Merkel (Bornschier 2010, 13).
[93] Arzheimer and Badinter 2006; De Wilde et al. 2019; Gastaldi 2018; Goodhart 2017.
[94] Frank 2005; Perrineau 2017; Fukuyama 2018; Lilla 2018; De Wilde et al. 2019; Sandel 2020.
[95] Fourquet 2018b; Fukuyama 2018; Giddens 2013; Olsen 2017; Sides, Tesler and Vavreck 2019.
[96] Cremer 2018; Immerzeel, Jaspers and Lubbers 2013; Montgomery and Winter 2015.

'"vaccinates" [Christian voters] against voting for a party of the radical right', by binding them to the established party and thus making them 'unavailable'.[97] The underlying logic here is that if a Christian electoral alternative is available, for instance in the form of Germany's Christian Democrats, Christian voters are comparatively immune to national populists' identitarian and civilisational references to Christianity. By contrast, if such an alternative is lacking or is 'hijacked' by populist movements (like the GOP by Trumpism in the USA) the religion gap could break down.

One example of this dynamic that we will investigate in more detail in Part III is the case of France, where Catholics had historically been bound to the centre-right *Républicains* and were therefore unavailable for the RN/FN. However, the former's gradual collapse in the context of the remaking of the French party system since 2017, has left France's Catholic electorate politically homeless. As a result, after the elimination of the centre-right candidate Francois Fillon in the first round of the 2017 presidential elections, and the underwhelming performance of his centre-right successor Valérie Pecresse in 2022, Catholics became more amenable to right-wing populist appeals when their only apparently realistic alternative was the socially liberal Emmanuel Macron (Chapter 11). A similar dynamic may have been at play during the Republican primaries in the USA in 2016, when practising Evangelicals were initially among the least supportive constituencies for Trump, instead favouring traditional Republican competitors like Ted Cruz, Marco Rubio, Ben Carson or Jeb Bush. However, most conservative faith voters fell in line and voted for Donald Trump during the general election once the other Republican candidates were eliminated and the only alternative to the national populist candidate was Hilary Clinton, who in many Christians' views represented a pro-abortion and increasingly secularist Democratic platform. By contrast, in Germany the abiding prominence of Angela Merkel's Christian Democrats, as well as the behaviour of mainstream left parties such as the Greens and the SPD, who had historically remained more open to religious voters than the French or American centre-left, played crucial roles in upholding a comparatively powerful and stable 'religious immunity'.

While the role of mainstream parties in shaping opportunity structures for right-wing populist parties is a hotly discussed topic in academia and the media, the role played by religious elites in this context has received significantly less attention. This is surprising as faith leaders' willingness

---

[97] Arzheimer and Carter 2009, 1006; Scarbrough 1984.

and ability either to condone and legitimise, or to challenge and create a social taboo around right-wing populists' religious references seem to correlate directly with the strength of religious immunity.[98] Scholars have long emphasised the importance of social taboos in determining social and political behaviour in general, and in voters' reaction to right-wing populist movements in particular.[99] Eric Kaufmann, for instance, describes how the erosion of the 'bounds of acceptable debate over immigration can set off the spiral of populist-right mobilisation' (Kaufmann 2018: 218).[100] Elite actors play a crucial role in either maintaining or eroding such social bounds. Mainstream parties or the media, for instance, often act as central gatekeepers in establishing social taboos around right-wing populists through a cordon sanitaire of non-cooperation or non-reporting.[101]

Church leaders may play a similar role within congregations through public statements, sermons and social norm-setting, which may increase the social costs among churchgoers of associating themselves with right-wing populist movements. Moreover, there is reason to believe that such taboos may be particularly powerful in religious communities, because of religious institutions' traditional role in defining social norms and because religious individuals tend to be more susceptible to social taboos than their secular neighbours.[102] Applied to the context of national populism, Chapters 7 and 11 therefore explore how in countries like Germany or France, where the churches have openly come out against right-wing populism, religious practice (and even religious affiliation) often remains a strong predictor for not voting for these parties. By contrast, Chapter 15 investigates how in a country like the USA, where church leaders have publicly been more ambiguous on their views of right-wing populists, this 'immunisation effect' is more limited.[103]

Of note, both the availability of Christian alternatives in the party system, as well as the strength of social taboos within congregations, are, however, also dependent on structural and institutional factors. For example, in strictly secularist systems like France's it may simply be more difficult or even illegal for mainstream parties to publicly present themselves as 'Christian alternatives' and to make faith outreach a prominent part of their policy platform, whereas in systems of moderate secularism like

---

[98] Cremer 2021a.
[99] De Jonge 2019; Haidt 2012; Douglas 2003.
[100] Kaufmann 2018, 218.
[101] Heinze 2018; de Jonge 2019.
[102] Haidt 2012.
[103] Elcott et al. 2021; Gorski 2019a; Whitehead, Perry and Baker 2018.

Germany links between faith communities and mainstream parties are more formalised and easily established.[104] Moreover, the historical relationship and institutional association between organised religion and the nation state can have a significant impact on the role of religion in national populists' politics in the first place, by shaping national populist's views as to whether religion is a useful cultural identifier or not.[105] When looking at faith leaders' willingness and ability to create social taboos around the populist right, institutional factors may be similarly important. For instance, more hierarchical or established churches are able to set stronger internal taboos and to communicate them more effectively. By contrast, decentralised denominations provide greater possibilities for individual clergy or lay leaders to challenge such norms internally and transmit less coherent positions externally. The institutional church–state settlement might further aggravate such discrepancies. For instance, a historical state church with an institutionalised voice in the public sphere may find it easier to communicate its stances and claim 'public ownership' over the definition of Christianity than churches in a secularist system that prohibits religious institutions' public expression.[106] Overall, church leaders may hence play a momentous role in shaping national populists' ability to redefine and re-politicise religion: either by riding on the populist tide and sanctifying right-wing populists' identity politics, or by reasserting their authority over religion in the public sphere and openly challenging contradictions between right-wing populist's religiously laden rhetoric and some of their less Christian policies.

To observe these dynamics in practice we now turn to Germany, where right-wing populists' attempts to co-opt Christianity heralded a bitter struggle with the churches about the future of religion in society.

[104] Cremer 2021b.
[105] Leustean 2008; Lichterman 2008; Smith 2008.
[106] Cremer 2021b.

PART II

The German Churches and the Alternative für Deutschland
Debunking Populist Sanctimony

Several thousand people had assembled around Dresden's Frauenkirche on a cold February evening in 2015.[1] Together they sang 'Silent Night', 'Rejoice, the Christ Child Comes Soon!' and other traditional Christian hymns as they began to parade their oversized crosses and candles through Germany's capital of Baroque. Their mission: to send a powerful message for the defence of the Christian West. Or at least that was what the name of the movement suggested: 'The Patriotic Europeans against the Islamisation of the Christian West', or simply PEGIDA. Considered, along with the AfD, to be Germany's main expression of right-wing populism,[2] PEGIDA's conspicuous use of Christian symbols, language and themes has been representative of Germany's populist movements writ large.[3] Whilst PEGIDA and its supporters carried candles and crosses through Dresden and other cities, the anti-Islamic 'Pro'-movement held their demonstrations in front of prominent churches,[4] and the AfD has claimed to defend Germany's 'Christian traditions' against radical Islam in its manifesto,[5] publicly presenting itself as the 'only Christian party that still exists'.[6]

As in other countries, observers were quick to interpret such religious references as expressions of a new reactionary alliance between the populist right and conservative Christians.[7] Some commentators even suggested an infiltration of German politics by the American Christian right, painting a bleak image in which networks of well-organised American 'Holy Warriors' are systematically undermining liberal democracy worldwide.[8]

---

[1] Contents of this chapter (though none of its primary research findings from the interviews) have also been published in a shorter contribution by the author in Elcott et al. 2021.
[2] Becher 2016; Bock 2019; Coury 2016.
[3] Havertz 2021; Coury 2021.
[4] Strohm 2011.
[5] AfD 2015.
[6] Focus 2017.
[7] Bednarz 2018; Höhne and Wensierski 2017; Morieson 2017.
[8] Brockschmidt 2021.

Yet, while such accounts were successful in grabbing the public's attention – perhaps not least because they align with some deeply rooted anti-American stereotypes in certain parts of the German population[9] – they often tend to hide a very different reality on the ground. Namely, that Germany is not just a prolific example of the right-wing populists' attempts to use Christian themes, but also of the churches' visceral rejection of such attempts, and of a strong empirical 'religious immunity' of Christian voters against the AfD. In fact, Germany's churches have become some of the most prolific public opponents of the AfD, with measures ranging from public condemnations, to the exclusion of AfD representatives from the national Church Day.[10] Meanwhile the party consistently and significantly underperforms among Protestants and Catholics when compared to irreligious voters across Germany.[11] What is more, surveys suggest that in Germany the re-politicisation of religion as a cultural identity marker has developed independently from, or even in negative correlation with, the development of religious belief and practice. An Allensbach survey in 2016 found, for instance, that whilst public support for the claim that Germany should be considered a 'Christian country' had reached an all-time high, church membership, church attendance and a proclaimed belief in God had reached an all-time low.[12]

Although at first glance such trends might seem contradictory, they largely align with the hypothesis outlined in this book of right-wing populists politicising religion as an ethno-cultural identity marker, while remaining distant from Christian institutions, doctrine and values. To analyse these dynamics in the German case study in more detail, Part II therefore applies the routes of enquiry outlined in the previous chapters and addresses four key questions: First, what are the social origins of the rise of the new populist right in Germany? Second, how do right-wing populist actors like the AfD seek to use religion? Third, how do German churches, Christian parties and voters react to these strategies? And fourth, what does this mean for the future relationship between politics and religion in Germany?

Accordingly, this part is organised in four chapters. Chapter 4 begins with a review of the historical development of church–state relations in

[9] Karnitschnig 2021.
[10] The largest assembly of Protestant lay people in Germany, bringing together biannually several hundred thousand believers, senior clergy and most of Germany's leading politicians and businesspeople. Bednarz 2018; Thielmann 2017.
[11] Konrad Adenauer Stiftung 2021; Montgomery and Winter 2015; Orth and Resing 2017.
[12] F.A.Z. 2017; Pollack and Rosta 2017.

Germany and the 'happy marriage of convenience' between religion and liberal democracy in Germany after the WWII. It examines the constitutional, institutional and political nature of Germany's constitutional settlement of 'benevolent neutrality' of the state towards the churches and analyses its implications for the behaviour of church elites and modern-day politics. Chapter 5 discusses how this settlement has been put into question by the rise of the right-wing populist AfD and its use of religion. It focuses on how the emergence of a new identity cleavage in German society has created the demand-side conditions and incentives for the AfD's transformation from an anti-Euro 'professors' party' into an identitarian right-wing populist party. Chapter 6 then turns to the AfD's use of religious themes. Relying on the elite interview material it shows how AfD leaders interpret Christianity primarily as a cultural marker against Islam in the context of a new brand of right-wing identity politics, whilst often remaining distanced from Christian social doctrine, values and institutions. Finally, Chapter 7 explains the reactions of Christian voters and the extent to which they are determined by supply-side actors such as the mainstream parties and churches. Particular attention is paid to how German Christians' 'religious immunity' to the populist right is shaped by the presence of 'Christian alternatives' in the German party system on the one hand, and by the strong social taboo around the AfD established by German faith leaders on the other. Overall, this case study shows that by categorically challenging the populist right's use of Christian symbols, Germany's institutional churches have not only had a significant impact on the AfD's electoral success, but also reclaimed a prominent place in the German political debate.

CHAPTER 4

Christianity and Democracy in Germany after World War II
From a Marriage of Convenience to Happily Ever After?

A country's institutional settlement of church–state relations can have a momentous impact on the dynamics between populism, religion and identity politics. By producing different incentive and opportunity structures, it can incite or discourage populist leaders' use of religious symbols and it can profoundly shape the ways in which mainstream party politicians and faith leaders perceive and react to the re-politicisation of religion and right-wing identity politics.

In Germany, since 1949 democratic politics and institutional religion have been tightly intertwined under a constitutional settlement of 'benevolent neutrality', in which the German state – though in principle secular – seeks to incorporate religious values and institutions as a civilisational antidote to totalitarianism.[1] This close relationship between politics and religion is visible in everyday politics. For instance, when Chancellor Angela Merkel, herself the daughter of a Protestant pastor, was sworn in to her fourth term in office by Federal President Frank-Walter Steinmeier in October 2017, three-quarters of the new cabinet were active members of one of the great German churches – compared with 62 per cent of the members of the Bundestag but only 54 per cent of the general population.[2] Federal President Steinmeier himself had been poised to become the President of the German Evangelical Church Assembly (Evangelische Kirchentag) prior to taking over the federal presidency from his predecessor Joachim Gauck, who in turn had been a Protestant pastor, before his election. Conversely, many Catholic bishops have traditionally been associated with Merkel's Christian Democratic Union (CDU/CSU), whilst a lot of their Protestant counterparts are said to be card-carrying Social Democrats (SPD). Politicians and faith leaders interviewed for this book confirmed that this high prevalence of religiosity in the top echelons of

[1] Dipper 2019.
[2] Deutscher Bundestag 2017; F.A.Z. 2018a.

53

German politics was nothing out of the ordinary. Instead, this personal proximity between the leadership of Germany's mainstream parties and ecclesiastical elites was also mirrored at the policy level. For example, a 2015 analysis of the German Protestant church's position papers placed it in the centre(-left) of German politics, and the churches' political statements often read like fierce defences of Germany's liberal order, resulting in the churches receiving infamous titles such as 'system churches' or 'government spokesmen' from AfD representatives.[3]

However, the interpretation of Christianity as a bulwark for liberal democracy was no matter of course. It is the result of a particular institutional and social settlement, which was shaped by the negative experience of secular totalitarianisms like Nazism and Communism, the rise of Christian Democracy, and an interpretation of religion not as politicised and exclusivist identity marker, but as source of shared norms, values and social cohesion. This chapter explores the genesis of this settlement and the ways in which it shapes the relationship between right-wing populism and Christianity in Germany today.

4.1   The Democratic Conversion of Germany's Churches after Nazism

The historical precondition for the intimate relationship between German democratic politics and the churches was the 'conversion' of Germany's churches to democracy after 1945. Prior to World War II neither the Protestant nor the Catholic Church were particularly enthusiastic supporters of democracy. German Protestantism had been closely associated with the Prussian throne, and even though most of the Protestant establishment would have preferred a Kaiser over a Führer, a majority of them still opted for the NSDAP over the Catholic Zentrum party or 'godless socialism' in 1933.[4] From 1933 to 1945, there was some notable Protestant resistance against Nazism in the form of the (minority) Confessing Church around Karl Barth, Dietrich Bonhoeffer and Martin Niemöller.[5] However, the majority of Protestants were loyal to the Führer and sided with the pro-Nazi 'German Christians', who sought to create a new 'positive Christianity' that was 'cleansed' of Christians of non-Aryan descent, 'free'

---

[3] Thieme and Liedhegener 2015.
[4] Günther Grass went so far as to argue that 'Christian churches assimilated themselves [into the Nazi state] with virtually no resistance' (van Norden 1979, 52; Strohm 2011; Scheliha 2019).
[5] Meier 1984; Cremer 2019.

from Jewish influences, and that substituted 'the traditional Trinitarian doctrine with a new Trinity of God, *Führer* and *Volk*'.[6]

Catholics, in whom the decades-long persecution as 'enemies of the Reich' in Bismarck's and the Kaiser's anti-Catholic *Kulturkampf* ('culture-struggle') in the nineteenth century had instilled greater suspicion towards the German state, voted for Hitler at much lower rates, and Catholic authorities remained significantly more critical of the Nazi ideal of a racially defined 'positive Christianity'.[7] In fact, being Catholic was one of the best predictors for not voting NSDAP in 1933 and Catholic clergy's reservations and resistance towards Nazism went so far that by 1945 more than half of all Catholic priests in Germany (10,315) had in one way or the other fallen victim to coercive measures of the regime.[8] However, pre-1945, political Catholicism was, as Kalyvas and van Kersbergen put it, still 'largely antiliberal … [and] challenged the ascendancy of liberalism in Europe from a "fundamentalist" and theocratic perspective'.[9]

It was only after the end of the war, once the horrors of Nazism had been revealed and Hitler's plan for an atheist 'final solution of the Church question'[10] shown to have been hardly more church-friendly than the communist persecution of believers in Eastern Europe, that the majority of German Christians and their spiritual leaders made a full conversion to liberal democracy. The Protestant church, which had amassed greater guilt under Nazi rule, felt the need to repent most urgently. In October 1945, in the 'Stuttgart Declaration of Guilt', the Council of the Evangelical Church professed, 'Through us, infinite wrong was brought over many peoples and countries. … [W]e accuse ourselves for not standing up to our beliefs more courageously, for not praying more faithfully, for not believing more joyously, and for not loving more ardently.'[11] In the following years German Protestantism reorganised itself into the new Evangelical Church of Germany (EKD). Internal church democracy was strengthened, and former protagonists of the anti-Nazi Confessing Church took up leading positions in the church. Perhaps most crucially, the neo-orthodox theology of Karl Barth, which had inspired the Barmen

---

[6]   Meier 1984, 19; Strohm 2011, 14ff.

[7]   Gruber 2006; Wehler 1994.

[8]   Falter 1991; Hehl and Kösters 1984, 79.

[9]   Kalyvas and Van Kersbergen 2010, 185.

[10]   In December 1941 Hitler claimed that 'The War will end, and I will make it my ultimate life's work to bring the Church question to its final solution. Only then will the German nation be fully secure.' Strohm 2011, 7.

[11]   EKD 1945.

Declaration against Nazism, replaced traditional liberal theology as the mainstream doctrine of the church.[12] Symbolising the Protestant church's break with nationalism, the Barmen Declaration itself became part of most regional churches' constitutions.[13] Pastors were ordained on it, and it was reprinted in every Hymnal ('Evangelisches Gesangbuch').[14]

German Catholicism seemed in less immediate need of a radical reversal. Yet, many Catholic activists and politicians were still inspired to re-evaluate liberal democracy more positively. This was partly due to the persecution they experienced alongside other democrats under the Nazis and the new Communist regimes in Eastern Europe. However, even more important was the influence of the new pro-democratic stream of Catholic thought that was gaining momentum around the middle of the century: Christian Democracy.[15]

4.2   Christian Democracy and the *Grundgestz*

Having originated in the late nineteenth and early twentieth centuries as 'a concept coined in opposition to liberal democracy',[16] after 1945 Christian Democratic thinkers and politicians began to apply themselves to the new challenge of 'how to reconcile Christianity and democracy; or failing a full reconciliation, how to render democracy safe for Christianity under modern conditions'.[17] Christian Democracy's crucial role in establishing liberal democracies throughout Europe is well established. Scholars have emphasised its importance in legitimising the free market economy, constructing the European project and pressuring the Catholic Church into opening itself up to democracy – a process ultimately crowned by the embrace of modernity and democracy at the Second Vatican Council.[18] Yet, its impact was also of special relevance in Western Germany, where, under the leadership of the Federal Republic's first chancellor Konrad Adenauer, the newly founded Christian Democratic Union and Christian Social Union (CDU/CSU) went beyond Christian Democracy's Catholic origins and brought

---

[12] Besier 1994, 343ff.
[13] Similar to the Federal Republic itself, the German Protestant Church (EKD) is in fact a federation of a number of relatively autonomous regional churches, each with their own constitutions and prelates.
[14] Bahr et al. 2009.
[15] Kalyvas and Van Kersbergen 2010.
[16] Kalyvas and Van Kersbergen 2010, 185.
[17] Müller 2013, 245.
[18] Linden 2009; Kaiser and Wohnout 2004.

together German Protestants and Catholics in one pro-democratic party for the first time. This not only gave Protestants a new democratic home, thus reconciling them with the new democratic system and with their traditional rivals of the Catholic *Zentrum* party. But it also helped Catholics to come to terms with the new German state and to emerge from their defensive and sometimes deeply antiliberal positions, informed by the *Kulturkampf.*[19]

Crucially, in 1945, as most other pillars of German civil society had either been eradicated by or fully assimilated into the Nazi state, the new movement also provided the population with a different narrative and connection point to 'another Germany'.[20] It was a vision of Germany that could be seen as a positive counterpart to the Nazi era, but that was still rooted in German history and civilisation and held together by ancient institutions relatively untainted by Nazism.[21] This narrative of a Christian Germany soon attracted millions of disillusioned Germans back into the pews as well as into the ranks of the CDU/CSU, which quickly grew to become Germany's largest political movement.[22] Importantly, this vision also appealed to the Western allies, who – on the lookout for an upbeat counternarrative to Nazism and trustworthy politicians and institutions with whom to (re)build the German state – keenly seized the opportunity to entrust Christian Democrats and Social Democrats with the creation of Germany's new constitution: the *Grundgesetz* ('basic law').[23]

'Conscious of their responsibility before God and man',[24] the *Grundgesetz*' authors echoed a Christian scepticism for secular ideology and direct democracy by establishing powerful courts and immutable foundational rights.[25] As political scientist Jan-Werner Müller observed, as elsewhere in Europe, Christian Democratic elites 'sought to constrain the demos ... internally through a revival of conservative forms of lay activism (hence a particular kind of "Christian demos") and externally through institutions such as constitutional courts and (supranationally) the European Court of Human Rights'.[26] In the hope that powerful and

---

[19] The *Kulturkampf* (culture struggle) refers to the conflict between the Protestant German imperial government and the Roman Catholic Church from about 1872 to 1878, in which Bismarck labelled Catholics as 'enemies of the Reich' (Clark and Kaiser, 2003).
[20] Ueberschär 2006.
[21] Ringshausen 2014.
[22] Pollack and Rosta 2017, 73ff.
[23] Schlaich and Heckel 1997.
[24] Grundgesetz 1949, 1.
[25] Pestalozza 1981; Püttmann 1994; Dipper 2019; Müller 2013.
[26] Müller 2013, 251.

vibrant churches could also help the new Republic to address the dilemma that, in the famous words of Grundgesetz co-author Ernst-Wolfgang Böckenförde, 'the liberal, secularised state lives by prerequisites which it cannot guarantee itself',[27] they created the explicitly church-friendly system of benevolent neutrality.[28] In this system, the new German state not only guaranteed religious freedom and equal rights for different religious groups, but also endowed religious institutions with a quasi-public status, collected their membership contributions through taxes, partly funded faith-run hospitals, schools and welfare organisations, and constitutionally enshrined religious education in schools and universities.[29] In doing so, the *Grundgesetz* formalised the expectation that churches, as protagonists of civil religion, would frame debates, instil social cohesion, foster shared values, virtues and identity as well as procure 'interior forces of regulation' that would allow the liberal state to refrain from coercive or authoritative measures.[30]

4.3　Benevolent Neutrality and the Depoliticisation of Religion

This formalised social, constitutional and institutional arrangement between church and state proved to be a relatively happy alliance over the decades, with the churches enjoying their constitutional privileges and high social status and the state relying on the churches to bridge public divides and fulfil social tasks.[31] In particular, Germany's churches have played an important role in mitigating the two traditional social cleavages in Western societies – the economic cleavage between workers and capitalists, and the cultural cleavage between social conservatism and social liberalism – by anchoring themselves on both sides of each cleavage. They advocated welfare distribution in tune with Catholic social doctrine whilst acting as a bulwark against Communism.[32] They supported Willy Brandt's new social and foreign policy, without giving up their role as guarantors of traditional values.[33] And they provided a platform for the peace and environmental movements of the 1980s, without questioning the legitimacy of Germany's political and constitutional system.[34] This is not to say that

---

[27] Böckenförde 1991, 112.
[28] Waldhoff 2013; Dipper 2019.
[29] Waldhoff 2013.
[30] Böckenförde 1991, 113.
[31] Pollack and Rosta 2017.
[32] Kaiser and Wohnout 2004, 2.
[33] Graf 2011; Hauschild 1968, 35ff.
[34] Zander 1989.

the churches' roles and positions were not highly contested at times or suffered significant losses in political and social influence, especially after Germany's reunification, as secularisation progressed and religious diversity increased.[35] Yet, their constitutionally endowed mediator role and ability to stand on both sides of the traditional cleavages saved them from being perceived as overly partisan and helped to depoliticise religion as a wedge-issue in German politics.[36]

As a result, Pollack and Rosta have shown that while religious authorities maintain a relatively high social status and moral authority in Germany, and religiosity continues to be seen as socially desirable, religion has also become increasingly privatised and more detached from traditional group identities, political tribes and even from party allegiances over the decades.[37] In terms of voting behaviour, Germany's Christians tend to be relatively evenly distributed across the mainstream party spectrum, with Catholic churchgoers and Evangelicals favouring the CDU/CSU, and Mainline Protestants predominately voting for the SPD, Greens or the liberal FDP.[38] These results are in line with the self-perceptions of party and church elites interviewed for this book. Former CDU General-Secretary Hermann Gröhe thus confirmed that 'in the CDU/CSU you find the whole spectrum of positions of German Catholicism, whereas liberal Protestantism is closer to the SPD and Greens'.[39]

Yet, beyond shaping the role of the churches in society, the arrangement of benevolent neutrality has also moulded the outlook and structure of Germany's churches themselves. For one, faith communities' legal status as bodies of the public law, and the collection of their membership contributions through the state in the form of taxes, required them to have a formal organisation with official legal and political representatives, clear hierarchies and official registers of their members.[40] Moreover, this system implicitly endowed the German state with the authority to distinguish

---

[35] Bertelsmann Stiftung 2016; Pollack and Rosta 2017.
[36] Püttmann 2016a.
[37] Pollack and Rosta 2017, 142.
[38] Whilst Chapter 7 shows that the CDU/CSU traditionally claimed to be the primary 'Christian party', other parties have come to represent and attract aspects of the Christian votership: for instance, the SPD became the main party of the liberal Protestant middle classes throughout the 1960s and 1970s after opening itself up to religion with its Godesberg Programme in 1959 (Inacker 1993), and the Greens originated as representatives of the largely religiously organised peace and environmentalist movement of the 1980s. See Zander 1989; Neu 2012; Pokorny 2018; Siegers and Jedinger 2021.
[39] Interview Gröhe 2018.
[40] Czermak 2019.

between denominations that qualify as 'religious communities' under public law and are therefore deemed worthy of receiving public support and privileges, and those that are not.[41] This formalistic approach naturally incentivises well-established, highly institutionalised and hierarchical churches, whose teaching closely aligns with the liberal-democratic basic order, set out by the *Grundgesetz*, over newer, less hierarchical and more state-critical denominations. As a result, it appears to have reinforced the institutional Protestant and Catholic churches' status and (self-)perception as the 'godparents' of Germany's liberal democratic system. This is a status that – as Chapter 7 will show – also profoundly shaped their vehement and outspoken opposition to the AfD.[42]

The elite interviews with faith leaders and politicians conducted for this book confirm this impression of relative harmony between the churches and the liberal democratic system. Even in times of accelerating secularisation and religious diversity the religion-friendly settlement of benevolent neutrality remained relatively uncontested and valued by both the political and the ecclesiastical elite. Of the twenty-one religious and mainstream political leaders interviewed in Germany, all but one displayed an unequivocally positive assessment of what interviewees largely referred to as Germany's 'benevolent neutrality model'. The then-president of the EKD synod (the highest decision-making body of the Protestant church), Irmgard Schwätzer, for instance, praised it as a 'wonderful system. Compared to the systems of other countries it's the best one I know, because it obliges the state to be neutral and to treat everyone the same, but it also obliges it to support religious communities.'[43] Germany's most senior Catholic cleric at the time, Cardinal Reinhard Marx, then president of the German conference of Catholic bishops, credited benevolent neutrality for having significantly 'contributed to the religious peace in our country' and for the fact that 'we in Germany do not have a strong anti-clericalism or anti-Christian attitudes as is the case in other countries'.[44] And even representatives of the more state-critical free churches such as Uwe Heimowski of the German Evangelical Alliance (DEA) judged that 'all in all, the German way is very good because we manage to rule out both extremes (state church and strong secularism)'.[45]

---

[41] Czermak 2019.
[42] Thieme and Liedhegener 2015; Kuzmany 2016; Thielmann 2017; Elcott et al. 2021.
[43] Interview Schwätzer 2018.
[44] Interview Marx 2018.
[45] Interview Heimowski 2018.

This assessment was also shared by senior political leaders like former CDU General-Secretary Hermann Gröhe, who argued that 'the churches in Germany still have a very high social status – also amongst those who are not religious'.[46] Katrin Göring-Eckardt, at the time of the interviews president of the Green party, maintained that, 'in principle the religious constitutional settlement is good the way it is'.[47] Meanwhile SPD politicians like Stephan Steinlein, the chief of staff of the German president, or Wolfgang Thierse the former president of the Bundestag, similarly positioned themselves as 'a supporter of the German model of the relationship between state and religion [because] the German model is more capable of solving the current problems and finding forms through which Islam, too, can be integrated',[48] and stated that 'the example of France shows that *laïcité* is the wrong way and counterproductive (whereas) our way – the German way – is much better'.[49]

Overall, throughout the second half of the twentieth century, benevolent neutrality seemed to ensure that religion remained recognised as a social bridge-builder over traditional cleavages, a moral authority and individual motivator for political action across parties. By contrast, religion, as a cultural group identifier or political wedge-issue, had lost much of its political salience. However, this 'happy marriage of convenience' between religion and politics has been fundamentally challenged by the emergence of a new social cleavage centred around identity and the subsequent rise of a new populist right in Germany around PEGIDA and the AfD. The latter's electoral success, with a strategy based on opposition to (Muslim) immigration and references to Germany's 'Judeo-Christian identity', suggests a fundamental transformation of Germany's political party system, and a return of religion as a political wedge-issue.

---

[46] Interview Gröhe 2018.
[47] Interview Göring-Eckardt 2018.
[48] Interview Steinlein 2018.
[49] Interview Thierse 2018.

CHAPTER 5

The Advent of the Alternative für Deutschland in the Context of the New Identity Cleavage

> The AfD [Alternative für Deutschland] clearly rejects an Islamic prac-
> tice of faith that is directed against the liberal-democratic basic order,
> our laws and against the Judeo-Christian and humanistic founda-
> tions of our culture.
>
> Party Programme, Alternative für Deutschland (AfD), 2015: 95

> We do not seek to defend Christianity in any religious sense, but as
> a traditional way of life in Germany, as a traditional sense of home
> [Heimatgefühl]. Christianity is only a metaphor for the customs
> inherited from our fathers.
>
> Alexander Gauland, President of the AfD, 2016

These AfD statements are emblematic, not only of the fact that religion
has returned as a politicised issue to Germany, but also of the way in
which the AfD has begun to employ Christianity in the context of the
new brand of right-wing identity politics; that is, less as an individual
faith and more as a culturalised marker of the nation against external others, and in particular Islam.

However, the AfD was initially not a natural candidate for politicising religious identity in such ways, let alone for challenging the system
of benevolent neutrality. When in February 2013 a few dozen 'concerned
citizens' came together in the Christian community centre of Oberursel, at
the invitation of the economics Professor Bernd Lucke, there was little talk
of the defence of 'German identity' or 'the Christian Occident' against the
dangers of 'Islamisation' or 'foreign infiltration'.[1] Like Lucke, most participants were well-educated members of the West-German upper middle
class (among them a disproportionate number of university professors).
And, again like Lucke, most were primarily concerned about the (in their
view) fiscally irresponsible economic policy of the German government

---

[1] Amann 2017, 59ff.; Arzheimer 2015; Dilling 2018.

during the Eurozone crisis.[2] In their minds the newly founded 'Alternative for Germany' was to be a 'party of a new type' as Lucke put it: different not only from the political mainstream but also from those right-wing populist parties surging throughout Europe.[3] It was to be economically (neo) liberal, but open to (qualified) immigration and moderately conservative on social issues, thus also providing an alternative to disappointed conservative Christian voters. Most importantly though, it was to be thoroughly 'respectable' and appeal to 'those middle-class and academic milieus, that consider themselves through their status as high-achievers'.[4] As Annette Schultner, the founding president of the 'Christians in the AfD' (ChrAfD) organisation, summarised the early AfD leaders' intentions in our interview, 'from the beginning it was completely clear to me that we wanted to build a middle-class conservative party in the style of the CSU'.[5]

Five years later the AfD had entered all sixteen German state parliaments, was the largest opposition party in the federal Bundestag and trailed only the CDU/CSU as the strongest party in the polls.[6] In some states there was even talk of the AfD assuming government responsibilities. But the party had also been fundamentally transformed. It had ousted personalities like Schultner, Lucke and most of their supporters from its ranks, adopted an economic policy that few would consider fiscally conservative, sourced its voters from the East-German working-class and was speaking of little else but the defence of 'German identity' and 'the Christian occident' against the dangers of 'Islamisation' and 'foreign infiltration'.[7] It was no longer a conservative party.[8]

What had happened? The AfD's path from a free-market 'professors' party', to an anti-Islam and anti-immigration 'precariat's party',[9] was paved by political infighting, reactions to social exclusion and ideological radicalisation. However, this chapter shows that its overall direction is most adequately explained by developments on the demand side of politics, and more specifically by the emergence of a new identity cleavage that has begun to fundamentally reshape German politics.

---

[2] Havertz 2020.
[3] Lucke in Die Welt 2013.
[4] Berbuir et al. for instance show that nearly half of the AfD sympathisers hold a university degree and earn above average. See Berbuir, Lewandowsky and Siri 2015, 168; See also Gebhardt 2013, 87; Dilling 2018.
[5] Interview Schultner 2018.
[6] Die Zeit 2018a.
[7] Hambauer and Mays 2018; Heimbach-Steins and Filipović 2017.
[8] Dilling 2018.
[9] Die Welt 2016.

5.1 The End of Germany's Populist Exception and the Emergence of a New Identity Cleavage

Germany has been a relative latecomer to the political manifestation of the new identity cleavage and of new political parties catering to it. Whilst in neighbouring countries such as France, the Netherlands, Austria and most Scandinavian countries, national populist anti-immigration parties appeared as early as the 1970s,[10] made an 'identitarian turn' in the 1990s,[11] established themselves as major political forces by the 2000s[12] and entered a number of governments by 2010,[13] by 2012 Germany could still be cited as an example of 'the lack of success of the populist right'.[14] Indeed, until the federal elections of 2017 no party right of the CDU/CSU had ever managed to score the 5 per cent necessary to enter the Bundestag, and those proto-right-wing populist parties that did emerge, such as the Republikaner[15] or the Schill party,[16] could only achieve isolated successes in regional elections and were generally short-lived.

The reasons for what Benner called 'Germany's populist exception' were manifold and remain contested.[17] Some observers point to demand-side factors in the electorate, arguing that the economic or moral cleavages were more deeply entrenched in German society than in other countries.[18] Others suggested that Germany's history and particularly its self-critical treatment of the Nazi era meant that German voters had learned from their past, thus reducing the prevalence of right-wing identitarian, nationalist, anti-universalistic and exclusionist attitudes.[19] However, such arguments have been challenged by findings of scholars like Backes and Mudde, Kriesi, van der Brug et al., Bornschier, or De Wilde et al., who point to survey data showing continuous approval ratings of between 10 and 20 per cent for nativist, authoritarian or nationalist statements in Germany since the end of the Cold War. Such numbers correspond

---

[10] Kaltwasser et al. 2017a; Mudde 2007; Mudde and Kaltwasser 2017.
[11] Betz 1994; Betz 2004.
[12] Kaltwasser et al. 2017a; Mudde 2014b.
[13] Albertazzi and McDonnell 2015.
[14] Benner 2016; Bornschier 2012, 121.
[15] A national conservative party that emerged in the 1980s and rose to some prominence in the 1990s gaining seats in several regional parliaments before largely disappearing in the 2000s. By 2013 it scored less than 0.2 per cent in the federal elections. Mudde 2003, 31–59.
[16] The Schill party or 'Party for a Rule of Law Offensive' was a minor right-wing populist party that rose to prominence in the early 2000s in Hamburg where it gained 19.4 per cent in the 2000 state elections before collapsing again and losing most of its support by 2003. F. Decker 2002.
[17] Benner 2016.
[18] Bornschier 2012, 126ff.
[19] Art 2006, 200; Berbuir, Lewandowsky and Siri 2015, 160.

with the European average.[20] Instead of focusing on the demand side, these scholars point at supply-side factors such as the role of Germany's electoral and constitutional system and the cordon sanitaire created by Germany's political elites to not cooperate with the far right.[21] It is beyond the scope of this volume to completely resolve such debates. Yet, with the meteoric rise of the AfD and its entrance into each regional parliament (*Landtag*) and the Bundestag in 2017, it appears clear that whatever the factors thwarting an earlier rise of a successful right-wing populist party had been, they could only delay but not prevent what Benner called 'the decisive end of German exceptionalism on populism'.[22] This suggests that under the surface of Germany's relatively stable-looking party system on the political supply-side, on the demand-side conditions for the rise of the new right had been growing and simmering for decades – just as in other western countries.

In response to the final 'thawing' of Germany's political landscape, academics have paid much more attention to these underlying demand-side developments. Specifically, scholars found indicators suggesting the emergence of a new social cleavage centred around identity since the end of the Cold War. A group of social scientists at the Berlin Social Sciences Centre, for instance, conducted a large-scale quantitative analysis of Germany's cleavage system and compared it with those in other countries. They found that 'there are good reasons to believe that a new fault line has emerged that pits opponents and proponents of globalization against one another' and that divides society into 'cosmopolitans' and 'communitarians' (De Wilde et al. 2019, 5). In line with scholars in other countries, who have found a new divide between 'somewheres' and 'anywheres',[23] between 'demarcationists' and 'integrationists',[24] or between 'nativists' and 'globalists',[25] De Wilde et al. argue that this divide is primarily identity-based rather than economic or moral, and that it is particularly concerned with questions of (national) identity, immigration and 'the status of communities and their relationship to individuals'.[26] On one side of the divide stand Germany's cosmopolitan elites, who, 'emphasising universalism, attribute moral value

---

[20] Decker, Kiess and Brähler 2016; Decker, Kiess and Brähler 2014; Decker, Kiess and Brähler 2012; Decker, Kiess and Brähler 2008; Backes and Mudde 2000; Kriesi et al. 2006; van der Brug, Fennema and Tillie 2005; Bornschier 2010; De Wilde et al. 2019.
[21] Givens 2005; Kitschelt 2007; Ellinas 2010; Bornschier 2012.
[22] Benner 2016.
[23] Goodhart 2017.
[24] Kriesi et al. 2006; Kriesi et al. 2012.
[25] Piketty 2020.
[26] De Wilde et al. 2019, 12ff.

exclusively to all human beings' (and therefore favour immigration). On the other side are the communitarian masses, who value national identity and view the 'constitutive communities we are born into (as) a core part of our identity' (and therefore oppose immigration).[27]

This line of argument was confirmed by other studies. For instance, Gaston and Hilhorst (2018) have found that German citizens 'feel they are witnessing the fragmentation of communities, as we enter an age of isolation', which renders them more pessimistic about 'the forces that once held us together – our shared culture, traditions and values – ... being displaced by an emphasis on pluralism'.[28] Similarly, the interpretation that the new cleavage is partly a result of the erosion of traditional identities and a confrontation with foreign identity corresponds with traditional 'individualisation theory' in Germany. Championed by sociologists such as Ulrich Beck or Jürgen Habermas and more recently by Andreas Reckwitz, individualisation theory emphasises how trends such as secularisation, globalisation and modernisation have eroded traditional group identity markers such as class, nationality, region and religion in German society.[29] This development has produced a new cosmopolitan economic and social elite comparatively free of social or geographical constraints, but left large parts of the population feeling insecure about their own identity and sensitive to any real or imagined threat to this identity from without.[30]

The result is a new divide between these two groups which appears to be – especially since the so-called refugee crisis of 2015/2016 – increasingly focused on the wedge-issue of (Muslim) immigration. Longitudinal survey data from the Eurobarometer (2007–2018) show that from the mid-2000s and throughout the 2010s immigration has continuously risen in relevance in German politics, and that from 2015 it has consistently topped the list of the main concerns amongst German voters.[31] As Dostal put it, whilst 'economic and social issues ... feature prominently on the public agenda ... all of these issues are still secondary when compared to the refugee and migration problem', as the latter has, 'since September 2015, become the ultimate "wedge"-issue of German politics'.[32]

---

[27] De Wilde et al. 2019, 12ff.
[28] Gaston and Hilhorst 2018, 18.
[29] Beck and Beck-Gernsheim 2001; Beck and Ritter 1992; Habermas 1985; Habermas 2006; Reckwitz 2018.
[30] De Wilde et al. 2019; Stubager 2008.
[31] Eurobarometer 2017; Forschungsgruppe Wahlen e.V. 2017.
[32] Dostal 2017, 591.

5.2   A Lack of Representation on the Supply Side?

While there is still debate in the academic literature about whether or not this demand-side phenomenon is really the result of a new social cleavage or just a short-term backlash against recent flows of immigration, on the supply side of politics, the practitioners interviewed were less divided in their interpretation, suggesting that their own actions and behaviour are increasingly shaped by such an interpretation of contemporary German politics.[33] Across the board and regardless of political or religious background, interviewees echoed, for instance, the assessment that (the erosion of) collective identities and the perceived threat of immigration are at the core of a new fault line. Wolfgang Thierse, former president of the Bundestag, asserted that 'the migration question divides all parties: CDU, CSU, SPD and Die Linke', and linked this development to a crisis of identity:

> Globalisation, digitalisation and terrorism are a wealth of changes that have created insecurity [across society]. This intrusion of the frightening and unfamiliar is personified by 'the refugee' … Through contact with the unfamiliar and the stranger, a feeling of the loss of home [Entheimatung] arises, as the familiar, which used to make up one's own identity, is suddenly put into question.[34]

Thierse's SPD party ally, and head of the Bundespräsidialamt (Office of the Federal President), Stephan Steinlein, gave a similar assessment, arguing that 'behind this debate about identity and culture is a sense of insecurity among many people, which they try to fight by finding something to cling onto. Ultimately, one has to look for the deeper causes of this search for home [Heimat] and identity [Beheimatung]'.[35] On the side of religious leaders, Martin Dutzmann, the representative of the Council of the Evangelical Church in Germany (*EKD*) to the federal government, explained that part of the reason for the rise of the new right is that 'in the face of globalisation, pluralisation and great uncertainty, people are in search of identity, asking: Who am I? Who are we? Who belongs to us?'[36] The head of the Conference of Catholic Bishops, Cardinal Marx, summarised the sentiment as follows:

---

[33] Bélanger and Meguid 2008; Bornschier 2012; De Wilde et al. 2019; Dostal 2017; Kriesi et al. 2012; Meguid 2005.
[34] Interview Thierse 2018.
[35] Interview Steinlein 2018.
[36] Interview Dutzmann 2018.

> There is a diffuse discomfort in Europe stemming from different sensations.
> Some say: 'We are losing ourselves; our homeland [Heimat], our identity,
> our social security are endangered by foreigners etc'. … If these diffuse feel-
> ings and fears are then exploited by right-wing populist forces this becomes
> dangerous. I would rather speak of the feeling of insult that people do not
> feel taken seriously and [feel] excluded which is also associated with envy
> and resentment towards the so-called established elites.[37]

While Germany's political and religious elite widely agreed in their assessment that the 'identity question' has become the new core divide in
German society, the grievances of the communitarian side were perhaps
most vehemently formulated by representatives of the AfD. For instance,
Armin-Paul Hampel the president of the AfD in Lower-Saxony and member of the Bundestag lamented the erosion of traditional norms, institutions and communities, arguing that 'we are partly living in late-Roman
decadence. Everything has become possible. Everything is arbitrary … We
are witnessing a cultural decay.'[38] Similarly, Volker Münz, MP and AfD
spokesperson for religious affairs, emphasised that 'the people … feel that
in a time when everything is put into question – from gender, marriage,
nationality, borders and the concept of the people – and in which there is
nothing that is not put into question, that they need something to hang
on to. One needs constants and identity.'[39]

   The fact that AfD representatives appeared particularly adept in formulating such grievances suggests that, as in other Western countries, right-
wing populists in Germany have been able to capitalise on a vacuum in the
traditional party system, as most mainstream parties seemed ill-equipped
to deal with the new identity cleavage on the demand side. For instance,
De Wilde et al. have observed that 'since the end of the Cold War, parties
of the mainstream Left and Right, … have converged on pro-globalisation
positions', leaving the communitarian side of the divide unrepresented.[40]
For instance, since the 2000s and 2010s, the mainstream left SPD, which
Bornschier had previously credited with 'averting the entry of an extreme
right competitor' by refraining from 'promoting a universalistic defence of
multiculturalism, [which] reinforces the extreme right's ownership of the
traditionalist communitarian position',[41] began to substitute old communitarian instincts of the working class, with a course towards 'the new centre'

---

[37] Interview Marx 2018.
[38] Interview Hampel 2018.
[39] Interview Münz 2018.
[40] De Wilde et al. 2019, 5; Mudde 2007; Arzheimer 2009.
[41] Bornschier 2012, 128.

(*Die neue Mitte*).[42] This opened the party to the cosmopolitan side of the new identity cleavage, with a more positive attitude towards the free movement of goods and people, and an increased emphasis on cosmopolitan core identity issues such as gay, women's and minority rights, but it often came at the expense of traditional appeals to communitarian positions and class identity.[43] Similarly, on the mainstream right, the traditional focus on patriotism, national identity and social conservatism has been increasingly replaced by a more 'cosmopolitan' vision of conservatism, incarnated in the personalities of Angela Merkel or her (short-lived) successor as CDU president, Annegret Kramp-Karrenbauer. In a process that political scientists called the 'social-democratisation of the Union parties',[44] Merkel and her entourage had replaced the old guard of conservatives around Wolfgang Schäuble, Edmund Stoiber, Roland Koch and Friedrich Merz, and led the party into the cosmopolitan mainstream with the abolition of military service and the introduction of gay marriage and, most crucially, the opening of Germany's borders to Syrian refugees in 2015/2016. As a result, Merkel's Grand Coalition of CDU/CSU and SPD is widely considered as 'perhaps the best example of the new mainstream pro-immigration consensus'.[45] After Merkel's departure from leadership and the CDU/CSU's crushing defeat in the 2021 federal elections under the leadership of the centrist Armin Laschet, Friedrich Merz, one of Merkel's most prolific conservative critics, finally succeeded (after several failed attempts in 2018 and 2021) to gain control of the CDU leadership and may seek to partly reverse the CDU's shift to the centre. Yet, at the time of writing it is still unclear whether the party will follow him on this path.

In either scenario, in the mid-2010s the consequence of the centre-left and centre-rights convergence on identity issues was a vacuum of representation for communitarians looking for collective forms of identity.[46] This trend was recognised by the interviewed experts and policymakers. For example, Christian Meißner, the director of the CDU's Protestant Association, stated, that he 'felt that there was a representation problem in conservative circles, when during the last campaign I spent hours on the phone talking to members, who have been in the CDU for decades but are now doing some soul searching'.[47] In a similar vein former CDU general

---

[42] Busch and Manow 2001; Giddens 2013.
[43] Bornschier 2012; Ohlert 2014.
[44] Klose and Patzelt 2016; Wiliarty 2021.
[45] De Wilde et al. 2019; Goodwin, Olsen and Good 2019; Kaufmann 2018.
[46] Meguid 2005; Bélanger and Meguid 2008; Dostal 2017.
[47] Interview Meißner 2018.

secretary and cabinet minister Gröhe claimed that within the party 'we certainly feel it when some conservatives wonder: "With Merkel in Berlin and Pope Francis in Rome: who's still fighting for the Christian Occident these days?"'[48] On the left, former SPD MP and now president of the renowned Federal Agency for Civic Education, Thomas Krüger, stated that 'through massive individualisation we now have a representation problem' and that part of the problem is that in particular the 'parliamentary Left is … globalist and cosmopolitan and that it has largely abandoned communitarian positions of community and solidarity'.[49]

5.3   The Advent and Transformation of the AfD

Throughout Europe political entrepreneurs on the populist right have recognised this political opportunity on the demand side and sought to politicise the new cleavage by increasing the salience of communitarian concerns through their own brand of identity politics. As discussed in Chapter 2, this right-wing identity politics prioritises the cultural identity of the ethnic majority, opposes (non-Western) immigration, feeds off feelings of victimhood and cultural decline, and challenges the globalist and liberal ideology of the 'elites'. It has dropped traditional 'biological' racism in favour of the 'ethno-pluralist' doctrine of 'equal but different', claiming to defend the 'rights' of (majority) cultures against mixture or 'dilution' with other cultures.[50] One important consequence of the concept of 'ethno-pluralism' is that culture – largely defined through religious identity – rather than race or ideology has become the key variable of differentiation between the 'us' and the 'external other'. The main opponent is no longer 'the Turk', 'the socialist', 'the welfare state', 'the euro' or 'the democratic deficit of the EU', but 'the Muslim immigrant' and the 'corrupted elite' who allow the former to enter the country and dilute the 'homogenous' people's cultural identity.[51]

While Betz notes that most western European right-wing populist parties made a corresponding 'identitarian turn' in their rhetoric and policies in the 1990s and 2000s, in the AfD, this development only took place amidst the heat of the 'refugee crisis' of 2015/2016.[52] Prior to this, the AfD appeared to be the exception to the right-wing populist rule. In its early

---

[48] Interview Gröhe 2018.
[49] Interview Krüger 2018.
[50] Jones 2016; Rydgren 2010; Jardina 2019; Havertz 2021.
[51] Casanova 2012a; Coury 2021.
[52] Betz 2004; Dilling 2018.

stages 'in contrast to the mainstream of European right-wing populist parties … the AfD party platform [did] not refer to migration in a strictly negative way'.[53] Hambauer and Mays, moreover, found that 'nearly half of the AfD sympathisers [held] a university degree', that it was 'the party of the well-off, as 34 per cent of AfD sympathisers were part of the richest fifth of the population', and that it attracted disproportionately former FDP or CDU/CSU voters.[54] Arzheimer's 2015 analysis of the AfD's 2013 manifesto and of hundreds of online party statements maintained that although the AfD did 'occupy a position at the far right of the German party system … it is currently neither populist nor does it belong to the family of the Radical right parties'.[55]

Crucially for this study, the early AfD also did not employ religion as a cultural identity marker in the ways it has become common for right-wing populist parties since 2010s.[56] Instead, in keeping with Germany's tradition of benevolent neutrality, early AfD leaders primarily referenced religion as a moral value system in the context of the traditional economic or moral cleavages. In a country where, as Mario Monti once put it, 'economics is still part of moral philosophy', the AfD hence occasionally appealed to the ideals of a 'Protestant fiscal ethics' in its opposition to Angela Merkel's commitment to the euro and the potential need to bail out southern EU members.[57] It also sought to appeal to those conservative Christian voters who felt alienated by the relatively liberal course of the mainstream parties and of the Protestant and Catholic churches on social and moral issues such as abortion, family values, sexual freedom or gay rights.[58] Combined with a leadership team including the practising Calvinist Bernd Lucke, the conservative journalist Konrad Adam, and the Grand-Duchesse and prominent Christian activist Beatrix von Storch, the early AfD displayed a public image of 'economics and faith'.[59]

Although religious values always remained secondary to economic issues in the early AfD's agenda, during our interviews several AfD representatives emphasised religion in their decision to take up a position of responsibility in the party. Annette Schultner, for instance, the former ChrAfD spokesperson, stated that 'in parts of the media Lucke's personal religiosity was strongly

[53] Berbuir, Lewandowsky and Siri 2015; Franzmann 2016.
[54] Hambauer and Mays 2018, 168, 136.
[55] Arzheimer 2015, 535.
[56] Roy, McDonnell and Marzouki 2016.
[57] Ankenbrand 2013; Tagesschau 2014; Matthews 2015; Chadi and Krapf 2017.
[58] Bednarz 2018; Thieme and Liedhegener 2015.
[59] Tagesschau 2014.

emphasized, which attracted conservative Christians including myself'.[60] Her successor, Joachim Kuhs, similarly stressed moral issues rather than identitarian concerns when describing his decision to join the AfD in 2013:

> In 2012 I participated for the first time in the [anti-abortion] March for Life in Berlin, where I was just shocked by the enmity from the counter-demonstrators … A few months later I read something about the AfD …, I then read their family programme and the rest of the manifesto and thought that I could agree with their position. Based on these considerations, I relatively spontaneously chose to enter the party.[61]

This early emphasis on personal religiosity and conservative Christian values, which led mainstream Protestant news outlets to wonder whether the AfD might be a 'Christian Alternative for Germany',[62] was quite distinct from later AfD references to Christendom as an exclusivist identity marker against Islam. Far from appealing to radical right-wing segments, Schultner explained that 'because Christians tend to be less receptive to radical opinions than people without this faith foundation, we believed that the ChrAfD would be a stabilising factor in the new party and would help to keep it free from radical influences'.[63]

However, like the early AfD's emphasis on the euro, such plans were soon thwarted by the refugee crisis and the AfD's subsequent identitarian turn. As over one million refugees from predominantly Muslim countries sought to settle in Germany and as it became increasingly clear that none of the mainstream parties had claimed the anti-immigration side of the new identity cleavage, the nationalist wing of the AfD saw its opportunity. To these individuals, 'professors' topics' like the euro or fiscal conservatism, as well as family or social issues, might have been valuable for middle-class respectability, but the core topics with which they could harvest the communitarian potential and which 'the established parties had left fallow' were immigration and national identity.[64] As one of the new right's intellectuals Götz Kubitschek put it, the euro 'topic is the posh topic, the door-opener topic, but our topics (identity, resistance, gender-, party- and ideology criticism) can now come rumbling in from behind, if we only put our foot in the door quickly and consistently'.[65]

---

[60] Interview Schultner 2018.
[61] Interview Kuhs 2018.
[62] Evangelisch.de 2014.
[63] Interview Schultner 2018.
[64] Amann 2017, 99.
[65] Quoted in Amann 2017, 117.

In the months following the first arrival of Syrian refugees, the party's internal struggle intensified between the moderate wing around Lucke and the nationalist camp around the newly founded patriotic platform, culminating in a dramatic showdown at the AfD party conference in Essen on 4–5 July 2015.[66] In what observers described as a 'turning point', which symbolised 'the decline of the moderate party wing' and where 'the bourgeois party tore the mask off its face', party founder and then president Lucke was shouted down by the delegates as he tried to promote dialogue with Islam and then – to his own surprise – was voted out of office in a coup orchestrated by the nationalist wing.[67] Subsequently, Lucke and 2,000 of his supporters (at that time 20 per cent of the membership) left the party citing the rise of Islamophobic and anti-immigrant positions as well as of populist and anti-parliamentarian tendencies in the party, with AfD co-founder Hans-Olaf Henkel later lamenting that he and Lucke had unwillingly 'created a monster'.[68]

By the early 2020 most indicators suggested that the former middle-class anti-euro 'professors' party' had fully transformed into an out-and-out right-wing populist and anti-immigration 'precariat's party',[69] not just in terms of its rhetoric, policy and the composition of its supporters, but also with a new religiously laden far-right identity politics position. In terms of rhetoric, the AfD now clearly displayed populist, anti-elitist discourse and ideology.[70] It was increasingly hostile towards Germany's political system and its institutions, including the 'system parties', the 'liars' press' and the 'chancellor-dictator', entities which they suggested were scheming together to destroy the German people's culture and its identity.[71] Similarly, in terms of policy, studies show a 'transformation of the Alternative für Deutschland (AfD) party from anti-Europe in sentiment to anti-Islamic'.[72] An analysis of the AfD's recent state and federal

---

[66] Like its successor organization der Flügel ('the wing'), the patriotic platform has been categorised as right-wing extremist and both have been investigated by Germany's domestic intelligence agency (Verfassungsschutz). While both organizations were ultimately dissolved in 2018 and 2020, respectively, most scholars agree that the radical current they represented has come to dominate the AfD as a whole. See Pfahl-Traughber 2020.

[67] Amann 2017, 152, 164.

[68] Püttmann 2016a, 41.

[69] Die Welt 2016.

[70] Ulrich, Kramer and Till 2022; Mudde and Kaltwasser 2017.

[71] Some like Alexander Gauland even went so far as to justify the violent anti-immigration riots and vigilantism in Chemnitz in 2018 as 'normal' reactions to what they consider to be a state failure (Die Zeit 2018b; Assheuer 2017; Pfahl-Traughber 2020; Dilling 2018).

[72] Strauß 2017, 3.

programmes found that by 2018 Islam had taken 'on a role as the main bogeyman in ways which were not even remotely perceivable in 2013'.[73]

This change in tone and content was mirrored in the AfD's electorate. In 2016 Andreas Püttmann pointed out a notable 'radicalisation [in attitudes] amongst AfD supporters in particular in the categories of chauvinism (19% increase), approval of dictatorships (10% increase) and social Darwinism (6% increase) whilst approval of these attitudes did not rise in the general population'.[74] Hambauer and Mays show that having left its middle-class origins behind, the post-2015 AfD 'seems to be more attractive for people from a lower social background and with lower incomes' as well as for those with 'lower and middle education'.[75] Its voters now shared 'a striking similarity in social structure with the votership of the (left-wing populist) party die Linke' rather than with the middle-class electorates of CDU/CSU and FDP.[76] Other studies found that AfD and die Linke supporters were also found to be disproportionately narcissistic, nostalgic and pessimistic, characteristics typical for supporters of populist parties throughout Europe.[77] These trends were also reflected in voting behaviour. In 2017 for instance over one in ten former Linke voters shifted their support to the AfD compared to just about one in twenty former CDU/CSU voters.[78]

In sum, the AfD had fundamentally transformed itself since its foundation. The evidence presented in this chapter suggests that it did so in response to the rise of a new identity cleavage on the demand side, which it has since sought to further politicise through its own brand of right-wing identity politics. To capitalise on a relative representative gap of communitarians on the political supply side, the AfD changed its personnel, shifted gears in terms of rhetoric and policy, and attracted a different demographic in the electorate. But was this transformation also accompanied by a fundamental change in gears in the AfD's relationship to religion? The next chapter's analysis of the AfD's policies, political personnel and its relationship to church institutions suggest that it was.

[73] Heimbach-Steins and Filipović 2017, 5.
[74] Püttmann 2016a, 45.
[75] Hambauer and Mays 2018, 134, 137.
[76] Hambauer and Mays 2018, 150.
[77] Yendell et al. 2018; Gaston and Hilhorst 2018.
[78] Tagesschau 2017.

CHAPTER 6

Defenders of the Faith?
The Alternative für Deutschland's Christian Credentials Under Scrutiny

Scholars have shown that in the context of other European right-wing populist parties' identitarian turns, such as the FN/RN's in France or the FPÖ's in Austria, religion often became crucial in defining national identity and making the distinction between 'us' and 'them'.[1] Religion is thereby primarily used as an *ex negativo* identity marker describing the 'external other' as 'Muslim', whereas Christianity is only considered as a secondary analogous identifier of the 'us' and, in the words of Jan-Werner Müller, 'purely about belonging, not about belief, let alone any concrete ethical conduct – a militant Christendom instead of a merciful Christianity';[2] or as Olivier Roy put it, a 'kitsch Christianity'.[3]

In the German context a renewed reference to Christian identity was initially most prominent in the right-wing populist PEGIDA movement and its spinoffs. Since its emergence in Dresden in late 2014 the movement has referenced the (Christian) Occident (*Abendland*) in their name, selected prolific churches as a backdrop for their rallies and prominently displayed Christian symbols. Since 2015/2016 the AfD had begun to follow this trend by accentuating its references to Germany's Christian identity in reaction to the refugee crisis. In its 2016 manifesto it prominently referenced its will to preserve Germany's 'Occidental (*abendländische*) Christian Culture', committed itself to a 'leading culture' (*Leitkultur*) sourced 'from the religious traditions of Christianity', and rejected an 'Islamic practice of faith that is directed ... against the Judeo-Christian and humanistic foundations of our culture'.[4] Furthermore, its leaders have sought to publicly portray the AfD as 'the only Christian party that still exists',[5] the 'natural

---

[1] Roy, McDonnell and Marzouki 2016; Casanova 2012a; Brubaker 2017.
[2] Müller 2018b.
[3] Betz and Meret 2009; Brubaker 2017; Marzouki 2016; Roy 2018; Elcott et al. 2021.
[4] AfD 2016, 11, 92, 95.
[5] Alice Weidel quoted in Focus 2017.

ally'[6] of the Christian churches or the place in which to find 'more active Christians than in all other parties'.[7] The AfD tried to substantiate such public declarations with 'informative meetings' about Christianity in the AfD,[8] brochures such as the 'Confessions of Christians in the AfD',[9] slogans like 'Christ for Germany'[10] and publicly advertised policy proposals in parliament against the persecution of Christians in the Middle East.[11]

Closer analyses have revealed that PEGIDA's references to Christianity were an example of the negative religio-cultural self-identification witnessed in other European countries and that their rallies were less about a positive appreciation of Christianity than about a reaction against Islam: participants turned out to be overwhelmingly irreligious, speeches were dominated by warnings about Islamisation, crosses were coloured in Germany's national colours, and Christian hymns were only hummed as most participants were unfamiliar with both the lyrics and the melody.[12]

Can a similar assessment be made about religiously laden identity politics of the post-2015 AfD? The following paragraphs explore the AfD's 'Christian credentials' more closely. They do so based on the empirical materials from manifestos, speeches and elite interviews and through the lens of what Lother Roos referred to as the 'cultural-ethical triangle' of values, ethics and institutions. Specifically, we will trace the AfD's Christian value orientation through three indicators: first, its policies' alignment with Christian social doctrine; second, its leaders' display of and commitment to Christian ethics in public life; and third, its relationships with the institutional churches.

6.1   Policies: Defending Christianity or Christendom?

The first corner of the 'cultural-ethical triangle' looks at whether a party's policies stand in direct agreement or disagreement with the dominant churches' social doctrine, policy positions and 'Christian values' as defined by the institutional churches and senior clerics. A review of the AfD's

---

[6] Jörg Meuthen quoted in Hermes 2016, 72.

[7] Jörg Meuthen quoted in Breyton 2017.

[8] See, for instance, the AfD Press conference 'Good Christians, Bad Christians?' on its relationship with the churches; or 'information' and 'discussion' events about charity in the Christian occident or other Christian themes; see Breyton 2017.

[9] AfD 2018.

[10] Deutschlandfunk 2018a.

[11] AfD Bundestagsfraktion 2018. The AfD's motion was strongly rejected by parliament and criticised as 'cheap propaganda' in Christian circles; see Katholisch.de 2018.

[12] Coury 2021; Bock 2019; Menzel 2014.

manifestos and of the elite interview material reveals not only striking contradictions between AfD positions and church doctrine but also that the
AfD's interpretation of 'Christianity' is primarily informed through a cultural, or even territorial, idea of Christendom and an opposition to Islam
rather than through a positive embrace of Christian values, beliefs and
institutions. This confirms earlier findings of Marianne Heimbach-Steins'
research team at Münster University, which conducted an extensive comparison of AfD positions proposed in federal and state manifestos with those
postulated by Catholic social ethics.[13] The researchers came to the conclusion that 'almost all of the topics considered in our analysis reveal profound
differences between the programme of the Alternative for Germany party
and Catholic social doctrine'.[14] They also found that the AfD's 'general references to Christian values and traditions leave it unclear what concretely
it wants to preserve and why' and point out that 'in the AfD's programmatic texts there is no independent, programmatic and identity-supporting
reference to either Christianity, the Christian concept of humanity or to
Christian values'.[15] Instead, the study argues that 'for the AfD it is only
about Islam; there is nothing about other religions and worldviews, except
for a few contrasting references to Christianity, which purely serve to rhe-
torically reinforce the rejection of Islam'.[16] Most academic and journalistic
observers in Germany come to similar conclusions. Püttmann has argued
that each supposedly Christian policy of the AfD 'always has a drawback:
pro-life activists suddenly push for the shooting command at borders or
consider abortion as a demographic problem'.[17] Seiterich has shown how
'the self-proclaimed defenders of the Christian Occident are trying to turn
an internationalist anti-racist Christianity of charity into a kind of anti-
Islamic white tribal religion'.[18] And Joppke has concluded that 'right-wing
populists' co-optation of Christianity is only an instrumental Christianism,
which can be just as easily be discarded again. It does not grow out of
religious conviction, but of an imagined cultural sense of belonging which
could equally be defined differently than in religious terms.'[19]

Such assessments are largely supported by the results of the interviews
conducted for this book. For instance, although AfD politicians were

[13] Heimbach-Steins and Filipović 2017.
[14] Heimbach-Steins and Filipović 2017, 71.
[15] Heimbach-Steins and Filipović 2017, ii, 25.
[16] Heimbach-Steins and Filipović 2017, 27.
[17] Püttmann 2016b, 51.
[18] Seiterich 2016.
[19] Joppke 2017.

slightly more vocal in their assessment that Germany's identity was and ought to be Christian than the clergy and mainstream politicians interviewed, they significantly differed when asked what exactly their party meant by 'Christian identity'. For instance, all clergy and almost all mainstream politicians answered this question primarily with references to theological elements of the Christian faith. They spoke about their belief in the 'verdicts of sinfulness, fallibility and the human limitedness' as informing their idea of Christian identity,[20] or about their conviction that 'I am not responsible on my own and that the good Lord has his plans for me',[21] that 'if I say "Jesus Christos kyrios" then this has consequences for the whole of my life' and that 'ultimately, it's the Last Judgement that decides'.[22] By contrast, most AfD representatives primarily referenced cultural aspects such as history, architecture, traditions or music when seeking to define Christian identity. For example, prominent AfD MP Paul-Armin Hampel spoke first of music, art, poetry, 'the Cathedral of Cologne or the Frauenkriche in Dresden: when one takes all this together then this is the basis of who we are. Germany and Europe *are* Christianity.'[23] This interpretation of Christian identity in civilisational rather than theological terms was mirrored by then AfD president Jörg Meuthen who explained that AfD references to 'Christianity' were about 'culture and a canon of virtues ... calling it "humanist-occidental" like [the AfD] in Hesse works for me, too. I know there are people who have issues with the term "Christian" – so I can also live with calling it "humanist".'[24]

Importantly, all AfD representatives I spoke to also (negatively) referenced Islam in their answers, whereas none of the mainstream politicians or clergy did so. Hampel emphasised in the same breath that he described Christian identity that 'when it comes to Islam, I see a great confrontation in Europe',[25] and Meuthen argued that discussions about Christian religion were rather unusual in the AfD: 'For many it's really a marginal issue. We rather talk about Islam, because of the migration crisis.'[26] Even those AfD politicians who emphasised personal faith as an important part of their identity, such as the AfD's Religious Affairs Spokesperson, Volker Münz, acknowledged that 'in the AfD the consensus is that when we

---

[20] Interview Meißner 2018.
[21] Interview Göring-Eckardt 2018.
[22] Interview Steinlein 2018.
[23] Interview Hampel 2018.
[24] Interview Meuthen 2018.
[25] Interview Hampel 2018.
[26] Interview Meuthen 2018.

say "Christian" or "occident" we mean it in historical and cultural terms rather than in theological terms. It's about defending our culture against other civilisations and the threat of civil war, which is more probable in multicultural states.'[27] Similarly, ChrAfD Spokesperson Joachim Kuhs described the evolution of Christian references in the AfD as follows:

> We are standing on Christian traditions and because these traditions are threatened, we want to restore them, also in defence against Islam. However, this thought only gained prominence in the context of the refugee question whereas other references [to religion] have moved more into the background.[28]

Whilst representatives of Christians in the AfD were careful to emphasise that personal religiosity and Christian values still mattered in AfD policy, former party grandees who at the time of the interviews had left the party were much more critical in their assessment. For instance, Joachim Kuhs's predecessor Annette Schultner, who left the party in 2016, explained that 'there are many people in the AfD, who outwardly say Christianity is extremely important to them and who say they're Christians themselves, but who have fought against Christians internally and were against Christians organising themselves in the party'.[29] Similarly, the former president of the AfD in North-Rhine Westphalia Marcus Pretzell postulated that 'the people [in the AfD], who are speaking of the Christian occident actually mean ethnic Germanity [*Deutschtum*]. ... This has nothing to do with Christianity. These are references to Germanic mythology – this is about a Germanic movement.'[30]

Statements from former AfD decision-makers, who have often parted on negative terms, ought to always be considered with some caution. Yet, they seem to align with the academic analysis of the AfD's positions discussed above, as well as with the verdicts of the senior theologians interviewed, who were unequivocal in their evaluation of AfD policies as being in blatant contradiction to Christian values. The Protestant Bishop of Berlin/Brandenburg, Markus Dröge, for instance, stated that 'in the AfD manifesto you cannot find what is essential in Christianity: namely a Christian concept of humanity'.[31] He further argues that 'trying to use Christianity to downgrade other religions or to encapsulate our country against refugees is a contradiction in itself'.[32] The chief representative of the Commissariat of German

---

[27] Interview Münz 2018.
[28] Interview Kuhs 2018.
[29] Interview Schultner 2018.
[30] Interview Pretzell 2018.
[31] Interview Dröge 2018.
[32] Interview Dröge 2018.

Bishops towards the Federal Government and the Bundestag, Karl Jüsten, similarly asserted that 'a party, which basically promotes racist stereotypes, and which excludes and fights people, can in my view not be a party that calls itself Christian', specifying that 'the core principles of what defines the "Christian" West are incompatible with the AfD programme'.[33] Even Uwe Heimowski, Jüsten's equivalent for the German Evangelical Free Churches (EAD), which are often rumoured to have greater sympathies for the AfD than Mainline Protestants or Catholics,[34] made clear that within 'PEGIDA or in the AfD Christianity is not seen as a faith, but only as a symbol or rejection against Islam and against everything foreign. Neither I personally nor the EAD are supportive of this.'[35] Taken together these findings suggest that the AfD's 'Christian policies' are not only primarily based on an ethno-cultural idea of 'Christendom' as an antidote to Islam, but also often stand in direct contradiction to Christian social and political doctrine. These findings match the results of the second part of the cultural-ethical triangle: the public ethics and personal virtues of the AfD's leadership.

6.2   Public Ethics and Virtues: Germany's Most Secular Party

When defining public ethics and virtues, it is important not to reduce them to the extent to which party leaders' personal lifestyle choices conform to conservative ideals of a pious lifestyle.[36] Instead, when speaking of 'personal virtues' in the context of the cultural-ethical triangle, this research is concerned with the party leaders' commitment to Christian virtues, ethics and beliefs in their *public* actions and policy statements. For this reason, this study bases its assessment on the analysis of the available data on leading AfD leader's public commitment to Christianity and the results from interviews with high-level AfD officials about the relevance and appreciation of Christian beliefs and ethics within the party. However, neither of these criteria suggests a particularly high importance

---

[33] Interview Jüsten 2018.

[34] See for instance Bednarz (2018); Höhne and Wensierski (2017); Jörgensen (2017). However, the assertion that Evangelical Christians are more sympathetic towards the AfD is highly contested and has been rejected by leading representatives of the Evangelical Churches in Germany (see Jörgensen 2016).

[35] Interview Heimowski 2018.

[36] For instance, the fact that AfD parliamentary group president, Alice Weidel, is bringing up her artificially inseminated child in a homosexual relationship, or that party president Jörg Meuthen and former party president Frauke Petry left their families and remarried following affairs while in office, might appear to stand in some tension with the AfD's self-declared ideals of traditional Christian family values, but need not have any bearing on these individuals' politics, nor are they necessarily expressions of the strength of their individual religiosity.

accorded to Christian virtues in AfD leadership circles. On the contrary their analysis even indicate the existence of an explicitly anti-Christian undercurrent within the party.

When it comes to the public commitment to the Christian faith, many leading politicians such as Alexander Gauland, Head of the AfD Parliamentary Group, or Björn Höcke, a prominent figurehead of the powerful far-right section of the party, openly identified as non-religious or outright atheist. Moreover, the official figures of the 2017–2021 Bundestag show that – along with the post-communist Die Linke – the AfD had one the highest rate of self-declared non-religious MPs in parliament. Less than one in three of AfD parliamentarians identified as Christian compared with 54 per cent of parliamentarians overall, and 85 per cent of Christian Democrats, 59 per cent of Liberals and 52 per cent of Social Democrats.[37] In the 2021–2025 Bundestag the share of self-declared Christians in the AfD parliamentary group fell further to just about one in four who stated that they identified with a Christian faith, while the share of AfD MPs declaring to be irreligious almost doubled.[38] These numbers contrast with an image of overall stability of religious affiliation in the Bundestag: 55 per cent of all MPs identified with a Christian faith in 2021, and in some parliamentary groups like the Christian Democrats or Greens the share of self-declared Christians even rose.[39] Certainly, that does not mean that there are not a number of highly religious AfD politicians such as Volker Münz or Joachim Kuhs, who were interviewed for this research. However, both Münz and Kuhs also acknowledged that in this 'we are a minority in the party'.[40] Münz indicated that the 'ChrAfD has about 500 members amongst a total 30,000 members in the AfD',[41] while Joachim Kuhs estimated that 'we are ca. 1 per cent of the members', in addition to stating that 'religion does not play a great role in the party anyway, except for the topic of Islam. Collectively practised faith is – with the exception of the ChrAfD – not particularly alive in the AfD.'[42] Both stressed that there are many more committed Christians in the AfD than just those organised in the ChrAfD. Yet even these estimates only tended to be between 10 and 30 per cent with another estimated 30–40 per cent of loosely associated 'cultural Christians'. There is no available

[37] Deutscher Bundestag 2017.
[38] Deutscher Bundestag 2017.
[39] Deutscher Bundestag 2017.
[40] Interview Kuhs 2018.
[41] Interview Münz 2018.
[42] Interview Kuhs 2018.

data to verify such estimates, but taken together and placed in the context of the Bundestag numbers, these data points suggest that the numbers and influence of Christians in the AfD remains marginal.

What is more, most interviewees indicated that the Christian influence within the party has further declined in recent years. AfD president, Jörg Meuthen stated in our interview that whereas 'initially the [Christian] impulse was stronger', today 'ChrAfD is neither contested nor particularly relevant … active Christians are more or less perceived as a welcome fringe group but have little real political power'.[43] Similarly, AfD MP and party president of Lower Saxony Paul-Armin Hampel stated that conservative committed Christians 'don't really play any role' in the party, and while 'in the beginning there were a few people who raised the [Christian] flag, … that went down again relatively quickly, because it was not in line with the vast majority of the party'.[44] This assessment was confirmed by Marcus Pretzell's account that in '2013 one had the impression that they [the Christians] might play a role [in the AfD] but that was a brief moment. It briefly flared up but quickly led to a countermovement – such a role was not wanted by the majority of the party'.[45]

Instead, several interviewees suggested the rise of a powerful and explicitly anti-Christian movement within the AfD. Jörg Meuthen for instance stated that 'we also have a number of radical atheists in our ranks, who absolutely cannot understand [the Christians] and who are positively church-hostile.'[46] Whilst Meuthen sought to emphasise that like the Christians in the party, their opponents 'don't have any political power either',[47] other interviewees were more critical of anti-religious influences in the party. Annette Schultner and Marcus Pretzell for instance described an outright inner-party campaign against Christians motivated by a post-religious right fuelled by radical atheism as well as by neo-pagan Christophobia.[48] Schultner hence described how 'the vision of the AfD as a Christian-conservative party, which I wanted to promote, was a thorn in the flesh for many. They really wanted to destroy us.'[49] Echoing the decline of Christian influence described by other interviewees, she argued that whilst 'there were initially many conservative

[43] Interview Meuthen 2018.
[44] Interview Hampel 2018.
[45] Interview Pretzell 2018.
[46] Interview Meuthen 2018.
[47] Interview Meuthen 2018.
[48] For the role of neo-pagan Christophobia in parts of the far right see in particular the influence of the philosophers of the 'nouvelle droite' in contemporary right-wing populist thought; see Rose 2021; François 2008.
[49] Interview Schultner 2018.

Christians in the party … they remained only a small minority for whom life was made hard in the AfD. By now the Christians in the party are so isolated that those who are still there have either assimilated themselves or have been marginalised.'[50] According to Schultner the reason for this was that 'at least half of the party is not just against religion in general, but also explicitly critical of Christianity'. She added that

> Never before have I met so many people who adhere to some Germanic creed or use pagan symbols as in the AfD … On the one hand you have people who are hostile to religion in general and on the other hand you have people who adhere to some pagan religion and say: 'Christianity is really a religion from the Near East, which does not fit into Germany.'[51]

Pretzell echoed this sentiment postulating that in the nationalist 'Höcke-wing' of the party 'it's not about Christianity and not even about cultural-Christendom, but about a Germanic tribal society … Germanic paganism plays a huge role for these people.'[52] He argued that

> whoever publicly says in the AfD that they are against combative atheism [*Kampfatheismus*] and national socialism, immediately reduce their electoral chances because they have at least 45 per cent of the party against them. One should not publicly display one's Christianity anymore. That's a fact. One could do that moderately in the beginning but it's no longer advisable today.[53]

Again, it is crucial to recognise how personal politics might play into such accounts. However, the detail in which each of these former officials described the events and the fact that their accounts align with the overall picture gathered from external observations and other interviews do suggest that a public commitment to Christian virtues and beliefs is neither particularly widespread amongst the AfD leadership, nor particularly advisable.[54] Even if one discards accounts such as Schultner's or Pretzell's, statements such as that of Joachim Kuhs (whose interest is certainly not to understate the role of Christianity in the party) that in parts of the AfD the ChrAfD 'has always been seen rather critically' and that the main reason why it is tolerated is 'because we try not to draw too much attention

---

[50] Interview Schultner 2018.
[51] Interview Schultner 2018.
[52] Interview Pretzell 2018.
[53] Interview Pretzell 2018.
[54] Off the record several AfD interviewees substantiated such claims by naming a number of prominent Christians in the party, who were internally pressured to increasingly downplay their Christian beliefs. One even stated that sections of the party sought to stop their own candidacy for the Bundestag because they considered 'Christians as too weak'.

to ourselves, restrain ourselves and fly under the radar in order to avoid provoking offense or opposition from others' would still stand in contradiction to the image of 'the only Christian party that still exists' (Weidel).[55] Such contradictions in terms of policy and public display of Christian commitment in the party ranks become even more stark when looking at the third part of the cultural-ethical triangle: the party's relationship with the institutional churches.

6.3   Institutional Relations with the Church: Towards a New 'Kirchenkampf'?

Whereas the AfD still seeks to maintain a public image as a party that defends Christian values and is attractive to Christians, it is quite outspoken in its criticism of, and even fundamental hostility towards, the institutional churches. A review of the AfD's official positions on religious liberty and state–church relations, as well as the disproportionately critical attitudes towards the churches displayed in the interviews, suggest that the AfD is perhaps the party in Germany that most radically questions the system of benevolent neutrality in favour of a more secularist system.

On the surface the AfD's hostility towards public religion is primarily directed against Islam. In its manifesto the AfD professes to be

> fully committed to the freedom of belief, conscience and creed. However, it demands that religious practice be restricted by state laws, human rights and our values. In particular, the AfD clearly opposes an Islamic practice of faith which is directed against the liberal-democratic basic order, our laws and against the Judeo-Christian and humanistic foundations of our culture.[56]

However, according to Heimbach-Steins et al., this qualification is symptomatic of a more fundamental willingness to reduce religious freedom to the freedom of private belief, whereas the public 'freedom to exercise one's religion as a group is restricted – and to Muslims it is largely denied'.[57] Indeed, the AfD explicitly rejects not only the practice of Sharia law, but also the wearing of headscarves, the ritual slaughter of animals (thus also undermining the Jewish practice of kosher butchering), the right to Islamic religious education in public schools and the establishment of Islamic theological faculties.[58] As this amounts to a denial of some of the very privileges

---

[55] Interview Kuhs 2018.
[56] AfD 2016, 95.
[57] Heimbach-Steins and Filipović 2017, 24.
[58] AfD 2015; Heimbach-Steins and Filipović 2017.

that the *Grundgesetz* grants to religious communities, such demands can be seen as an implicit challenge to the system of benevolent neutrality itself. It is more indicative of a French *laïcité*-style ideal of church–state relations, according to which the state can and should ban religion from the public sphere instead of considering it as an equal and indispensable partner in civil society and public debate, as the *Grundgesetz* does (see Chapter 8). Heimbach-Steins at al. have laid out the implicit risks, asking, 'Why should a party advocating such positions [against Islam] today, not demand the same restrictions for other religious communities, including the Christian churches, tomorrow?'[59]

Considering recent AfD policy demands, and the stances of high-level officials interviewed, this concern did not seem unfounded. In its 2017 electoral programme the AfD made a first public step in this direction by demanding that Germany 'abolish the remuneration of church representatives such as Bishops etc. through tax money'.[60] Manifestos in subsequent state election such as in Bavaria went further, demanding the collection of church taxes through the state to be abolished, church privileges in education to be cut, the personal ties between church and state to be severed, and church officials' voices in politics to be shut down.[61] A motion to include such demands in the federal manifesto was only narrowly defeated at the 2017 party conference, where several high-ranking AfD officials such as Paul-Armin Hampel and Björn Höcke publicly called for AfD members to leave the churches.[62] Such rhetoric is representative of an increasingly critical tone vis-à-vis the churches and their authorities, with AfD officials referring to them as 'system churches', 'profiteers of the asylum-industry' and 'government spokesmen'.[63]

This anti-clericalism is particularly striking when compared to the position and rhetoric of other parties. The CDU/CSU, SPD, FDP and the Greens do not fundamentally question the system of benevolent neutrality or the public roles and rights of the churches.[64] Only the post-communist Die Linke comes close in its secularism to the position of the AfD, yet without echoing the latter's harsh public attacks against the churches.[65] Indeed, as shown earlier in this chapter, during our interviews all mainstream party

---

[59] Heimbach-Steins and Filipović 2017, 31.
[60] AfD 2017, 45.
[61] AfD Bayern 2018.
[62] Die Welt 2017.
[63] AfD Heidelberg 2018; F.A.Z. 2016b; Kuzmany 2016.
[64] CDU/CSU 2017, 72ff.; FDP 2017, 82; Grüne 2017, 120ff.; Katholisch.de 2017; SPD 2017, 6, 79ff.
[65] Die Linke 2017, 124.

representatives univocally supported the system of 'benevolent neutrality' and praised the position of the churches. This is not to say that these politicians had no specific criticisms vis-à-vis particular church positions or aspects of the current constitutional setting. CDU official Christian Meißner, for instance, vocally criticised the EKD for their liberal policies in areas such as 'gay marriage, EKD gender institutes or the ideological way in which such questions are forced upon society', and argued that 'the Protestant Church has over the last four decades pushed away middle-class conservatism'.[66] Meanwhile, Green party leader Katrin Göring-Eckhardt demanded that the 'constitutional law of religion needs to be constantly updated' to ensure the same constitutional privileges to Islam as to Christianity and to avoid religious discrimination in labour laws.[67] Yet, none of the mainstream politicians interviewed questioned the churches' participation in the public debate or their constitutional privileges.

By contrast most active AfD officials voiced fundamental criticisms, not only about specific aspects of the churches' policies or individual church leaders, but against the role of the church in society as a whole. For instance, AfD president Jörg Meuthen stated that 'the public relevance of the official church is in continuous decline and given the nonsense that they are currently creating, I am pretty happy about that'.[68] Armin-Paul Hampel argued that 'we are for the abolishment of the church taxes because I think that the church needs to reform itself in humility and poverty'.[69] And Volker Münz, the AfD's Spokesperson for Religious Affairs, defended the AfD's position asserting that 'the institutional settlement needs to change. ... Overall, there is too close an intertwinement between church and state in Germany.'[70] Instead he demanded 'a stricter separation of state and church'. Of particular relevance to this volume's findings about the AfD's cultural interpretation of religion as a cultural identity marker as opposed to a faith, he argued that

> Symbols like crosses should be kept in the public spaces, but the political influence of the churches has to be pushed back: church officials should not be allowed to engage in politics or even become members of a political party, and similarly politicians should not be allowed to hold high offices in churches.[71]

---

[66] Interview Meißner 2018.
[67] Interview Göring-Eckardt 2018.
[68] Interview Meuthen 2018.
[69] Interview Hampel 2018.
[70] Interview Münz 2018.
[71] Interview Münz 2018.

Joachim Kuhs went a step further, stating his belief that 'Only radical measures towards the separation of church and state will help. Adjusting the current system is only of limited use. It's much better in France and Italy', where according to him, 'there is not such strong politicisation [of religion] and where the church is less in bed with the state. I am relatively radical in this respect: we need a laicist model.'[72]

It is important to emphasise that such sentiments may be in part motivated by other factors than general hostility towards public religion, or against Christianity. As I will discuss in more detail in Chapter 7, it may partly be a reaction to the churches' own hostility towards the AfD. Volker Münz for instance argued that the fact that the Bavarian AfD section 'focuses its manifesto on the separation of state and church and calls the churches lobby groups ... is a reaction to the broadside fire we get from the churches'.[73] For others, criticism from within the AfD might genuinely be motivated by an attempt to protect religion from state influence. Kuhs for example lamented that the proximity of church and state has 'totally changed the identity of the house of Christ. The people realise that the soul of the church has changed and that there are only formal remnants of the church's core business of preaching the gospel, social welfare work and its educational vocation.'[74]

However, when placed in the broader context of the AfD's programmatic disregard for the freedom of religious practice, radical tone in which AfD leaders have frequently attacked church authorities, and the apparent lack of appreciation for religious institutions as independent actors in the public sphere and political debate, it is hard to imagine that the AfD's strained relationship with the churches is a mere result of the latter's criticism of the AfD or of theological disagreements. Rather, they appear to confirm the overall assessment that like PEGIDA, the AfD is more interested in 'Christendom' as a cultural identity marker against Islam than in Christianity as a set of beliefs or as an independent force in the political debate. As Catholic commentator Andreas Püttmann summarised it in our interview,

---

[72] Interview Kuhs 2018.
[73] Interview Münz 2018.
[74] Interview Kuhs 2018. This view is shared by some voices across parts of the (Evangelical) religious spectrum, like Helmuth Matthies, the former president of an Evangelical news agency, who lamented that 'because of the politicisation [of the church] many conservatives have already left the church – and not because they lost their faith but because they increasingly miss it within the church'. Interview Matthies 2018.

the AfD wants a compliant Church, and if the church does not obey then
you insult it … [I]t is only about [Christianity's] political instrumentaliza-
tion, whereas the spiritual and social effect of Christianity in the formation of society are not appreciated or even recognised, because everything
remains on the surface of identity politics.[75]

In sum, this chapter's exploration of the AfD's Christian references
through the cultural-ethical triangle suggests that the self-declared defender
of Germany's Christian identity may in fact be one of the most secularist parties in the German political landscape. AfD policies show strong
discrepancies with Christian doctrine and are indicative of a conception
of 'Christendom' that is primarily informed by cultural-identitarian ideas
about Christian civilisation as an antidote to Islam, rather than through
theological notions about Christian ethics and beliefs. The AfD's leadership appears disproportionately irreligious when compared to most
other German parties, and there are indications of a powerful and actively
Christophobic, post-religious right movement within the party. Moreover,
the AfD's attitude towards religious institutions is characterised by a
strong anti-clerical sentiment and a level of hostility towards the system
of benevolent neutrality that stands out in the German political sphere.
All this suggests that the AfD's 'Christian credentials' are scarcely more
convincing than those of PEGIDA. Yet, at least as important as the question of whether the AfD should be considered a Christian party in theory
is whether it is perceived as such in practice. Chapter 7 therefore turns to
Christian voters' reactions to the AfD's religiously laden identity politics
and how this reaction is shaped by the actions of mainstream parties and
the churches themselves.

[75] Interview Püttmann 2018.

CHAPTER 7

Religious Immunity
Voting Behaviour and the Church's Social Firewall

Voters are unpredictable. On the evening of Sunday 14 October 2018, when the results of the Bavarian state election arrived at the governing Christian Social Union's (CSU) election party in Munich, the usual image of leder-hosen, dirndls and Augustiner beer was overshadowed by the gloom on the participants' faces. The CSU had just experienced its most traumatic defeat in Bavaria since 1950. In one of Germany's most Catholic state, where for decades the CDU's sister party had scored between 50 and 60 per cent of the votes, they had fallen to a mere 37 per cent. Meanwhile, the AfD had achieved a record score of over 11 per cent. Many CSU officials had long feared such a result. In the months prior to the election, they had even begun to co-opt some of the AfD's formulas: the party took an aggressive stance on immigration, challenged the CDU/CSU's own chancellor's more open refugee policy and copied the AfD's attempts to politicise Christian symbols as cultural identity markers. Minister President Markus Söder for instance ordered the display of crucifixes in public buildings 'not as religious symbol, but [as] a profession of identity and Bavaria's cultural legacy'.[1] While Catholic and Protestant Bishops condemned such a culturalised use of the cross, CSU strategists, haunted by the fear of losing their Catholic constituency, paid little heed to such warnings.[2] On election night it became clear that some of their concerns were not unfounded: of the 530,000 voters who had deserted the CSU on this day, 54 per cent said they had done so because 'the CSU had given up on its Christian convictions'.[3] However, to the surprise of most observers and strategists the majority of former CSU voters had not migrated as expected to the AfD. Instead, they had largely voted for the left-wing lib-eral, pro-migration, Green party.[4]

[1] Bayrische Staatszeitung 2018.
[2] Wetzel and Drobinski 2018.
[3] Steppart and Giesel 2018.
[4] Steppart and Giesel 2018.

Though perhaps counter-intuitive at first glance, these results are representative of many Christian voters' reactions to national populists' religiously laden identity politics across Western Europe and particularly in Germany.[5] Studies have found that Christians tend to be empirically more 'immune' to voting right-wing populist than their irreligious neighbours in countries like the Netherlands, where secular voters were the most likely to vote for Geert Wilders,[6] in France or Italy, where church attendance has historically been one of the strongest predictors for not voting right-wing populist (see also Chapter 11),[7] or in Denmark, where 98 per cent of the supporters of the Danish People's party reported that they never or rarely attend church.[8] However, it appears to be particularly pronounced in Germany.[9] Election results show that the AfD – in spite of its forceful references to Germany's 'Christian traditions' and 'Judeo-Christian identity' – has performed significantly worse among Catholics and Protestants as among irreligious voters (see Figure 7.1). For instance, in the federal election of 2013 the AfD only scored 4 per cent among Protestants and Catholics compared to 7 per cent amongst irreligious voters. Four years later AfD support had climbed to 17 per cent amongst the irreligious but was still only 9 per cent amongst Catholic voters and 11 per cent amongst Protestants.[10] Moreover, the AfD underperformed amongst Christians consistently across both Western and Eastern German states, suggesting that this 'vaccination effect' is independent of where in Germany voters live (see Figure 7.2).

The impact of religion on voters' propensity to vote for right-wing populist parties remains a relatively untouched topic in the literature, and especially so for the case of Germany.[11] However, there are a handful of hypotheses emerging from research in related fields and from the interviews undertaken for this book to be considered. These range from demand-side factors such as intrinsic attitudes amongst Christian voters, to supply-side factors such as the role of other parties or of the institutional churches themselves.

---

[5] Daenekindt, De Koster and Van Der Waal 2017; De Koster et al. 2014; Immerzeel, Jaspers and Lubbers 2013; Montgomery and Winter 2015; Guth and Nelsen 2021.

[6] De Koster et al. 2014.

[7] Du Cleuziou 2016a; Montgomery and Winter 2015; Perrineau 2014; Roy 2016.

[8] Betz and Meret 2009.

[9] Siegers and Jedinger 2021; Cremer 2021a; Cremer 2021b.

[10] Konrad Adenauer Stiftung 2021.

[11] Mudde 2007, 296; Akkerman, Mudde and Zaslove 2015; Achterberg 2009; Arzheimer 2009; Siegers and Jedinger 2021.

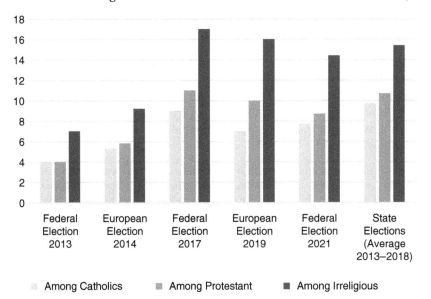

Figure 7.1   AfD results in Germany by religious affiliation (in percentages)
Source: Konrad Adenauer Stiftung 2021.

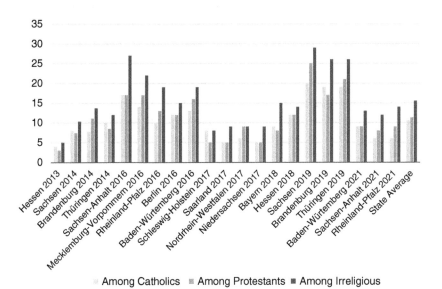

Figure 7.2   AfD results in regional state elections by religious affiliation (in percentages) *Source*: Konrad Adenauer Stiftung 2021.

7.1 The Demand Side: Between Usual Attitudes and Unusual Voting Behaviour

Perhaps the most intuitive explanation for Christians' comparative hesitancy to vote for right-wing populist candidates might be to point to how the (in)compatibility of certain Christian beliefs with right-wing populist ideology might affect Christians' voting behaviour. The rationale for such a hypothesis has been vocalised by political scientist Kai Arzheimer as follows:

> After all, the values, beliefs, and traditions associated with most contemporary versions of the Christian faith are those of tolerance, compassion and altruism, and these find little in common with the authoritarian, xenophobic and even racist ideologies and appeals of the parties of the radical right, and the practice of targeting some.[12]

Given that the AfD has evolved into an increasingly radical right-wing populist party, embracing exclusivist forms of identity politics, and that it appears more interested in 'Christendom' as a culturalised identity marker than in 'Christianity' as a faith, one might think that the main factor preventing German Christians from casting their vote for the AfD is an incompatibility of Christian universalist beliefs and AfD ideology.

This view was popular amongst politicians, church representatives and experts interviewed. State Secretary Stephan Steinlein argued for instance that the 'deeper reason' for why Christians are less attracted to the AfD might be 'that someone rooted in faith, who knows where they come from and where they are going, just has a different resilience and is less spiritually homeless [*heimatlos*]'.[13] Hermann Gröhe (CDU) similarly focused on the relevance of Christian beliefs when noting that the 'World church and racism just don't fit together, and therefore very conservative Catholics are usually immune against right-wing ideology.'[14] On the side of the churches, Bishop Dröge explained that 'Christians vote for the AfD less frequently than the average person because Christians realise that what the AfD represents does not correspond to the Christian faith.'[15] Similarly, Thomas Sternberg, the president of the Central Committee of German Catholics (the main Catholic lay organisation in Germany), argued that 'from a Christian viewpoint nobody can really vote AfD because its views

[12] Arzheimer and Carter 2009, 989.
[13] Interview Steinlein 2018.
[14] Interview Gröhe 2018.
[15] Interview Dröge 2018.

are so anti-religious and anti-Christian'.[16] Experts such as Liane Bednarz concurred, claiming that 'the relative resilience of those close to the church vis-à-vis the AfD is caused by the mental presence of Christian charity and humility, through which you see other people – including Muslims – primarily as God's creatures'.[17]

Yet, while this hypothesis appears widespread and intuitive, there is only inconclusive empirical evidence for it in the literature. Even though many studies have found that Germany's Christians tend to be slightly less open to right-wing populist positions and significantly more tolerant of foreigners and religious minorities than their secular neighbours,[18] there are also some studies suggesting the reverse. Most prominently, a study by Norris and Inglehart found that individuals who state that religion plays a greater part in their lives have a greater affinity to right-wing populist parties and positions.[19] Similarly, a 2018 Pew study on Christianity in Western Europe suggested that in most European countries, including Germany, 'religion [is] strongly associated with nationalist sentiment' and that 'on balance self-identified Christians … are more likely than religiously unaffiliated people to express negative views of immigrants as well as of Muslims and Jews'.[20] On closer inspection this deviation from other studies may stem from methodological factors, rather than empirical differences.[21] Moreover, De Koster, Van der Waal and others have pointed out that under the heading of 'cultural conservative attitudes' studies often lump together religious traditionalist attitudes (such as opposition towards gay marriage or traditionalist views towards gender equality), which are empirically linked to Christian orthodox beliefs, with nativist authoritarian positions (such as racial resentment or opposition to immigration), which are not linked to such beliefs.[22] In fact, a growing number of studies

---

[16] Interview Sternberg 2018.
[17] Interview Bednarz 2018.
[18] Rebenstorf 2018; Ribberink, Achterberg and Houtman 2017; Pickel 2018, 306.
[19] Norris and Inglehart 2019.
[20] Pew 2018, 20.
[21] For instance, the Pew study found significantly higher levels of Christians in Germany (71 per cent) than suggested by either the numbers provided by the German churches (54 per cent) or most other surveys. The same is true for indicators such as church attendance, which is consistently higher in Pew than in other data sets. This might be because the Pew study was primarily based on phone interviews, which are often associated with overreported levels of religiosity due to the social desirability effect (see Wuthnow 2015). In Germany where the churches still enjoy relatively high social prestige, the use of phone interviews might hence have incited survey participants who would otherwise be counted as 'irreligious' or merely as 'cultural Christians' to overstate their religiosity and to thus skew the results.
[22] De Koster and Van Der Waal 2007; Daenekindt, De Koster and Van Der Waal 2017; De Koster et al. 2014.

have shown that while religious practice may be correlated with greater prejudice towards gay marriage or women's reproductive rights, it also tends to make individuals more open towards immigration, and *less* hostile towards racial or religious minorities.[23] Yet, these findings currently still remain too limited in scope and geographical coverage to be generalisable.[24] As a result, Pickel concludes after a detailed review of a number of empirical surveys such as Pew, the ESS, the Bertelsmann Religionsmonitor, the Allgemeine Bevölkerungsumfrage der Sozialwissenschaften (Allbus), the German Longitudinal Election Study (GLES) and the Leipziger Mitte-Studien (Mitte), that in spite of some differences there is 'no clear directional effect of Christian religiosity' in Germany on voters' attitude towards right-wing populist positions.[25]

In other words, attitudinal divergence between Germany's Christians and the AfD's policy platform alone appear to be neither sufficient to fully account for the strength of their immunity towards the populist right at the ballot box, nor to understand why this immunity should be stronger in Germany than in other Western countries such as the USA or Poland, where Christian theology arguably proclaims similarly universalist values, but voters have been much more open towards right-wing populist parties (see Chapter 14). A review of supply-side explanations and in particular the behaviour of political and religious elites helps to better understand the strength of religious immunity to populism in Germany and its variation from other countries.

7.2   The Political Supply Side: Christian Alternatives in the Party System

Most existing studies of the supply side in this context focus on mainstream conservative parties' ability to bind Christian voters, thus making these voters unavailable to far-right parties. Arzheimer and Carter, for instance, argue that in countries with strong Christian democratic parties, like Germany or the Netherlands, Christian voters are simply 'not "available" to these [right-wing populist] parties, because they are still firmly attached to Christian Democratic or conservative parties'.[26] This view

---

[23] Daenekindt, De Koster and Van Der Waal 2017; Cremer 2021a; Rebenstorf 2018; Ekins 2018.
[24] De Koster and Van Der Waal 2007; De Koster et al. 2014; Daenekindt, De Koster and Van Der Waal 2017.
[25] Pickel 2018, 278; Rebenstorf 2018.
[26] Arzheimer and Carter 2009, 985; see also Montgomery and Winter 2015; Siegers and Jedinger 2021.

assumes that, in spite of its overall decline, the traditional moral cleavage still disproportionately structures Christian voters' partisan alignment independently from their agreement or disagreement with far-right parties' ideologies. According to this logic, rather than being intrinsically repelled by the policies of the populist right, it is primarily their traditional partisan 'attachment [to centre-right parties that] "vaccinates" Christian voters against voting for a party of the radical right'.[27] This hypothesis seems to be supported by several cross-country studies and to be of particular relevance in Germany, where recent research confirmed that observant individuals continued to be significantly more likely to identify with the CDU/CSU.[28] As Pascal Siegers and Alexander Jedinger from the GESIS Leibniz Institute for Social Sciences explain, 'Church attendance reduced the probability to report an AfD vote intention mediated both by lower anti-immigrant attitudes … and a higher probability of identifying with the Christian Democratic parties.'[29]

This continued alignment of practising Christians with mainstream parties in Germany is partly a result of traditional cleavages, but also of these parties' policies and behaviour. As we have seen in Chapter 5, the centre-right's continued 'ownership of the issues related to traditionalism and immigration' has often been referenced as a key explanatory variable for the long-term absence of a right-wing populist party in Germany.[30] The interviews conducted for this book suggest that same dynamic has made most Christian voters unavailable for right-wing populist parties as long as mainstream parties, and in particular the CDU/CSU, maintained ownership over issues relevant to these voters. As former CDU general secretary Gröhe argued, 'it is certainly also a task of the CDU to provide conservative Christians with a political home' and, as a result of it fulfilling this role, 'social debates such as those surrounding gay marriage have not been turned into a "culture war" in the same way as in other countries'.[31] Similarly, Cardinal Marx emphasised that historically 'many Catholics have often had a close bond with the CDU/CSU but going beyond this and further to the right has never been imaginable for Catholics'.[32] Compared to France, where after the defeat of François Fillon in 2017

---

[27] Arzheimer and Carter 2009, 1006; Scarbrough 1984.
[28] Van der Brug, Fennema and Tillie 2005; Montgomery and Winter 2015; Siegers, Franzmann and Hassan 2016; Siegers and Jedinger 2021; Elff and Roßteutscher 2017.
[29] Siegers and Jedinger 2021, 162.
[30] Bornschier 2010, 13.
[31] Interview Gröhe 2018.
[32] Interview Marx 2018.

the Républicains' ability to provide a political home for French Catholics appeared undermined, leaving these voters up for grabs for Marine Le Pen (see Chapter 11), in Germany the CDU/CSU appeared still to bind many Christian voters, thus making them unavailable for the AfD and contributing to the 'religion gap'.

Often overlooked in the literature, this historical unavailability of Christian voters in Germany was further amplified by the actions of other mainstream parties. Thus, although the CDU/CSU is regarded as the primary party for Christian voters, the SPD, Greens and Liberals have also offered political homes to different Christian streams in Germany.[33] Siegers and Jedinger have shown, for instance, that 'Protestant identification with the Social Democrats results in a similar immunisation effect against the RWP vote as Catholic identification with the Christian Democrats.'[34] This dynamic may partly be a result of the fact that Germany's Social Democratic Party had hitherto refrained from overemphasising identity politics, thereby blocking the AfD's attempts to reshape the debate in identitarian terms and to re-politicise religion as a cultural identity marker.[35] Crucially moreover, unlike other Western European mainstream-left parties or the Democrats in the USA, which in the last decade have often embraced increasingly secular politics and rhetoric in reaction to the far right's attempts to instrumentalise Christianity (see Chapters 11 and 15), SPD and Green representatives emphasised that their parties had largely resisted this temptation. As former Bundestag president Wolfgang Thierse (SPD) put it,

> So far, secularists and atheists have not gained the upper hand in the SPD. This would be a step backwards for our party, because the initiation of the Godesberg programme and the opening to Christians and the churches were a decisive step for the SPD in becoming a people's party [*Volkspartei*] and that should not be reversed. All this has also not shifted in the last few years, even in light of the AfD.

Similarly, Katrin Göring-Eckardt, parliamentary leader of the Green party, emphasised that there have so far been no tendencies towards

---

[33] Siegers, Franzmann and Hassan 2016; Cremer 2021a.

[34] Siegers and Jedinger 2021, 163.

[35] For instance, Bornschier has shown that part of the reason why the FN/RN was able to establish itself in France in the 1970s, whereas the AfD arose in Germany only four decades later, was that 'the Socialists in France pursued an "adversarial strategy" regarding traditionalist-communitarian issues, making multiculturalism a central claim, while the SPD employed a "dismissive strategy"'. Assuming a similar 'dismissive strategy' towards the AfD's references to religion may have helped to keep religious identity widely depoliticised and the SPD (as well as the Greens) open as 'Christian alternatives' to the Union. See Bornschier 2012, 138; Siegers, Franzmann and Hassan 2016.

secularist reactions to the AfD's references to religious symbolism in her party 'because what the AfD is doing there is so dubious that it is not taken seriously by us'.[36]

Yet, whilst Germany's mainstream parties' traditional binding of Christian voters might go a long way in explaining the latter's immunity to the AfD in the past, a number of indicators suggest that this may begin to change in the near future, as a result of significant policy shifts on the centre-left and a crisis of identity in the CDU/CSU after the election defeat of 2021. Thus, after their election victory the 'traffic light coalition' of Social Democrats, Greens and Liberals made explicitly secular and progressive positions on social and moral issues a centrepiece of their coalition contract, entitled 'Daring More Progress'.[37] Among its first measures, the new government set out plans to further liberalise German abortion laws, to facilitate adoption and surrogacy for gay couples and to restructure the institution of marriage by introducing what critics referred to as a 'marriage light' for non-monogamous partnerships.[38] It also appointed Germany's first ever 'queer commissioner' to oversee a 'LGBTQ national action plan'.[39] Meanwhile, many German Christians will have noted with concern that then SPD leader Saskia Esken had publicly called prominent Christians in the party, like Wolfgang Thierse, 'embarrassing' and 'backward' after the latter had raised doubts about the party's gradual embrace of left-wing identity politics.[40] Such concerns have likely become even more acute, as the SPD later ran a much-criticised negative campaign ad that ridiculed one of the CDU-chancellor candidate's advisors as an 'arch-Catholic … for whom sex before marriage is a taboo'.[41]

What is more, such secularisation trends were not just limited to the centre-left. After the unexpected election defeat of Armin Laschet, who was a representative of the Catholic social wing of the party, Germany's Christian Democrats have entered a profound crisis of identity and purpose. One of the key outcomes of this development has been a new debate about whether or not to drop the word 'Christian' from its name and to

---

[36] Given the nature of the new identity cleavage between communitarians and cosmopolitans, some scholars suggest that continuing such a stance might even create new electoral and coalition opportunities for the centre-left, as 'the ongoing transformation of the European political space might further put together holistic-spiritual Greens and church-religious Christian Democrats fighting against the right-wing populist challenge' (Siegers, Franzmann and Hassan, 2016, 203).

[37] SPD, Bündnis 90/Die Grünen and FDP; Wiese 2021.

[38] Riehl 2021; Wiese 2021; SPD, Bündnis 90/Die Grünen and FDP.

[39] Weichert 2022.

[40] Carstens 2021.

[41] Die Zeit 2021.

remove the centrality of the 'Christian view of man' from its programme.[42] While at the time of writing it remains to be seen whether CDU will really follow through with such a radical change, this debate, alongside with the policy agenda of the centre-left, is symptomatic of a broader shift within German politics. It is a shift that risks fundamentally undermining the historical alignment of church-attending Christians and Germany's mainstream parties that had historically helped to 'inoculate' these voters against the far right.

Already prior to the 2021 elections, the presence of many conservative Christians in the early AfD and its potential attraction amongst some conservative (Evangelical) Christians had indicated that a surge of left-wing identitarian issues such as gay marriage, the treatment of trans- and gay issues in schools or the push towards a further liberalisation of abortion by parts of the SPD and Greens combined with the lukewarm response of the CDU/CSU, may alienate certain segments of conservative Christian voters and create new opportunities for the AfD.[43] For instance, almost all Christian AfD politicians interviewed emphasised their disappointment with the CDU's course in the 2010s as a reason for their migration to the AfD. Annette Schultner for instance argued that Christian conservatives 'have no political counterpart outside Bavaria anymore', which according to her led to the fact that 'people who normally would never even have considered a party like the AfD, but have lost their political home for years, have the feeling that … they have barely another choice but to vote for the AfD'.[44] Such views were echoed amongst representatives of some Christian organisations like Michael Inacker, the president of the international Martin Luther Foundation, who spoke of 'dissatisfaction in parts of the middle class, because one does not feel politically and religiously represented anymore'.[45] He explained that part of the problem 'are the legal developments in Germany that introduce secularism through the backdoor …, [which] lead to further alienation and create the setting for the [religious] crocodile tears of the AfD'.[46] Similarly, Helmuth Matthies, then president of the conservative Evangelical news outlet Idea, claimed that when it comes to issues like abortion or family values, 'the CDU has unfortunately watered down many Christian ethical positions in

---

[42] Carstens 2022.
[43] De Wilde et al. 2019, 127; Klose and Patzelt 2016.
[44] Interview Schultner 2018.
[45] Interview Inacker 2018.
[46] Interview Inacker 2018.

the Merkel era. ... Here the AfD can easily position itself.'[47] Meanwhile, Thomas Arnold, the director of the Catholic Academy Dresden-Meißen, lamented that 'if it is true that the CDU has created a gap of representation by moving too far to the left, then it is also true that it has created a representational gap amongst Christians and then it is in principle legitimate for another party to try to fill this gap'.[48] Even within the CDU some interviewees such as Christian Meißner have recognised a certain uneasiness within the Christian middle class in recent years:

> For the last ten to fifteen years, it [the middle class] has been overrun by the left-wing forces in our republic. Therefore, there is now a certain homelessness. The CDU has not always been completely innocent in this because in some political decisions the difference between us and the Greens and the SPD was no longer visible.

In sum, it appears that Germany's political parties have played a crucial role in the existence and size of the religion gap in Germany in the past, as their binding of Christian voters of all backgrounds through a general openness to religion and their avoidance of combative identity politics helped to make Christian voters unavailable to the AfD and avoided a politicisation of religion as a culturised identity marker. However, recent trends suggest that these factors might be evaporating as Germany's centre-left adopts a more assertive stance on issues such as gay marriage and abortion, whilst the CDU/CSU has lost much of its Christian profile. To be sure, SPD chancellor Olaf Scholz or the new CDU president Friedrich Merz may have recognised such risks. Scholz for instance explicitly sought to avoid left-wing identity and to re-emphasise traditional economic issues in his 2021 campaign;[49] and Friedrich Merz may well seek to strengthen the social conservative profile of the CDU.[50] Yet given recent trends, as well as the general weakening of party ties, one should not take for granted the continued alignment of Christian voters with mainstream parties in the long run. Interestingly, however, even as party allegiances are waning, the fact that those Christian voters who deserted the CSU in October 2018 have not migrated to the AfD but to other parties, suggests that there are still factors other than demand-side attitudes, or traditional party loyalty that prevent Christian voters from casting their lot with the populist right: the behaviour of the Christian churches themselves.

---

[47] Interview Matthies 2018.
[48] Interview Arnold 2018.
[49] Läsker 2021; Sievert 2021.
[50] Kissler 2021.

7.3 The Religious Supply Side: The Churches' Social Firewall

One of this book's key findings is that the behaviour of institutional churches and religious leaders is one of the most important, but also one of the most underestimated factors in shaping right-wing populists' ability to co-opt religion for political gain. Specifically, religious leaders' willingness and ability to either condone and legitimise, or to challenge and taboo right-wing populists' religious references emerge as critical factors in explaining the existence and strength of religious immunity.[51] The logic here is that by speaking out unequivocally and publicly against right-wing populism, elite actors can raise the social cost of association with the populist right, thus discouraging voters from electorally supporting these parties even if they agree with some of their policies. Conversely, Olivier Roy observed that in many Western countries 'Christianity has been taken hostage by the populists and is turning into a kitsch Christianity' primarily 'due to the Church's lack of credibility and clarity'.[52] In Germany, faith leaders seem to have been able to avoid such pitfalls and instead capitalised on their privileged public position in the system of benevolent neutrality to create precisely such a social firewall around the AfD among Christians.

Although initially not in principle opposed to a new right-wing party, Germany's churches have emerged as one of the most prolific public adversaries of the AfD and its use of religion after it became apparent that anti-immigration policies and nativist ideals were becoming the AfD's core issues. The churches positioned themselves, for instance, clearly in the pro-immigration camp, shouldering most of the refugee aid in Germany through Christian organisations, and publicly arguing – often with explicit slights directed at the AfD's reference to Christian identity – that 'our Christian identity is particularly evident when every person who seeks refuge in our country receives humane treatment',[53] or that welcoming refugees and immigrants is a 'commandment of Christian responsibility'.[54] The church leadership also directly attacked the AfD's reference to religion as 'perverted',[55] condemned its rhetoric as 'hate speech'[56] and declared the positions of its leadership to 'stand in profound contradiction to the Christian faith'.[57] In a further step the churches repeatedly banned AfD

---

[51] Cremer 2021a; Cremer 2021b.
[52] Roy 2018.
[53] Deutsche Bischofskonferenz 2016.
[54] EKD 2015.
[55] Die Welt 2015.
[56] Deutsche Bischofskonferenz 2016.
[57] Evangelisch.de 2018.

politicians from speaking at the Protestant or Catholic Church annual assemblies, where Germany's two dominant churches organise mass gatherings to discuss social issues with politicians of all backgrounds.[58]

When discussing the source of churches' resolute opposition to the AfD, interviewees were keen to emphasise that this was no pre-meditated top-down 'strategy' but was born out of almost unanimous support from the Christian grassroots across Germany. For instance, the president of the Central Committee of German Catholics, Thomas Sternberg, stated, 'I know that in my demarcation [from the AfD] I am in complete agreement with church members, the representatives of the Catholic associations and organisations as well as the dioceses.'[59] The Protestant Bishop of Berlin Markus Dröge reported that he received 'a lot of positive feedback from parish pastors who were grateful that the church is so clearly taking a stance [against the AfD] in the public sphere'.[60] Some church representatives even spoke of a push for stronger opposition against the AfD from the bottom, stressing that 'many local church groups go much further with their criticism against the AfD than leading church authorities do'.[61] Similarly, Stefanie Rentsch, the Programme Director of the German Evangelical Church Assembly 2019, reported that 'if there is substantive criticism, it is that the church still does not distance itself clearly enough from the AfD and that it should do more'.[62]

Nonetheless, Germany's system of 'benevolent neutrality' seems to have also played an important role in encouraging this outcome by favouring highly centralised churches whose leaders enjoy a high social status, perceive themselves as integral part and defenders of the current system, and are therefore both willing and able to create social taboos against right-wing populism. For instance, the interviews revealed that, while faith leaders may have been responding to popular requests from congregations in their condemnation of the AfD, doing so was also in the churches' self interest. For rather than seeing the populist right as a potential ally against a secularist system, many German faith leaders recognised the AfD's anti-system stance as an important threat to the religion-friendly reading of the *Grundgesetz*. As Thomas Arnold, director of the Catholic

---

[58] F.A.Z. 2018b; Focus 2016.
[59] Interview Sternberg 2018.
[60] Interview Dröge 2018.
[61] Interview Dutzmann 2018.
[62] At the grassroots many Christian congregations rejected donations from AfD officials because they consider the AfD to be 'irreconcilable with Christian values' (Handelsblatt 2018), demonstrated at AfD party conferences with slogan's such as 'our cross has no hooks' (the German word for swastika literally translates as 'hook cross') (Spiegel 2018) or asked AfD members to step down from parish councils and other church positions.

Academy in Dresden, put it, 'the AfD's position on church–state relations is extremely problematic. The programme and the statements of AfD politicians strongly suggest that they are striving for a very secularist order and that they do not represent a positive interpretation of religious freedom as we currently have in Germany'.[63] Markus Dröge, the Protestant bishop of Berlin, concurred claiming that 'just as it became clear in the 1930s that the National Socialists were hostile to Christianity at the moment when the Christians did not follow their ideology, we already have tendencies that the AfD is becoming increasingly hostile to the church'.[64]

Interviewees also recognised that Germany's Christians' religious immunity importantly hinged on the social status and normative authority of faith leaders; something the system of benevolent neutrality formally endowed them with. As Andreas Püttmann, a prolific Catholic commentator, put it, 'the [German] churches have managed to maintain a moral high ground, which has largely crumbled in the secular context, where everything seems relative'. As a result, 'sermons from the pulpit or public statements [from church leaders] play an important role in maintaining a social taboo against the far right'.[65] The then president of the Protestant National Synod, Irmgard Schwätzer, concurred, saying that 'the difference in electoral behaviour is, above all, a result of the continuing social influence and moral authority of the churches'.[66] Likewise, the director of the Protestant Academy in Berlin, Christian Staffa, argued that, due to the church leadership's clear positioning, 'acting on right-wing attitudes is "blocked" differently as a Christian. [A Christian] knows that: "If I act on these attitudes, I'm really part of 'them' [the populist right] and somehow I know that's wrong".'[67] He further emphasised this point by stating that

> The moral leadership in the church is very important. There is no [anti-elite] 'Merkel must go motive' in the church, because there is a different appreciation of leading clergy in the church and people know that the leading clergy are against the AfD. In this regard, the episcopal faith of Protestants is no less pronounced than that of Catholics.[68]

---

[63] Interview Arnold 2018.
[64] Interview Dröge 2018.
[65] Interview Püttmann 2018. This could also help account for the AfD's comparatively strong performance in East Germany, where after fifty-two years of atheist Nazi and Communist dictatorships levels of secularisation are among the highest in the world, religious institutions are significantly weakened and the sway of religious leaders much more diminished than in West Germany; see Siegers and Jedinger 2021.
[66] Interview Schwätzer 2018.
[67] Interview Staffa 2018.
[68] Interview Staffa 2018.

Catholic representatives agreed with this assessment. Karl Jüsten maintained, for instance, that the reason why Catholics are less likely to vote
AfD is 'that the church and its leadership have openly taken a clear-cut
position in rejecting this ideology. The bond to the Christian faith then
makes many people fundamentally more resistant to left- and right-wing
radical temptations.'[69] Similarly, Cardinal Marx stressed that 'it's about
long-term bonds; not just daily politics, but longer-term inhibitions
against going to the right'.[70] These assessments were confirmed through
outside perspectives such as that of Thomas Krüger, the president of the
Federal Agency for Civic Education, who pointed to an 'inner resilience
[among Christian voters] created by the clergy and their relatively clear
positions against right-wing populism'.[71]

Indeed, even former AfD officials like Marcus Pretzell admitted that
many Christians within the AfD struggle, 'precisely because they are
Christians, … actually have a very hard time with the AfD … These conservative Christians are very sensitive to warning calls and social taboos.'[72]
Other AfD interviewees explained that the 'exclusions' and 'accusations'
they experienced through the churches have discouraged the AfD from
further attempts to associate itself with the churches or to use Christian
symbols.[73] Instead many AfD leaders publicly distanced themselves from
earlier pro-church positions, called on party members to leave the 'system
churches', denounced the churches as 'red-green filth' or 'asylum lobby
groups', and redefined the AfD as 'not a Christian party'.[74]

Overall, these observations substantiate the impression that Germany's
system of benevolent neutrality has encouraged and enabled German faith
leaders to create a powerful social taboo for Christians around casting their
vote for the AfD.[75] However, the reactions of AfD leaders also reveal some
of the political, social and religious risks associated with the churches'
'social firewall'. Some interviewees suggested that what may appear as a
radicalisation of the party is partly a reaction to the often-intense social
isolation AfD members feel as a result of the open attacks by the church.
AfD politician Armin-Paul Hampel hence explained that, 'At the party
congress in Cologne, I asked AfD members to quit the church. Why?

---

[69] Interview Jüsten 2018.
[70] Interview Marx 2018.
[71] Interview Krüger 2018.
[72] Interview Pretzell 2018.
[73] Interview Meuthen 2018; interview Hampel 2018.
[74] F.A.Z. 2016a; AfD Thüringen 2019; Hofmann 2019.
[75] Pollack and Rosta 2017.

Because the churches attack the AfD in ways that no church leader is entitled to. We have experienced this exclusion for years.'[76] AfD president Jörg
Meuthen similarly described his frustration over the fact that the churches
profess to 'believe that AfDers, who're demonstrating in Chemnitz are
all masked Nazis'.[77] He emphasised that 'such accusations trigger anger
and make me emotional. ... At the beginning, I reached out and offered
to talk ... but none of those conversations ever took place. Since then I
have given up completely. The churches are not interested in a dialogue.'[78]
Others held the church implicitly responsible for radicalising tendencies
within the party. Volker Münz hence declared that

> Being Christian is denied to us, people no longer greet us, some of us even
> experience attacks. ChrAfD is therefore also a mutual 'support system' for
> us Christians struggling with these hostilities in our neighbourhoods and
> communities. But our response to the church's confrontational course is
> 'now more than ever'.

Ex-spokesperson of the Christians in the AfD, Annette Schultner, made
this accusation more explicitly when she lamented that

> The media and the churches with their undifferentiated criticism have
> contributed to a siege mentality and radicalisation in the AfD. I know
> a number of people who ... lost their jobs or businesses because of their
> involvement with the AfD ... Many have entered the party as perfectly
> respectable [*bürgerlich*] individuals, but ... have seen their social environ-
> ment be decimated. This has caused them to say, 'This can't have all been
> in vain' and so these are people who have essentially been radicalised within
> the party through this [outside criticism].

Certainly, these accounts should be read with caution, given what one
interviewee off-the-record identified right-wing populists' strategic use of
a 'victim- and martyr rhetoric, whereby they develop a narrative in which
they are the silent majority'.[79] Moreover, grievances about the attacks
from the church also cannot fully account for the strong resistance against
Christians from within the AfD, which interviewees confirmed was present
from the party's beginning, nor for the stark discrepancies revealed between
AfD policies and Christian doctrine (see Chapter 6). In fact, even the AfD's
positions of anti-clericalism and secularism appear too radical and fundamental to be solely explained as a reaction to the churches' criticism.

---

[76] Interview Hampel 2018.
[77] Interview Meuthen 2018.
[78] Interview Meuthen 2018.
[79] Müller 2017; Nestler and Rohgalf 2017.

Nonetheless, the fact that several of the concerns raised by AfD officials were shared by some church and mainstream party representatives suggests that the risk of isolation, polarisation and politicisation associated with the churches' social firewall is real. For instance, EAD Representative Heimowski asserted that 'the course of the churches has gone too far, because it has marginalised people and contributed to their radicalisation. This has made the AfD great and allows them to present themselves as victims.'[80] EKD-Synod president Irmgard Schwätzer said that 'at the beginning we were perhaps too exclusionary and ostracising. I have turned against this because we have to remain open to our own members.'[81] And former CDU general secretary Hermann Gröhe emphasised that although he agrees with the churches' strong stance against the far right, 'churches are not political parties and must be able to offer people of different political beliefs a home of faith'.[82] These concerns were echoed by the empirical findings in the literature that the position of the churches might lead to further divides within society, but also to an 'increased polarisation amongst church members'.[83]

Given this risk of isolation, radicalisation and politicisation, many church and party officials interviewed have considered new ways of amending the churches' position. Irmgard Schwätzer for instance called for the need to 'distinguish between a necessary public confrontation and internal discussion. There must be sheltered spaces in the church to speak with doubters … [O]ur task is to strengthen cohesion in our society and to counter fragmentation. That's where the question of identity comes in.'[84] Similarly, Bishop Dröge emphasised that 'we need to find ways to reach out to people in the public debate who feel attracted by the AfD and give them the opportunity to voice their problems, concerns and criticisms so that they do not see right-wing populist events as the only space in which they can express their concerns'.[85] On the Catholic side, Karl Jüsten emphasised that 'the church would be ill-advised to simply fence itself off [from AfD voters]. The church is better advised to approach these people and convince them of the truth of our own message.'[86] These assessments about the churches' duty but also particular ability to provide sheltered spaces for common debate was shared by former Bundestag president Wolfgang Thierse:

---

[80]   Interview Heimowski 2018.
[81]   Interview Schwätzer 2018.
[82]   Interview Gröhe 2018.
[83]   Pickel 2018, 277.
[84]   Interview Schwätzer 2018.
[85]   Interview Dröge 2018.
[86]   Interview Jüsten 2018.

Churches must be the place and space for conversation and peaceful debate, where fears are taken seriously and not immediately denounced; a place where right-wing extremists are not confirmed, but where people are taken seriously and can voice their insecurities. This is only possible to a limited extent in the political sphere and parties simply cannot do this in the way Christian congregations can.[87]

In addition to this provision of internal spaces for open discussion with AfD supporters on a micro-level, which one interviewee off-the-record compared to the Catholic Church's concept of 'hate the sin but love the sinner', church officials also appeared to consider a change in the church's public reaction to AfD on the macro-level. For instance, several interviewees sought to tackle accusations about a politicisation and left-wing bias, levelled in particular against the Protestant church, through a stronger emphasis on theology over politics. In this context, the Director of the Protestant Academy in Berlin, Christian Staffa, argued, 'We have the images; we have the language. We don't need to talk like Social-Democrats because we have much more radical sources about equality for all people. … We have to be theological – we have everything we need, we just don't use it enough.'[88] He maintained that 'if one challenges them [the right-wing populists] on the grounds of theology and Holy Scripture rather than asylum law, then one quickly gets to their absurd claims like that "love thy neighbour" should be interpreted geographically, and then you can take it apart biblically-theologically'.[89] The Protestant Bishop of Berlin, Markus Dröge, similarly praised the advantages of using theology to challenge the AfD's superficially religious position, saying that, 'in my weekly newspaper column "What Would Jesus Say?",[90] I argue with the AfD from our point of view. That means that I am not discussing politics with the AfD, but first and foremost theology.'[91]

Such a renewed emphasis on theological rather than political arguments was not only popular amongst church officials, but also in otherwise often critical conservative Protestant circles. For instance, the president of the International Martin Luther Foundation, Michael Inacker, argued that 'what is most important is that the churches must challenge the AfD in

---

[87] Interview Thierse 2018.
[88] Interview Staffa 2018.
[89] Interview Staffa 2018. One recent project exemplifying this new strategy to re-emphasise theology in the dispute is the 'Netzteufel' project, in which theologians analyse online hate speech and respond to it with theologically informed 'hopespeech' (Deutschlandfunk 2018b).
[90] Dröge is referring to his regular column in the *Berliner Zeitung* (Dröge 2020).
[91] Interview Dröge 2018.

their own language. Secular left-wing liberal arguments do not help to put right-wing populists on the path of virtue.'[92] Even many mainstream party representatives, who would profit from the alleged political bias of the churches, such as SPD member Stephan Steinlein, stated that 'I hope that theology can help to positively steer this debate and put it on firmer footing. I believe that religion can be a force of good here to solve the current crisis.'[93] CDU official Meißner concurred saying, 'I would discuss theology very concretely with these people and ask how they can reconcile their Christian principles with this party. I believe that [AfD supporters] are not helped by exclusion. ... This task cannot be left to the Greens, the Linke or the SPD.'[94]

However, all church officials, lay representatives and mainstream party politicians were adamant that neither a potential opening to more internal debates, nor a renewed focus on theology should soften or lower the social firewall that the churches' harsh public confrontation with the AfD has helped to create. Rather they stressed that with such additional measures in place to reduce the 'negative externalities' of isolation, radicalisation and politicisation associated with the social taboo, the churches could make their differences with the AfD even clearer. Bishop Dröge for instance argued that through the theological challenging of AfD positions, 'I believe that [the relationship between the churches and the AfD] has become clearer and thus more distant.'[95] Some interviewees even suggested that the provision of safe spaces for open discussions and identity concerns might amplify Christians' internal resilience against the AfD's identity politics by reaffirming their own sense of identity and community within the church. Furthermore, interviewees have expressed the hope that a focus on public theology rather than on politics may also help curtail the spread of religious illiteracy, thus undermining the credibility of the far right's use of religion and expanding resilience to such appeals in the population.[96]

In sum, the reaction of Christian voters, parties and institutions to the AfD's use of Christian rhetoric appears to be characterised by a 'vaccination effect' amongst voters, and prolific criticism from the churches. Supply-side factors such as the behaviour of mainstream parties, the settlement of benevolent neutrality and the behaviour of church leaders themselves

---

[92] Interview Inacker 2018.
[93] Interview Steinlein 2018.
[94] Interview Meißner 2018.
[95] Interview Dröge 2018.
[96] Brink 2012; Moore 2007.

appear to have played a critical role in this context. Specifically, the historical openness of Germany's mainstream parties to Christian voters, and their relative abstinence from identity politics, have kept Christian voters unavailable for AfD. Meanwhile the system of benevolent neutrality has boosted the churches' willingness and ability to publicly condemn the AfD's uses of religion and thereby create a powerful social taboo around this party among Christians.

7.4   Conclusion

Part II set out to explore the social origins of the rise of the new populist right in Germany, the ways in which right-wing populist actors like the AfD seek to use religion, how German churches, Christian parties and voters react to these strategies, and what this means for the future of the relationship between politics and religion. Four conclusions emerge from this analysis.

First, Chapter 4 showed that after 1945, the *Grundgesetz* produced a relatively 'happy marriage of convenience' between religion and democratic politics in Germany through the system of benevolent neutrality, in the context of which the churches largely functioned as a bridge-builder across social cleavages and a defender of the liberal democratic order. Second, Chapter 5 revealed how this settlement has recently been put into question by the emergence of a new identity cleavage between cosmopolitans and communitarians, and the subsequent rise of the AfD, which has sought to re-politicise religious identity to capitalise on the new divide. Third, the analysis of the AfD's 'Christian credentials' in Chapter 6 demonstrated that this renewed reference to Christianity is not necessarily representative of a return to religiosity in German society, but rather of the attempt of a comparatively secular – and at times openly secularist – party to employ Christianity as a secularised national identity marker against Islam. Fourth and finally, Chapter 7 has showed that irreligious voters were much more drawn to the AfD than practising Christians, who seemed to be 'inoculated' against the radical right partly as a result of demand-side factors, such as attitudes or theological beliefs, but mainly because of supply-side factors such as the role of mainstream parties and the institutional churches, which through their clear and public condemnation of the AfD's use of religion have created a powerful social taboo surrounding the AfD.

Returning in the light of these results to the cold February night in Dresden in 2015, it appears evident that although PEGIDA's demonstrators used religious symbols and language during their rally, this was not based on a positive appreciation of Christianity, but rather on an ethno-cultural rejection of the Islamic 'other'; that PEGIDA used 'Christendom' as a cultural identity marker without necessarily subscribing to 'Christianity' as a faith. Part II has shown that in this respect the PEGIDA demonstration in Dresden was representative of the use of religion by Germany's populist right writ large and by the AfD in particular, whose exclusivist use of Christian references as secularised identity markers was strongly rejected by Christian voters, parties and the churches. Interestingly, a keen observer could have come to many of these conclusions without surveys on the religious beliefs of participants and systematic analyses of speeches and policy positions, but simply by looking more closely at the Frauenkirche itself. For shortly after the beginning of the gathering its pastor had turned off the church's lights to stop it from being 'instrumentalised as a backdrop to xenophobic rallies'.[97] His colleagues in other prolific German churches like the Cologne Cathedral soon did the same, heralding the new struggle over the meaning of Christian identity in contemporary Germany between populists' identitarian interpretation of Christendom, and the universalist reading of the Christian faith put forward by the churches. This was reminiscent of a struggle that had been going for decades on the other side of the Rhine between the French Catholic Church and the right-wing populist Front National, which the following chapters will explore in more detail.

[97] Die Welt 2015.

French Catholicism, the Rassemblement National and Laïcité
Between the Devil and the Dark Blue Sea

The first of May is Labour Day in France. On this 'high day' for the country's secular left, hundreds of thousands of protesters traditionally parade through the streets of Paris to demonstrate for higher wages as well as to celebrate the country's republican – and at times revolutionary – tradition.[1] However, for several decades, these left-wing demonstrations were contrasted by another very different rally in the heart of Paris. Every year on this day several thousand demonstrators would gather around the statue of a Catholic saint, deposit flowers and march through Paris' streets venerating that saint. In the heartland of *laïcité* such a religiously flavoured rally is surprising enough. Yet, perhaps even more surprising is the fact that these marches were not organised by the Catholic Church or any other religious organisation, but by the right-wing populist Front National (FN) in honour of France's national Saint, Joan of Arc.

Founded in 1972 by Jean-Marie Le Pen and renamed as the Rassemblement National (RN) in 2018 under the leadership of his daughter Marine Le Pen, RN is one of the oldest and most prominent right-wing populist party in Europe.[2] Since the mid-2010s, just when Germany's far right turned to the defence of the 'Christian Occident', the RN also began to make increasing references to France's Catholic identity. In addition to the long-established marches in veneration of Joan of Arc, RN politicians sought to reclaim France's status as the *Fille aînée de l'eglise*,[3] pushed for the ostensible display of nativity scenes in city halls, and presented the RN as a

---

[1] Tartakowsky 2005.

[2] Betz 2018b; Brustier and Escalona 2015; Mayer 1999; Mudde 2007; Perrineau 2014

[3] 'The first-born daughter of the church' is an informal title that had its roots in the French king's title as 'first-born sons of the church' and re-emerged in the nineteenth century when France often acted as the military protector of the Vatican. In the twentieth century it has mainly been used to emphasise the country's Catholic identity (Poupard 1986).

champion against the vandalisation of France's churches.[4] More recently, the RN has been joined in its reference to France's Catholic identity by Éric Zemmour, a journalist turned politician who has become a rising star on the French far right and has challenged Marine Le Pen's leadership status through his candidacy for the French presidency in 2022. Zemmour who, although being Jewish, calls himself 'steeped in Christianity', has attracted much attention by publicly proclaiming that Catholicism has a 'birth right' to cultural hegemony in France, and by calling for the reaffirmation of 'Catholicism's cultural pre-eminence'.[5]

Both the rise of Zemmour and the RN's turn towards religious symbols coincided with what some observers called 'France's Catholic Moment', or 'the emergence of a French Christian right' after millions of French Catholics took to the streets to demonstrate against gay marriage in 2012 and subsequently organised themselves in political movements like the *Manif pour Tous* or *Sens Commun*.[6] As a result of this temporal overlap, many observers were quick to speak of a 'Tea Party French style', assuming an alliance or even an identity between the populist right and French Catholicism.[7] However, as the following chapters will show, the relationship between the two is much older and much more complicated than such narratives would suggest. For instance, while many French Catholics seem to have shifted further to the right and while France's traditionally powerful Catholic left has all but disappeared, high levels of religious practice have been one of the strongest statistical predictors *against* voting for the RN for decades, and church authorities have continuously clashed with the RN not only on immigration but also on abortion, gay marriage and *laïcité*.[8] Meanwhile, the RN, in addition to being steeped in a history of neo-paganist influences, has more recently begun to stylise itself as the key defender of a radically secularist reading of *laïcité*, with the declared aim to reduce any religion's visibility in the publish sphere.[9]

Part III seeks to better understand these paradoxical dynamics in the context of France's shifting political landscape, which since 2017 has been fundamentally reorganised around the new bipolarity between the far right and Emmanuel Macron's centrist *La Republique En Marche* movement

[4] In recent years France has seen a significant wave of church vandalisations and anti-Christian attacks with up to 875 reported incidents in one year alone (Cornevin 2019; Sugy 2019).
[5] Zemmour 2016; Zemmour and Leclerc 2018; Neuville 2021.
[6] Gregg 2017; Fourquet 2018a; Du Cleuziou 2019.
[7] Bizeul 2018; Davies 2010; Stille 2014.
[8] Dargent 2016; IFOP 2019; IFOP 2017a; Tevanian 2013; Pelletier and Schlegel 2012; Cremer 2021c.
[9] Almeida 2017.

(LREM). To do so, Part III first locates these developments within the historical and institutional context of religion and politics in France (Chapter 8). It then analyses which socio-demographic shifts might have led to the remaking of France's political landscape (Chapter 9), before studying how the RN and Zemmour have sought to re-politicise religion and *laïcité* in this new context (Chapter 10). Finally, it explores how French Catholics have reacted to this development, and what this means for the future relationship between politics, religion and *laïcité* in France's new political constellation (Chapter 11).

CHAPTER 8

La République Laïque *vs.* La France Catholique
The Rise and Decline of French 'Catho-Laïcité'

Religion was and remains a touchy and treacherous topic for French politicians. French President Emmanuel Macron experienced this for himself when, in early 2018, he attended the national funeral of one of France's most celebrated pop icons, Johnny Halliday. As a former Jesuit school pupil, Macron walked up to the coffin and raised his hand to make the sign of the cross. At the last second, he remembered the presence of cameras, stopped in the middle of the movement and withdrew his hand. But the damage was done. The incident was followed by a torrent of criticism.[1] Although, Macron had always keenly avoided publicly speaking about his faith (or lack thereof), many defenders of *laïcité*, who already suspected him of being insufficiently *laïque* for the office, now saw their suspicions confirmed.[2]

This incident was by no means out of the ordinary for twenty-first-century French politics. It illustrates the explosive potential of the return of politicised religion for French politics. Other recent examples include the 'scandal' that broke out in 2019 around the LREM's lead candidate for the European elections, Nathalie Loiseau, because her public agenda revealed her attendance at Catholic Mass.[3] Similarly, her competitor from the centre-right party, Les Républicains (LR), François-Xavier Bellamy, was criticised for his private but religiously motivated views on abortion, as had been the LR's candidate for the 2017 election, François Fillon, after he had publicly acknowledged that his personal faith also informed his political engagement.[4] To make sense of these episodes and to comprehend the explosive potential of the RN's re-politicisation of religion, it is necessary to examine the nature, history and importance of the concept of *laïcité*, which is considered to be one of the strictest institutional separations of

---

[1] 20 Minutes société 2017; Herreros 2017; Jeanpierre 2017.
[2] Corre 2018; Dosse 2017; Michelon 2018.
[3] Sautreuil 2019.
[4] Berdah 2019; Du Cleuziou 2019; Journal du Dimanche 2017; Saint Clair 2017.

church and state in the world.[5] This chapter will show that *laïcité* is far more than a legal settlement of state–church relations in French politics. Instead, as almost all political and religious elites interviewed agreed, it has become a crucial part of French national identity. As Nino Galetti, the head of the conservative Konrad Adenauer foundation in France, put it during our interview, 'It would be more coherent to extend the French Republic's motto to *Liberté, Égalité, Fraternité, Laïcité*.'[6]

8.1 *La République Laïque* vs. *La France Catholique*: The War of the Two Frances

How could a legal principle acquire such a revered status? *Laïcité* has been the central point of contention in a two-century-long struggle between two competing visions of French identity. As Philippe Portier emphasises, 'The Revolution of 1789 separated France into two parts: on one side, *la France Catholique*, on the other, *la France Républicaine*.'[7] *La France Catholique* was the product of a millennium-old, almost symbiotic relationship between the Catholic Church and the French monarchy.[8] Tracing back its own origins to the conversion and coronation of Clovis as the first king of France in Reims in 496, the kings of France defined themselves as the *fils ainés de l'eglise* and defenders of the Catholic faith.[9] In spite of a strong Gallican tradition, the French kings never completely broke with Rome and even after the end of the wars of religion and the peace of Westphalia, when in other parts of Europe a certain level of tolerance of religious minorities became the norm, the *ancien régime* continued to double down on its policy of religious 're-Catholicisation'.[10]

By contrast, *la République laïque* was born of the French Revolution and largely constructed in opposition to this close – and in the view of many French Enlightenment philosophers – troubling entanglement between

---

[5] Baubérot, Milot and Portier 2014; Dieckhoff and Portier 2017; Hurd 2009.
[6] Interview Galetti 2019.
[7] Portier 2016, 1.
[8] Tracing back its own origins to the conversion and coronation of Clovis as the first King of France in Reims in 496, the kings of France defined themselves as the *fils ainés de l'eglise* and defenders of the Catholic faith Leclerc 1933; Portier 2016; Poupard 1986. In spite of a strong Gallican tradition Martimort 1973, the French kings never completely broke with Rome and even after the end of the wars of religion and the peace of Westphalia, when in other parts of Europe a certain level of tolerance of religious minorities became the norm, the *ancien régime* continued to double down on its policy of religious 're-Catholicisation' (Portier 2016, 23–35).
[9] Portier 2016; Poupard 1986.
[10] Martimort 1973; Portier 2016, 23–35.

earthly and spiritual power.[11] The revolutionaries of 1789 therefore juxta-
posed an idea of a rationalist and revolutionary national identity that was
anti-clerical and often anti-religious in outlook.[12] No less ambitious than
Catholicism in its claim for absolute truth, aspiration to transform humanity and to create a new moral order, this secular universalism became the
guiding ideology of *la République laïque*.[13]

Sociologists and historians have shown that in the early nineteenth century the conflict between these two irreconcilable identities gave birth to
a social cleavage that decisively structured society and politics for the next
two centuries.[14] Victory for Republican over Catholic France appeared
only to be achieved in the Third French Republic with the codification
of *laïcité*. From 1880 to 1905 the secularist 'fathers of the Republic' led
by Jules Ferry, Émile Combes, Jean Jaurès and Léon Gambetta, passed
several laws to establish *laïcité* as a political principle: the *Loi Ferry* of 1886
suppressed religious schooling in favour of a 'public, free, obligatory, and
secular School', which was to become 'the Church of the Republic'.[15] The
Loi du 9 décembre 1905 enshrined the separation of church and state, stating
in Article 2 that 'The Republic does not recognise, pay, or subsidise any
religious sect', thus demoting Catholicism from the religion of the state to
a simple association under private law.[16] To be sure, moderates like Astride
Briand sought to emphasise the freedom of worship and belief guaranteed
in the law, yet under the Third Republic a 'separationist model' of *laïcité*
prevailed, where, as Phillipe Portier summarised, 'nothing was left of the
traditional alliance between the two powers'.[17]

This legal victory of Republican over Catholic France did not lead
to a cooling of tensions, however. On the contrary, the social cleavage
deepened as the Catholic Church began to create a parallel universe of

---

[11] Willaime, Langlois and Chatellier 2009.
[12] Baubérot 2005; Seippel 1905; Vovelle 2002.
[13] Baubérot 2005; Portier 2016.
[14] For instance, the *terreur* of Robespierre of 1792, the revolutions of 1830 and 1848, and the com-
mune of Paris can be interpreted as anti-clerical, republican France fighting the church and the old
regime; just as the restoration of monarchies and empires from 1804–1814, 1818–1848 and 1852–1870
can be seen as attempts of *la France Catholique* to fight back. Fourquet argues that even secular
divides such as those between the left and right, monarchists and republicans, conservatives and
liberals, or workers and the bourgeoisie could ultimately be traced to the antagonism between *la
France Catholique* and *la République laïque*, which 'always remained predominant in the sense that
it constituted the backbone that ultimately organised the political contest'; see Fourquet 2019, 10;
Le Bras and Todd 2013; Portier 2016; Portier 2011.
[15] Gambetta famously declared on the 4 May 1877 to the Assemblée Nationale, 'Le cléricalisme? Voilà
l'ennemi.' See also Chevallier 2014; Ozouf 1992.
[16] Baubérot 2005; Combes 1905; Loi de 1905 2019.
[17] Portier 2016, 313; Bellon 2015.

Catholic education, newspapers, healthcare, labour unions and social clubs.[18] Meanwhile, a new political movement emerged, which claimed to defend the old *France catholique, eternelle et charnelle*. Inspired by the integral nationalism of (the self-declared agnostic) Charles Maurras and organised since 1899 in the Action Française (AF), this movement went beyond the conservatism of the church and promoted a secularised but more radical ideal of an ethnically purified French national Catholicism.[19] Acting in many ways as a precursor and inspiration for modern-day right-wing populists movements, the AF was less interested in the restoration of the Catholic faith and the church's authority than in Catholicism as a cultural identifier of the French nation.[20] As Maurras himself put it, 'a true nationalist places his country above everything' (including God and His church).[21] The church itself remained sceptical towards the AF and in 1926 Pope Pius XI put Maurras's writings on the index of forbidden books and condemned the movement.[22] Yet, Republican France had no eye for such nuances. To most Republicans, Maurras and the AF were proof of the abiding threat that Catholicism posed to the Republic. After the end of WWII the Republic therefore struck back and, in an attempt to unassailably enshrine *laïcité* into the fabric of France, included it in the 1946 constitution of the Fourth Republic. From then on France was forever to be '*une République indivisible, laïque, democratique et sociale*'.[23] However, just at the moment when the principle of *laïcité* seemed set in stone, its interpretation began to change.

8.2   De Gaulle, Mitterrand and the Reconciliation of the Two Frances

In the second half of the twentieth century, through developments in Catholic and Republican doctrine and under the leadership of presidents De Gaulle and Mitterrand, the separatist model of *laïcité*, which had characterised the Third Republic, gradually gave way to a more cooperative

---

[18] Portier and Willaime 2012, 196.

[19] Joly 2015.

[20] Many contemporary right-wing populist leaders in France and in other Western countries have directly referenced Maurras as an intellectual influence, in particular with regards to the identitarian use of religion Jenkins 2019. Steve Bannon for instance 'approvingly cited Maurras' as precursor for his nationalist-populist project (Crowley 2017).

[21] Lawrence 2016, 95.

[22] Prévotat and Rémond 2001.

[23] Constitution de la IVe République 1946.

'model of recognition'.[24] Scholars have long emphasised that the law of 1905
itself never prescribed a staunchly separatist model.[25] What had rendered
laïcité so divisive in preceding decades was the anti-clerical and ideological
zeal that, according to Portier, had 'merged [the law] with a Republican
ideology that intended to reorganise society around an all-encompassing
and educating state spreading reason and progress'.[26] However, after 1945
this Republican ideology was in crisis. Disillusionment over the secular
utopias of Communism and Fascism and the crisis of France's overseas
empire, which had been inspired by a republican *mission civilisatrice*, had
shaken the very belief in reason and secular progress upon which *laïcité* was
based. At the same time, French Catholicism had also begun to change.
Since the 1930s the Catholic Church had undergone a slow but fundamental conversion to modernity and democracy, crowned by the Vatican II
Council in 1965.[27] In addition, the Catholic Church's role in the construction of the European project alongside the rise to prominence of Christian
democracy in Europe and its expression through Mouvement Républicain
Populaire (MRP) in France made it harder to denounce Catholicism as the
reactionary arch-enemy of democracy and progress.[28]

By the 1950s the divide between the two Frances softened and religion was losing much of its explosive potential. However, it was not
until the Fifth Republic that this détente produced a lasting institutional
settlement. Two French presidents were of particular importance in
forming and reinforcing a compromise: Charles de Gaulle and François
Mitterrand. Both presidents were steeped in France's secular as well as
Catholic traditions. De Gaulle, an army general and part of the nobility,
was a product of the old Catholic France, and a devout believer. Yet, he
was also the incarnation of the French Resistance and was celebrated as
the saviour of the Republic in 1945.[29] Mitterrand was France's first post-
war Socialist president. Yet he too came from a devoutly Catholic family,
had been associated with a number of reactionary Catholic movements
in his youth and was amongst the first Socialist politicians to recognise
and capitalise on the emergence of the new Christian left, which rose to

---

[24] Willaime 2008.
[25] For instance, the two legal elements of *laïcité* – the teleological element, to guarantee the freedom
of belief and worship (including in the public sphere), as well as the instrumental element, to assure
the religious neutrality of the state – are in themselves no stricter than the American 'wall of separation' (Portier 2016, 10).
[26] Portier 2016, 193.
[27] Roy 2019, 43.
[28] Descamp 1980; Kalyvas and Van Kersbergen 2010; Müller 2013.
[29] Roussel 2002.

prominence in the 1960s.[30] These deep roots in France's Catholic and Republican identities allowed both men to establish a settlement that was committed to the system of *laïcité* but also appreciative of France's Catholic identity and open to utilising all the potential for compromise that the law allowed.

De Gaulle, for instance, helped to reconcile Catholics with the Republic through the Debré law of 1959, which allowed the public financing of the Catholic private education system, as well as with a broader shift to a '*laïcité* of dialogue and recognition' that entailed the symbolic inclusion of Catholic authorities at certain official ceremonies.[31] Mitterrand meanwhile welcomed the Catholic left into the Socialist party, and set the precedent for a pact of non-aggression between the secular left and Catholic France by retracting a law of his education minister that would have curtailed the independence of the Catholic schools in 1984.[32] Hence, both presidents laid the foundation of what Jerôme Fourquet calls *Catho-laïcité*, a 'gentlemen's agreement' that largely depoliticised the question of religion and *laïcité* for the decades to come.[33] De Gaulle' and Mitterrand's successors fostered these mechanisms of cooperation between state and church, integrating the latter into the political decision-making process through 'reflexion fora', or annual meetings between the bishops and the government.[34] Under the new system Fourquet argued that 'Catholics were at ease with the *modus vivendi* … lived their faith in a discreet way and did not feel the need to mobilise, because, although the churches were emptying, the Republic and society did not question their fundamental values.'[35] In return, the left tolerated a certain level of religious expression and references to France's Christian heritage in the public sphere, as long as the church did not interfere with daily politics.[36]

The acceptance of *Catho-laïcité* and the pacification of the war of the two Frances was confirmed by political and religious elites interviewed for this book. *Laïcité* was praised by representatives of secular republicanism,

---

[30] Pelletier and Schlegel 2012; Védrine 2017; Winock 2016.
[31] Loth and Picht 1991; Baubérot 2015; Willaime 2008.
[32] Fourquet 2018a.
[33] Fourquet 2018a, 9.
[34] Portier and Willaime 2012.
[35] Fourquet 2018a, 11.
[36] Some left-wing politicians like Jean-Pierre Chevènement even publicly recognised the connection between Christian and republican values, stating that 'The values of the Republic owe much to our Judeo-Christian heritage. No doubt, our idea of modern democracy has its source in the Athens of Pericles. No doubt our conception of citizenship borrows much from that of Rome. But these republican values, it must be admitted, are largely secularised Christian values' (Chevènement 1997).

such as former Socialist Education minister Najat Vallaud-Belkacem, who
called it an 'an element of national identity' and 'extremely positive',[37]
or the LREM politician Françoise Dumas, for whom '*laïcité* is in itself
a superior principle'.[38] It was also approved of by the representatives of
the traditionally pro-Catholic centre-right and the Christian churches.
For example, Gérard Larcher, Senate president and interim president of
the centre-right LR, declared himself 'profoundly attached to the concept
of *laïcité*' and emphasised the abiding strength of *Gaullisme* as a guiding
principle.[39] Meanwhile Jean-Frédéric Poisson, then president of the Parti
Chretien-Democrate (PCD; renamed VIA, la voie du people in 2020),
declared that '*laïcité* is in its essence a very good thing for the French
Church, because it saves it from former Gallican tendencies'.[40] Within
the Protestant church the president of the Protestant Federation of France
(FPF), François Clavairoly, emphasised 'that the law of 1905 is very important to us',[41] while the president of the United Protestant Church of
France (Reformed and Lutheran), Emmanuelle Seyboldt, explained that
'Protestants are happy about the separation law of 1905 because it allows
them to exist.'[42] On the Catholic side Pascal Wintzer, the Archbishop
of Poitiers, declared that 'most French Bishops are quite happy with
this model of *laïcité*', adding that 'it's a guarantee of liberty',[43] while
Dominique Quinio, the president of France's largest Catholic lay organisation, the *Semaines Sociales*, and former editor-in-chief of France's main
Catholic Newspaper *La Croix*, praised the system's advantages, saying that
'we must not touch the base of *laïcité*. ... Catholic education, taxes paid to
social religious organisations; things are possible and it works.'[44] However,
several religious leaders and centre-right politicians also emphasised that
the depoliticisation of religion and *laïcité* depended upon the upholding
of the 'pact of non-aggression'. Grégoire Catta from the Conference of
Catholic Bishops for instance argued that 'I do not agree with interpretations [of *laïcité*], which say that religion has no place in the public space.'[45]
Christophe Billan of the conservative *Sens Commun* movement (SC) made
a similar distinction:

---

[37] Interview Vallaud-Belkacem 2019.
[38] Interview Dumas 2019.
[39] Interview Larcher 2019.
[40] Interview Poisson 2019.
[41] Interview Clavairoly 2019.
[42] Interview Seyboldt 2019.
[43] Interview Wintzer 2019.
[44] Interview Quinio 2019.
[45] Interview Catta 2019.

The law of 1905 can be read in two ways: either as the law of a strict separation where there is no relationship whatsoever, or as a more nuanced distinction in the way that we always wanted it. Today *laïcité* can be a good thing if interpreted correctly, or it can become very bad if one thinks, like the far left, that it should become a strict separation.[46]

On the Protestant side, Emmanuelle Seyboldt concurred, explaining that 'problems arise when we try to turn *laïcité* into something that imposes silence in the public space on believers'.[47]

8.3   A Fragile Equilibrium Challenged Once More

Notably, interviewees reported the return of precisely such a 'separationist model' of *laïcité* since the turn of the twenty-first century. Dominique Lebrun, the Archbishop of Rouen hence observed 'a tentative push … to put religion back into the private sphere',[48] while PCD/VIA president Jean-Frédéric Poisson lamented 'a form of prohibition in the name of the sacrosanct principle of *laïcité*, to the extent that we are totally forbidden from speaking about faith or even issues directly concerning Christians'.[49] Xavier Breton, another centre-right politician and member of the LR, observed that 'a very aggressive militant, restrictive and aggressive *laïcité* is on the attack',[50] and the prominent Catholic blogger and author Erwan Le Morhedec described how 'an extensive understanding of *laïcité* in France increasingly meant that when I started to publicly express myself as a Christian, people would tell me "you have no right to speak in this way"'.[51] Jean-Pierre Delannoy from the Catholic chaplaincy to the French *Assemblée Nationale* even testified an increase in anti-Catholic incidents in parliament, reporting 'several instances of parliamentarians going so far as to ban the use of religious vocabulary in the everyday language in the name of republican *laïcité*', or the Archbishop of Paris being 'attacked by a radical left-wing parliamentarian who flatly insulted him'.[52]

Such experiences were not limited to Catholics in public life. Protestant leaders, who had historically been strong proponents of *laïcité*, voiced similar concerns. Reformed leader Emmanuelle Seybold worried that 'there has

---

[46]   Interview Billan 2019.
[47]   Interview Seyboldt 2019.
[48]   Interview Lebrun 2019.
[49]   Interview Poisson 2019.
[50]   Interview Breton 2019.
[51]   Interview Le Morhedec 2019.
[52]   Interview Delannoy 2019.

really been tension in the last ten to fifteen years. There is a real drift towards a secularist society, but in fact a secularist society can become totalitarian.'[53] Even socialist politicians recognised with concern the return of religion versus *laïcité* as a political wedge-issue, with former Socialist Education minister Najat Vallaud-Belkacem emphasising that while she was in office the issue of *laïcité* had been more and more 'instrumentalised and exploited by politicians, the media and polemicists who tried to turn it into an electoral asset'.[54] Former socialist minister and now president of the *Observatoire de la Laïcité*, Jean-Louis Bianco summarised this re-politicisation of religion and *laïcité* as follows: 'today there is once again extreme tension around the law of 1905 … [W]e are facing an almost religious taboo about *laïcité* [and there exists] the idea that it is not enough to have the secular legal framework. Their argument is: "Stop considering it legally, make it political."'[55]

A look at recent surveys confirms these assessments of elite actors and shows that *laïcité* and religion have made a powerful comeback as political wedge-issues in the 2010s. For instance, in the 2017 elections 60 per cent of voters said that *laïcité* was an important determinator of their vote and a major survey in 2019 found that three-quarters of people (74 per cent) estimated that *laïcité* was in danger.[56] The same survey showed that the proportion of those demanding to 'reduce the influence of religion in our society' had more than doubled from 9 per cent in 2005 to 20 per cent in 2019. Large majorities now supported the ban on religious ceremonies and processions in public (86 per cent), an extension of the ban on religious symbols to users of all public services (including public transport) (76 per cent) and a ban on religious symbols at universities (76 per cent), each of which were permitted by the law of 1905.[57] These changes in public sentiment were mirrored by a number of legal changes such as the ban on religious symbols and forms of dress in schools and on nativity scenes in city halls. In the political sphere the change manifested itself through the formation of anti-religious movements such as the left-wing *printemps républicain* (Republican Spring)[58] or the far-right *riposte laïque* (Secular Response)[59] and a heightening sensitivity around politicians' public (and private) attitudes towards religion.

[53] Interview Seyboldt 2019.
[54] Interview Vallaud-Belkacem 2019.
[55] Interview Bianco 2019.
[56] Fondation Jean-Jaurès 2019; IPSOS 2017.
[57] Fondation Jean-Jaurès 2019; Observatoire de la Laïcité 2019.
[58] Bui and Le Bailly 2018.
[59] Nilsson 2015.

In sum, the incidents around Emmanuel Macron, Nathalie Loiseau, François-Xavier Bellamy or François Fillon described at the outset of this chapter are only the tip of the iceberg of renewed tensions surrounding religion and *laïcité*. What had caused religion's re-politicisation? Was this the infamous *revanche de Dieu*, the return of the war of two Frances and the reopening of the old social cleavage, or were new forces at play? The next chapter will show that while the battlefields of religion and *laïcité* were the same, the frontlines, opposing parties and *casi belli* had changed. Rather than being dominated by the old divide between Catholics and *laïcards*, the conflict was now driven by a new cleavage between globalists and communitarians, in the context of which religion and *laïcité* had become elements of right-wing identity politics.

CHAPTER 9

France's New Identity Cleavage
and the Rise of the Far Right

On 23 April 2017 France's traditional party system collapsed. In the first round of the presidential election the *Parti Socialiste* (PS) and the Union pour un *Mouvement Populaire* (UMP), the mainstream centre-left and centre-right parties that had dominated French politics since the end of the Third Republic and that had still assembled 56 per cent of voters in the first round of the 2012 presidential election, were humiliatingly defeated. Neither of their candidates qualified for the second round of the election, their combined voting share was halved to 27.7 per cent, and the sitting president's party, the PS, was decimated to 6.4 per cent. In their stead, a new electoral bipolarity emerged with two political outsiders entering the run-off for the presidency. On the one side was the politically unaffiliated former minister of the economy, Emmanuel Macron, supported by his newly founded progressive-liberal *La République En Marche* (LREM). On the other side was Marine Le Pen, the leader of the right-wing populist RN. Five years later, in the run-up to the 2022 presidential elections, the only serious challenge to this new bipolarity seemed to emerge from the rise of other populist outsiders: the left-wing populist Jean-Luc Mélenchon and the far-right firebrand Éric Zemmour. By contrast, the historically dominant centre-right LR and centre-left PS were reduced to marginal actors, with their candidates scoring 4.8 per cent and 1.7 per cent, respectively, in 2022, while their parties were ridden with continued internal turmoil and crisis.

Since the electoral shock of 2017 much ink has been spilled to analyse this political upheaval. Some observers have sought to understand the election result as an exceptional short-term reaction to current political crises. Others saw it as a reconfiguration of the political supply side, with the PS and the UMP being supplanted by the LREM and the RN, but with the latter pair still catering to the same traditional cleavages.[1] Yet, as the new

---

[1] Clift and McDaniel 2017; Duyck and Quéméner 2017; Lees 2017; Prissette 2017; P.-A. Taguieff 2017; Wormser 2017.

bipolarity persisted in all major elections since, more observers have begun to suspect that behind the transformation of the political partly landscape were deeper socio-demographic causes in the electorate.[2] Indeed, both the populist right and the LREM have claimed to transcend France's traditional left–right divide and to respond to a new social antagonism. Macron's advisers called this the new divide between 'progressives and nationalists'.[3] Marine Le Pen referred to it as the opposition between 'globalists and patriots', while her far-right competitor Éric Zemmour has spoken of a 'new profound, philosophical and identitarian cleavage between populists and progressives'.[4] Whatever the nomenclature, each of these readings suggest that the future of France is no longer to be fought between left and right, workers and capitalists, Catholics and *laïcards*, but between those embracing liberal cosmopolitan values and individualist forms of identity against those favouring nationalist communitarian values and traditional group identities. The following section discusses the social roots of this new cleavage and how it has contributed to the re-politicisation of religion and *laïcité* in French political discourse.

9.1   Roots of Revolution: The Collapse of the Catholic Matrix and the Rise of a New Identity Cleavage

Although the return of tensions surrounding religion and *laïcité* observed in the previous chapter might at first glance appear to be a revival of the old divide between *la Republique laïque* and *la France Catholique*, closer analysis suggests that it is the very decline of Catholicism that has importantly contributed to the reshaping of French politics by undermining traditional sources of identity and thus paving the way for the new identity cleavage. Since 1945 France has been one of the most rapidly de-Christianising countries in the world.[5] Its share of Catholics, which in 1945 was still 98 per cent, dropped to 80 per cent in the 1980 and to 48 per cent in 2019.[6] The rate of children's baptisms fell from 92 per cent in 1961 to 30 per cent in 2012,[7] while the proportion of Catholics stating they go to Mass 'as often

---

[2] The LREM won 61 per cent of the seats in the Assemblée Nationale in 2017, whilst the RN topped the poll of the 2019 European elections. Both were parties' candidates competing for supremacy in the local elections in 2020, and the presidential elections of 2022.

[3] Emelien and Amiel 2019.

[4] Galiero 2017; Sapin 2022.

[5] Du Cleuziou 2018; Fourquet 2019; Portier 2016; Portier and Willaime 2012; Todd 2008.

[6] IFOP 2010; Observatoire de la Laïcité 2019; Pew 2016a.

[7] Fourquet 2019, 25.

as possible' or 'every Sunday' dropped from 38 per cent in 1961 to 7 per cent in 2012 (less than 2 per cent of the overall population).[8] The physical presence of the Catholic Church in society almost halved from over 20,000 priests in 1990 to fewer than 10,000 in 2012, with a large number of the clergy approaching retirement age.[9] As a result, whilst Portier and Willaime emphasise that 'until the years following the Second World War France presented all the apparent traits of a Catholic nation',[10] by 2019 Fourquet concluded that 'we are today almost at the end of the [secularisation] process; and France, which once was said to be the *"fille aînée de l'eglise"*, has mostly become de-Christianised'.[11]

This colossal secularisation has had enormous consequences not only for French Catholic identity and the institutional church, who have come to terms with their new minority status, but also for the structure and cohesion of society and politics writ large.[12] Prominent historian and sociologist Emmanuel Todd, for instance, argued that after almost two centuries in which predominant group identities have been defined in relation to the divide between *la France Catholique* and *La République laïque*, the disappearance of the Catholic Church as a landmark has destroyed France's key organising ideological principle.[13] Combined with the global trends of globalisation, de-industrialisation, individualisation and immigration, Fourquet similarly identified the 'dislocation of the Catholic matrix of French society' as 'the primary cause for the process of the increasing "archipelagoisation" [fragmentation] of society'.[14]

In our interviews religious and political elites overwhelmingly shared this analysis. The Bishop of Nanterre Matthieu Rougé reported, for example, that 'many people today feel like strangers in their own country, not because they are of foreign origin, but because the loss of Christian culture means that they do not know where they are from and who they are'.[15] His colleague, Bishop Stenger, emphasised that in France 'the problem is that for many this [Christian identity] does not mean anything anymore and suddenly they find themselves in a quest for identity'.[16] Erwan Le

---

[8]   Fourquet 2019, 25.
[9]   Fourquet 2019, 27.
[10] Portier and Willaime 2012, 195.
[11] Fourquet 2019, 21.
[12] Du Cleuziou 2018; Dreher 2017; Duchesne 2016.
[13] Todd 2008.
[14] Fourquet 2019, 10; Le Bras and Todd 2013.
[15] Interview Rougé 2019.
[16] Interview Stenger 2019.

Morhedec echoed this analysis, stating that 'there is clearly a strong desire to ask, "Who are we?" – and since we're not really Catholic anymore we do not know how to answer it'.[17] Other interviewees stressed that this crisis of identity extended beyond the Catholic orbit. The author and public intellectual Thibault Collin, for example, emphasised that 'the *combat républicain* [of the Left] took its purpose from its opposition to Catholicism, … but the collapse of the Catholic enemy meant that today there is also no republican myth anymore'.[18] Jean-Louis Bianco explained that the result was 'a massive search for and closure of identity that affects people from all political traditions'.[19]

However, whilst the loss of the Catholic matrix and associated group identities has cut across all traditional cleavages, it has not impacted all parts of society equally. Rather it has helped create a new division between those who have embraced and profited from the disappearance of collective ties and those who have remained attached to them and view their erosion as a cultural threat. Indeed, observers found an increasing ideological and psychological empowerment of the elite whereby the most privileged, mobile and educated parts of the population have emancipated themselves more and more from traditional group identities.[20] For example, Fourquet argues that what he calls the *nomades* have embraced a mixture of universalist cosmopolitanism and individualist forms of identity leading 'over the last thirty years to a progressive decline in their sense of belonging to the national community'.[21]

This trend is in marked contrast to developments in other parts of society, where in 2019 a majority (61 per cent) perceived globalisation as a threat and lamented the disappearance of France's national identity (59 per cent).[22] Rather than embracing the globalism of the elite, these *sédentitaires* – to stick with Fourquet's vocabulary – often reacted to the erosion of traditional identities with a renewed attachment to the national community or a desire to protect France's national culture and borders.[23] This split not only seems to align with Macron's and Le Pen's claims about a new divide between

---

[17] Interview Le Morhedec 2019.
[18] Interview Collin 2019.
[19] Interview Bianco 2019.
[20] Fourquet 2019, 93; Fourquet 2018b; Algan, Beasley, Cohen and Foucault 2019; Perrineau 2017; De Wilde et al. 2019.
[21] Fourquet 2019, 108; Todd 2008.
[22] More in Common 2017.
[23] Four out of ten, for instance, demanded the closing of national borders (More in Common 2018; Fourquet 2018b; Illouz 2017).

'progressives and nationalists' or 'globalists and patriots', but is also borne out by the data gathered by Thomas Piketty, who in turn speaks of a new distinction between 'nativists' and 'globalists'.[24] Crucially, we also recognise the traits of the identity cleavage that scholars have identified in Germany and other Western countries between 'cosmopolitans' and 'communitarians',[25] 'anywheres' and 'somewheres'[26] or 'integrationists' and 'demarcationists'.[27]

As in Germany, the main political wedge-issue through which this identity cleavage manifests itself in France is immigration and the place of Islam in society (further politicised in recent years through several Islamist terrorist attacks in France). For example, a 2017 IFOP study revealed that 85 per cent of the French think that the rhythm of immigration has accelerated in recent years (even though it remained unchanged in the years prior to the survey), and 56 per cent had 'negative' or 'very negative' attitudes towards this.[28] The longitudinal analysis of the Eurobarometer confirms such findings, showing a steady increase in the concern over immigration, with those considering it one of the two top priorities that France is facing, rising from about 6 per cent in the late 2000s to around 15 per cent in the late 2010s.[29] Moreover, concerns over immigration are subject to high degrees of polarisation between the two camps of the identity cleavage. For instance, during the first round of the 2017 presidential elections, the fight against immigration was the top priority among Le Pen voters, with 92 per cent of them saying 'it played a determinant role in their vote'. By contrast, only 18 per cent of Macron voters said the same.[30] This 74 per cent gap was the greatest level of disagreement between the two camps during the election, underlining immigration's role as the key wedge-issue shaping the new identity cleavage. The run up to the 2022 presidential election saw a similar polarisation with 61 per cent of RN supporters and 76 per cent of Zemmour's supporters stating that immigration is their principal preoccupation, compared to just 16 per cent of Macron's supporters.[31]

---

[24] Piketty 2020.
[25] De Wilde et al. 2019.
[26] Goodhart 2017.
[27] Bornschier 2010; Kriesi 2008.
[28] IFOP 2017b.
[29] There was an even greater explosion in concern about Islamic terrorism, rising from 1–2 per cent in the 2000s to 36 per cent in 2018. Whilst the spike is partly due to the successive Islamic terrorist attacks in France since 2015, it is also a manifestation of deeper concerns about the role of Islam and the re-politicisation of religion in society. Indeed, studies show a concomitant expansion of anti-Islamic sentiment (38 per cent of French perceive Islam as incompatible with French society). Fondation Jean-Jaurès 2019; Perrineau 2017; Eurobarometer 2018.
[30] Fourquet 2018b, 139.
[31] Teinturier, Doridot and Vacas 2021.

9.2   (A Lack of) Supply-Side Responses: The Vacuum of Representation amongst French Communitarians

This new divide has not gone unnoticed among elite actors on the political and religious supply side. Catholic lay leader Dominique Quinio, for instance, drew a distinction between 'parts of the metropolitan population [who] are very comfortable, because they studied in France, in Germany and in England, so globalisation does not scare them' as opposed to 'the people who are not comfortable with globalisation and who feel that Europe does not protect them and that elites do not care about them'.[32] The Archbishop of Poitiers Dominique Wintzer highlighted 'the fear of a part of the population in response to the demographic evolution' of immigration, noting that, 'faced with this identitarian or cultural anxiety, there is a tendency to cling to what is considered the identity of France'.[33] Meanwhile, the editor-in-chief of the right-wing newspaper *l'Incorrecte*, Jacques de Guillebon, pointed out that people thought 'that one could live only through materialism, but that is not enough for an existence so one seeks for natural roots. We want to fit into a story and a civilisation.'[34] *Sens Commun* leader Christophe Billan summarised this sentiment saying, 'people are afraid for their children and for their cultural identity because they believe that the globalism they are offered is harmful to them'.[35]

However, it was RN representatives, and especially many of those who would later defect to the campaign of Éric Zemmour, who expressed the grievances and attachment to traditional identity markers of the new divide's 'sedentary' side most emphatically. Gilbert Collard, RN MEP, who was a member of the RN's national committee until he defected to Éric Zemmour's campaign in January 2022, criticised the globalist liberalism of the *nomades* as 'a sort of hatred against one's own identity' and emphasised that 'we have a new cleavage today: on one side you have … men and women for whom there is no history and for whom postmodernity is a time that goes beyond history … And on the other side you have modest people who have in them untouchable historical sanctuaries.'[36] Marion Maréchal-Le Pen, who caused some family drama in the spring of 2022 by declaring her support Éric Zemmour's rather than for her aunt Marine, and who was mentioned by Zemmour as a potential

[32] Interview Quinio 2019.
[33] Interview Wintzer 2019.
[34] Interview de Guillebon 2019.
[35] Interview Billan 2019.
[36] Interview Collard 2019.

prime minister for his government should he have won,[37] analysed the consequences of these developments in strikingly similar terms to the academic literature, claiming that 'the cleavages are clearly being redefined … but what is certain today is that there are … two blocs, or even three archipelagos, which confront one another: the archipelago of communitarised immigrants, the archipelago of big city globalists and the archipelago of "yellow vests"'.[38] Particularly, Maréchal-Le Pen continued, the 'part of French society who live in the big cities – the "anywheres", the winners of globalisation – are barely confronted with the difficulties of rural and peripheral France, because France today lives in archipelagos; they no longer see each other, they no longer frequent each other, in reality they no longer live in the same country'.[39]

The fact that RN politicians and Zemmour supporters appeared more attuned to the new identity cleavage and *sédentitaires'* identitarian concerns than other politicians interviewed is indicative of the traditional party system's difficulties in representing the new demand-side divide on the political supply side. Mainstream parties' unresponsiveness might appear surprising, given that French political scientists and sociologists have emphasised that the cleavage is not new to France, but had manifested itself for over thirty years, for example during the referendum about the Maastricht treaty in 1992 or over the European constitution in 2005.[40] Similarly, tensions regarding the place of Islam in society and the role of *laïcité* in addressing it already rose to prominence in the 1990s surrounding the banning of Islamic headscarves in schools.[41]

Still, prior to 2017, France's mainstream parties seemed to barely react to the demands of the *sédentitaires* for years and even decades, converging instead on the cosmopolitan and pro-globalisation position, thereby creating space for the RN to steadily grow. On the left, Bornschier argues that the socialist party's decision in the 1980s to 'regularise illicit immigrants' and to promote 'anti-racism as a central issue, defending a multiculturalist recognition of differences … contributed to the rising salience of the cultural rather than economic dimension of conflict', and thus to the RN's emergence as a key defender of the

---

[37] Le Point 2022.
[38] Interview Maréchal-Le Pen 2019. This refers to the protest movement against social injustice that paralysed parts of France for several months in 2018 and 2019 and was known by the characteristic yellow vests worn by the demonstrators (Algan, Beasley, Cohen, Foucault et al. 2019; Grunberg 2019;).
[39] Interview Maréchal-Le Pen 2019.
[40] Fourquet 2018b; Perrineau 2014; Perrineau 2017.
[41] Banon 2016; P. Taguieff 2017.

communitarian stance.[42] Pascal Perrineau added that 'the left has abandoned its great historical references – solidarity, the central role of the state and equality – and has instead embraced the charms of individualisation, privatisation and equity'.[43] In line with the empirical data gathered by scholars like Piketty, Perrineau argues that the French left's shift from communitarian to individualist and cosmopolitan policy positions was accompanied by its 'social and cultural gentrification [*embourgeoisement*]', which produced 'a profound cultural rupture with the social presentations and expectations of the working class'.[44]

During interview, socialist MP Dominique Potier confirmed this rupture with regret, admitting that 'the left has often lost its balance in its quest for autonomy and emancipation at the expense of the question of community. One of the most profound dramas of our civilisation today is perhaps the great solitude generated by this focus on individualism and materialism.'[45] Yet, other left-wing actors such as the progressive Terra Nova think tank argued that this dissociation from the communitarian camp should be embraced, claiming that 'the working class is no longer at the heart of the left vote, it is no longer aligned with all of its values'.[46] Instead, the left was to represent a new coalition of university graduates, the young, minorities, women and non-Catholics (in other words the *cosmopolitains*) as champions of 'cultural liberalism'.

The left was, however, not alone in its focus on the cosmopolitan side of the new cleavage. On the centre-right, France's Gaullist movement equally failed to provide a new home for disappointed communitarians for many years. Thus, scholars observe that from the 1980s onwards the centre-right gradually gave up on communitarian positions such as traditional values and patriotism, played down the immigration issue, failed to oppose cultural liberalism and in the 2000s 'converged with the left on a libertarian-universalistic position'.[47] During our interviews centre-right politicians like Xavier Breton and Christophe Billan emphasised this historical dominance of 'the libertarians' (Breton) around Jacques Chirac and Alain Juppé, which, according to Billan, resulted in a situation where 'the classical right stopped investing in its doctrine, its principles and its

---

[42] Bornschier 2012, 135.
[43] Perrineau 2017, 128.
[44] Perrineau 2014, 190; Piketty 2020.
[45] Interview Potier 2019.
[46] Terra Nova 2011.
[47] Bornschier 2012, 136; Brustier and Escalona 2015; Richard 2017.

identity. An electoral vacuum emerged as the centre-right limited itself to economic liberalism, and economic liberalism only' (Billan).[48] As a result, when in the 2010s and 2020s centre-right politicians like Nicolas Sarkozy, François Fillon or Valérie Pécresse sought to reclaim the communitarian stances, such attempts largely failed due to the fact that communitarian issues had already been occupied by the populist right.[49]

9.3   The Rise of the Populist Right and the Return of *Laïcité* and Religion

For decades the FN (RN since 2018) was the undisputed champion of right-wing populist politics in France. Founded in 1972 by Jean-Marie Le Pen it succeeded over the years in tapping into the electoral vacuum around communitarians with its own brand of right-wing identity politics. It thereby not only became one of the most successful right-wing populist parties in the Western world, but also prepared the conditions for the collapse of France's traditional party system in 2017.[50] However, although the convergence of the mainstream parties on the cosmopolitan end of the new cleavage created the necessary opportunity structure for the RN's rise, it was not a forgone conclusion that the RN could seize it. Indeed, in its early stages the FN was an unlikely candidate to fill the communitarian void. Founded in direct response to decolonisation and the Algeria War, it began as a neo-fascist fringe movement, which consisted of *Pieds Noirs* (former colonists returning from Algeria), die-hard monarchists, former Vichy supporters and Nazi-collaborators, and had extremely limited support within the electorate.[51] As Perrineau observed, the early FN lived in 'anonymity' and 'for ten years … remained a marginal force regularly shaken by internal quarrels and splits that often mark the life of such fringe groups'.[52]

---

[48] Interview Breton 2019; interview Billan 2019.
[49] Understanding why exactly France's mainstream parties failed to react to the lack of representation of communitarians and allowed this political supply-side vacuum to grow over the decades goes beyond the scope of this study. However, some observers point to the role of the French majoritarian electoral system, as an explanatory variable. See Mayer, Crépon and Dézé 2015; Ehrhard 2016. As the German ambassador to France Mayer-Landrut put it in our interview, the two-round system allowed France's mainstream political parties to 'ignore this problem [of communitarian discontent] over many years based on the motto that "if you only have 20 per cent of the vote it's not a problem"'; interview Meyer-Landrut 2019. This allowed the FN to score consistently high results with over 10–15 per cent in the 1980s and 1990s and results close to 20 per cent in the 2000.
[50] Betz 2018b; Mayer, Crépon and Dézé 2015; Mudde 2010.
[51] Camus 2015; Comtat 2009; Lebourg 2015; Mayer and Perrineau 1996; Roy 2016.
[52] It scored only 0.7 per cent in the 1974 presidential election, 0.3 per cent in the European elections of 1979 and 0.1 per cent in the parliamentary elections in 1981. Perrineau 2014, 18.

Crucially, in these early years the FN made little to no reference to religion or *laïcité*. That is not to say that ultra-conservative Catholics have not played their role in the party. For instance, there has always been a group of Neo-Maurrassian Monarchists, who, in the tradition of the *Action Française*, favoured a pre-Vatican II vision of Catholicism as an ordering principle for society and who rallied around (the later excommunicated) Bishop Lefevbre.[53] To please this strand of opinion, Jean-Marie Le Pen tolerated Catholic traditionalists such as Bernard Antony in leadership positions, and permitted the celebration of a Latin tridentine mass (which had been banned by Rome since Vatican II) at the margins of the annual meetings of the FN. Yet, these movements always remained marginal and as Olivier Roy emphasised, 'the FN never aligned itself with the religious right and always played down religion in policy terms'.[54]

This can partly be explained by the fact that the 'Catholic' wing was outsized by a strong neo-pagan current within the FN in these years.[55] Yet, perhaps even more important was the fact that religion played no role in the early FN's construction of 'the other'. Thus, Roy emphasised that 'opposition to immigration was at this point expressed in "culturalist" and ethnic terms and not yet in religious ones ("immigrants" and "Arabs" not "Muslims")'.[56] Pascal Perrineau similarly observed that 'when the FN was founded in the 1970s there was no reference to Islam whatsoever'.[57] In his early career Jean-Marie Le Pen even praised Islam, proclaiming 'that there is nothing in the Muslim religion that would morally inhibit a believer or practising Muslim from becoming a perfect French citizen. On the contrary its precepts are essentially the same as those of the Christian religion that are the fundament of Western civilisation.'[58] As a result, initially there appeared little risk of a re-politicisation of religion and *laïcité* emanating from the FN.

However, this radically changed as the FN began to transform under the influence of the new identity cleavage. As the issues of immigration, globalisation and national identity rose to greater prominence throughout the 1980s and early 1990s, the FN began to morph from a neo-fascist fringe movement into one of France's most prominent parties and an early champion of modern-day right-wing identity politics. The first steps

---

[53] Camus 1992; Levillain 2010; Roy 2016, 81.
[54] Roy 2016, 85.
[55] François 2007; François 2008; Camus 2015; Roy 2016.
[56] Roy 2016, 83; Rydgren 2008.
[57] Perrineau 2014, 96.
[58] Le Pen 1958, 310.

towards this transformation were made under the influence of the *nou-velle droite.* This school of thought, which loosely connected a number of intellectual movements such as the GRECE, the *Club d'Horloge* or the *Nouvelle Droite Française,* had conducted the philosophical groundwork for the new right-wing identity politics by developing the concept of eth-nopluralism (see Chapter 3).[59] As Roy emphasises, 'these new thinkers replaced references to "race" with the concept of "culture" and "ethnic-ity" as developed by anthropologists and social scientists … In short they replaced racism with culturalism.'[60]

The FN embraced this intellectual current as one of the first far-right parties in Europe, effectively pioneering these movements' 'identitarian turn' in the 1990s.[61] The electoral pay-off was almost immediate with the FN's breakthrough in the 1984 European elections, when Jean-Marie Le Pen's party scored almost 10 per cent, followed by consistently strong results of up to 15 to 20 per cent in most subsequent elections up to Jean-Marie Le Pen's qualification for the second round of the presidential elec-tions in 2002. That this success was largely due to the new support of the FN by communitarians has been shown by scholars such as Nonna Mayer and Pascal Perrineau, who emphasise that the FN's electorate was fundamentally restructured in these years, with its traditional cohorts of *Pieds Noirs,* Ultra-royalists and former Vichy supporters increasingly being outnumbered by new swathes of former left-wing working-class and lower middle-class voters (in particular elderly males), who after the col-lapse of the Communist Party felt abandoned by the individualist and multi-culturalist left.[62]

Despite this success, the FN's transformation into a modern national populist movement that could appeal to all sectors of society remained incomplete until the change of leadership from Jean-Marie Le Pen to his daughter Marine in 2011. Prior to this, Jean-Marie and his paladins still sporadically fell back into old habits, uttering racial or antisemitic slurs, downplaying the Holocaust as a 'historical detail', or openly maintaining connections to Neo-Nazi groups.[63] All this continued to limit the party's appeal to younger, female and formerly left-wing voters. Marine Le Pen recognised this and, once in office, drove a notably different public course from her father. In her strategy of *dédiabolisation* she cleansed the FN

---

[59] Camus 2015; Rydgren 2008; Spektorowski 2000.
[60] Roy 2016, 83.
[61] Betz 2004; Rydgren 2008.
[62] Mayer 2013; Mayer 2015a; Mayer 2017; Mayer and Perrineau 1996.
[63] DeClair 1999; Fourquet 2015; Lebourg 2015; Winock 2015.

national bureau of her father's old grandees and promoted a new generation of politicians around Florian Philippot, Louis Alliot, Sebastien Chénu, Jordan Bardella and Nicolas Bay, who had no personal connection to the party's roots in Vichy France or the *Pieds Noirs*' Algeria, but distinguished themselves through an air of respectability and their loyalty to Marine.[64] On a policy level, Marine Le Pen also broke with her father's economic liberalism and embraced economically 'left-wing' positions favouring protectionism, a strong welfare state and state interventionism.[65] In terms of rhetoric, the FN now sought to explicitly pick up on the new identity cleavage by condemning the 'globalist totalitarianism' of the 'nomad-elite' as an 'ideology whose objective is to destroy all natural structures that reassure the people: the family, the nation, borders, and the belonging to a history'.[66]

Although Dézé argues that this was a *dédiabolisation* in style only and that the FN had not actually 'modified its doctrinal software in a substantial manner', election results showed that the strategy was highly effective in attracting new segments of the population.[67] Whereas Jean-Marie Le Pen's electorate in the 2002 presidential election still consisted primarily of elderly, lower middle-class males, in the 2012 elections his daughter had made significant inroads amongst working-class voters where the FN was now by far the most popular party (31 per cent) amongst women (+2 percentage points), the 18–24-year-olds (+5 percentage points), the 25–34-year-olds (+8 percentage points) and the irreligious (+5 per cent).[68] The culmination of this process came with the 2017 and 2022 presidential elections, which left no doubt about the RN's ability to appeal to a large part of the population and of its advancement to being the main representative of the identity cleavage's communitarian end.

The RN's transformation was also accompanied by a marked change in its relationship to religion. Completing the 'identitarian' turn, it shifted from an ethnic to a culturalist and civilisational discourse in its definition of the 'external other'. Perrineau hence emphasised that 'as the ethnic reading of immigration became unfashionable the [FN/RN's] focus shifted to the rise of radical Islam'.[69] During the interviews Jean-Louis Bianco, the president of the *laïcité* Observatory, confirmed this development, reporting

---

[64] Balent 2013; Dézé 2015a; Dézé 2015b; Mayer 2015b; Mestre and Monnot 2015.
[65] Gougou 2015; Ivaldi 2015; Perrineau 2017.
[66] Le Pen 2012.
[67] Dézé 2015b, 46.
[68] Mayer 2017; Perrineau 2017.
[69] Perrineau 2014, 65; Betz and Meret 2009; Brubaker 2017.

a marked evolution of the FN's rhetoric, … between the traditional discourse that was against immigrants, and the contemporary discourse, which is in the name of secularism against Islam. There is a semantic change, a vocabulary change, but from a political and philosophical point of view it is always the other: the foreigner.[70]

Indeed, during our interviews, RN leaders made no mention of 'Arabs', 'Meghrebiens' or 'Africans' but emphasised the cultural threat of Islam as they saw it. RN general secretary and later Zemmour supporter Nicolas Bay, for instance, argued that 'the rise of communitarianism and of politico-religious demands coming from Muslims, who base themselves on an integralist version of Islam … touches the basis of our customs, our habits of life, our traditions, of what we are – that is to say, our identity'.[71] His RN colleague Wallerand de Saint-Just stressed that 'the weight and the importance of Islam in France today is a political and sociological fact that policymakers must absolutely take measures against to ensure that it does not become too important'.[72] And Marion Maréchal-Le Pen stated that the question of Islam 'is omnipresent and poses great difficulties because of its demands'.[73] These testimonies confirm the RN's shift from nationalism to 'civilisationism', which as Brubaker observes, 'has been driven by the notion of a civilisational threat from Islam'.[74] Éric Zemmour's campaign, while based on economic and cultural issues more closely aligned with the old FN of Jean-Marie Le Pen than with that of his daughter, seems to have followed or even exceeded the latter's discourse of civilisationist and anti-Islamic othering.[75] For instance, *Reconquête*, the name of Zemmour's newly founded party, was a direct reference to the Spanish 'Reconquista', which sought to purge Muslims from the Iberian peninsula in the middle ages.[76] 'Islam' (or rather Islamophobia) featured as its own 'primary pillar' in Zemmour's election programme, and dystopias about the Islamisation of France have been a focal point in Zemmour's rhetoric, both as a presidential candidate and in his earlier career as a journalist.[77] This focus on Islam is mirrored in attitudes of his supporters. Thus, with 83 per cent of them claiming that they see Islam as 'a threat to the Republic',

[70] Interview Bianco 2019.
[71] Interview Bay 2019.
[72] Interview de Saint-Just 2019.
[73] Interview de Saint-Just 2019.
[74] Brubaker 2017, 1191.
[75] Finchelstein et al. 2021.
[76] Forcari 2021.
[77] Raynaud 2021; Zemmour 2021.

Zemmour's supporters showed themselves to be even more hostile towards Islam than RN voters (73 per cent).[78] It was therefore perhaps no coincidence that both Nicolas Bay and Marion Maréchal Le Pen, who were particularly outspoken in their criticism of Islam during our interviews, were also among those RN figures who first defected from Marine Le Pen to Zemmour in 2022.

Overall, the RN's transformation from a neo-fascist fringe party into a modern right-wing populist party in response to the new identity cleavage has paved the way for a new brand of radical right-wing identity politics in which religion in general and Islam in particular have become the focal point of political contestation. Éric Zemmour's rise in 2021/2022 based on a staunchly Islam-critical platform has further accentuated this development. But what does this re-politicisation of religious identity in these movements' discourse of othering mean for their attitude towards *laïcité* and Christianity? The next chapter will analyse the French populist right's relationship with Christianity through the lens of the cultural ethical triangle, focusing on the policies and political personnel and their relationship with the institutional churches.

---

[78] Finchelstein et al. 2021.

CHAPTER 10

La Fille Ainée de l'Église? *Christianism and Secularism in the French Populist Right*

To conduct the elite interviews for this case study, I spent several months living in a small room in the centre of Paris a few hundred meters away from the *Ile de la Cité*. In the early evening on Monday 15 April 2019, I came home from a run to discover an enormous cloud of smoke dominating the sky: at 6 p.m. that evening the Cathedral of Notre Dame de Paris, the 'heart of Catholic France', had burst into flames.[1] The fire sent shock waves around France and the globe: campaigns for the European elections were suspended, billions of euros donated within hours, and from my window I witnessed thousands of Parisians gathering at the banks of the Seine, falling on their knees and singing Christian hymns.[2] In this time of national sorrow and religious emotion, most politicians limited themselves to messages of grief and empathy. Yet, a number of commentators and politicians did not hesitate to seize this opportunity to pose as defenders of Catholic France against the dangers of Islam. For example, Jean Messiha, a member of the RN's national bureau encouraged rumours about a potential Islamic terrorist attack noting obscure 'sources', which 'spoke of the *true* origins of the fire'.[3] His party colleague, Julien Leonardelli, appealed to the fears of French Christians, tweeting, 'Hallucinating! We really have a serious problem in France when we see the number of bastards who are happy to see the cathedral of #Notre Dame de Paris burst into flames. By denying the acts of Christianophobia in France, the political class trivialises them!'[4] Meanwhile Éric Zemmour, then still a journalist rather than a presidential candidate, claimed in his *Le Figaro* column that 'on social networks, Muslims exulted without shame [about the fire], calling for the vengeance of Allah on those infidels'. He continued by portraying the fire as part a broader threat to French Catholics, claiming that

---

[1] Rougé 2019.
[2] Vaillant 2019.
[3] Messiha 2019; Sénécat 2019.
[4] Leonardelli 2019.

The fire of Notre-Dame was not a first, but merely the apotheosis of a succession of sackings of churches that have taken place for months and which have scandalized no one. A Pakistani was arrested and sentenced for destroying sacred objects in Saint-Denis Cathedral; the police have been following a criminal trail after the fire in Saint-Sulpice church; courts have passed judgment on a jihadist, Inès Madani, who had tried to set fire to a car filled with explosives in front of Notre-Dame Cathedral in Paris. This was in 2016. Already.[5]

Such declarations about the need to protect Christianity against the perceived threat of Islam are no outliers but indicative of an ongoing trend in French far-right rhetoric. Just as religion had become central to its definition of the (Islamic) 'other', far-right politicians also intensified their references to France's Catholic identity and culture when defining the 'us'. In addition to holding its marches and celebrations of Joan of Arc, RN representatives began to demonstrate their Christian credentials by displaying large nativity scenes in city halls, condemning the mounting vandalisation of churches and raising the issue of Christian persecution internationally.[6] Marion Maréchal-Le Pen, who had been schooled in the elite conservative Catholic school Saint-Pie X before becoming the youngest MP for the RN, had long been the figurehead of this trend, publicly displaying her Catholic credentials through the attendance of pilgrimages, participation in the anti-gay marriage demonstrations with *Manif pour tous*, and repeated references to France's status as *la fille aînée de l'Église*.[7] During the 2022 presidential campaign Éric Zemmour employed a similar strategy, proclaiming that while he was Jewish himself, he was 'steeped in Catholicism' and that he wanted to 'reclaim France's Catholic Civilisation'.[8]

This surge in references to Christianity is noteworthy, not only because it has re-politicised religion at a moment when France appears more secular than ever, but also because it coincided with the broader trend among Western right-wing populist parties to make the defence of Christendom a centrepiece of their rhetoric.[9] Part II of this book showed that in the case of the AfD and PEGIDA, this return of religious references was mainly about deploying a secularised idea of Christendom as a cultural identity marker against Islam rather than about a reawakening of faith. Were similar dynamics at work in France? The following analysis of the French populist

[5] Zemmour 2019.
[6] Almeida 2019; Roy 2019; rtl.fr 2014; Chenu 2019; Aliot 2019; Cornevin 2019.
[7] Deharo 2016; Denis 2013; Fourquet 2018a; Gélie 2018; Hacot 2016; Krug 2016.
[8] Lindell, Jova and Tournier 2021; Lesueur 2022.
[9] Roy, McDonnell and Marzouki 2016; Haynes 2020; Brubaker 2017.

right's 'Christian credentials' through the lens of the cultural-ethical triangle addresses this question by focusing on its policies, its leadership's display of 'Christian virtues' and its institutional relationship with France's Christian churches. This chapter thereby focuses primarily on the RN, but will also make references to the more recent phenomenon of Éric Zemmour.

10.1   Policies: Identity Politics between *la France Catholique* and the Strategy of *Dédiabilisation*

The first step in applying the cultural-ethical triangle, is to examine the extent to which politicians' policies align with 'Christian values' and social doctrine, as defined by the churches. The examination of the RN's and Zemmour's manifestos, and of thirty-eight interviews with elite RN politicians (several of whom have subsequently shifted their allegiance to Zemmour), church leaders and mainstream policymakers in France, reveals marked policy clashes with Christian doctrine. What is more, both the RN's and Zemmour's approaches to Christianity appear dominated by an identitarian and largely secularised idea of Catholic France, which stands in tension to Christian teachings.

In terms of policy clashes, it is notable that despite their outward turn to Christian identity, neither Marine Le Pen's nor Éric Zemmour's manifestos make any programmatic mentions of Christianity, except for one reference to the preservation of churches as historical monuments in a 2014 RN manifesto.[10] Instead, the first electoral promise in Marine Le Pen's 2017 presidential manifesto was to organise 'a referendum about our membership in the European Union' followed by demands to 'make it impossible to naturalise illegal immigrants' and to 'reduce legal immigration to an annual balance of 10,000'.[11] Zemmour's 2022 programme similarly focused first and foremost on promising tougher punishments for crime, stopping and reversing immigration, improving the economy and reducing the visibility of Islam in French society.[12]

Such demands are representative of the populist right's priorities of Euroscepticism, anti-globalism and anti-immigrationism, but they vehemently clash with the position of the churches.[13] Stefan Lunte from the Catholic Church in the European Union (COMECE), for example, stated

---

[10] Front National 2017; Roy 2019, 8; Roy 2016, 88.
[11] Front National 2017.
[12] Zemmour 2021.
[13] Balent 2013; Mayer and Perrineau 1996.

that the RN's aims 'with regards to Europe – the end of the Euro, the reintro-
duction of borders – are completely wrong … [I]t is unacceptable that they
invoke Christian identity for themselves.'[14] With regards to immigration bishops such as Dominique Rey and Dominique Lebrun said that 'the RN itself
rejects any association with Catholicism' (Rey), and that 'the leaders of the
RN clearly set themselves up against the word of the bishops' (Lebrun).[15] RN
interviewees were candid about this clash, with Jean-Marie Le Pen explaining that 'the church is a global accomplice of global migration and in this
context the RN does not hesitate to criticise the church'.[16] His former deputy
and RN national bureau member, Bruno Gollnisch, similarly declared that
'we are hostile to mass immigration and members of the clergy can criticise
this in good faith, given that it's a breach of the duty of Christian charity, of
the universalism which is theirs, and of their moral obligation to welcome
the stranger'.[17] Éric Zemmour, whose anti-immigration stance often even
exceeds those of the RN, went so far to publicly declare that 'Pope Francis is
an enemy of Europe' because of his openness towards immigration.[18]

However, policy clashes were not limited to Europe and immigration.
Another more recent yet no less profound divergence between the church
and the far right was revealed regarding societal issues such as abortion
and gay marriage. Whereas senior clergy emphasised that 'the Catholic
Church has hardened in its positions on societal problems' (Bishop Marc
Stenger) and that the Protestant Church has seen 'a hardening of positions on ethical issues … such as abortion and homosexuality' (FPF president François Clavailory), the contrary was the case for the RN.[19] Scholars
like Crépon observe that 'whilst the FN of Jean-Marie Le Pen maintained
the image of a conservative party in terms of morals, the policy positions
of Marine Le Pen's RN point at an inflection in the matter'.[20] Indeed,
under the new president, the RN abandoned its opposition on abortion,[21]
remained largely at the sidelines of the anti-gay marriage movement[22]

---

[14] Interview Lunte 2019.
[15] Interview Rey 2019; interview Lebrun 2019. Similarly, the president of the United Protestant
Church, Emmanuelle Seybold, pointed to tensions between the RN and the Protestant church,
which had 'the same demands from the general synod for decades … to push harder for the welcoming of refugees and migrants'; interview Seyboldt 2019.
[16] Interview Le Pen 2019.
[17] Interview Gollnisch 2019.
[18] Valeurs Actuelles 2020.
[19] Interview Stenger 2019; interview Clavairoly 2019.
[20] Brubaker 2017; Crépon 2015, 185; Roy 2019.
[21] Bastié 2016; Perrineau 2014, 77.
[22] Domenach 2016; Du Cleuziou 2019; Nouvel Observateur 2016.

and showed itself open to the expansion of surrogacy.[23] In addition, the
RN increasingly posed as the defender of gay and women's rights against
Islam, with for instance RN speaker Sébastien Chenu organising the gay
pride parade in Marseille, and the RN's 2017 manifesto proclaiming to
'defend the rights of women [and] fight against Islam'.[24] In our interview former RN MP Bernard Antony even lamented that 'Marine Le Pen
has made abortion a fundamental value and an untouchable issue in the
Front National'.[25] And although some of his former colleagues sought to
emphasise that the RN still supports 'the right of all life' (Bay) or that they
personally 'know by heart the religious pains' surrounding abortion (de
Saint-Just), they also admitted that the defence of conservative values on
such topics was now off the table.[26] Wallerand de Saint-Just, a member
of the RN national committee, for instance, stated that the 'sociological
reality is that homosexuality is not viewed negatively as it once was' and
praised Marine Le Pen for her decision to not attend the *Manif pour Tous*,
adding that 'as politicians we are not moralists'.[27]

Éric Zemmour has often been said to defend more socially conservative
positions, offering an alternative to those voters who were disenchanted by
the RN's left-wing turn on social issues.[28] For instance he publicly opposed
a further liberalisation of abortion laws (though rather for demographic
than for religious reasons) and showed himself more critical of surrogacy
than Marine Le Pen.[29] Yet, Zemmour also made it publicly clear that such
social issues were of no great importance for him because 'my priority is
the fight to save France from the big replacement [through Muslim immi-
grants] and therefore I do not want to disperse myself [with such social or
moral issues]'.[30] Moreover, during the interviews, those RN representatives
who subsequently defected Zemmour showed themselves not significantly
more conservative on societal issues than others. Former RN general secretary Nicolas Bay, who prominently defected to Zemmour in February 2022,
for instance stressed that 'we talk about politics, not morality',[31] and his

---

[23] Lambrecq 2019; Sapin 2019.
[24] Front National 2017; Crépon 2015; Parrot 2017; Brubaker 2017; Roy 2019.
[25] Interview Antony 2019.
[26] Interview Bay 2019; interview de Saint-Just 2019. One top-level RN politician interviewed even
      stated that 'this topic [opposition to abortion] is now absolutely taboo' and asked for anonymity on
      this subject to avoid negative consequences from within the RN.
[27] Interview de Saint-Just 2019.
[28] Lindell, Jova and Tournier 2021.
[29] Robien 2021.
[30] Robien 2021.
[31] Interview Bay 2019.

national committee colleague Gilbert Collard, who had joined Zemmour's campaign even earlier in 2022, emphasised that 'everyone can live their sexuality as they want – this really doesn't bother me'.[32]

Given these approaches church officials were largely unanimous in their assessment that especially the RN was 'very liberal from a societal perspective and totally accepting of abortion, homosexuality and even surrogacy' (Clavailory).[33] Even the Bishop of Toulon Dominique Rey – renowned for being less critical of the RN than many of his colleagues – emphasised that the gulf between the RN and Catholic doctrine has widened in recent years, not just because of the RN's 'position regarding the question of welcoming refugees to France, but also with regards to non-negotiable issues such as the defence of unborn life and abortion, which it [the RN] no longer prioritises'.[34] Such findings confirm Roy's claim that despite its Christian rhetoric, in terms of policy, the French populist right 'rejects Christian values, either because these values are too "leftist" (i.e. charity and hospitality) or because they are too conservative (i.e. moral positions on sexuality)'.[35]

Yet perhaps the greatest tensions between the far right and the churches emerged over the former's identitarian interpretation of Christian identity itself. Asked during the interviews how they would define Christian identity, the responses from RN politicians differed significantly from those of clergy and most mainstream politicians. Church officials referenced theological beliefs or Christian social values, and some explicitly rejected any links between Catholic and French national identity. The Archbishop of Rouen Dominique Lebrun for instance noted that Christian identity meant 'to be a disciple of Christ, living the gospel to the best of one's ability in one's personal, intimate, family, social and professional life',[36] while Pascal Wintzer, the Archbishop of Poitiers, emphasised that 'the Catholic Church is the universal church; there's an old song that say "always Catholic, always French", but that is wrong'.[37] On the Protestant side, Emmanuelle Seyboldt stressed that 'for me, France's Christian identity does not exist – one receives one's identity from God, but it is something personal and under no circumstances can a society call itself Christian'.[38] Meanwhile among mainstream politicians, LR parliamentarian Xavier

[32] Interview Collard 2019.
[33] Interview Clavairoly 2019.
[34] Interview Rey 2019.
[35] Roy 2016.
[36] Interview Lebrun 2019.
[37] Interview Wintzer 2019.
[38] Interview Seyboldt 2019.

Breton stressed that 'political reflections I have on the subjects of bioethics are inspired by the enlightenment of religious values and in particular of Catholicism'.[39] On the centre-left, Françoise Dumas from Macron's LREM movement explained that for her, 'Christian values are the values of universalism, fraternity and solidarity', and socialist MP Dominique Potier declared that 'to have a Christian identity is to be a disciple of Christ and to recognise one God who is Jesus Christ'.[40]

By contrast, most RN politicians, and particularly those who subsequently defected to Éric Zemmour, defined Christian identity primarily in cultural, historical and identitarian terms. RN general secretary and later Zemmour supporter Nicolas Bay, for instance, argued that Christian identity is 'our law, our architecture, our heritage, it's a reality that makes the Christian heritage foundational to our national identity'.[41] His former RN colleague and fellow Zemmour backer Gilbert Collard stated that 'for me Christian identity is historical … It means that at the foundation of France there was a Frankish king who was baptised at the Cathedral of Reims by a bishop'.[42] To be sure far-right politicians were not entirely alone in making this link between Catholic and French national identity. However, what singled out RN officials' statements was that – mirroring the tradition of Charles Maurras and the *Action française* – they often explicitly disassociated Catholicism as a cultural identity marker from Christian religious belief.[43] Bay thus added that, for him, France's Catholic identity existed regardless of religious belief: 'believing or not, practising or not … It's who we are – a country of Christian tradition and culture.'[44] Similarly, Gilbert Collard drew a distinction between the 'religion of God [which the church defends] and the religion of history [which the RN defends]'.[45]

Furthermore, reflecting the *ex-negativo* religious definition of the 'us' discussed in Part I of this book, almost all RN politicians interviewed negatively referenced Islam in their definition of Christian identity, whereas only a few mainstream politicians and no members of the clergy did. Former vice president of the RN, Bruno Gollnisch, thus stated that 'our identity is under demographic threat because of the population replacement. It is threatened culturally and even physically by the push of Islam. … When

---

[39] Interivew Poisson 2019; interview Breton 2019.
[40] Interview Dumas 2019; interview Potier 2019.
[41] Interview Bay 2019.
[42] Interview Collard 2019.
[43] Jenkins 2019.
[44] Interview Bay 2019.
[45] Interview Collard 2019.

people react against that they are brought closer to the Christian identity of their country.'[46] Marion Maréchal-Le Pen stressed that 'the religious question will necessarily be central, but it will be in relation to the question of political Islam; and perhaps in relation to political Islam, there will be a will to defend what defines us; and when it comes to what defines us today it is still hard to avoid Christian identity'.[47] When asked whether a return to religious faith was central to this defence of France's culture, she specified that 'it's rather something cultural'.

Such statements raise the question of whether many of the far right's 'Christian' policies, such as the push for nativity scenes in public places, are driven by an identitarian version of Christendom in opposition to Islam, rather than by an appreciation of Christianity as a faith. And indeed, far-right politicians like Gilbert Collard emphasised that 'although people want nativity scenes ... many of them are atheists. This is a historical struggle and not necessarily a religious one. It's a fight for the survival of a certain idea of the nation and of our civilisation.'[48] Thibault Collin, a Catholic public intellectual who backed Marine Le Pen in 2017 and serves on the academic council of Marion Maréchal-Le Pen's ISSEP school in Lyon, similarly recognised that 'the problem [with the RN's references to Christianity] is the danger of folklorisation ... This is also true for the nativity scenes: people are attached to the fact that there are still Christian references in society, but the reasons are extrinsic. ... It's not living faith.'[49] This analysis seems to apply in equal measures to Éric Zemmour's campaign. For instance, while Zemmour's spokesman Sébastien Pilard declared that Éric Zemmour 'seeks to defend the Christian roots of France, not Christianity as such',[50] Zemmour himself made the distinction even more explicit when explaining in an interview that he was 'for the church but against Christ'.[51]

Overall, these findings support the analysis that despite increased references to Christianity, both the RN and Éric Zemmour clash with Christian social and political doctrine in areas such as immigration, Europe and societal issues and that even their explicitly pro-Christian policy stances are often driven by an ethno-cultural conception of Christendom as an exclusivist identity marker against Islam, rather than by Christian doctrine and beliefs.

---

[46] Interview Gollnisch 2019.
[47] Interview Maréchal-Le Pen 2019.
[48] Interview Collard 2019.
[49] Interview Collin 2019.
[50] Lesueur 2022.
[51] Lindell 2022.

10.2   Public Ethics and Virtues: From Neo-Paganism to *Laïcité*

The impression of a secularised and transactional attitude towards Christianity in the RN and Zemmour's campaign also emerged in the analysis of the cultural-ethical triangle's second corner: the extent to which the political style of the party leadership aligns with traditional ideas of Christian public virtues and ethics. As mentioned before, 'public ethics and virtues' are not to be reduced to politicians' *private* lifestyle choices, as they are insufficient reflections of a politician's public ethics or of their personal faith (or lack thereof). Therefore, this section focuses on the reflection of Christian ethics and virtues in politicians' *public* service: for example, through public commitment to Christianity, or through the way in which Christians and their beliefs shape the inner life of the party.[52]

However, analysis of these indicators does not suggest a particularly important role of Christian ethics or virtues in either the RN's or Éric Zemmour's values, actions and beliefs.[53] This dynamic is particularly clear in the case of the RN, where despite the RN's public posturing as the defender of France's Catholic identity, the role of Christians and Christianity appeared smaller than in most French parties, and to have suffered further internal marginalisation in recent years, due to the rise of a secularist current under Marine Le Pen. Jean-Pierre Delannoy noted, for instance, that during his twenty-plus years as the Catholic deacon to the National Assembly, he had 'never seen an MP from the FN' in the chaplaincy, adding that in recent years the RN has increasingly 'criticised the church with the rhetoric of the left' and has become 'much more secularised today than in the 1980s, especially with regards to moral issues'.[54]

At first glance claims about the marginalisation of Christian influence within the RN might appear surprising, not just because of the RN's increased references to Christianity, but also because the 'neo-pagan contingent that was strong at [the FN's] birth',[55] and which had opposed the influence of Christianity, had significantly declined in recent years.[56] Thus,

---

[52] It is, moreover, extremely difficult to measure the role of religion in French political organisations, not only because, unlike in Germany, there are no official statistics on the religious affiliation of French office holders, but also, because *laïcité*'s re-politicisation has made politicians generally keen to avoid mentioning their religious beliefs in public.

[53] Due to the novelty of Éric Zemmour's Reconquête party, there was insufficient empirical data to conduct a similarly thorough analysis of the role of Christianity in the inner workings of the Zemmour campaign.

[54] Interview Delannoy 2019.

[55] Roy 2016, 79.

[56] François 2008; François 2007.

whilst former party grandee Bernard Antony emphasised that in earlier decades 'it was not easy for me in the FN [as a Christian], because there were many who objected to my vision – in particular those who would be defined as the [neo-pagan] new right',[57] other interviewees like Bruno Gollnisch emphasised that 'there is only a very marginal contingent of neo-pagans today'.[58] Gilbert Collard, for instance, stressed that 'there are no neo-pagans anymore'[59] and Marion Maréchal-Le Pen insisted that 'the neo-pagan current no longer exists in the FN. It existed during the 1980s and 1990s, but it has disappeared today.'[60]

However, the neo-pagan current's decline has not coincided with a strengthening of Christian voices within the RN. Rather, as we will see in more detail in the next section, it has been replaced by a new religion-critical contingent of defenders of *laïcité*, spearheaded by Marine Le Pen. Jean-Marie Le Pen himself stated, for example, that 'the FN became the RN in 2015. This change has some significance: there was at this juncture a sociopolitical shift to the left' with the result that 'today there is a very strong secularist current in the FN'.[61] His former deputy Bruno Gollnisch similarly acknowledged that 'there is no doubt there has been a secularist [*laïciste*] drift in the FN in recent years'.[62] These statements are in line with academic assessments of a 'secularist turn' in the RN, under the leadership of personalities such as Florian Philippot, Sebastien Chenu and Jordan Bardella.[63]

It might strike the observer as odd that this embrace of a secularist reading of *laïcité* chronologically coincided with RN's increased references to France's Catholic identity. Yet, closer analysis reveals that, like Christianity, *laïcité*, in the RN's right-wing identity politics, is an *ex negativo* identity marker against Islam.[64] Jean-Marie Le Pen for instance claimed that 'the law of 1905 now appears to us as a defence in relationship to Islam. When accused of Islamophobia we respond that it's the law of 1905',[65] and Bruno Gollnisch stated that 'Marine Le Pen told me that the defence of *laïcité* is a way to oppose Islamist tendencies in society.'[66] It is therefore perhaps not

[57] Interview Antony 2019.
[58] Interview Gollnisch 2019.
[59] Interview Collard 2019.
[60] Interview Maréchal-Le Pen 2019.
[61] Interview Le Pen 2019.
[62] Interview Gollnisch 2019.
[63] Almeida 2017; Brubaker 2017; Nilsson 2015; Perrineau 2017; Roy 2016; Cremer 2021c.
[64] Baubérot 2015, 103–18; Brubaker 2017; Du Cleuziou 2019; Roy 2019.
[65] Interview Le Pen 2019.
[66] Interview Gollnisch 2019.

too surprising that the RN tends to perform best among those voters who are also most concerned about the weakening of *laïcité* in France.[67]

Whatever the reasons behind the RN's 'secularist turn', interviewees agreed that it led to Christian influences within the RN being sidelined. Thus, although Marion Maréchal-Le Pen sought to downplay the RN's secular current's hostility towards Catholicism, saying that 'I wouldn't go quite so far as to say they are anti-religious',[68] the testimonies of other leaders suggest that Christian voices have increasingly been stifled within the RN. Former party Vice President Bruno Gollnisch for instance reported that 'one does not talk a lot about religious questions in the RN anymore. I think there has been a change – back in the day we evoked religious questions much more.'[69] Jean-Marie Le Pen, whilst observing that historically 'religion was an element that had an influence on a part of the electorate and was therefore welcomed and not rejected', similarly commented that 'this politico-religious aspect is much less important today'.[70] And Bernard Antony went so far as to claim that he left the party because 'the Christian contingent became so marginalised in the FN … for me it was a drama of conscience because I felt I was denied the right to voice my opinion'.[71]

This impression was underscored by statements from RN leaders, who acknowledged Christians' minority status in the party. For instance, Bruno Gollnisch noted that 'there is no [organised] Christian group within the RN – there are Catholics but not a significant number',[72] while then RN General Secretary Nicolas Bay explained that 'religion [in terms of faith] is not very present in the daily life of the RN'.[73] Thibault Collin, moreover, remarked that 'Marine Le Pen has typically nothing to do with Christianity',[74] while Jacques de Guillebon, editor of the right-wing magazine *l'Incorrecte* and advisor to Marion Maréchal-Le Pen, emphasised that Marine 'has always been contemptuous of Catholics. I don't know if it is an electoral choice or rather issue that she has with Catholics whom she

---

[67] Finchelstein et al. 2021.
[68] Interview Maréchal-Le Pen 2019.
[69] Interview Gollnisch 2019. Gollnisch, for instance, a representative of Catholic voices in the RN, not only lost the election for the RN leadership to Marine Le Pen in 2011 but was also deselected from leading the RN into the European elections for 2019 and has since retreated from politics. Marion Maréchal Le Pen similarly retreated from politics in 2017, leaving the Catholic camp within the RN leaderless and marginalised.
[70] Interview Le Pen 2019.
[71] Interview Antony 2019.
[72] Interview Gollnisch 2019.
[73] Interview Bay 2019.
[74] Interview Collin 2019.

considers as bourgeois'.[75] Some RN officials privately admitted their own
Christian faith, but asked for anonymity, while several of their colleagues
criticised conservative Christians within the party. One for instance called
Christians in the party the 'one group that can be a little dissident', and
noted a desire to silence their beliefs, saying, 'You want an ideal society
where everyone shares your values? So, don't do politics, go to a con-
vent.' These insider accounts were underlined by some of Marine Le
Pen's public declarations in the 2022 election campaign. At a major rally
in Reims in early 2022 she explained, for instance, that 'there are some
[Christians] in the RN, but they are not organised with the objective of
influencing our political project', while accusing her far-right challenger
Éric Zemmour of not being sufficiently secular and being too welcoming
to conservative Christians.[76] Zemmour, who had indeed been successful
in attracting a certain number of prominent conservative Catholic activists and politicians, as we shall discuss in Chapter 12, responded, however,
by downplaying their role in his party, with campaign officials calling Le
Pen's accusations 'nonsense' and stressing that their candidate was merely
defending France's Catholic heritage but not Christianity itself.[77]

Overall, despite its outward references to France's Catholic identity and
the demise of neo-pagan currents, Christian voices and values within the RN
appeared increasingly marginalised due to the rise of new secularist currents
under Marine Le Pen. And while Zemmour's campaign showed itself to be
somewhat more open towards Catholic traditionalists in its ranks, its representatives too were adamant to emphasise that Christians did not play a major
role in their movement. Public commitments to the Christian faith, it seems,
had become a handicap in France's populist right, which instead adopted an
increasingly secularist reading of *laïcité*. This secularist shift also had important consequences for these movements' relationship with the institutional
Christian churches, the final element of the cultural-ethical triangle.

10.3   Institutional Relations with the Church: A Tumultuous History and an Ambivalent Present

The findings from the interviews suggests that despite the populist right's
public focus on the need to defend France's Christian heritage, its transformation into a staunch defender of a secularist reading of *laïcité* has

[75] Interview de Guillebon 2019.
[76] Lesueur 2022; Equating 'Zemmourism' with 'communitarianism', Le Pen accused Zemmour of aggre-
gating 'chapels filled with sulphurous characters', 'Catholic traditionalists', 'pagans' and 'some Nazis'.
[77] Lesueur 2022.

caused it to vehemently question not only specific church policies or leaders, but the church's place in the public sphere altogether.

Relations between the populist right and the churches have never been cordial. For example, Jean-Marie Le Pen emphasised during our interview that 'from the beginning there was hostility from the Assembly of Bishops' and the FN made no secret of its own hostility towards church representatives, whom they perceived as having shifted to the left since the Second Vatican Council.[78] In the 1990s Jean-Marie Le Pen accused bishops of Freemasonry and argued that, because they would betray the French nation in favour of the interests of the Church Universal, 'we do not need the advice of the Bishops'.[79] This animosity towards church leadership persists.[80] During our interviews, RN representatives, including those who later defected to Zemmour, criticised Catholic bishops as 'conformists, pharisees and cowards' (Gilbert Collard),[81] as 'bishops and priests who don't hide their left-wing tendencies' (Nicolas Bay),[82] or as 'diverted and having lost their way and their ministry' (Wallerand de Saint-Just).[83] Interestingly for a party that previously claimed to defend 'true' (pre-Vatican II) Catholicism and strong ecclesiastical hierarchies, not even the authority of the Holy Father was spared. Mirroring Zemmour's comments about Pope Francis as an 'enemy of Europe', Wallerand de Saint-Just argued that 'we have a pope who talks a lot of nonsense about the migration crisis ... but on issues like that the popes have always said a lot of nonsense'.[84] Jean-Marie Le Pen questioned the pope's authority (whilst refusing to use his pontifical name) stating that 'Mr Bergoglio is an Argentinian and a son of immigrants who confuses things. He does not understand the Muslim dimension of immigration in Europe.'[85]

Moreover, while in earlier decades it was primarily discontent with specific church leaders that soured relations, in the context of Marine Le Pen's 'secularist turn' the far right also began to question the legitimacy of religious institutions' very presence in the public sphere. Jean-Louis Bianco,

---

[78] Interview Le Pen 2019.
[79] Dubertret 1996; Roy 2016, 86; Senneville 2015; Tabard 2015; Mayer and Perrineau 1996.
[80] Some RN individuals, however, have sought to break with this antagonism and spearhead a rapprochement towards the church. During the interviews Marion Maréchal Le Pen claimed to have 'generally good relations with Catholic circles; and a relationship with parts of the Church of France ... [T]hings have changed a lot.' Yet, given the other interviewees' comments, this strategy does not appear to have had a lasting impact.
[81] Interview Collard 2019.
[82] Interview Bay 2019.
[83] Interview de Saint-Just 2019.
[84] Interview de Saint-Just 2019.
[85] Interview Le Pen 2019.

president of the *Observatoire de la Laïcité*, hence observed that 'the personality who has employed the word of *laïcité* the most, is Marine Le Pen' and that 'you can now find very similar propositions between the extreme right and the secularist [*laïciste*], anti-religious left'.[86] Scholars like Almeida emphasise the centrality of *laïcité* in policy terms, showing that '*laïcité* played a pivotal role in Marine Le Pen's [2012] campaign. Not only did the topic appear as a guiding theme in almost every campaign speech, but the FN was also one of the few parties whose manifesto featured an entire chapter devoted to the issue.'[87] In 2017 the FN even proposed the banning of 'all public funding (state, regional authorities …) for places of worship and religious activities'; 'to inscribe in the constitution the principle that "the republic does not recognise any religion"', and to 'restore *laïcité* everywhere, to extend it to the entirety of the public sphere and to inscribe it into the labour code'.[88] Even in secular France such measures would go far beyond the law of 1905 and critically infringe on religious communities' rights and believers' freedom to express religious beliefs in public.[89]

Certainly, the main target of such measures is Islam rather than Christianity, as many interviewees sought to emphasise during the interviews. Former RN general secretary and subsequent Zemmour backer Nicolas Bay for example explained that '*laïcité* is the philosophical and religious neutrality of our institutions. It should not go against our identity, our civilisation, our tradition, our culture, but of course this *laïcité* is today a tool to stop politico-religious claims from radical Islam.'[90] His colleague and fellow Zemmour supporter Gilbert Collard similarly highlighted that his vision of *laïcité* made special allowance for Christendom as a historical identity marker, saying that 'to be *laïc* is to be neutral, that is to say it is not to promote a specific religion, but to promote evidence, such as that the kings of France were Catholic, that they were crowned in a cathedral and not in a synagogue or mosque'.[91] Marion Maréchal-Le Pen asserted that 'we are never confronted with problems with the Catholic religion. It's a religion that has constructed *laïcité* so it is perfectly assimilated … [T]here is nothing today in our code of society that would bring Catholics into confrontation with our model of society. It is the question of political Islam that is dominant.'[92]

[86] Interview Bianco 2019.
[87] Almeida 2017, 249; Baubérot 2015; Brubaker 2017; Perrineau 2017; Badinter 2011.
[88] Front National 2017.
[89] Almeida 2017, 255; Bianco 2016; Roy 2019.
[90] Interview Bay 2019.
[91] Interview Collard 2019.
[92] Interview Maréchal-Le Pen 2019.

Still, the Christian churches might equally suffer from the far right's secularist policies. As François Clavairoly, the president of French Protestant Federation (FPF), put it, 'If one day the far right came to power, I'm certain that there would be indirect negative consequences for Christianity.'[93] Similarly, Jean-Louis Bianco, when asked whether the Christian churches could become collateral damage in the hardening of *laïcité* against Islam on the populist right, answered, 'exactly, exactly, they even say so explicitly'.[94] Several RN officials freely admitted to such negative effects on Christianity, with Bruno Gollnisch explaining that 'we insist on the importance of *laïcité* in order to ban religious symbols – knowing that it is really aimed against the Islamic scarf, but if we want to be impartial we also have to say, "no headscarf but also no cross"'.[95]

A number of scholars claim that this attack on Christianity is not an unwanted side effect but welcomed and intended. Brubaker for instance argues that *laïcité* was not only 'embraced [by the populist right] as a way of minimizing the visibility of Islam in the public sphere – but also as a way of excluding or delegitimizing substantively Christian arguments for openness towards, or solidarity with, migrants and refugees'.[96] Roy similarly points out that 'behind the debate on Islam there is indeed a deeper debate on the very nature of Europe, and on its relationship with religion in general'.[97] Interviewees like Bishop Stenger supported such claims stressing that 'because religion became the enemy [of the far right] and because little by little they discovered that religion was an obstacle to certain xenophobic positions, it became necessary for them to put the church back in the village, and to reduce religion. It is a way to privatise religion … to neutralise it.'[98]

Indeed, during our interviews, many far-right leaders' criticisms of the church were accompanied by a fundamental questioning of its legitimacy as a public actor. Nicolas Bay for example made it clear that Catholicism's reconcilability with his idea of *laïcité* was dependent on the church's refraining from weighing in on political questions. He emphasised that 'historically Catholic representatives have moved away from this principle [of political silence] and there is today an intrusion of religion and clergy in the public sphere, which is a distortion of

---

[93] Interview Clavairoly 2019.
[94] Interview Bianco 2019.
[95] Interview Gollnisch 2019.
[96] Brubaker 2017, 1199.
[97] Roy 2019, 10.
[98] Interview Stenger 2019.

[the church's] role'.[99] Wallerand de Saint-Just put it even more plainly:
'A French Bishop should shut his mouth on political questions ... he
should shut up and care for his flock and his church ... we need to more
severely apply the rules of *laïcité à la française* here.'[100]

In sum, these results from the analysis of France's populist right's
Christian credentials through the socio-ethical triangle suggest that the
RN, while a self-declared saviour of *la France Catholique*, is in fact one
of the most secularist parties in France. Its policies not only clash with
Christian doctrine on immigration, Europe and societal questions, but are
also indicative of an underlying identitarian conception of Christianity,
one that seems more concerned with 'Christendom' as a civilisational antidote to Islam than with Christianity as a faith. Whilst the Christophobic
neo-pagan current within the party apparatus has waned, there is evidence that it has been supplanted by new secularist anti-clericalism.
This turn towards a radically secular reading of *laïcité* has had significant
consequences for the RN's attitude towards religious institutions, whose
legitimacy as public actors they fundamentally questioned. While on the
surface, Éric Zemmour's campaign seemed to assume a less openly hostile
position towards Catholicism, catering to some of the demands of conservative Catholics with regards to social issues and being less radically
secularist in his rhetoric, at the time of writing it is still too early to make
a full assessment about the extent to which this may change the dynamics
between Catholicism and the far right in the long run. Still, first indicators, such as Zemmour's open hostility towards the pope, his attempts to
dissociate France's Catholic heritage from the Christian faith, as well as
his readiness to downplay or deny Christian influences in his party when
they are perceived as politically inconvenient, all suggest that under the
surface the rising star of the far right is driven by a similar interpretation
of Catholicism as his far-right competitors in the RN. As Yann-Raison
du Cleuziou put it, for the French far right it is 'not about restoring a
Christian State or defending the truth of the faith. Their relationship with
Catholicism is more secular; they defend French identity against the threats

---

[99] Interview Bay 2019.
[100] Interview de Saint-Just 2019. Whilst the RN's criticism of the Catholic Church appeared tempered
by the appreciation of Catholicism as a cultural identity marker, such aspects were absent in its
view of minority Protestantism. In declarations such as Marion Maréchal-Le Pen's that 'Provence
is a land of identity and resistance ... resistance against the Saracen invasion, resistance against
the revolutionary terror, against Protestant Reformation, against German occupation, against the
disastrous project of the EU in 2005', Protestantism is put on a par with external others like Nazism
or Islam.

of globalism and Islam.'[101] Yet, while this might be the assessment emerging from scholarly and theoretical examinations, it is even more important whether it is shared by French Christians. Chapter 11 therefore turns to Christian voters' reaction to the RN's religious references and assess the role of mainstream parties and of the churches in shaping it.

[101] Du Cleuziou 2019, 302.

CHAPTER II

A Successful Dédiabolisation?
Factors in Understanding the Weakening of Religious Immunity to Populism in France

On the respective evenings of the 2017 and 2022 presidential elections, when collective sighs of relief went through the salons and offices of France's social, political and cultural establishment at the news that Emmanuel Macron had defeated Marine Le Pen, there may well have been one notable exception on both occasions: the Headquarters of the French Bishops Conference. This was not because the bishops had hoped for a different outcome (as this section will show their scepticism towards the far right has little changed over the decades), but because the RN's *dédiabolisation* seemed to finally have reached the Catholic electorate. In 2017, in the ballot 38 per cent of Catholics had voted for Le Pen, compared with only 34 per cent of the overall population, and in 2022 that number had risen to 45 per cent (compared to 42 per cent in the general population).[1] Certainly, with 62 per cent and 55 per cent, respectively, most Catholics had still opted for Macron, and among practising Catholics the support for Le Pen was still disproportionately low at 29 per cent in 2017 and 39 per cent in 2022.[2] Yet, the result still seemed to put into question the old truism that Catholicism was one of the most formidable electoral bastions against the far right's march to power.

For decades polling data and election results had shown a significant 'religious immunity' to the far right in France, with Catholics supporting the FN/RN at much lower rates than the rest of the population.[3] In this respect French Catholics were representative both of France's Christians in

[1] IFOP 2017a; IFOP 2022a.
[2] IFOP 2017a; IFOP 2022a.
[3] Roy emphasises that whilst 'throughout the history of the French Republic, practising Catholics have tended to vote in large numbers for the right or more precisely different rights ... after WWII they kept away from the extreme right identified with pro-Nazi and neo-pagan trends' (Roy 2016, 87). De Cleuziou similarly finds that Catholics 'constituted an electorate of very low propensity to vote FN' (Du Cleuziou 2019, 312), and Fourquet that Catholics were 'up to now one of the most refractory categories to vote against the FN' (Fourquet 2018a, 87; cf. Mayer and Perrineau 1996; Perrineau 2014).

general, with Protestants proving similarly reluctant to cast their lot with the RN,[4] as well as of their brethren in other Western European countries. Moreover, France's Catholics had proven more resilient to the RN's *dédiabolisation* and electoral expansion than other traditional bastions against the populist right such as women, the young, the working-class or the irreligious.[5] Davies even observed that 'the amount of practising Catholics voting for the FN halved between 1984 and 1997, and the proportion of those with "no religion" in its ranks more than trebled'.[6] These observations align with Perrineau's findings that between 2002 and 2012 the RN 'progressed by 2% with women, by 5% with the 18–24 year olds, by 8% with 25–34 year olds, by 9% among working-class voters and by 5% among the irreligious', but that 'the nationalist drive that feeds the far right in France always stumbled against the block of practising Catholics who yield far less to the temptation of the FN than most other parts of the population'.[7] As late as in the first round of the 2012 presidential election the religion gap appeared as powerful as ever: only 4 per cent of practising Catholics chose Marine Le Pen compared to 18 per cent of the general population.[8]

Yet, in the 2017 and 2022 this religion gap seemed to have vanished. What is more, in the first round of the 2022 presidential elections, the dynamic was even reversed with 11 per cent of practising Catholics favouring the far-right candidate Éric Zemmour, compared with only 7.1 per cent of the overall population.[9] What could explain this change in Catholic voting behaviour? This chapter analyses the extent to which the religious immunity disappeared or transformed and what might have driven this development. Applying this book's theoretical framework, I review both demand- and supply-side explanations, focusing firstly on potential connections to shifts at Catholic grassroots, secondly on the role of the other parties and thirdly on the influence of church leaders.

11.1   The Demand Side: A Conservative Counter-Revolution?

One popular explanation for the progress of the RN and Éric Zemmour amongst Catholics is an alleged right-wards shift within this electorate that would have landed it on the same side of the new identity cleavage as the

---

[4] Dargent 2005; Ipsos 2017; Schwengler 2005.
[5] Mayer and Perrineau 1996.
[6] Davies 2010, 582.
[7] Perrineau 2014, 39.
[8] Du Cleuziou 2019, 312.
[9] IFOP 2022b.

RN. Specifically, observers reference the *Manif pour tous* demonstrations against the legalisation of gay marriage in 2013, and the subsequent foundation of the conservative *Sens Commun* (SC) movement as evidence. Commentators spoke for instance of 'an anti-gay marriage Tea party French style',[10] claimed that 'the far right is in the first line of the *Manif pour tous*',[11] or that the *Manif pour tous* is fuelled by 'the toxic right'.[12] During our interview former Socialist Education Minister Najat Vallaud Belkacem aptly summarised this hypothesis: 'At the moment of the *Manif pour Tous* a rapprochement took place between the Catholic milieus and the far right. The famous rapprochement which we found in 2017 ... is I believe linked to the fact that she [Marion Maréchal-Le Pen] has demonstrated with them [the Catholics] at the *Manif pour tous*.'[13]

However, the findings of this book cast some doubts upon this logic. Certainly, most scholars agree that 'France's Catholic Moment' in the early 2010s was primarily driven by conservative currents.[14] Fourquet for instance speaks of 'Catholics' identitarian awakening', and de Cleuziou of 'a Catholic Counter-Revolution'.[15] Interviewees like Bishop Marc Stenger similarly shared this view, saying 'that Catholic opinion has hardened. It has hardened in its positions towards societal questions, and it has become more charismatic'.[16] Grégoire Catta, director of the department for 'Family and Society' at the French Bishops Conference, similarly observed that whereas 'after Vatican II there were many Catholics engaged in politics and especially in social issues, ... since my generation and the next, there has been a return of a more conservative political commitment, especially on societal issues'.[17] The *Manif pour tous* in particular was seen as a turning point, with Christophe Billan, the co-founder and former president

---

[10] Stille 2014.
[11] Boumediene 2014.
[12] Destal 2013; Du Cleuziou 2018; Milet 2014.
[13] Interview Vallaud-Belkacem 2019.
[14] Gregg 2017.
[15] Scholars link the surge of conservative Catholics to the community's demographic decline, the associated mentality shifts towards a more confrontational minority mindset, and the nature of the gay marriage project itself. Fourquet stressed, for instance, that whereas for a long time Catholics had sought to reconcile their faith with society and to avoid conservative culture wars, 'the debate on gay marriage was to break this equilibrium and represented not only a true casus belli for the Catholic world but also a scathing illustration of its loss of influence' (Fourquet 2018a, 9). De Cleuziou argues that this development was compounded by the fact that 'the pious [observants] are gaining importance in the Church because, in the context of general religious decline, they are better able than other Catholics to perpetuate their faith from one generation to the next' (Du Cleuziou 2019, 17).
[16] Interview Stenger 2019.
[17] Interview Catta 2019.

of the SC, arguing that 'the Taubira law [which introduced gay marriage] showed that the revolution of May 1968 made laws' and that in response 'we created *Sens Commun*, which seeks to reverse the absurdity of this deconstruction of our civilisation'.[18] Father Jacques Enjalbert the chaplain of Sciences Po Paris – the French elite school for politics some of whose students played a key role in the Catholic mobilisation – similarly reported that 'the turning point was the introduction of gay marriage. … [M]any [Catholic students] were now clearly saying: "It's enough – the conciliarism between faith and modernity is no longer viable."'[19] This sense of social marginalisation and an associated shift towards conservativism was, moreover, not limited to Catholics but also extended to the Protestant minority. François Clavailory, the president of the French Protestant Federation, claimed that the 'slow but real erosion of the influence of religious views in the political debate' resulted in 'a risk that Christians feel humiliated, forgotten and fall back on very conservative postures. This is the unwanted side effect of secularisation and eradication of religious reference points.'[20]

However, whilst these statements confirm a shift towards social conservatism along the traditional moral cleavage, several indicators suggest that this did not necessarily lead to a rapprochement between Christians and the far right on the new identity cleavage. Rather two parallel but inherently distinct right-wing movements emerged, with the social-conservative Catholic 'counter-revolution' on the one hand and a more secular populist right on the other. Most interviewees, for instance, observed that the new Catholic movement's core was diametrically opposed to the RN both politically and socio-culturally. Thus, politically, we have seen that the RN embraced an anti-clerical identitarian nationalism, radically rejected immigration, defended protectionist economic policies and advocated greater liberalism on societal issues. By contrast, François Euvé, editor-in-chief of the influential Jesuit *Revue Etude* journal emphasised that 'the classical Catholicism of Versailles, which found its expression in the *Manif pour tous* is not identitarian. It's classical: they are for the Pope; the immigration question is debated but the central question is the family – everything else is secondary.'[21] Likewise, Bishop Rougé confirmed that those driving the new conservative activism were 'sometimes wrongly confused … as

---

[18] Interview Billan 2019.
[19] Interview Enjalbert 2019.
[20] Interview Clavairoly 2019.
[21] Interview Euvé 2019.

being people of far-right political sensibilities, which is not at all true'.[22]
Instead he emphasised that it is 'a fairly balanced and purified Catholicism,
which constitutes a "significant and creative minority", as Benedict XVI
put it'.[23] Representatives of conservative grassroots movements similarly
highlighted their policy disagreement with the RN. Former SC president
Christophe Billan repeatedly insisted that 'there is nothing Christian or
Catholic in the RN. The RN follows a strictly materialist and jacobine
logic favouring a centralist and collectivist state ... which is in opposition to Christianity.'[24] Similarly, in 2014, his predecessor Madeleine de
Jessey refused any cooperation with the RN or Marion Maréchal-Le Pen,
because of the former's 'statist' positions and the latter's support of the
'great replacement' hypothesis,[25] which de Jessey called 'dangerous'.[26]

That does not mean that there are no connection points between
Catholic conservatives and the new identitarian and populist right. Bishop
Marc Stenger for instance worried that the sense of marginalisation and
shift towards a combative minority mentality among Catholics might
open the gates to 'a strong entryism from far-right movements'.[27] Catholic
author and influencer Erwan Le Morhedec suggested that 'identitarian
groups such as génération identitaire are trying to create confusion among
Catholics, which convinced me that there is a strategy to enter Christian
spaces of discussion to introduce an identitarian logic'.[28] A number of interviewees also stressed the potentially decisive role of Marion Maréchal-Le
Pen as a bridge-builder into this milieu for the far right. Thibault Collin,
for instance, claimed that 'Marion has a greater centrality in the French
right than Marine, because she can bring voters together that Marine cannot.'[29] And Marion Maréchal Le Pen herself confirmed that 'the question
of identity is clearly the bridge [between Catholics and the RN] because it
connects the archipelago of the Catholic middle class who live in the big
cities and the France of the yellow vests'.[30] This dynamic may also help

---

[22] Interview Rougé 2019.
[23] Interview Rougé 2019.
[24] Interview Billan 2019.
[25] First put forward by far-right author Renaud Camus in 2010, the 'great replacement' is a conspiracy theory holding that there is a deliberate attempt by 'replacist elites' to substitute the French
and European population with non-European populations, originally from black Africa and the
Maghreb through mass migration (Camus 2011; Gourévitch, 2019).
[26] Du Cleuziou 2018, 107.
[27] Interview Stenger 2019.
[28] Interview Le Morhedec 2019.
[29] Interview Collin 2019.
[30] Interview Maréchal-Le Pen 2019.

explain Éric Zemmour's relative success in attracting not only a greater share in Catholic votes, but also prominent Catholic lay activists and politicians, including VIA (formerly Parti Chrétien Democrate) president Jean-Frédéric Poisson, or Christophe Billan's successor as president of *Sens Commun*, Laurence Trochu.[31]

Still, recent election and polling data suggests that as the new identity cleavage is becoming more prevalent the attitudinal gulf between practising Catholics and the far right's positions had actually widened. Two 'More in Common' studies found, for instance, that 'Catholics seem to be more sympathetic towards migrants than the French in general', with 41 per cent of them supporting the idea that migrants show a willingness to integrate (compared to only 22 per cent in the general population) and 61 per cent opposing a closing of borders (compared to only 29 per cent in the general population).[32] Openness towards immigration, moreover, strongly correlates with religious practice: whereas in 2017 60 per cent of practising Catholics supported the welcoming of migrants, only 38 per cent of non-practising Catholics did so (compared to 42 per cent in the general population).[33] Other studies found that 'practising Catholics are paradoxically more open towards Islam',[34] whereas 'in terms of moral values [the electorate of the RN] is more liberal' than France's Catholics.[35] Such findings suggest that when it comes to identitarian policy issues conservative Catholics are not only far away from Marine Le Pen's RN but also from Éric Zemmour, who has shown himself, if anything, even more radical than the RN on identitarian issues.

One key difference between Zemmour and the RN was, however, that the former seemed to be able to overcome some of the cultural and socio-demographic barriers (at least among non-practising Catholics) that compounded the attitudinal divergences between the RN and conservative Catholics. These barriers were not only a result of the fact that, as Archbishop Pascal Wintzer explained, 'the Catholic community today is polycultural and polychrome. There are African and Indian Catholics in almost all the parishes',[36] which sits uneasily with the RN's ethno-nationalist

---

[31] Lesueur 2022.
[32] More in Common 2018; More in Common 2017.
[33] IFOP 2017b.
[34] Geisser 2018, 6; Béraud 2014.
[35] Dargent added to the list of discrepancies that 'a certain attachment to [economic] liberalism remains central among most practising Catholics', whereas the RN clearly embraces a more statist view (Dargent 2016, 19).
[36] Interview Wintzer 2019.

tendencies.[37] The barriers were also a result of France's most devout Catholics and the electorate of Marine Le Pen coming from opposite ends of the social ladder. Bishop Matthiue Rougé thus emphasised that

> today living Catholicism in France is often the Catholicism of the upper middle class or of a certain intellectual class in the west of Paris and some large cities … [P]art of the working class in the RN does not feel at all comfortable with this bourgeois Catholicism, meaning that if Catholics vote RN it's not because of their Catholic identity – on the contrary they'd do so in opposition to it.[38]

Marion Maréchal-Le Pen's confidant Jacques de Guillebon similarly observed that whilst 'it is practically only the bourgeoisie who have transmitted their faith and Catholic teaching to their children, the electorate of the RN is rather the disinherited and obsolete, who aren't very concerned by religious questions'.[39] Building on such observations FPF president François Clavairoly explained that 'what characterises the voter of the FN is the fear of the future, the fear of declassification and the promise of personal consideration and recognition: "With Marine Le Pen and the FN I will really exist, and I will be recognized."'[40] By contrast, Clavairoly claimed that 'Christians who find their identity in Christ are immune to that. They do not need to find an identity of substitution.'[41] These observations closely align with the findings of Nonna Mayer or Pascal Perrineau, who show that the RN electorate is primarily young, rural, male and working class, whereas the contrary is true for France's practising Christians, among whom women, the elderly and well-off city dwellers are overrepresented.[42]

In the light of these findings, it is perhaps unsurprising that at least when it comes to the RN, recent polling and election data reveal that rather than

---

[37] Studies show that French congregations are becoming increasingly multi-ethnic and multicultural, with in particular believers with sub-Saharan and South-East Asian origins playing an increasingly important role in parishes in terms of numbers and engagement (Fourquet and Le Bras 2014; Landron 2004). Béraud shows that this is also increasingly true for the French clergy, whose new recruits often come from the global south (Béraud 2015).

[38] Interview Rougé 2019.

[39] Interview de Guillebon 2019.

[40] Interview Clavairoly 2019.

[41] Interview Clavairoly 2019.

[42] Mayer 2016; Mayer 2015a; Perrineau 2017. Fourquet's research supports these findings showing for instance that in addition to pensioners, highly educated senior executives and professionals are among the most avid churchgoers (10.1 per cent and 9.3 per cent, respectively), whereas manual workers are the least likely to be practising Catholics (6.3 per cent) (Fourquet 2018a, 28). A study from the Jean-Jaurès foundation similarly found that the traditional gap between more religious rural areas and less religious cities has largely disappeared and that today 'practice is all the more high as the district is bourgeois' (Fourquet and Le Bras 2014, 48, 54).

disappearing, the religion gap has actually only limited itself to practising Catholics.[43] Thus, whereas the latter were drivers of the *Manif pour tous* but less likely to vote RN, it is amongst non-practising Catholics with the loosest links to the church that Marine Le Pen proved most popular.[44] In the first round of the 2022 election, for instance, 29 per cent of non-practising Christians voted for Le Pen compared with only 21 per cent of frequent churchgoers.[45] Indeed, the RN's inroads among Catholics appeared rather to be a consequence of the secularisation of the French working class than of a cultural and political convergence with Catholicism. The result was a growing schism amongst right-wing voters. On one side stands the traditional religious right which remained focused on the old moral cleavage, recruited largely from the churchgoing and more educated middle classes, was socially conservative but open to immigration, committed to democratic values, and aligned with the centre-right LR. On the other was a new secular right defined by the identity cleavage, which appeals to working-class voters and combines socially more 'progressive' values with cultural nativism and authoritarian tendencies.

In 2022 Éric Zemmour has proven able to bridge this divide at least partly by catering to Catholics' core social issues, recruiting key Catholic activists to his campaign and by capitalising on his reputation as an intellectual in middle-class circles. While still focused on the same identitarian key issues as the RN, he polled significantly better than Marine Le Pen among upper middle-class, elderly and urban voters in the lead-up to the election, and performed particularly well among regular churchgoers, scoring 16 per cent compared with just 7.1 per cent of the general population.[46] Zemmour's comparative success among Catholics when compared to the RN makes Catholics' traditional 'religious immunity' towards the far right, as well as the apparent erosion of this immunity in recent years, appear to be less a function of a major right-ward shift in Catholic attitudes than of changes on the political and religious supply side.

11.2   The Political Supply Side: The Implosion of the Centre-Right between Le Pen, Macron and Zemmour

The first factor to consider on the supply side is the role of mainstream competitor parties and specifically the ability of centre-right or Christian Democratic

---

[43] IFOP 2019; IFOP 2017a.
[44] Dargent 2016; Du Cleuziou 2017; IFOP 2019; IFOP 2017b.
[45] IFOP 2022b.
[46] IFOP 2022b.

parties to bind Christian voters and to thus make them 'unavailable' for the populist right. In Germany the historical association of Christians with the CDU/CSU and the latter's continued issue-ownership over moral and religious questions was an important factor in explaining the empirical 'religion gap' (see Chapter 7). In France, Christians' association with the centre-right is less straightforward, due to the stricter separation of politics and religion and the subsequent absence of a major Christian Democratic party.[47] Thus, although during the interviews Senate president and interim leader of the LR Gérard Larcher acknowledged that 'until the end of WWII, [the right's] main difference with the left rested on the defence of the faith and the church against the anti-clerical claims of the left', he was also keen to emphasise that, unlike Christian Democracy elsewhere, French Gaullism always openly embraced *laïcité* and explicitly avoided defining itself as a Christian party.[48] Clergy and centre-right politicians interviewed agreed that 'there isn't really an explicitly Catholic party in France' (Bishop Dominique Rey),[49] that 'in France we don't have a Christian Democratic party and if we had one they wouldn't talk about it' (Xavier Breton),[50] and that 'we never had a Christian Democratic party. We don't have the German CDU' (Grégoire Catta).[51]

This lack of an explicit association notwithstanding, for decades the centre-right attracted most Catholic voters. Dargent for instance found a 'strong orientation towards the right among Catholics, particularly the practising ones',[52] and Bréchon showed that in the 2000s and 2010s about 60 to 70 per cent of practising Catholics voted for centre-right parties.[53] Moreover, after a partial abandoning of Christian references by a generation of centre-right politicians around Jacques Chirac or Alain Juppé since the 1980s, throughout the 2000s and early 2010s the LR sought to restore its 'Christian credentials'.[54] Inaugurated by Nicolas Sarkozy's positive

[47] Descamp 1980; Kalyvas and Van Kersbergen 2010; Müller 2013.
[48] Interview Larcher 2019.
[49] Interview Rey 2019.
[50] Interview Breton 2019.
[51] Interview Catta 2019. Interestingly, some interviewees highlighted the lack of a Christian democratic dimension of the French centre-right as an important disadvantage when compared to the German CDU/CSU, due to their reduced ability to confederate and long-term bind conservative, liberal and Christian voters and thus limit the electoral potential for the far right. Nino Galetti, the head of the Parisian office of the Konrad Adenauer Stiftung, hence observed that 'in Germany, we regularly have the debate in the CDU in particular about 'what does the C mean to us?' This debate allows the CDU to reassure itself of its identity again and again, and it is missing in politics here [in France].' Interview Galetti 2019.
[52] Dargent 2016, 20.
[53] Bréchon 2018.
[54] Le Bras and Todd 2013; Rémond 2014; Richard 2017.

references to Christianity, this strategy reached its apex with the candidatures of the practising Catholics François Fillon at the presidential election in 2017 and François-Xavier Bellamy at the European elections 2019.[55]

During our interview Archbishop Wintzer asserted that Catholics 'have overwhelmingly voted Fillon in the first round of the presidential elections, because he knew how to talk to Catholics: He picked up societal issues again but from a centrist way and with a social fibre, and the same is true with François-Xavier Bellamy during the European elections.'[56] Sciences Po chaplain Enjalbert stressed that 'Bellamy is the great hope for the classical Catholics'.[57] These comments are in line with the findings of Bouthors and De Cleuziou who found that 'for practising Catholics, Fillon is one of them',[58] and that 'a moderate figure in his expressions and strong in his convictions, François Fillon finally gave Catholics a public presentation of the "respectability" with which they identified .... His internalised rather than identitarian Catholicism appealed to them.'[59] Another expression of this realignment was the incorporation of the SC into the LR in 2017. Church representatives like François Euvé or Bishop Stenger hence emphasised that 'the *Sens Commun* are LR, not RN' and that '*Sens Commun* was clearly with François Fillon' and even RN general secretary Nicolas Bay conceded that 'the LR has been able to use *Sens Commun* to capture a part of the electorate of the *Manif pour tous*'.[60]

During the first round of the 2017 presidential elections 46 per cent of practising Catholics and 55 per cent of the most frequent churchgoers casted their vote for François Fillon, compared to only 20.1 per cent of the general population.[61] However, whilst these statistics demonstrated the LR's success in appealing to practising Christians, they also epitomised a new electoral dilemma for Catholics. For the result was insufficient to enable Fillon to enter the second round of the presidential elections, and was indicative of the centre-right's profound decline from France's historically dominant political movement to a party with little power perspective.[62] Indeed, rather than recovering from its poor showing advancing to become the main opposition party to Macron after the 2017 elections, the LR – afflicted by infighting and

---

[55] Du Cleuziou 2019; Du Cleuziou 2016a; Pruvot 2016; Saint Clair 2017; Schlegel 2015.
[56] Interview Wintzer 2019.
[57] Interview Enjalbert 2019.
[58] Bouthors 2016.
[59] Du Cleuziou 2019, 266.
[60] Interview Bay 2019.
[61] IFOP 2017a.
[62] Raynaud 2019; Richard 2017; Rougé 2018.

secessions – only scored 21.5 per cent in the parliamentary elections 2017 and fell to 8.5 per cent in the European elections in 2019. In the 2022 elections the LR's freefall continued even further with its candidate Valérie Pécresse, winning only 4.8 per cent of the vote. Though Précresse still overperformed among practising Catholics, 9 per cent of whom voted for her compared to just 2 per cent of irreligious French, this poor performance placed her only in fifth place behind both Zemmour and Le Pen and far off the prospect of qualifying for the second round.[63]

In France's structurally bipolar political system the centre-right's erosion poses a significant predicament for Catholic voters: being no longer numerous enough to sustain the LR as one of France's top two parties, many Catholics may feel increasingly forced to look at political alternatives.[64] However, unlike in Germany, where not only the centre-right but also the centre-left and Greens still appealed to Christian voters, a large part of the French centre-left historically defined itself in opposition to Catholicism (see Chapter 9). With the advance of secularisation and the re-politicisation of *laïcité*, this tendency only strengthened, thus reversing the efforts of François Mitterrand.[65] Interviewees such as LR MP Breton hence emphasised that 'it's clear that today there are far fewer Christian politicians in the left than at the end of the twentieth century, ... on the level of office holders this is quasi non-existent today'.[66] Former Socialist Education Minister Belkacem similarly confirmed the rise of 'a current towards a more radical *laïcité*' within her party,[67] while PS MP Dominique Potier acknowledged 'anti-Christian sentiments in parts of the left'.[68]

In light of the PS's humiliation in the 2017 presidential election and near annihilation in the subsequent European and presidential elections, when it received only 6 per cent and 1.7 per cent of the votes, respectively, one might think that its secularist current could be of lesser concern for French Catholics. However, the very erosion of the PS was linked to a development of much greater consequence for Catholic voters' political choice elsewhere. As Socialist MP Dominique Potier noted, the socialists' secularist current did not simply disappear: 'by contrast they rather joined the new *En Marche* movement'.[69] Given the emerging new electoral bipolarity

---

[63] IFOP 2022b.
[64] Feré 2017.
[65] Baubérot 2015; Bui and Le Bailly 2018.
[66] Interview Breton 2019.
[67] Interview Vallaud-Belkacem 2019.
[68] Interview Potier 2019.
[69] Interview Potier 2019.

between the LREM and the far right, a secularist turn of Macron's party under the influence of this influx might dampen its prospects of replacing the LR as Catholics' new political home and last alternative to the RN or Zemmour.

At the time of writing, such a development was no foregone conclusion. Indeed, many Christian leaders interviewed still expressed great hopes for Macron, referencing his upbeat remarks about religions' positive influence in society and hints at a more inclusive reading of *laïcité* during speeches to the Protestant and the Catholic leadership in 2018.[70] Bishop Matthieu Rougé emphasised that whilst 'the PS and LR are in a dire state, today there is this new emergence of the *En Marche* movement, in which there are also many Catholics'.[71] His colleagues at the Bishops Conference stressed that 'the last visit of the President to the Collège des Bernadins was seen as a historic moment where Catholics felt that "finally they recognise we exist"' (Archbishop Pascal Wintzer),[72] and that 'if we really want religion to have its structuring place in the social construction we must have a common project ... Macron's speech to the bishops at the Bernadins spoke in that sense' (Bishop Marc Stenger).[73] Protestant leaders were even more enthusiastic, with François Clavairoly claiming that 'Macron and his team have a great interest in religion. We have never had such a good dialogue with the state as under Macron.'[74]

Yet interviewees also reported that recent developments had gradually stifled many such hopes. One was the growing influence of the formerly socialist *laïcard* current within the LREM. Jean-Louis Bianco, the president of the observatory of *laïcité*, emphasised that although 'Emmanuel Macron had more liberal positions ... there was a strong *laïcard* influence around Emmanuel Valls [the former socialist Prime Minister] when he joined the LREM', and increasingly 'this tendency ... is detectable in the remarks of Jean-Michel Blanquer [Macron's Education Minister] to teach a secularist, republican catechism at school under the cover of civics classes'.[75] Jean-Pierre Delannoy, chaplain to the Assemblée Nationale, similarly observed that there is 'a fairly large group within *En Marche* who are former socialist MPs and very secularist'.[76] LREM politician Françoise

---

[70] Mongin 2018.
[71] Interview Rougé 2019.
[72] Interview Wintzer 2019.
[73] Interview Stenger 2019. For a detailed analysis of his Bernadin speech see Bourdin 2018, 67ff.
[74] Interview Clavairoly 2019.
[75] Interview Bianco 2019.
[76] Interview Delannoy 2019.

Dumas confirmed that in the debate 'between a more liberal Anglo-Saxon conception [of state–church relations] and a much more secular conception framed by the law of 1905, the president has now ruled: It's the law [of 1905] pure and hard.'[77] This shift was keenly felt among church leaders interviewed. In our interview, Bishop Rougé for example reported that in a recent conversation 'with someone from the Macron team, when I asked whether we will continue on the path developed in the president's speech at the Bernadins, his face hardened and he immediately said "No. We don't want any division anymore."'[78]

However, even more decisive in stifling Catholics' hopes for the LREM might have been the latter's increasingly libertarian positions on social issues, as it put forward a number of controversial law projects to liberalise embryo research, assisted suicide, surrogacy (GPA) and assisted reproductive technology (PMA) for gay couples.[79] The LREM also put severe pressure on those within the party who were opposed to such measures for religious reasons, excluding for instance Agnès Thill, the perhaps most vocal socially conservative voice in the LREM parliamentary group, from the party.[80] Delannoy confirmed this rift between Catholics and the LREM, explaining that 'most [LREM politicians] are rather sympathetic to the general ideal of contemporary individualism … and in such a perspective the question of ethics is non-existent'.[81] Matthieu Rougé similarly lamented that 'many young cabinet ministers don't have any link to the church anymore, which becomes clear over societal questions such as abortion or the PMA'.[82]

These developments have not yet stopped the LREM from becoming the main electoral beneficiary of the LR's decline, with Macron's party scoring 71 per cent among practising Catholics in the second round of the 2017 presidential election (compared to 65 per cent in the general population), 37 per cent in the 2019 European elections (compared to an overall score of 22.5 per cent) and 61 per cent in the second round of the 2022 presidential election (compared to 58 per cent in the general population).[83] Moreover, Macron sought to explicitly strengthen his appeal in conservative and

---

[77] Interview Dumas 2019. On 18 March 2019 Macron had buried his reform plans in favour of a more liberal *laïcité* in a widely publicised discussion with intellectuals (Bourmaud 2019; Corre 2019).
[78] Interview Rougé 2019.
[79] Favereau 2018; Gorce 2019; Priol 2019.
[80] Chazaud 2019; La Croix 2019.
[81] Interview Delannoy 2019.
[82] Interview Rougé 2019.
[83] IFOP 2019; IFOP 2017b.

Catholic circles, with the public defections of some centre-right heavy-weights such as Éric Woerth or Christian Estrosi to his campaign, reports that former conservative President Nicolas Sarkozy also supported Macron behind the scene, and by floating the idea in 2022 that he had been considering making centre-right politician and ECB president Christine Lagarde his next prime minister.[84] Yet, given the LREM's shift towards greater secularism and social libertarianism and with their traditional choice (the LR) in continued decline, an increasing number of Catholics seem to have begun to share Christophe Billan's 2017 perception of being left with a 'choice between the chaos of Marine Le Pen or the decay of Macron', or to consider casting their vote for Éric Zemmour.[85] Yet, the question to what extent Catholics really will turn to a right-wing populist candidate also depends on another set of supply-side actors: the institutional churches and their willingness to uphold the social taboo around the far right.

11.3   The Religious Supply Side: The Catholic Church between Internal Paralysis and the 'Benedict Option'

When in 2002 Jean-Marie Le Pen reached the second round of a presidential election for the first time, the Catholic Church's position could hardly have been clearer in its anti-far-right stance. Bishop Matthieu Rougé, at that time secretary to France's most senior cleric Cardinal Jean-Marie Lustiger, described the situation during our interview: 'the success of Jean-Marie Le Pen came as a great shock … [W]e immediately had all the bishops issue press releases, and a great public engagement of the bishops against the FN, in particular from Cardinal Lustiger who strongly opposed Jean-Marie Le Pen.'[86] The Conference of Bishops quickly issued a common statement urging Catholics not to vote FN and to remember that 'in the current period we must use our intelligence rather than instinct, our discernment rather than spontaneity, our serenity rather than fear'.[87] This intervention was remarkable, given that *laïcité*, as the former president of the United Protestant Church Laurent Schlumberger put it, usually ensured 'a high level of discretion from the churches on politics … [T]o say for example what Bedford-Strohm says in Germany that "the AfD is no alternative for Christians" … would be understood as a political incursion

---

[84] Lair 2022; Nouvel Observateur 2022.
[85] Pruvot 2017.
[86] Interview Rougé 2019.
[87] Lesegretain 2017; Ricard 2002.

by the church in France.'[88] Yet, for decades France's bishops had made the far right a noteworthy exception to this rule. With repeated interventions, warning Catholics that the FN's positions were 'incompatible with the gospel and the teaching of the church' (Cardinal Decourtray), individual clergy denying FN politicians the holy sacraments, priests refusing to baptise Jean-Marie Le Pen's granddaughter and ubiquitous sermons against the FN and their positions, the institutional church appeared committed to maintaining a strong social taboo against the FN.[89] As in Germany, scholars argued that this taboo was a key explanatory variable for Catholics' religious immunity to the far right, with Réné Remond emphasising in 2002 that 'the Church constitutes a barrage to the influence of the FN; its decline is one of the main causes for the rise of the FN'.[90]

Fifteen years later, the position of the church's leaders in the face of another Le Pen in the run-off of the presidential election once again attracted public attention. However, this time it was not because of the bishops' clarity, but because of the lack thereof. Unlike in 2002 and in contrast to their Protestant, Muslim and Jewish colleagues, in 2017 the Catholic hierarchy decided not to give any voting instructions against the FN, but simply referred voters to 'their own discernment'.[91] This decision, which bishops repeated in 2022, crowned a gradual process of demobilisation in the church's position vis-à-vis the FN/RN since 2012.[92] On the one hand, decision-makers interviewed reported that the church had become less outspoken in its condemnation of the RN, with the then RN general secretary Nicolas Bay proclaiming, 'we can say today that we hardly hear bishops making such statements anymore'.[93] Moreover, incidents such as Marion Maréchal-Le Pen's invitation by Bishop Dominique Rey to speak at his diocese's summer academy in 2015 appeared to put an end to the church's traditional cordon sanitaire around the RN.[94] As Maréchal-Le Pen herself put it, 'my invitation by Bishop Rey was a bit of a first in recent political history because prior to that the church had largely kept its distance from our movement'.[95]

What had led to this apparent reversal of the church's public stance towards the RN and what were its political consequences? The findings from

[88] Interview Schlumberger 2019.
[89] Interview Collard 2019; interview de Guillebon 2019; Senneville 2015.
[90] Tincq 2017.
[91] Ribadeau Dumas 2017.
[92] Le Normand 2022.
[93] Interview Bay 2019.
[94] Du Cleuziou 2016b; L'Express 2015; Tincq 2015.
[95] Interview Maréchal-Le Pen 2019.

the interviews suggest that it was not a result of a fundamental change of attitude within the institutional church. To be sure some clerics interviewed warned that 'Maurrassianism is resurging in parts of the clergy' (Jacque Enjalbert) or that the church remained silent because of the perceived '*dédiabolisation* of the RN' and 'the incapacity nowadays to support anyone at all' (Archbishop Dominique Lebrun).[96] Still, when asked for their own view, Catholic leaders were united in their rejection of the far right and confirmed that this remained the overwhelming view within the church. Archbishop Lebrun of Rouen for instance asserted that 'in the RN's positions there is a certain egoism that compatible with the Gospel' and that 'the RN is a party that has not understood that salvation is universal'.[97] Bishop Rougé stressed that 'the RN is still also a neo-pagan and atheist right, and it is also a highly secularised working-class right – even some sort of a revisited communism, all of which has no affinity with Catholicism at all'.[98] Archbishop Wintzer further confirmed that such views were overwhelmingly shared: 'overall the activists of the far right know very well that the bishops of France are not favourable towards them. ... That's why their rhetoric is so very anti-episcopal.'[99] And even Bishop Rey sought to relativise his invitation of Marion Maréchal-Le Pen, stressing that 'there is no relationship between the far right and the church: I invited Marion Maréchal-Le Pen, but I also invited a representative from the radical left the following year'.[100]

Instead, most interviewees pleaded pragmatic reasons for the toning down of their public opposition to the far right, such as the perceived futility of the tabooisation strategy, and the wish not to divide the Catholic community. Bishop Stenger for instance explained that 'I have the impression that many of my colleagues are very afraid of taking a stance too publicly ... there is still the fear of separation within the Catholic community'.[101] Bishop Rougé stressed the 'Catholic hierarchy's declining capacity to influence' adding that 'at the time of Lustiger and the bishops' communiqué in 2002, these things still had great influence, but if bishops had tried to forbid Catholics to vote for Marine Le Pen in 2017 this just wouldn't have had any influence'.[102] Similarly, LR politician Xavier Breton explained that 'the difference [between 2002 and 2017] is a logical

[96] Interview Enjalbert 2019; interview Lebrun 2019.
[97] Interview Lebrun 2019.
[98] Interview Rougé 2019.
[99] Interview Wintzer 2019.
[100] Interview Rey 2019.
[101] Interview Stenger 2019.
[102] Interview Rougé 2019.

evolution in the context of the *dédiabolisation* of the FN in society: the church has realised that the *dédiabolisation* does not work'.[103] Interestingly the interviewees among whom this argument was most popular were far-right politicians themselves. Nicholas Bay thus linked the fact that 'there is less of a taboo around us than before … to our electoral weight. If you score 10 per cent of the vote, people can treat you like a marginal party, but if you get into the second round of the presidential election and rally one-third of the French population, the marginalisation strategy becomes unsustainable'.[104] Gilbert Collard concurred, explaining the shift of the bishops' position with 'just more conformism: they have realised that a part of their faithful don't follow them anymore – that's all'.[105]

Yet, two factors suggest that pragmatic reasons alone are not the whole truth and that the church might be not quite as powerless as such statements suggest. The first are reports of strong grassroots opposition to the bishops' new conciliatory position, which – in line with this research's earlier findings on the demand side – cast doubts on the proclaimed identitarian and far-right pressure from the Catholic base. Archbishop Lebrun, for instance, described how he 'faced protests because I had invited the author Laurent Dandrieu [who is close to the far right on issues such as immigration]',[106] while Matthieu Rougé spoke of a significant 'commotion' in 2017 with 'many people who told me that they regretted that the bishops had not taken a clear position [against the far right]'.[107] And indeed, many prominent Catholic lay organisations, media outlets and individual bishops explicitly diverted from the Bishops' Conference's public position by issuing their own appeals to Catholics to vote against the populist right.[108] Grégoire Catta, who in 2017 had been working with the Jesuit *Revue* magazine, described how

> in a great cooperation with La Croix and a large number of Catholic lay organisations we made a special issue of *Revue Project*, which was distributed to over 80,000 readers. The idea was to help think about the far right between the two rounds between Macron and Marine Le Pen and we took a very clear position saying that not all votes are possible if one is Catholic.[109]

[103] Interview Breton 2019.
[104] Interview Bay 2019.
[105] Interview Collard 2019.
[106] Interview Lebrun 2019.
[107] Interview Rougé 2019.
[108] Catta et al. 2016; Coq et al. 2017; Vaillant 2017.
[109] Interview Catta 2019. The appeal was supported by a large array of major Catholic lay organisations including representatives of Caritas France, the Scouts of France, the Catholic Press, the Jesuits and the Semaines sociales. Projet Revue 2016.

Dominique Quinio, the former editor-in-chief of France's largest Catholic newspaper *La Croix*, similarly emphasised that its anti-RN stance was 'about the only subject on which the newspaper took a firm stand during the elections'.[110]

The second indicators are observations that the church's traditional tabooisation attempts against the populist right actually still had significant impacts on the Catholic electorate. Jean-Louis Bianco, former socialist minister and subsequent president of the government's *laïcité* observatory, emphasised that 'among practising Catholics the public statements of the church and the sermons of the priest at Sunday Mass saying "let us help the poor, let us help our immigrant brethren" have a huge impact on the faithful ... I believe that this creates a formidable barrier of protection [against the far right].'[111] These claims are substantiated by quantitative data showing not only a continuously strong correlation between relative immunity to the populist right and religious *practice*, but also an explicit 'institution' or 'Pope Francis effect', effectively working to attenuate Catholics' sympathies with the right-wing populist positions.[112] Geisser thus claims that 'the Catholic Church maintains its role as a "guide of conscience" ... in terms of openness to the world and to cultural and religious otherness'.[113]

However, perhaps the most revealing indicators for the strategy's continued effectiveness were the testimonies of far-right politicians themselves. For instance, Marion Maréchal-Le Pen reported that 'the social taboo around the RN continues to exist in parts of the population and in particular amongst Catholics'.[114] And Gilbert Collard, the RN MP who later became a prominent figure in Éric Zemmour's campaign specifically singled out the role of the bishops and of social pressure saying, 'Look at the clergy we have: in my experience I've met a lot of priests and Catholics who are not even that hostile to us but are subjected to the bishop and afraid of criticism. It's conformism: they have demonised us and it has worked.'[115] These indicators, combined with the fact that the bishops themselves still admitted the 'doubtless influence of clergy' (Archbishop Dominque Lebrun) and the fact that 'the taboo might have evolved but it's certainly still there' (Bishop Matthieu Rougé), suggest that pragmatic

[110] Interview Quinio 2019.
[111] Interview Bianco 2019.
[112] IFOP 2019; IFOP 2017a; Teinturier, Doridot, and Vacas 2021; Geisser 2018.
[113] Geisser 2018, 12; More in Common 2018.
[114] Interview Maréchal-Le Pen 2019.
[115] Interview Collard 2019.

reasons or ecclesial impotence are not the only reasons for the shift in the church's public stance.[116] Rather the church's rhetorical demobilisation vis-à-vis the far right appeared driven by an internal re-conceptualisation of its own relationship with politics and society.

In fact, the interviews revealed a broader mentality shift within the Catholic hierarchy: *en lieu* of a vision of a broad national church, senior clergy appeared increasingly to embrace an ideal more akin to what Rod Dreher called 'the Benedict option', in which the church embraces its minority position and seeks to save the Christian community by distancing it from secular politics and society.[117] Bishop Matthieu Rougé for instance asserted that 'today the question of our relation to politics is rather secondary in the priorities of the church. Today we are rather mobilised on the advance of faith', stressing that this is primarily a result of 'our marginalisation in society ... with parishes made fragile and a church that has entered into a minority phase'.[118] Bishop Dominique Rey echoed such interpretations, emphasising that 'today the church's voice in politics is much more delicate ... because the place of the church in society has evolved: fifty years ago Catholics were still a majority ... today there is a profound separation between Christian values and political values in general'.[119]

However, whilst the reasons for the church's re-conceptualisation might have been primarily demographic, social, theological or personal, its consequences were highly political. Indeed, rather than being an inevitable consequence of the far right's *dédiabolisation* and the religious immunity's erosion, the church's own policy shift might have inadvertently contributed to these developments in the first place, by putting a self-imposed end to the church's public opposition to the populist right. Bishop Stenger made this dynamic explicit when he explained that the new 'spiritual reconstruction does not express itself through the confrontation with the far right, but on the contrary through a spirituality that can make space for everyone [including those sharing extremist views]. It's really a loss of the political dimension of religion.'[120] This shift towards a more apolitical 'Benedictine' mentality contributed to the erosion of religious immunity in two crucial ways. First, directly, by discouraging clergy from using their position of authority to openly criticise the RN, thus giving Catholics the

---

[116] Interview Lebrun 2019; interview Rougé 2019.
[117] Dreher 2017; Fourquet 2018a; Roy 2019.
[118] Interview Rougé 2019.
[119] Interview Rey 2019.
[120] Interview Stenger 2019.

impression that the latter was indeed *dédiabolisé*.[121] And second, indirectly, by further separating religion and politics, and thus implicitly undermining the church's moral authority in political issues in general. This risk was highlighted by Bishop Stenger who emphasised that 'one of my hypotheses for why the taboo [around the FN] is blowing up is that religion is increasingly being privatised; it's becoming a private thing that does not interact anymore with the development in society ... so more and more Christians feel able to separate their conscience from the gospel during the elections'.[122] The result has been a growing normative vacuum that has created new opportunities for pro-far-right voices in the Catholic sphere and undermined traditional inhibitions. This effect has been importantly compounded in the 2022 campaign by the decision of several prominent Catholic lay leaders and politicians to publicly support Éric Zemmour. Thus, Jean-Frédéric Poisson, president of VIA (formerly Parti Chrétien-Démocrate) officially announced his support for Zemmour in 2021 at the same time as prominent *Sens Commun* leaders like Laurence Trochu and Sébastien Pillard, who had formerly been associated with the centre-right LR (Pillard even became Zemmour's official campaign spokesman in 2022).[123] While representing a minority among Catholic lay leaders and politicians, the defection of these formerly centre-right Catholic politicians is critical because they epitomise the erosion of the traditional taboo around the far right in some conservative Catholic milieus, but also because they are likely to further undermine it by setting an important public precedent for others. Critically in this context, the church's silence makes it easier for such figures to present themselves as representative of Catholicism writ large, thereby normalising support for the far right, while contributing to further secularisation of Catholic symbols and identity through their dissociation from Catholic doctrine and institutions.

Certainly, it is important not to overemphasise the church's influence in halting such a process. As we have seen, the social taboo around the RN began to erode in other strata of society much earlier and quite

---

[121] Archbishop Wintzer and Archbishop Lebrun epitomised this shift when they doubted their own earlier decisions to publicly speak out against the RN. Archbishop Lebrun hence emphasised that 'I publicly said when I arrived as the Bishop of Saint-Denis ... that I wouldn't vote either communist or FN ... but I think today that I was perhaps a bit harsh in my statement', whereas Archbishop Wintzer declared that 'I don't know whether I was right' because 'even just doing it as a private person is a form of exercising pressure – Is this my role as a bishop?' This logic was also recognised in Bishop Rey's statement when he responded to the question of why more and more Catholics are now voting for the RN that 'we try less to tell believers what to vote for or what not to vote for'.
[122] Interview Stenger 2019.
[123] Du Cleuziou and Boucaud-Victoire 2021.

independently of the position of the church.[124] We have equally seen that, given the church's internal crisis, external marginalisation and general trends towards secularisation, religious institutions' sway amongst their members is in continuous decline.[125] Nonetheless, the findings of this section suggest that the public behaviour of church authorities can still play a critical role, either by maintaining the social taboo around the far right and thereby slowing down the process of *dédiabolisation*, or, on the contrary, by abandoning their public opposition, which in turn might lead to a self-accelerating process whereby the church's refusal to uphold the taboo encourages more Catholics to publicly support the far right, which in turn further discourages senior clerics to speak up publicly against the RN or Zemmour.

11.4   Conclusion

Taken together the analyses of Part III enable us to reconsider questions about the origins of the far right's rise in France, its use of religious references in the context of *laïcité* and the reactions of Christian communities' mainstream parties and church leaders in a new light. Chapter 8 has shown that the hard-fought and fragile compromise of *Catho-laïcité* that had been established after two centuries of social and political conflict between *la France Catholique* and *Republique Laïque*, has recently been challenged by a return of political tensions surrounding religion and *laïcité*. Chapter 9 revealed that this re-politicisation was not linked to a revival of Catholicism but, on the contrary, to the emergence of a new identity cleavage in French society, partly rooted in France's rapid secularisation and Catholicism's demise. Under the pressure of this new identity divide between cosmopolitans and communitarians, France's political system has undergone a fundamental transformation leading to a new bipolarity between the liberal-cosmopolitan camp of Macron's LREM and the populist-communitarian camp around the RN and Éric Zemmour. Chapter 10 demonstrated how in the context of this transformation the French far right rediscovered religion and *laïcité* as political wedge-issues and cultural identity markers against Islam. However, instead of a rapprochement with Christian policy positions, ethics and institutions, Chapter 10 revealed clashes with the church over policy, the populist right's identitarian conception of

---

[124] Mayer, Crépon and Dézé 2015; Perrineau 2014.
[125] Du Cleuziou 2019; Fourquet 2018a; Portier 2016.

Christendom and it secularist reading of *laïcité*, all of which suggested a further secularisation of Christian symbols in the hands of the populist right rather than a Catholic revival in French politics. Finally, Chapter 11 showed that these discrepancies notwithstanding, Catholics' traditional religious immunity to the far right has begun to erode in recent years. Whilst this development chronologically coincided with the emergence of the conservative Catholic movement around the *Manif pour tous*, the analysed evidence suggests that Catholics' electoral opening towards the far right was primarily driven by political and religious supply-side factors. In particular, the narrowing of electoral alternatives for Catholics and the softening of the bishops' language against the far right, in the context of the church's gradual shift from a politically engaged national church, towards a more inward-looking minority church, have all contributed to the relative *dédiabolisation* of the RN and Zemmour amongst Catholics.

Returning in the light of these findings to the RN's 1st of May demonstrations in honour of Joan of Arc, it might seem less surprising that a formerly neo-pagan movement was parading through the streets of Paris in veneration of a Catholic saint whilst elsewhere calling for a stricter separation of politics and religion in the name of *laïcité*. After all, both the RN's embrace of *laïcité* and its references to Christianity were primarily motivated by an identitarian fight against Islam. Still, even more revealing of the future relationship between the far right and Catholicism than the decade-long existence of these marches may have been the way in which they were abandoned. Rather than yielding to earlier criticisms from church officials, Marine Le Pen cancelled the demonstrations in 2015 just when the church's rhetoric became more accommodating; simply because the embrace of *laïcité* now seemed the more modern and coherent cultural identifier of secular France. This development suggests that the retreat from politics by the church is unlikely to significantly influence the far right's attitudes towards religion. However, it may well further reduce the church's still sizeable sway over its flock and encourage more and more French Christians to follow the example of some of their brethren in the USA, who, as we shall see in part IV, had become some of the most loyal defenders of the USA's perhaps most openly irreligious president to date.

PART IV

A Faustian Bargain?
American Christianity and Trumpism

Tens of thousands had congregated on the National Mall in Washington, DC on the afternoon 6 January 2021. Some participants had brought oversized crosses, others staged sit-in prayers or waved 'Jesus Saves Flags'. Christian rock was blaring loudly from their speakers as the crowd keenly awaited their leader to address them. This leader was no popular evangelist nor a megachurch pastor, but the outgoing US President, Donald J. Trump, who had called on his supporters to gather in Washington, DC to protest against his electoral defeat a month earlier.[1] In his speech to the crowd, Trump repeated his unfounded claims that the election was 'rigged' and 'stolen', and encouraged attendees to march on the US Capitol, where Congress was in the process of certifying the election results. By the time he stepped down from the podium, the sound of Christian rock had been replaced by chants of 'Fight for Trump' and 'Hang Mike Pence'.[2] Shortly afterwards the crowd took President Trump by his word and stormed the US Capitol. Killing several policemen and threatening lawmakers, the rioters sowed death and destruction at the very heart of American democracy.

Just four years earlier Donald Trump had been inaugurated on Capitol Hill after defeating fifteen established Republican competitors and the then long-hailed Democratic favourite, Hillary Clinton.[3] From the outset and throughout his presidency, Trump and his campaign displayed all the anti-elitist, nativist and identitarian hallmarks of right-wing populist politics present in Western Europe.[4] Notably he also displayed a highly ambiguous relationship with religion.

---

[1] Green 2021.
[2] Pence was Trump's vice president, who presided over the proceedings in Congress and refused the president's request to block the certification of Trump's defeat (something he also had no constitutional right to).
[3] Alberta 2019; MacWilliams 2016; Sides, Tesler and Vavreck 2017; Wolff 2018; Woodward 2019.
[4] Bonikowski 2019; Goodheart 2018.

Although, as a former pro-choice Democrat and thrice-divorced New York real-estate tycoon Trump was an unlikely champion of religious conservatives, he had overtly courted faith voters. In addition to adding religious elements to rallies, he had picked Evangelical stalwart Mike Pence as his vice president, appointed several pro-life judges to the Supreme Court and promised to protect religious freedom and defend 'America's Christian heritage'.[5] During the BLM protests in the summer of 2020 Trump also prominently posed with a Bible in front of St John's Church in Washington, DC after having instructed the National Guard to use tear gas and batons to clear his path through the peaceful protesters.[6]

This strategy seemed to pay off as over 80 per cent of white Evangelicals, and majorities of white Mainline Protestants and Catholics, voted for him at the 2016 and 2020 presidential elections.[7] Given this overwhelming electoral support as well as the prominence of Christian symbols at the Capitol riots and other Trump rallies, many observers have concluded that religious voters and 'white Christian nationalism' formed the base of Trump's national populist revolt and that his election was a direct continuation of the historical 'culture war' between secular progressives and religious conservatives in the USA.[8]

However, several indicators suggest that an interpretation of Trumpism as a movement primarily driven by religious fervour may be premature. For instance, despite the record number of white Evangelicals supporting Trump in the general election, survey data revealed that the same Evangelicals had also perceived him to be the least religious GOP candidate in recent history, and during the 2016 Republican primaries, Trump actually did best among those voters who indicated to never attend church, whereas he performed worst among frequent churchgoers.[9] Moreover, large parts of the otherwise conservative Evangelical establishment had openly spoken out against Trump, calling him 'an awful candidate', Christians' support for him a 'scandal and a disgrace' (Russell Moore), and some would go on to demand his removal from office during the 2019 impeachment process.[10]

---

[5] Fea 2018; Gorski 2019b; Trump 2016; Washington Post 2017.
[6] Bennett et al. 2020.
[7] Smith and Martinez 2016.
[8] Alberta 2017; Jones 2016; Kidd 2019; Norris and Inglehart 2019; Whitehead, Perry and Baker 2018.
[9] Carney 2019; Ekins 2018; Pew 2016b; Smith and Martinez 2016.
[10] Alexander 2016; Beyerlein and Ryan 2018; Crouch 2016; Economist 2018; Galli 2019; Showalter 2016.

These contradictory indicators invite a closer examination of the relationship between Trump-style national populism (or 'Trumpism') and America's Christian communities. In a by now familiar structure, the US case study (Chapters 12–15) explores the demand-side origins of the remaking of America's party landscape and of the rise of Trump's right-wing populist platform; how the Trump campaign has approached religion on the supply side; how this differed from traditional appeals to Christianity in American politics; how Christian communities reacted; and what the role of elite actors such as the Democratic and Republican establishment and Christian faith leaders was. Finally, we raise the question of what these developments mean for the future of religion in America's new social and political constellation.

In response to these questions, Part IV proceeds in four steps. First, Chapter 12 sets out the historical and institutional context, focusing on how the institutional separation of state and church through the First Amendment evolved into the compromise of 'American civil religion',[11] and on how this compromise has been challenged from the religious right, the secularist left and most recently by the populist right. Chapter 13 then explores how the emergence of a new identity cleavage on the demand side, itself partly linked to the rapid decline of American Christianity, has shifted American politics away from the old faith-driven culture wars, towards a new more secular and race-driven identity politics. Chapter 14 analyses how in the context of this new brand of right-wing identity politics Trump's use of religion was not only at odds with America's civil religious tradition but also represented a radicalisation and secularisation of America's tradition of white Christian nationalism. Finally, Chapter 15 looks at the reactions of America's Christian communities, noting the apparent absence (or even reversal) of the 'religious vaccination effect' that has been observed in Europe, as well as the choice of many Christian leaders to remain silent vis-à-vis their criticism of Trump. Overall, the American case study explores the possibility that rather than being a victory for the Christian right, Trump's ascent to power may be indicative of the former's crisis and decline, and of the rise of a post-religious identitarian right in its stead. However, due to structural factors undermining American faith leaders' willingness and ability to challenge right-wing

---

[11] Civil religion is here defined as the religiously inspired but non-sectarian creed of common values that undergirds American politics and identity (Bellah 1967; Gorski 2019b; Squiers 2018; Weed and Heyking 2010).

populism, many American Christians have chosen to strike what some observers have called a 'Faustian bargain' and to support right-wing populist politics at much higher rates than their European brethren. To appreciate the extent to which recent dynamics between Trumpist populism and Christian communities constitute both continuities and important breaks in the relationship between politics and religion in the USA, it is crucial to first consider this relationship's historical and institutional background.

CHAPTER 12

'A Nation under God'?
American Civil Religion between the Wall of Separation and Christian Nationalism

One can witness an instance of the mixture of politics and religion in America on the first Thursday of February every year in the Hilton Hotel's Ballroom in Washington, DC: on that morning the social, political, economic and religious elite of the country – including the US president, his cabinet, leaders of Congress and high-ranking international guests – gather to contemplate scripture and pray together at the National Prayer Breakfast.[1] An institution like the Prayer Breakfast might appear surprising in a nation in which state–church relations are supposedly governed by a 'wall of separation'.[2] Yet, along with the pledge of allegiance to 'one nation under God', the swearing of office oaths on the Bible, legislative prayers and the slogan 'in God we Trust' printed on the US dollar, the National Prayer Breakfast is just one of many examples of America's civil religious tradition. It is a concept that denotes the idea that American politics and identity are based on a religiously inspired but non-sectarian creed of common values and symbols.[3] This chapter investigates the historical, institutional and conceptual genesis of American civil religion, its relationship with religious pluralism and Christian nationalism, and the challenges it has encountered in recent decades, culminating in the emergence of the new identity cleavage and the rise of a post-religious populist right in American politics.

---

[1] Founded in 1953, it is hosted each year by two senators and two members of the House of Representatives (one Democrat and one Republican for each chamber) and remains a highlight in America's social and political calendar (Lindsay 2007; Sharlet 2008; Johnson 2012; Lienesch 2019).
[2] Dreisbach 2002; Soper, Dulk and Monsma 2017; Sorauf 2015.
[3] Gorski 2019a; Bellah 1967.

12.1   The Institutional Settlement of the First Amendment:
Between Pluralism and Christian Nationalism

'French *laïcité* was designed to protect the State from the Church. By contrast the American wall of separation was designed to protect the Church from the State.' This statement by former French ambassador to the USA Gérard Araud during a Harvard lecture in 2016 encapsulates a key difference between the two nominally secular French and American republics and points to the centrality religion has held within the United States since its founding.[4] Scholars like Gorski have shown that historically the First Amendment's disestablishment clause was less preoccupied with separating the secular nation from religious influences than with reconciling two competing but constitutive parts of what would become American civil religion: on the one hand a 'covenant narrative' of America as a chosen Christian nation, and on the other hand an 'exodus narrative' of America as the country of religious refugees, tolerance and pluralism.[5] As Gorski and others (like Sam Perry and Andrew Whitehead) have shown, in their extreme form, the 'covenant' and 'exodus' narratives could turn into incompatible concepts of white Christian nationalism and radical secularism, respectively.[6] Yet, in more moderate forms, both are important components of America's civil religious tradition to this day.

Both narratives were present since the arrival of the first European settlers in America. Thus, many of those who arrived as religious refugees from the established churches in Europe interpreted their plight as an 'exodus' from religious persecution and intolerance, akin to Moses' and the Israelites' flight from Egypt. Yet, at the same time, like the Israelites, they also perceived themselves as part of a new 'covenant' with God, in which America was to become a Christian utopian 'New Canaan'.[7] Throughout the colonial period potential tension between the two ideals of religious tolerance and religious nationalism remained muted by a Protestant focus on the individual's rather than society's relationship with God and the political reality of being subjected to British colonial rule.[8] However, after the War of Independence, as the founding fathers considered how to organise the new republic, the question of whether it was to have an established

[4] Araud 2016.
[5] Gorski 2019a; Gorski 2020; Murphy 2001; Nussbaum 2008; Skillen 2020.
[6] Gorski 2019a; Whitehead and Perry 2020; Gorski and Perry 2022.
[7] Gorski 2019a; Murphy 2001; Skillen 2020; Wald and Calhoun-Brown 2014.
[8] Wills 1990.

church, and which church it should be, rapidly came to the fore, and with it tensions between religious pluralism and the concept of America as a Christian nation.[9]

At first glance, the disestablishment clause seemed to favour the exodus narrative of religious freedom. This was partly because for many founding fathers the separation of state and church on the federal level appeared to be the only way to avoid sectarian strife and conflict between states in an already religiously pluralistic country.[10] However, in contrast to French *laïcité*, the First Amendment was never meant as a wholehearted endorsement of secularism, let alone as an attempt to ban religion from the public sphere. On the contrary, the covenant ideal of America as a Christian nation always remained central to the founders' vision of the new republic, which was not only to be a political 'New Rome' but also a religious 'New Jerusalem'.[11] As a result, the founding fathers set out to establish a concept of pro-religious but pan-denominational 'civil religion', which in its intent resembled more the German system of benevolent neutrality than British 'state religion' or French *laïcité*.[12] However, unlike the authors of the *Grundgesetz*, the authors of the US constitution were convinced that 'true' religion could best prosper if it was freed from the stifling influence of the state and could operate in a comparatively unregulated religious marketplace.[13]

By allowing new innovative religious entrepreneurs to challenge traditional churches and to transform the religious landscape, this model laid the fundaments for what Nathan Hatch has called the 'democratization of American religion'.[14] Proponents of religious economic theory have argued that, as a result of this settlement, religious life in America was much more diverse, flexible and able to adapt to changing circumstances than the hierarchical and often state-controlled religious landscape of the old world.[15] However, in the eighteenth century American civil religion was also still decidedly Protestant, and often served as a source for white Christian nationalism.[16] Kaufmann for instance has pointed out that up until the

---

[9] Hamburger 2009; Wald and Calhoun-Brown 2014; Wills 1990.
[10] Though the fact that on the state level many of the new commonwealths did establish their own state religions, and often continued to do so until the mid-nineteenth century, demonstrates the limitations of this philosophical commitment to religious pluralism (Wills 1990).
[11] Gorski 2019a; McDougall 1997; Preston 2012.
[12] Bellah 1967; Gorski 2019a; Tocqueville 1990.
[13] Cousins 1958; Finke 1990.
[14] Hatch 1989.
[15] Stark and Iannaccone 1994.
[16] Casanova 2012a; Jones 1992; Kaufmann 2018.

mid-twentieth century, 'the "W-A-S-P"[17] trinity of white appearance, unaccented English, a British or Dutch surname, and Protestant religion' formed the 'ethnic boundary markers' of what it meant to be American.[18]

In the early years of the republic, such limitations caused little political tension, because in 1776, 98 per cent of America's free population was made up of White Protestants, and over 80 per cent were of British descent.[19] However, by the middle of the nineteenth century, when many Catholics and Jews had started to arrive, tensions rose as it became clear that, just as American democracy provided unparalleled levels of political participation for white males while excluding black slaves, Native Americans and women, American civil religion allowed for religious tolerance for Anglo-Saxon Protestants of different denominations, but not for other faith traditions.[20]

As a result, throughout the late nineteenth century religion was re-politicised in two important ways: first through what Casanova called 'a renewed Protestant crusade to Christianise the Republic' by way of social reform; a movement fuelled by the 'Second Great Awakening', which sought to prophetically hold America to the moral standards of covenant narrative and inspired the anti-slavery, temperance and women's suffrage movements.[21] The second manner of re-politicisation came by the rise of anti-Catholic 'Anglo-American nativism', epitomised by the rise of the proto-populist 'American People's' and 'Know-Nothing' parties.[22] The latter trend contributed to further segregation and discrimination against Jews and Catholics, who, as Casanova points out, were painted as 'a radical threat to Christian America, to the Democratic Republic and to modern civilisation',[23] demonstrating the early limitations of American civil religion. In fact, it was only after 1945 that American civil religion was fundamentally reframed to include Catholics, Jews and eventually black Christians and Americans of other faiths in 'one nation under God'.

12.2   The Expansion of American Civil Religion after World War II

The roots behind civil religion's post-WWII expansion included theological developments in Mainline Protestantism, lower immigration levels and

---

[17] 'White-Anglo-Saxon-Protestant'.
[18] Kaufmann 2018, 34; Smith 1991.
[19] Kaufmann 2018, 32.
[20] Kaufmann 2018.
[21] McLoughlin 2013; Billington 1939; Casanova 2012a.
[22] Kaufmann 2018.
[23] Casanova 2012a, 489.

the steady social integration and upward mobility of many second- and third-generation Catholics and Jews.[24] However, perhaps the most important trigger was the geopolitical context of WWII and the Cold War. As Gorski put it,

> The struggle against fascism and then communism gave birth to both a new 'them' and a new 'us'. The new 'them' was a 'secular' or 'political religion', that was, 'paganistic', fascist and 'Godless' qua ersatz religions. The new 'us' consisted of Protestants, Catholics, and Jews, or, more broadly still, those under the Judeo-Christian tradition.[25]

Building on this new 'us', during the post-WWII period President Eisenhower – though not a particularly avid churchgoer himself, but cognisant of the potential of civil religion as a source for national unity – added the words 'under God' to the pledge of allegiance in 1954, inscribed 'in God We Trust' on American currency in 1956 and supported the foundation of the National Prayer Breakfast in 1953.[26] Unlike the Protestant civil religion of the nineteenth century, the post-WWII civil religion was kept explicitly inclusive and non-sectarian. As Eisenhower himself famously phrased it, 'Our form of government has no sense unless it is founded in a deeply felt religious faith, and I don't care what it is.'[27]

This did not mean that post-war civil religion was void of religious substance, however. Rather it sought to reconcile and expand the exodus and covenant narratives by promoting a ceremonial deism, emphasising pan-Christian religious themes and conferring quasi-sacred status to documents and personalities such as the US Constitution, the Declaration of Independence, the Bill of Rights and the founding fathers.[28] It also reinforced the 'deep-rooted belief in American culture that political and personal virtue should be inseparable' and emphasised that the new 'American creed' still clearly embraced 'Judeo-Christian values'.[29] Putnam and Campbell have stressed that the subsequent 'high tide of Civil Religion' in the 1950s transcended religious, as well as partisan divides as worship

---

[24] Gorski 2019a; Kaufmann 2018; Putnam and Campbell 2012.
[25] Gorski 2019a, 170.
[26] Bellah 1992; Putnam and Campbell 2012.
[27] Given these very visible expressions of the expansion of civil religion it was perhaps no coincidence that the sociological concept of 'American civil religion' was now for the first time theorised and distinguished from traditional Protestantism as America's 'founding myth' and the 'religious dimension, … through which it [the American people] interprets its historical experience in the light of transcendent reality' (Bellah 1975, 8; 1967).
[28] Gorski 2019a; Lienesch 2019; Squiers 2018.
[29] Sennett 1987, 42.

attendance and affiliation 'skyrocketed' across all religious denominations and as 'Republicans and Democrats, liberals and conservatives were all equally represented among those in the pews'.[30] Hence, the post-WWII brand of civil religion largely succeeded in reconciling America's new political and demographic realities with its religious founding myths. Importantly, it also provided a cultural and political rallying point as well as a source of prophetic criticism for the nation.[31]

Examples of civil religion's integrative function range from the invocation of civil religious discourse at national ceremonies such as state funerals and presidential inaugurations, to countless invocations of civil religion by American presidents and other political and social leaders.[32] Meanwhile, civil religion's potential as prophetic critic of politics, which had been evident during the anti-slavery and women's suffrage movements, resurfaced most prominently in the Civil Rights movement.[33] Gorski, for instance, points out that the civil religious rhetoric of Martin Luther King Jr accounted for much of the Civil Rights movement's ability to bring 'together a diverse coalition of social reformers that bridged long-standing divides of race and religion, as well as the growing chasm between religious and secular worldviews'.[34]

Such positive views of civil religion's potentials were also voiced by American religious and political leaders who were interviewed for this book. US Senate Chaplain Barry Black, for instance, emphasised that in US politics the 'dichotomy between the sacred and the secular is artificial. You bring your spirituality with you, and it will affect your political views, even as Martin Luther King's spirituality affected the Civil Rights movement.'[35] Others like Archbishop Allen-Henry Vigneron, the vice president of the United States Conference of Catholic Bishops, emphasised that without its Judeo-Christian civil religion, 'the country would be a very different place. From my own perspective I don't know that the civil order we have can be maintained by a postmodern set of convictions.'[36] Galen Carey, vice president of Government Relations for the National Association of Evangelicals (NAE), emphasised the Christian churches' 'role as witnesses' and the 'fundamental' importance of America's 'pluralistic environment',[37] and then

[30] Putnam and Campbell 2012, 83–85.
[31] Gorski 2019a; Putnam and Campbell 2012; Wald and Calhoun-Brown 2014, 55.
[32] Bellah 1992; Cristi 2006; Wald and Calhoun-Brown 2014, 54.
[33] Braunstein 2017; Marsh 2008; Smith 2014.
[34] Gorski 2019a, 156.
[35] Interview Black 2020.
[36] Interview Vigneron 2019.
[37] Interview Carey 2020.

president of the Mainline Protestant National Council of Churches, Jim Winkler, summarised that 'the state should not attempt to control the church and the church should not attempt to control the state, but the church should speak truth to the state'.[38]

Moreover, this positive assessment of the civil religious compromise was not limited to faith leaders. Democratic and Republican representatives equally testified to civil religion's continued importance. For instance, former Republican speaker of the House Paul Ryan related that

> Our system of government and the moral vision that created it is encapsulated in the Declaration of Independence and codified in our constitution. It is an expression of natural rights and natural law that derives from Christianity, but it's also a system that believes in pluralism.[39]

Meanwhile Barack Obama's faith advisor, Michael Wear, stressed that 'our Christian history isn't history. It's still a central part of the narrative of our story.'[40] Both Republicans and Democrats, moreover, praised specifically civil religion's integrative ability. Former Republican Congressman and National Prayer Breakfast co-host Randy Hultgren, for example, explained that civil religious institutions allowed politicians 'to build friendships, build relationships, to talk about faith journeys across the aisle',[41] while Democratic Congressman Thomas Suozzi stated that he was 'very concerned' about the weakening of religious institutions as sources of 'common values', and called the Prayer Breakfast 'a very positive event, offering a shared journey that allows us to build trust and relationships across partisan divides'.[42] Yet, while these testimonies highlight the positive potential of civil religion to this day, it has been repeatedly challenged over the years.

12.3 Challenges to Civil Religion: The Culture Wars and the Religious Right

Some challenges to civil religion have come from Christian conservatives, and more recently from identitarian right-wing populists. However, civil religion's first post-war challenge arose neither from the religious nor from the populist right, but from an unlikely coalition of hippies and Supreme

---

[38] Interview Winkler 2019.
[39] Interview Ryan 2020.
[40] Interview Wear 2020.
[41] Interview Hultgren 2020.
[42] Interview Suozzi 2020.

Court justices in the middle of the twentieth century.[43] From the early 1940s onward, just when civil religion was becoming more inclusive, the US Supreme Court broke with 150 years of jurisprudence and embraced a more separationist interpretation of the First Amendment, turning it 'from one of the least-litigated provisions of the Constitution … to one of the most frequent topics of federal jurisprudence'.[44] Though driven by the wish to bolster religious freedom for minority faiths like Jehovah's Witnesses and Seventh-day Adventists, some scholars have argued that the shift towards enforcing 'a wall of separation' between state and church was perceived by many Americans as an anti-religious move that came 'without warning, and without immediate provocation by any development in American religious life' and was largely at odds with public opinion and the mood in Congress.[45]

The ensuing conflict over religion's place in society was exacerbated when the judiciary's and minority faiths' challenge to civil religion of the 1940s and 1950s was joined by the sociocultural revolution of the 1960s, which, according to Putnam and Campbell, 'presented a perfect storm for American institutions of all sorts – political, social, sexual and religious'.[46] Thus, as a separationist Supreme Court seemed to codify many of the protesters' demands, for example through their *Roe* vs *Wade* decision to de facto legalise abortion, many Americans became worried that 'almost overnight, it seemed, America had turned from God's country to a godless one'.[47] As a result, the cultural shock of the 1960s was soon followed by a conservative 'aftershock', which turned traditional moral cleavages into a 'culture war' that fundamentally threatened civil religion's integrative potential.[48] This aftershock was primarily (though not exclusively) concentrated around a reinvigoration of Evangelicalism in the 1970s and 1980s.

Evangelicalism itself had been part and parcel of the American experience since the seventeenth century and had repeatedly been demographically and spiritually renewed through the so-called religious 'Great Awakenings' of the eighteenth and nineteenth century.[49] Hunter even argues that in

---

[43] Beinart 2017; Campbell and Layman 2015; Putnam and Campbell 2012; Wilcox 2018.
[44] Wald and Calhoun-Brown 2014, 79. It now ruled, for instance, that the disestablishment clause and even Jefferson's private correspondence about 'a wall of separation between church and state' should apply not only to the federal but also to the state level (*Everson* vs *Board of Education*, 1947), and that there could be no more state-sponsored school prayer or devotional uses of the Bible in schools (*Engel* vs *Vitale*, 1962, *Abindton School District* vs *Schempp*, 1962).
[45] Powers 2010, 238; Elifson and Hadaway 1985; Wald and Calhoun-Brown 2014; Pacelle 2019.
[46] Putnam and Campbell 2012, 91.
[47] Putnam and Campbell 2012, 100.
[48] Green et al. 1996; Hunter 1992; Lipset and Rokkan 1990; Putnam and Campbell 2012.
[49] Kidd 2008; Joustra 2019.

the mid-1800s Evangelicalism was 'unquestionably predominant, not only in the religious life of America, but in the broader culture'.[50] Yet, in the early twentieth century many Evangelicals had retreated from politics and the public world after the fundamentalist–modernist controversy and the Scopes Monkey Trial over evolution, which was legally won by fundamentalists but led to their marginalisation in American public opinion.[51] It was only now after the end of the WWII that Evangelicals slowly re-emerged from this self-imposed retreat from politics and became determined to re-engage culturally, intellectually and politically with the world.[52]

Organised around the newly founded NAE, and the charismatic preacher Billy Graham, these 'neo-Evangelicals' were initially very supportive of the bipartisan and pan-denominational post-WWII civil religion, to which they sought to contribute their own prophetic voice.[53] However, this non-partisan approach was soon challenged, when, throughout the 1970s and 1980s, conservative Evangelical leaders such as Pat Robertson and Jerry Falwell drew on the backlash among religious, cultural and political conservatives against the 1960s cultural revolution to create the 'religious right'.[54] Institutionalised in the form of Falwell's 'Moral Majority' and Robertson's 'Christian Coalition', the religious right was open to trading political allegiance in return for policy commitments. In turn Wilcox has described how the Republican Party quickly realised 'that fundamentalists and other Evangelicals might be induced to become more involved in politics and that it might be possible to mould that political action into support of Republican candidates'.[55] The result was an increasingly symbiotic relationship between the GOP and white Evangelicals, who, although primarily concerned about religious freedom and sexual morality, became closely associated with right-wing politics more broadly.[56] While the new coalition was highly successful politically, sweeping Ronald Reagan into the White House, providing Republicans with decades of congressional dominance and culminating in the election of self-identified Evangelical George W. Bush to the presidency in 2001, it came at the cost of undermining civil religion's bipartisan appeal. The culture wars pitted secular against

---

[50] Hunter 1983, 24.
[51] Fea 2018; Wilcox 2018.
[52] Kidd 2019, 75.
[53] Joustra 2019; Kidd 2019; Lindsay 2007.
[54] Fea 2018; Kidd 2019; Putnam and Campbell 2012, 120; Wilcox 2018.
[55] Wilcox 2018, 61.
[56] Fea 2018; Olsen 2017; Putnam and Campbell 2012; Wilcox 2018.

religious Americans along party lines and created an electoral 'God gap' between 'God's Own Party' and the Democrats.[57]

Moreover, the re-politicisation of religion through the culture wars of the 1960s and 1970s also soon contributed to what Putnam and Campbell describe as the 'second aftershock', namely the unprecedented rise of secularist sentiment from the 1980s.[58] Campbell, Green and Layman emphasise that opposition to the GOP–Christian right coalition has driven an important minority of religious 'nones' to embrace 'an affirmative secular identity and positive commitment to secular principles'.[59] The rise of this constituency further undermined civil religion, not only because the latter's integrative and prophetic functions largely relied on the fact that historically almost all Americans had identified with a religion or at least held religious institutions in high esteem,[60] but also because it put into question civil religion's core institutions such as public displays of religious symbols, ceremonial deism and the paramount importance accorded to religious freedom.[61] This view was shared among observers interviewed for this study, such as the former president of the American Enterprise Institute (AEI) Arthur Brooks, who claimed that 'over the past several decades, the First Amendment has been applied more and more in a way that is antagonistic towards religion',[62] or Barack Obama's former faith advisor, Joshua Dubois, who described an 'overreaching among some progressives seeking not just to have a different opinion on issues, but to communicate to Christians that their opinion has no place in the public square at all'.[63]

Whilst Chapter 14 discusses how the new secularist constituency has reshaped the Democratic Party's platform in particular, growing secularism also exacerbated the culture wars in the minds of many conservative Christians by creating a sentiment of fear and being under siege.[64] During our interview former Republican Governor of Kansas and then

---

[57] Claassen 2015; Putnam and Campbell 2012; Sullivan 2008.
[58] Putnam and Campbell 2012.
[59] Campbell et al. 2018, 551; Campbell, Layman and Green 2020.
[60] Historically, even among religious 'nones', only a tiny minority self-identify as atheists and in 2010 almost half of them believed in God (Pew 2016a).
[61] The National Prayer Breakfast epitomises some of these trends. In 2020 it took place under the shadow of a secularist outcry in the context of the culture wars after a number of books and a documentary series had depicted it as a conspiratorial weapon of the religious right to undermine American democracy (Fea 2019; Sharlet 2008).
[62] Interview Brooks 2019.
[63] Interview DuBois 2020.
[64] Claiborne et al. 2018; Fea 2018; Kidd 2019.

Ambassador at Large for Religious Freedom Sam Brownback argued, for instance, that 'we used to have a pretty homogenous culture in the United States ..., but now there's a very clear opposition between a post-Christian view and a Judeo-Christian view'.[65] Christopher Demuth, another former AEI president, and later co-organiser of the National Conservatism conference, stated that Christians 'fear that the secular world is closing in on them and not giving Christians and Jews the sort of respect that in American life has traditionally been given to minorities'.[66] Republican Congressman Doug Collins even spoke of an 'an attack on faith in the country'.[67] Numerous interviewees from both sides of the political aisle emphasised that such fears have contributed to an important shift in priorities from religious to identitarian issues among some conservatives, making them more attune to national populist appeals. As Conservative commentator Henry Olsen put it, for many of those who felt under attack from the secular left, it was increasingly less about the traditional culture war issues such as sexual morality or religious freedom and more about identitarian issues. Olsen suggests that there is 'something about saying "I'm a Christian", that is reassuring and matters to them, even if it does not find itself in the expression of caring about the independence of "my church" etc. It may be something as simple as Trump's talk about the war on Christmas.'[68]

The next chapter explores the rise of such identitarian fears in more detail and looks into how Donald Trump has sought to capitalise on them through a new brand of right-wing identity politics. However, the ways in which this new politics has impacted America's civil religious tradition were also perceivable at the 2020 National Prayer Breakfast. Whilst the event still showcased civil religion's integrative potential, by bringing together bitter rivals like Donald Trump, Democratic Speaker of the House Nancy Pelosi and Democratic House majority leader Chuck Schumer in one room on the very day after a historic vote to impeach the president had failed, Trump's own speech exemplified an important shift in American politics. Rather than employing the civil religious tones his predecessors used to bridge divides and to conjure shared values, Trump used the event to present himself as the defender of the pure and virtuous people against a cosmopolitan elite, whom he described as 'very dishonest

---

[65] Interview Brownback 2020.
[66] Interview DeMuth 2020.
[67] Interview Collins 2020.
[68] Interview Olsen.

and corrupt people [who] have done everything possible to destroy us, and by so doing, very badly hurt our nation'.[69] America's civil religion, rooted in the exodus and covenant narratives of America's founding, appeared undermined by a populist and identitarian rhetoric, which seemed less reflective of America's old religious culture wars than of a new social divide between liberal cosmopolitans and populist communitarians reminiscent of secular Europe.[70]

[69] Gerson 2020.
[70] Betz 1994; De Wilde et al. 2019; Kaufmann 2018.

CHAPTER 13

The New Social Cleavage
From Religious Culture Wars to White Identity Politics

'During the Bush years European observers saw American politics as pro-foundly alien. By 2016 it was to become thoroughly familiar.'[1] This statement from political scientist Eric Kaufmann points to a long-standing assumption that for decades the persistence of religiously fuelled culture wars had made American politics inherently different from that of secular Europe.[2] Thus, American politics in the late twentieth and early twenty-first centuries still focused on the moral cleavage and its wedge-issues of abortion, gay marriage and religious freedom. By contrast, identitarian core issues around immigration or the role of Islam, which had become major dividing lines in Europe since the 1980s, continued for a long time to be comparatively less controversial in the USA.[3] Kaufmann draws a connection between these two developments when he argues that, since the 'religious right was universalist, not white nationalist', and 'pitted the faithful of all races and religions against seculars and moderates ... religious issues took precedence over immigration in the public mind'.[4] This assessment has been echoed by sociologist of religion José Casanova, who argued that, 'due to the general pro-religious attitudes dominant in the United States as well as to the weakness of secularism as anti-religious ideology', concerns about Islamist terrorism after 9/11 'failed to develop into a general ideological discourse against Islam as a religion'.[5] As a result, 'xenophobic anti-Muslim nativism has been much weaker in the United States than in Europe'.[6]

By 2016, however, all this seemed to have changed. Donald Trump had won the American presidency on a platform that only made cursory remarks about abortion, gay marriage or religious freedom, and instead

---

[1] Kaufmann 2018, 88.
[2] Casanova 1994; Cesari 2007; Kaufmann 2018; Norris and Inglehart 2011; Pollack and Rosta 2017.
[3] Betz 1994; Green et al. 1996; Bornschier 2010; Putnam and Campbell 2012; Fowler 2018.
[4] Kaufmann 2018, 85, 78; Beinart 2017; Hunter 1992.
[5] Casanova 2012a, 493.
[6] Casanova 2012a, 493, 485; Cesari 2007; Leonard 2003; Strum and Tarantolo 2003; Bilici 2011.

focussed on 'building a wall' against immigrants, issuing a 'Muslim ban' and monitoring American mosques.[7] Indeed, research by Sides and others has shown that attitudes related to immigration, race and identity were more salient in 2016 than in any previous election,[8] and that 'issues like immigration, race, and Islam were central not only to Trump's election but also [had] become core to his presidency'.[9] American politics it seemed had gotten a European taste.

Much ink has been spilled seeking to understand this shift. Some scholars have argued that Donald Trump's surprise election victory was a cultural backlash of religious traditionalists who felt under threat or was simply the true face of America's tradition of white Christian nationalism.[10] Others have interpreted it as a long-term consequence of economic dislocation and rising inequality following the 2008 financial crisis.[11] Both accounts offer important insights. However, this chapter looks more closely at findings such as Sides's and examines the possibility that the root causes of this shift often ran deeper than the traditional moral or economic cleavages alone. Instead, it investigates the extent to which the apparent 'Europeanisation' of American politics and the shift towards a white identity politics on the political right may have been less related to the resurgence of religious culture wars than to the emergence of a new social cleavage around the question of identity, which appears partly linked to rapid secularisation of American society itself.

13.1   Falling from Grace: The Crisis of American Civil Society and the Rise of a New Identity Cleavage

'The secularisation of America gave us Trump.'[12] Political scientist Tim Carney's claim might appear surprising given the historical vitality of American religion, the traditional alliance between the GOP and the religious right, and Trump's overwhelming support from white Evangelicals.[13] Yet, several indicators suggest that there may be validity in Carney's claim. Thus, while for most of the twentieth century America was characterised by remarkably high and stable rates of religiosity, surveys show that by the

---

[7] Sides, Tesler and Vavreck 2019.
[8] Sides 2017, 3.
[9] Sides, Tesler and Vavreck 2019, 202.
[10] Guth 2019; Norris and Inglehart 2019; Whitehead and Perry 2020.
[11] Finger 2017; Judis 2016; McQuarrie 2016; Piketty 2015.
[12] Carney 2019, 233.
[13] Norris and Inglehart 2019; Whitehead and Perry 2020.

end of the 2010s this had begun to change dramatically. The GSS and the Pew Religious Landscape Survey, for example, both found that while the percentage of American Christians had remained relatively stable at around 90 per cent until the 1990s, it has since experienced a rapid decline to only 65 per cent in 2019.[14] These values are not just close to the rates of religious affiliation in many Western European countries, but also mean that Protestants, traditionally the dominant religious group in the USA, lost almost a third of their share in the population (down from 61 per cent in the 1990s to 43 per cent by 2019), and became a minority for the first time in US history.[15] By contrast the share of religious 'nones' – only 8 per cent of the population in the 1990s – more than tripled and by 2019 had bypassed Catholicism, whose share had fallen from 27 per cent to 20 per cent in the same timeframe, to become the second largest 'religious group' in the country. Indicators of practice such as church attendance were still disproportionately high by Western standards. Yet they, too, showed signs of decline, as the proportion of weekly churchgoers sank from 37 per cent to 31 per cent in the decade from 2009 to 2019, while the proportion of Americans who never attend church jumped from 11 per cent to 17 per cent.[16]

These trends coincided with a profound institutional, financial and reputational crisis of American Christianity.[17] Chaves, for instance, notes that America's churches have been facing overwhelming difficulties in terms of membership and finances, and that clergy 'have lost ground in recent decades when it comes to reputation, social prominence, and attractiveness as a career choice for young people'.[18] Indeed, Gallup polls show that whereas in the 1980s 65 per cent of Americans still said they had 'a great deal' or 'quite a lot' of trust in organised religion, only 37 per cent said so in 2021.[19] Echoing such findings, prominent Pastor John Dickerson has written about a 'great Evangelical recession',[20] and during our interview Mark Tooley, president of the Institute on Religion and Democracy, reported the 'erosion of institutions in the Evangelical community' emphasising that 'the older religious hierarchies are almost entirely gone and the great denominational agencies and bureaucracies have almost been erased'.[21]

---

[14] Pew 2019a; T. W. Smith et al. 2019; Pew 2018.
[15] Pew 2019a.
[16] Pew 2019a.
[17] Carney 2019; Chaves 2011; Dickerson 2013; Levin 2020; Norris and Inglehart 2011; Putnam 2016.
[18] Chaves 2011, 87.
[19] Brenan 2021.
[20] Dickerson 2013.
[21] Interview Tooley 2020.

Alongside other major demographic trends such as rapid ethnic change, broader individualisation and mechanisation of working-class jobs, this sharp decline of American Christianity has contributed to a shift in politics in two important ways. First, by weakening the religious right and decreasing the salience of traditional culture-war issues. Thus, numerous scholars and insiders have described the profound demographic, organisational, financial and even spiritual crisis of the Christian right. Historians of Evangelicalism such as Kidd and Fea speak of 'a movement in crisis' that is driven by fear.[22] Others like Moreton or Dickerson observed drops in donations and significant staff layoffs.[23] And during our interview, Russell Moore, then president of the Southern Baptist Convention's Ethics and Religious Liberty Commission, stated that 'the old Christian rate is diminishing very quickly because it's not reproducing itself'.[24] This loss of organisational weight was echoed within the population writ large through the decreasing prominence of and polarisation around issues such as abortion, gay marriage and religious freedom as well as through greater scepticism about religious actors' role in American public life.[25] For instance, the share of Americans who think that churches or other religious institutions have little or nothing at all to contribute to solving social problems has almost doubled from 21 percent in 2001 to 39 percent in 2016.[26] In fact, 63 percent of Americans would now prefer that religious figures stay out of political matters all together (up from 49 percent in 2016).[27] As a result, some observers announced 'the coming end of the American Culture War'.[28] Yet while the view that a more secular politics may be a desirable antidote to populism, nationalism, extremism and religious bigotry appears to have become more popular, and while cross-carrying Capitol rioters seem to be making secularists' case for them, there are several indicators suggesting that rapid secularisation has thus far failed to produce an any less virulent, aggressive or polarised political culture. Rather, the second way in which Christianity's decline seems to have reshaped American politics was by fuelling a crisis of group identity and belonging, which like in many European countries, has paved the way for a new identity cleavage and a subsequent surge in identitarian right-wing populism in American politics.[29]

[22] Kidd 2019.
[23] Dickerson 2013; Moreton 2015.
[24] Interview R. Moore 2021.
[25] Pew 2017a; Campbell and Putnam 2011; Pew 2017b.
[26] Street et al. 2016; G. A. Smith et al. 2019.
[27] G. A. Smith et al. 2019.
[28] Teixeira 2009.
[29] Beinart 2017; Teixeira 2009.

This crisis of identity has been particularly pronounced within the white working class, a demographic that had already been severely impacted by some of the negative side-effects of globalisation, individualisation, de-industrialisation and immigration.[30] The rapid erosion of religious institutions and belonging seems to have further alienated these voters. Thus, Wilcox, Campbell and Putnam highlight that the decline of religious practice was not only much sharper among working-class Americans than among their white-collar compatriots,[31] but also that the least- and moderately educated Americans had been 'especially likely to benefit from the social support and civic skills associated with religious institutions'.[32] This is mainly due to religious communities' traditional role as a cost-free provider of social capital in America's working-class communities. Putnam for instance has shown that 'nearly half of all associational membership in America is church-related, half of all personal philanthropy is religious in character and half of all volunteering occurs in a religious context'.[33] Without this resource secularisation may, thus, confront white working-class communities with even steeper declines of social connectedness, employment, marital stability and cultural conservatism, leading many to feel like 'strangers in their own land', as sociologist Ari Hochschild put it.[34] Tim Carney even argues that 'the woes of the white working-class are best understood not by looking at the idled factories but by looking at the empty churches'.[35]

Scholars have long shown that socially alienated and atomised communities are often more susceptible to nationalist reactions.[36] The fate of America's secularised white working class seems to confirm this hypothesis. Thus, political scientist Francis Fukuyama argues that within this group the erosion of traditional identities has produced a 'crisis of identity [that] leads in the opposite direction from expressive individualism, [namely] to the search for a common identity that will rebuild the individual to a social group and re-establish a clear moral horizon. This psychological trend lays the groundwork for nationalism.'[37] This development is contrasted by an embrace of individualistic and cosmopolitan values by Americans with

---

[30] Case and Deaton 2020; Eatwell and Goodwin 2018; Fukuyama 2018; Hochschild 2018; Kaufmann 2018.
[31] As Robert Putnam pointedly put it, 'If you listen carefully, hymns in American houses of worship are increasingly sung in upper-class accents' (Campbell and Putnam 2011, 253).
[32] Wilcox et al. 2012, 125.
[33] Putnam 2000, 66.
[34] Hochschild 2018; Campbell and Putnam 2011; Cherlin 2011; Cherlin 2010; Wilcox et al. 2012; Sandel 2020.
[35] Carney 2019, 122.
[36] Arendt 1973; Hariri 2017; Holmes 1995; Norris and Inglehart 2019.
[37] Fukuyama 2018, 56.

high levels of social capital, education and mobility.[38] The result has been a growing social divide between an increasingly cosmopolitan part of the population, which embraced and profited from the erosion of communal ties, and a communitarian camp, which suffered from these developments and resorted to national and ethnic identity as alternative forms of collective belonging. These are familiar characteristics of the new identity cleavage, which has reshaped European politics since the 1990s, and which pits 'cosmopolitans' against 'communitarians', 'globalists' against 'nationalist', and 'anywheres' against 'somewhere'.[39]

Like in Europe, this new identity cleavage has manifested itself in US politics primarily through increased polarisation around identitarian wedge-issues like immigration and Islam.[40] The American National Election Study, for instance, has shown that after decades where white Republicans and Democrats were only 2 to 5 percentage points apart on their views of immigration, this gap had widened to 12 per cent in 2012 and to 48 per cent by 2016.[41] Scholars also observed a marked increase in Islamophobic sentiment and the emergence of 'serious partisan cleavages' around how Americans feel towards Islam, with 'Democrats moving toward more favourable attitudes, Republicans moving toward less favourable attitudes.'[42] These trends seem to confirm observers like Beinart when they argue that after decades of religious culture wars progressives' assertion that the 'new secularism would ease cultural conflict, as the country settled into a near-consensus … was naïve'. Instead, Beinart suggested that 'as Americans have left organized religion, they haven't stopped viewing politics as a struggle between "us" and "them". Many have come to define "us" and "them" in even more primal and irreconcilable ways.'[43]

13.2   The Rise of Identity Politics on the Political Supply Side

The rise of Donald Trump on a radical, populist and identitarian platform seems to confirm this hypothesis on the political supply side. His unorthodox 2016 electoral campaign, which turned Democrats' 'blue wall' of white

---

[38] Fukuyama 2018; Kaufmann 2018.
[39] De Wilde et al. 2019; Fourquet 2019; Goodhart 2017; Piketty 2020; Sobolewska and Ford 2020; Levin 2020; Sandel 2020.
[40] Brubaker 2017; Hamid and Dar 2017; Sides, Tesler and Vavreck 2019.
[41] Some 69 per cent of white Republicans now favoured limitations to immigration whereas only 21 per cent of white Democrats agreed. Kaufmann 2018, 113.
[42] Sides 2017, 3, 5; Hamid 2019; Hamid and Dar 2017; Sides, Tesler and Vavreck 2019; Wajahat 2011.
[43] Beinart 2017.

working-class voters into a red sea of Trump support, did so primarily by tapping into identitarian and demographic fears and by focusing on identitarian issues like building 'a wall' against immigrants and enacting a 'Muslim ban'. Pete Wehner, a senior official in three Republican White Houses, emphasised this shift when during our interview he explained that Trump's success has not only 'been more a question of cultural identity rather than faith' but also that

> It was not economic dislocation and anxiety that explained Trump's popularity among whites. It was the idea of lost cultural power and privilege: that feeling that for demographic and other reasons, ... the country is changing. And Trump particularly tapped into this because he played anti-Muslim and anti-immigrant cards so often.[44]

On the Democratic side, President Obama's senior adviser, Joshua Dubois, concurred, stressing that the Trump base's 'overarching ethos is that "we are losing our place in society and we need to fight to reclaim it"'.[45] Meanwhile John Carr, the director of the Department of Justice, Peace, and Human Development at the USCCB, stressed the importance of polarisation around identity when stressing that 'the people who identify themselves as citizens of the world, drive others to say "That's not me ... if that group is for globalisation ... then I'm for nationalism."'[46]

Yet strikingly, the interviewees who made the drivers underlying the new identity cleavage most explicit were those who identified with the national populist movement itself. Republican congressman and Trump confidant Doug Collins, for instance, voiced the resentment of blue-collar Americans at 'being lectured that they will have to become more diverse' as well as their wish to 'stand up for who they are'.[47] Michaël Modrikamen, the Managing Director of Steve Bannon's national populist 'The Movement' organisation, explained the new cleavage to be a divide between 'a globalist vision of a universalist world, where everyone is replaceable, there are no

---

[44] Interview Wehner 2019.
[45] Among religious observers, John Carr, the director of the Department of Justice, Peace, and Human Development at the USCCB, emphasised the dynamics between the new divide's two sides, claiming that 'the people who identify themselves as citizens of the world, drive others to say "That's not me ... if that group is for globalisation ... then I'm for nationalism."' Similarly, Francis Maier, from the Catholic Archdiocese of Philadelphia explained that 'the irony is that the same people who revile Donald Trump in places like the *New York Times* made him unavoidable by their arrogance and behaviours' and that his supporters 'want to feel like they have a home, they want to feel grounded'. Meanwhile Evangelical Gordon College President, Michael Lindsay summarised, '[these voters] are pro-military, they love the flag, they are nostalgic for an era of greater American sensitivity. It's not a cosmopolitan approach. It's a populist approach.'
[46] Interview Carr 2019.
[47] Interview Collins 2020.

borders, everything can mix, and the political financial and educated elites profit' on the one hand, and, on the other hand, 'the common people, who are forgotten by globalism. ... It is economic but also about culture and identity.'[48] This view was echoed by Rusty Reno, the editor-in-chief of *First Things* magazine and co-organiser of the National Conservatism conference who argued that 'Populism is a rejection against that utopianism of a world without borders', and emphasised the role of secularisation in this development, claiming that it is the 'disappearance of this shared [Christian] identity oriented toward the transcendent that drives people towards populism: No father at home, no father in heaven and then all you have left is the political community to shelter you.'[49]

While earlier Republican candidates like Nixon, Reagan or Wallace also tapped into the potential of white working-class voters, Trump's appeal to these 'forgotten men and women' was particularly strong. This can partially be explained by the fact that in the run-up to 2016, both Democrats and mainstream Republicans seemed to have largely failed to represent the new social cleavage.[50] Some commentators and scholars suggest that the Democratic Party, in particular, had not just failed to represent communitarians' cultural concerns, but that many of its twenty-first-century policy shifts, and specifically its embrace of left-wing identity politics, actually further aggravated them.[51] Indeed, empirical studies have shown a fundamental refashioning of the Democratic 'base' away from working-class union voters and Catholics towards a new coalition of affluent, highly educated whites on the one hand and racial minorities on the other.[52] Observers like Thomas Frank have argued that, because since the 1980s the Democratic Party has increasingly abandoned its communitarian instincts and focus on class solidarity in favour a 'liberalism of the rich', this is built on the principles of competitive individualism, meritocracy and a new brand of identity politics.[53] Another self-identified liberal commentator,

---

[48] Interview Modrikamen 2019.

[49] Interview Reno 2019.

[50] While sources of this divide had been growing for decades, and signs of communitarian identitarian concerns had manifested themselves politically in the candidacies of Pat Buchanan or Ross Perot as well as in the context of the Tea Party movement, this did not lastingly change both parties' convergence on a cosmopolitan, pro-globalisation and pro-migration 'Washington consensus' in relation to the new identity cleavage (Braunstein and Taylor 2017; Burghard 2010; Formisano 2012; Jones and Cox 2010; Stanley 2012).

[51] Eatwell and Goodwin 2018; Frank 2005; Fukuyama 2018; Haidt 2012; Kaufmann 2018; Lilla 2018; Sides, Tesler and Vavreck 2019.

[52] Abramowitz 2018; García Bedolla and Haynie 2013.

[53] Frank 2005; Sandel 2020.

Mark Lilla, has claimed that the Democratic Party 'has slipped into a kind of moral panic about racial, gender and sexual identity that has distorted liberalism's message and prevented it from becoming a unifying force capable of governing'.[54] Meanwhile political scientist Eric Kaufmann has claimed that this 'left-modernism' identity politics was in turn based on a 'new moral order', in which the antagonist was no longer the business elite, but 'white ethno-racial oppression' and 'the image of the retrograde white "other"'.[55] Fukuyama even stated that because left-wing identity politics has 'only tended to legitimise certain identities, while ignoring or denigrating others, such as European (i.e. white) ethnicity', it has alienated many white working-class voters and thus 'stimulated the rise of identity politics on the right'.[56]

This book does not seek to discuss the merits of and justifications for left-wing identity politics, which are manifold, but seeks to understand how it interacts with right-wing identity politics. And during the interviews with religious and political elites conducted for this research, many explicitly echoed Fukuyama's hypothesis that by politicising the social cleavage around identity left-wing and right-wing identity, politics made each other more salient. For instance, former AEI president Arthur Brooks stressed that 'the identity politicians and identity politics of both sides are making each other stronger',[57] while Rusty Reno from *First Things* argued that 'the alt-right fills the vacuum left by multiculturalism and an increasingly marginal Christianity. ... It's a reverse reaction to identity politics. Whites ask: "why can't I have my own identity politics If everybody else can?"'[58] This analysis was not limited to conservative commentators. Progressive leaders such as former Obama White House official Joshua DuBois similarly recognised a tendency among parts of the left to 'overstate their numbers ... suggesting that if the party can mobilise every person of colour, progressive woman and member of the LGBT community, we'll have enough to win'.[59] DuBois's former colleague in the Obama campaign and advisor to dozens of Democratic presidential, senatorial and gubernatorial campaigns Eric Sapp similarly reported a significant shift in tone with the rise of 'liberal rich, educated elites among Democratic staffers who support the idea of a "majority minority country", where "we

---

[54] Lilla 2018.
[55] Kaufmann 2018, 3.
[56] Fukuyama 2018, 117.
[57] Interview Brooks 2019.
[58] Interview Reno 2019.
[59] Interview Sapp 2019.

don't need white people anymore"'.[60] And even Democratic Congressman Thomas Suozzi voiced his concern that 'we used to be the blue-collar working people's party, but Trump has done a good job of talking about "the politically correct Democrats" and saying to these people, "I hear you as white blue-collar rural workers, and the fact that you're concerned."'[61]

These findings suggest that the Democratic Party's shift towards 'left-wing identity politics' has not just further politicised the identity cleavage, but also broadened a gap of representation among Democrats' traditional working-class constituency.[62] As former White House official Michael Wear noted, this shift has led to 'an environment where left-wing and right-wing identity politics fuel one another in a vicious cycle' and where white working-class voters looked for a new champion – and found one in Donald Trump.[63]

13.3 'A Hostile Takeover'? Trumpist Populism and the GOP in the 2016 Presidential Election

It was, however, by no means a foregone conclusion that a Republican candidate would be able to tap into communitarians' concerns. In fact, for most of the late twentieth and early twenty-first centuries the GOP was no natural home for white working-class voters. Rather, Republicans' traditional 'three-legged stool' of a neo-conservative emphasis on strong defence, a neo-liberal focus on limited government and a social con-servative embrace of traditional family values, remained largely at odds with a demographic that was becoming increasingly anti-globalist, pro-government intervention and less religious.[64] As conservative analyst Henry Olsen put it in our interview,

> The best way to understand these blue-collar voters is that they don't want competition from foreigners at home, which is immigration, and they don't want competition from foreigners abroad, this is trade … but they don't want to be on a religious crusade either. These voters did not like George W. Bush. They did not move in his direction. It's why there was a blue wall in the early 2000s.[65]

This discord between communitarians and the GOP was intensified by the latter's post-2012 attempts to come terms with recent demographic and

---

[60] Interview Sapp 2019.
[61] Interview Suozzi 2020.
[62] Sides, Tesler and Vavreck 2019, 167.
[63] Interview Wear 2020.
[64] Finger 2017; Goodhart 2017; Norris and Inglehart 2019; Olsen 2017; Olsen and Scala 2016.
[65] Interview Olsen 2020.

cultural changes through the 'Growth and Opportunity Project Report' (commonly known as the 'Autopsy'). In this report, leaders of the Republican National Committee had called for the party to 'campaign among Hispanic, black, Asian and gay Americans' and specifically to 'embrace and champion comprehensive immigration reform'.[66] Recognising that many minority voters were at odds with parts of the new Democratic agenda (specifically its move towards a more radical secularism; see Chapter 15), the report put special emphasis on the old culture war cleavage and on faith as a shared point of reference between the GOP's core constituency of white Evangelicals and minority groups. As Republican Congressman Francis Rooney explained in our interview, 'the idea was to change the Republican Party into a party that is more focused on diversifying its membership, in particular by using faith to unite immigrants and Latinos'.[67]

Initially, the line-up of 2016 Republican primary candidates provided optimism for this strategy: the long-hailed favourite, Jeb Bush, was ideationally close to his brother George W.'s faith-driven compassionate conservatism as well as a Catholic convert, married to a Hispanic wife, fluent in Spanish and had won Hispanic majorities in his home state of Florida.[68] His two main rivals, Ted Cruz and Marco Rubio, presented themselves as devout Christians of Hispanic descent and all three had campaigned on a platform of comprehensive immigration reform.[69] However, in spite of the 'autopsy's' recommendations, by the end of 2016 the GOP had been reshaped in the opposite direction.

Donald Trump, who had opened his campaign with a speech describing undocumented Mexican immigrants as 'rapists' and 'murderers', followed by a call for a 'Muslim ban' and refusals to condemn the racist Ku Klux Klan, won the GOP primaries and was elected president.[70] His platform constituted a radical break from traditional conservatism and was recognised as such by Republican officials.[71] Former Republican Governor of Kansas, Sam Brownback for instance described Trump's victory as 'a hostile takeover of the party' and Republican Congressman Andy Hultgren emphasised that 'among my [Republican] friends in Congress and beyond there were many people who said, I could never support him.'[72] In 2016

---

[66] Barbour et al. 2013, 6, 8.
[67] Interview Rooney 2020.
[68] Alberta 2019; Coppins 2015; Olsen 2017; Sides, Tesler and Vavreck 2019.
[69] Alberta 2019; Sides, Tesler and Vavreck 2019.
[70] Holley 2016; Washington Post 2015.
[71] Barber and Pope 2019a; Coppins 2015; Olsen 2017.
[72] Interview Brownback 2020; interview Hultgren 2020.

Republican Speaker of the House, Paul Ryan stressed that 'I didn't see it coming in the beginning: I didn't think he was going to win because I didn't think people support that.'[73] And Ryan's chief of staff, Jonathan Burks summarised that

> Donald Trump's attachment to the Republican Party was marginal, and so the idea that he was going to win the nomination was certainly a surprise, especially for a party that was conservative and that had approached 2016 very much taking the view of the autopsy about how the party needed to become more inclusive, especially of Hispanic minorities. The president adopted a very different strategy.[74]

Rather than appealing to traditional conservative core issues around economic cleavages or religious culture wars to create a multi-racial coalition, Trump and his team explicitly sought to tap into the demand created by the identity cleavage, with a pronounced departure in tone and content from other Republican campaigns.[75] Paul Ryan described this difference in tone as follows:

> It was that people saw Mitt Romney and me as polite men who play by the rules of decorum and debate … and people were sick of losing with what they thought were good and godly men – they wanted an apex predator, they wanted a fighter, they wanted a junkyard scrapper who was going to attack all this political correctness.[76]

In terms of content, the key figure in the Trump campaign's move from the GOP's traditional emphasis on religious culture wars and laissez-faire economics towards a more European right-wing populist-style identity politics was Steve Bannon.[77] Intellectually influenced less by William Buckley, Milton Friedman or George Will than by European ethno-nationalist writers such as Charles Maurras, Jean Raspail and Alain de Benoist, Bannon and the new generation of campaigners around him explicitly identified themselves and the Trump campaign as 'national populist'.[78] Bannon also drew rhetorical and institutional connections between Trumpism and the European populist right (including the RN and the AfD) through the creation of transnational populist organisations such as the 'Academy of the Judeo-Christian West' or 'The Movement'.[79] This 'Europeanisation' of

---

[73] Interview Ryan 2020.
[74] Interview Burks 2019.
[75] Abramowitz 2018; Alberta 2019; Bonikowski 2019; Sides, Tesler and Vavreck 2019.
[76] Interview Ryan 2020.
[77] Abramowitz 2018; Kaufmann 2018; Sides, Tesler and Vavreck 2019.
[78] Crowley 2017; Green 2017; Haynes 2017; Wolff 2018; Rose 2021.
[79] Baume and Borellie 2019; Horowitz 2018; Keohane 2018.

the American right under Bannon and Trump manifested itself in terms of policies through a focus on identitarian and civilisational issues, such as immigration and national identity, as well as through a markedly different approach to religion.[80] This became especially clear in the context of Islam. Whereas George W. Bush had sought to integrate Islam into American civil religion and the Tea Party had a Muslim constituency, the Trump campaign followed European right-wing populists' tendencies to reconceptualise Islam as the 'external other' and as an 'enemy ideology'.[81] Sides for instance has shown that Islam had unprecedented salience in the 2016 election, while Brubaker observed a rhetorical shift on the American right from 'nationalism to "civilisationism"', driven by the notion of a civilisational threat from Islam'.[82] Occasionally, the Trump campaign's rhetoric even picked up on Western European national populists' tendencies to present themselves as defenders of liberal values against Islam. Trump for instance stated that 'radical Islam is anti-woman, anti-gay and anti-American. I refuse to allow America to become a place where gay people, Christian people, Jewish people are targets of persecution and intimation by radical Islamic preachers.'[83] Such rhetoric is remarkable given the relatively low levels of Muslim immigration in the USA, their successful integration into society and Republicans' traditionally critical positions vis-à-vis gay rights and feminism.[84]

Overall, a new divide between communitarians and cosmopolitans, which has been fuelled by globalisation, de-industrialisation, immigration and the rapid decline of Christianity, appears to have fundamentally reshaped American politics. Accelerated by a lack of representation on the political supply side and greater salience of left-wing identity politics, this identity cleavage facilitated Donald Trump's 'hostile takeover' of the GOP in 2016 and, according to Kaufmann, created 'an opening on the political right', which ethno-traditionalist Americanism stood ready to enter'.[85] The next chapter shows how this shift away from America's religious culture wars towards European-style secular identity politics also profoundly transformed the American right's relationship with Christianity.

---

[80] Thus, although aspects of Trumpism have a strong genealogy in American populism, and while civilisational concerns were also expressed in US politics by politicians like Buchanan and authors like Huntington since the 1990s, Trump's and Bannon's focus on Islam and national identity were much more redolent of European far-right discourse in recent decades. See Casanova 2012a; Stanley 2012; Haynes 2019.

[81] Berg 2014; Brocke 2004; Haynes 2017, 66.

[82] Brubaker 2017, 1191; Sides, Tesler and Vavreck 2019; Sides 2017.

[83] Beckwith 2016.

[84] Putnam and Campbell 2012; Bilici 2008; Cesari 2007.

[85] Kaufmann 2018, 87.

CHAPTER 14

The Saviour of Christian America?
Trumpism's Christian Credentials through the Lens of the Cultural-Ethical Triangle

Presidential inaugurations are highpoints of American civil religion. New presidents – sometimes referred to as the 'High priests of civil religion'[1] – would use vocabulary from the 'American creed' to reconcile the nation after often divisive electoral campaigns and recall America's shared higher principles and quasi-divine mission. President Joe Biden, for instance, who was sworn into office on a century-old family Bible, used his inauguration speech on 20 January 2021 to conjure America's civil religious tradition by praising the healing power of faith for a divided nation, appealing to Americans to hold true to the nation's higher ideals, citing Saint Augustine, and leading the nation in silent prayer.[2] The contrast to the inauguration speech of his immediate predecessor could not have been starker.[3] While in terms of liturgy and symbolism Donald Trump, too, had gone to great lengths to make his inauguration ceremony on 20 January 2017 one of the most explicitly religious in recent history,[4] the tone of his inauguration address ostentatiously broke with the civil religious tradition of his predecessors and successor. Trump did not reference universalist principles of compassion and reconciliation, nor America's God-given mission.[5] Instead he spoke of the 'American carnage', the 'red blood of

---

[1] McDougall 1997; Wald and Calhoun-Brown 2014.
[2] Cremer 2021d; Graham 2021.
[3] By contrast Biden's rhetoric was representative of that of other US presidents. Barack Obama for instance used religious language during his inauguration speech, invoking America's 'God-given promise that all are equal, all are free, and all deserve a chance to pursue their full measure of happiness'; see The White House 2009. His predecessor, George W. Bush, similarly reminded Americans that 'we are not this story's author, who fills time and eternity with His purpose. Yet His purpose is achieved in our duty, and our duty is fulfilled in service to one another'; see The White House 2001.
[4] McDougall 2017.
[5] In fact, Trump barely referenced any traditional aspects of civil religion. Whereas appeals to dignity, freedom and liberty appear twenty-four times in Obama's inaugural speech, thirty-nine times in Reagan's and sixty-two times in George W. Bush's, Trump only mentioned freedom once (and only for Americans) and made no reference to dignity or liberty.

208

patriots', 'the forgotten men and women' and of 'Making America Great Again'.[6] This combination of Christian symbolism with secular national populist content mirrored Trump's references to religion throughout his campaign and raises questions about the extent to which Trump's 'hostile takeover' of the American right also transformed the latter's approach towards Christianity and civil religion.

As discussed in Chapters 6 and 10, in Germany and France national populist movements often referenced Christianity primarily as a civilisational identity marker between the homogenous 'us' and the (Islamic) external 'other', but remained distanced from Christian doctrine, values and institutions. This chapter explores differences and similarities in the American context by analysing Trumpism's 'Christian credentials' through the lens of the cultural-ethical triangle. Specifically, it focuses on (1) the compatibility of Trump's policies with Christian social doctrine, (2) his and his entourage's public displays of Christian ethics, and (3) their relationship with the institutional churches and faith leaders. The chapter finds that although the Trump campaign remained more closely aligned with conservative Christianity than the RN in France or the AfD in Germany, the overall trajectory was the same: towards a gradual secularisation of America's right and the 'culturalisation' of Christianity in the context of the new right-wing identity politics that has fused with a secularised form of white Christian nationalism.

14.1   Policies: Frenemies with Benefits?

The first step in applying the cultural-ethical triangle is to examine the extent to which Donald Trump's policy platform aligned with 'Christian values' as expressed by official church doctrine.[7] At first glance, Trump's brand of national populism appears much more closely aligned with conservative Christian doctrine on questions of sexual morality and religious freedom than its German and French counterparts. The Trump administration for instance catered to conservative Christian policy demands by

---

[6] The White House 2017.
[7] Given America's much more diverse religious landscape, it is less straightforward to establish a clear definition of 'Christian values' or 'Christian social doctrine'. This study therefore relies on positions published by the largest church denominations, such as the USCCB for Catholicism (USCCB 2020), the Southern Baptist convention's Ethics and Religious Liberty Commission (ERLC 2020), position papers from associations, which encompass large numbers of denominations such as the Evangelical NAE (NAE 2018) or the Mainline Protestant National Council of Churches (NCC 2020) as well as on the statements put forward by major para-church organisations, Christian lobby groups and the twenty-eight American religious leaders interviewed for this book.

appointing pro-life Supreme Court justices and judges in lower courts, moving the US Embassy in Israel to Jerusalem,[8] making the global persecution of Christians a top priority of US diplomacy, and issuing an executive order 'to defend the freedom of religion and speech' by easing the Johnson Amendment.[9] During our interviews, religious leaders overwhelmingly praised these efforts. Unsurprisingly, the Evangelical leaders closely associated with the president were most enthusiastic. Robert Jeffress, Pastor of First Baptist Church Dallas, and a member of Donald Trump's White House Faith Advisory Board, called Trump 'without dispute the most pro-Israel, most pro-life, most pro-religious candidate in history, who has fulfilled every promise he has made to Evangelicals'.[10] Fellow board member Jay Strack argued that 'Donald Trump has done more in his first two years in office than any other president'.[11] And Jim Garlow, another board member, emphasised that 'unlike almost all other candidates, he's kept his word'.[12] But praise also came from those less closely associated with the Trump administration. Travis Wussow, vice president of the Southern Baptist Convention's Ethics and Religious Liberty Commission (ERLC), for example, emphasised that 'on issues of religious freedom, issues of protecting human life, issues of rights of conscience, this administration has done a number of great things'.[13] IRD president, Mark Tooley, stressed that from a Mainline Protestant perspective Trump 'has delivered for his conservative religious supporters'.[14] And even those faith leaders who had openly criticised President Trump, such as the Catholic Bishop of El Paso Mark Seitz, stressed that 'on issues such as life and religious liberty, which are very important to the Catholic Church, they [the Trump administration] have been amazing'.[15]

This praise is noteworthy as moral and social issues were not a priority at the outset of Trump's campaign. During the primaries, candidate Trump, known for his earlier pro-choice views, barely mentioned abortion or religious freedom and the campaign had no specific faith outreach

---

[8] Moving the US Embassy to Jerusalem has been a long-standing policy demand of conservative Christian leaders in the USA, many of whom adhere to a Christian Zionism. According to this belief, the return of the Jews to the Holy Land and the establishment of the Israeli state are preconditions for the fulfilment of biblical prophecy (Bump 2018; Spector 2009).

[9] Risse 2020; Addicott 2018; Moten 2018; Aprill 2018.

[10] Interview Jeffress 2020.

[11] Interview Strack 2020.

[12] Interview Garlow 2020.

[13] Interview Wussow 2020.

[14] Interview Tooley 2020.

[15] Interview Seitz 2020.

programme.[16] Former Kansas Governor Sam Brownback, who and under Trump became the US Ambassador for International Religious Freedom, observed that 'when he [Trump] came into office [religious freedom] really was a bit of a new topic to him'.[17] The Trump campaign's later religious outreach director Pam Pryor similarly noted that it was only at the end of the primaries that the Trump campaign 'recognised that we really needed more intensive faith outreach'.[18]

Yet, things changed fundamentally after the Republican convention in the summer of 2016. At this point, the Trump campaign hired Pryor for faith outreach, made stalwart Evangelical Mike Pence its vice-presidential candidate, and invited large numbers of Evangelical leaders to Trump Tower. His campaign also directly appealed to faith voters by publishing a list of potential pro-life Supreme Court justice nominees, and promising to protect Christianity, which according to Trump was 'under siege in this country and elsewhere'.[19] Interviewees emphasised the importance of this post-convention volte-face. Paul Ryan's former chief of staff, Jonathan Burks, for example, confirmed that 'the key turning point was really when they released the list of judges that they would be drawing from for Supreme Court nominations'.[20] Then Republican congressman and co-host of the National Prayer Breakfast Randy Hultgren stressed the importance of 'the selection of Mike Pence and some of the commitments he made for judges'.[21] Certainly, many faith leaders – including those on Trump's faith advisory board – still lamented that Trump's 'position is a lot softer on the gender issue or on homosexuality … [H]e gets cooked for that in the faith world because we think he could be stronger in that area.'[22] Others such as the Senior Director of the bipartisan Institutional Religious Freedom Alliance, Stanley Carlson-Thies, cautioned that 'Trump presents himself as the big champion of religious freedom, but he came in and didn't do anything initially about it.'[23] Yet, overall, the Trump administration's policies on social issues remained much more aligned with conservative Christian doctrine than many of its Western European national populist counterparts did.

---

[16]   Benen 2015; Crouch 2016; Jung 2016.
[17]   Interview Brownback 2020.
[18]   Interview Pryor 2019.
[19]   Boorstein and Bailey 2017; Rappeport and Savage 2016; Sargent 2016; Trump 2016.
[20]   Interview Burks 2019.
[21]   Interview Hultgren 2020.
[22]   Interview Strack 2020.
[23]   Interview Carlson-Thies 2019.

This apparent alignment with conservative Christianity on social issues, however, did not translate to national populist trademark issues of immigration, race relations and Islam. Like in France and Germany, the US interviews revealed major clashes between the Trump administration's positions and the views of the churches and faith leaders on these issues. USCCB vice president Archbishop Vigneron, for instance, emphasised that 'immigration is certainly a significant problem',[24] while his colleague Bishop Paprocki of Springfield confirmed that our 'bishops and especially our new president, Archbishop Gomez, have been very, very strongly in favour of the rights of immigrants. In this area, not only Pope Francis but also the leadership of the Bishops Conferences have not been in sync with the Trump administration.'[25] The president of the Mainline Protestant NCC and former general secretary of the American Methodist Church, Jim Winkler, similarly stressed that whereas 'the sentiment fuelling Trumpism is a view that white men in particular should control the country …, the churches have been at the forefront of struggles for equality and justice against racism'.[26] And NAE vice president, Galen Carey, emphasised tensions around the 'Muslim travel ban' as a 'clear violation of religious freedom for Muslims' and registered his 'strong concern around refugee settlement, the sharp curtailing of immigration numbers and more general policies that are very harmful to immigrants'.[27] Off the record one top-level Evangelical leader added that 'even more troubling is what is underneath the anti-immigration policies – the racial attitudes. It's terrifying that this has brought racial drivel back into the conversation that was completely out just a few years ago.'

These claims also align with the experience of political operatives. For instance, the Biden 2020 campaign's national faith engagement director Josh Dickson noted that

> it's remarkable how many conservative and traditionally Republican voting faith voters have come out to support us during the [2020] campaign, because of the race issue. These voters are often multi-issue voters who might be pro-life and conservative on many social issues, but who are really concerned about systematic racism and the ways in which this administration is fostering it through its rhetoric [especially during the BLM protests].[28]

---

[24] Interview Vigneron 2019.
[25] Interview Paprocki 2019.
[26] Interview Winkler 2019.
[27] ERLC vice president Travis Wussow similarly stated that 'Where we have publicly opposed the administration, the predominant issues have been immigration policy and rhetoric surrounding race.'
[28] Interview Dickson 2020.

Moreover, clashes over identitarian core issues were also confirmed by representatives of the national populist movement themselves. Pam Pryor, the 2016 Trump campaign's faith advisor for instance emphasised that 'when it comes to points of friction, I think immigration is one big issue'.[29] Michaël Modrikamen, director of the national populist 'The Movement' organisation pointed out that

> The problem that we have in the Christian world is immigration. The church sees a person– a Syrian or an African, etc. – as an individual who must be helped in the context of a fraternal vision of welcoming the stranger. But then you have the populist common man who says 'I want to [welcome the stranger], but these people who are coming, are in my neighbourhood.' And then you have the populist leader who says, 'I want to help, but today you have 1.5 billion Africans of whom about two-thirds are in poor circumstances and how many can we host? 10 million? 50 million? 100 million? It is endless.' This is the conflict we have with the church.[30]

Such comments suggest that underlying the policy clashes between the churches and Trumpism is also a divergence about the very conception of America's 'Christian identity'. Scholars like Gorski, Brubaker or Haynes have argued that the Trump campaign's attitude towards Christianity is characterised by a 'reactionary and secularised version of white Christian nationalism',[31] or by an identitarian 'Christianism',[32] whereby 'Judeo-Christian' is a general term to differentiate between 'them and us'.[33] Such an identitarian approach to Christianity would echo developments on the populist right in Western Europe, but constitute a significant break from the American conservative tradition.[34]

Yet, interviewees spoke of precisely such a break. As George W. Bush's former speechwriter, Pete Wehner, put it,

> Trump is much less personal about religion. He doesn't talk like George W. Bush did about 'how Jesus changed my life'. There is nothing about Christianity and justice, Christianity and compassion, Christianity and care. For Trump I think it is transactional and I think it is cultural identity tapping into fear and anger.[35]

---

[29] Interview Pryor 2019.
[30] Interview Modrikamen 2019.
[31] Gorski 2020, 7.
[32] Brubaker 2017.
[33] Haynes 2017, 70.
[34] Brocke 2004; Knippenberg 2010.
[35] Interview Wehner 2019.

This impression was shared not only by progressive faith leaders, such as Rabbi Jack Moline, who argued that Trumpism's conception is 'not Christian, per se. It's Western. ... It's more civilisational than theological',[36] but also by conservative Christian leaders such as ERLC vice president, Travis Wussow, who observed 'a kind of identity politics that exists on the right, where you are trying to lay out a tribal marker of belonging'.[37] Even members of Trump's own faith advisory board, like Johnnie Moore, stated that 'Steve Bannon is a Catholic, but it seems to me that his nationalism, like a lot of European nationalism, begins with immigration, whereas the Evangelical patriotism begins with religious freedom and individual liberty.'[38] National populist leaders like Modrikamen confirmed such shifts in priorities from religious to secular identity issues when explaining that 'limiting immigration, giving priority to our citizens ... These are themes where we all agree [in the national populist movement] and then there are themes that we don't address because there is a real division, like the question of religion.'[39] Rusty Reno, co-host of the national conservatism conference, put it even more plainly, saying that '"taking back our country" now doesn't mean Christianity in the way that it meant in the eighties. Now it means nationalism. So, it's less religious and more political. There's no doubt about that.'[40]

Taken together, alignments between Trump's policy platform and conservative Christian positions on social issues were contrasted with policy clashes on identitarian wedge-issues like immigration, race relations and Islam, as well as by the Trump campaign's shift away from universalist civil religious rhetoric towards an ethno-cultural idea of (white) 'Christendom' as an exclusive marker of national belonging rather than religious believing. This shift also manifested itself in the second part of the cultural-ethical triangle: the extent to which the public ethics and virtues displayed by Trump and his team corresponded with Christian ethics.

14.2   Public Ethics and Virtues: King David 2.0?

There is no denying the number of people who have spoken out to condemn the incompatibility of Trump's personal lifestyle with Christian ideals of traditional family values.[41] A thrice-divorced, formerly pro-choice real-estate

---

[36] Interview Moline 2020.
[37] Interview Wussow 2020.
[38] Interview J. Moore 2019.
[39] Interview Modrikamen 2019.
[40] Interview Reno 2019.
[41] Benen 2015; Crouch 2016; Gerson 2020; Guardian 2017; Jung 2016.

tycoon and reality TV star, who has repeatedly displayed his unfamiliarity with Christian scripture and liturgy, refused to ask God for forgiveness and openly boasted of his extramarital affairs, was, as Governor Sam Brownback put it, 'an unlikely candidate' for the Christian right.[42] However, while the *private* life choices and personal sexual morality of political leaders may have historically been given high priority in America's Christian right, this is not the focus of this study.[43] Instead, this book is chiefly concerned with leaders' displays of Christian values, ethics and beliefs in their *public* actions and statements. The following analysis is therefore based on two indicators: first President Trump's and his leadership team's public commitment to civil religious and Christian values, and second, the ways in which Christians and their beliefs have shaped the inner life of the campaign and administration. Both indicators yield ambiguous results, suggesting that while Christian influences remain much more important within the Trump administration than within many European national populist parties, they are significantly less important than in earlier Republican administrations.

In terms of public commitments to Christianity, President Trump has stood out for his often-blatant public disregard for civil religious traditions and Christian ethics. The key point here is not just that President Trump was unable to name his favourite Bible verse in an interview,[44] misquoted 'the second letter to the Corinthians' as 'the two Corinthians',[45] referred to Holy Communion as 'drinking my little wine and eating my little cracker',[46] or that he tried to put dollar notes on the communion plate.[47] Rather, it is the fact that on several occasions he directly voiced his lack of interest in traditional Christian virtues in public life. During a campaign interview Trump declared for instance that he had never asked God for forgiveness and did not have time for prayer.[48] Similarly, at the 2020 National Prayer Breakfast President Trump not only failed to use civil religious language during his speech, but, after the keynote speaker Arthur Brooks called for politicians to remember Christ's commandment to 'love your enemies', Trump replied, 'Arthur, I don't know if agree with you on that.'[49] He then proceeded to criticise Republican Senator Mitt Romney

---

[42] Interview Brownback 2020.
[43] Putnam and Campbell 2012; Wilcox 2018.
[44] Moran 2019.
[45] Taylor 2016.
[46] Burnett 2015.
[47] Voorhees 2016.
[48] C-Span 2015; Scott 2015.
[49] C-Span 2020; Gerson 2020.

and Democratic Speaker of the House Nancy Pelosi, who had referenced the role of their faith in their political decisions in the impeachment process, saying, 'I do not like people who use their faith as a justification for doing what they know is wrong. Nor do I like people who say, "I'll pray for you", when I know that is not so.'[50]

This disregard for Christian ethics and civil religious traditions did not go unnoticed. During our interview House Chaplain Father Patrick Conroy noted that 'Donald Trump has never apologised for one thing in his life. That is the definition of a non-Christian ... I don't think he'd be offended by my saying, I don't think he has a single Christian virtue.'[51] Trump's own faith advisor Jim Garlow acknowledged that 'he would not be seen as one of us. He functions differently than most of us do.'[52] And Mark Tooley from the IRD added that

> Trumpism is far more irreverent and brash in style and does not resort to or rely on the rhetoric of American civil religion. Ronald Reagan and George W. Bush obviously relied on it heavily, but there's a quote from Donald Trump where he dismissed the idea of civil religion, and obviously its language does not appear in his rhetoric.[53]

Indeed, the contrast between Trump's attitudes towards Christian public ethics, and those of former Republican presidents was a recurring theme during the interviews. Former NAE Vice President for Governmental Affairs, Richard Cizik for instance emphasised that 'Trump's approach is very different from Bush's approach to religion. I wouldn't have ever questioned Bush's faith ... but I don't think it's genuine for Trump.'[54] Similarly, former Bush White House official and veteran of the Romney/Ryan 2012 campaign, Jonathan Burks explained that 'religion was not a big piece of the 2016 campaign ..., which is interesting for a conservative movement in this day and age, not to have the religious component front and centre'.[55] By contrast he emphasised that 'the role of conservative Christianity was just pervasive in how we thought about problems in the Bush administration'.[56] Jackie Johns from Cleveland Pentecostal Theological Seminar was representative of many interviewees' views when stating that

[50] C-Span 2020.
[51] Interview Conroy 2019.
[52] Interview Garlow 2020.
[53] Interview Tooley 2020.
[54] Interview Cizik 2019.
[55] Interview Burks 2019.
[56] Interview Burks 2019.

Trump represents a major break [in the GOP]: The Republicans of my life-
time who have been national leaders have believed that they were operating
out of a well-grounded Christian identity, Christian faith and of a fundamentally Christian worldview. And I think Trump operates out of a post-
Christian worldview.[57]

What is more, several political and religious leaders interviewed suggested
that the Trump campaign had brought new explicitly irreligious alt-right
currents into the Republican coalition. While former American Enterprise
Institute president Arthur Brooks emphasised that 'the alt-right had an outsized influence on the Trump campaign',[58] several members of the Trump
administration and the Republican National Committee confirmed off the
record that 'there are now a lot of people from far-right fringe movements in
the room that wouldn't have been there a couple of years ago'. This is a significant development, as numerous studies have emphasised that the irreligious, and at times explicitly anti-Christian nature of the alt-right was one of
the reasons for its historical marginality in American conservatism.[59] Rusty
Reno explained, for instance, that 'the alt-right are entirely non-religious. I
don't know any religious person that would fit into that camp. … And it's
precisely because the religious right is so strong in the Republican Party that
white identity politics has not had played a bigger role.'[60]

Precisely this seemed to change, however, under Trump as alt-right groups
associated with his campaign were gaining more influence in the GOP and
the administration.[61] In his analysis of the influence of the post-religious
right in American politics, Matthew Rose, for instance, argued that 'in congressional offices, Republican politicians won't know the [post-Christian,
identitarian thinkers of the alt-right], but their young aides will'.[62] This
assessment was echoed by several interviewees who reported growing tensions
between secular nationalist elements from the campaign on the one hand,
and Christian conservative members of the administration and in Congress
on the other. White House faith advisory board member Johnnie Moore for

---

[57] Interview Johns 2019.
[58] Interview Brooks 2019.
[59] Berry 2017; Berry 2018; Hawley 2017; Jones 2018; McAlister 2018b; Rose 2021.
[60] Interview Reno 2019. Several interviewees confirmed that the abiding presence of a strong religious
constituency in the Republican Party was the main barrier to the growing influence of the irreligious
far right. Indeed, Pew research has shown, for instance, that in 2019, 99.2 per cent of Republicans in
Congress self-identified as Christian, with a majority of 69.7 per cent being Protestant, compared
to 78.4 per cent of Christians and only a minority of 41.5 per cent of Protestants among Democrats
(Sandstrom, 2017, 2019), suggesting that the secularisation of the American right on the supply side
appears to be largely limited to the Trump campaign and administration.
[61] Cremer 2021e.
[62] Rose 2021, 4.

instance claimed that within the Trump administration 'the religious community isn't part of the worst inclinations of nationalism. We're actually the solution', and that 'Steve Bannon was trying to get some Evangelicals out of the White House, but I would say that Evangelicals played a role in getting him out of the White House.'[63] Samuel Rodriguez, the President of the National Hispanic Christian Leadership Conference similarly acknowledged tensions between the old Christian and the new secular populist right referencing that he often 'encountered critical elements within the administration that may run counter to what I believe with regards to immigration'.[64]

Certainly, most members of the faith advisory board interviewed still sought to argue that they had been successful in taming identitarian populists' worst inclinations. Rodriguez for instance claimed that 'I critiqued and rebuked the [far-right] rhetoric I came against, and this rhetoric has tempered down extremely.'[65] And Johnnie Moore argued that

> We as Evangelicals have actually very often held off the nationalist right in Republican politics. Take just one specific example: The president did not run on reforming our justice system [to make it less discriminatory against racial minorities]. The exact opposite. ... But as Evangelicals we went down and we sat with him and in the end, we got the largest reform of our justice system in thirty years with the president's support. The people that were trying to derail it were people on the far right, but it was the conservative Evangelical community that shut down that far-right nationalistic element.[66]

Interviewees, such as the Evangelical insider on Capitol Hill Rob Schenck, confirmed the non-negligible influence of Christian elements in the administration when stressing that '[Mike] Pence is the Evangelical influence within the administration. I know personally of several instances where Pence has paraded Evangelical candidates for posts into the Oval Office and said, "here's your pick". And the president has said, "okay if that's going to make them happy. I need the Evangelicals to be happy."'[67] Pam Pryor even suggested that some of these religious individuals might have changed President Trump's own view on faith-related issues, claiming that 'just a decade ago, he was not pro-life, but he listened to people like Kellyanne Conway who talked to him about this issue, and he became, to my thinking, enlightened about the life issue'.[68]

[63] Interview J. Moore 2019.
[64] Interview Rodriguez 2020.
[65] Interview Rodriguez 2020.
[66] Interview J. Moore 2019.
[67] Interview Schenck 2020.
[68] Interview Pryor 2019.

However, the extent to which these anecdotes reflect Christians' real influence in the administration remains doubtful. Schenck for instance also stressed that 'the Trump administration itself is overwhelmingly not Evangelical, and on a personal level often even anti-Evangelical. Many high-level appointments that came from [Trump's] personal sphere would be opposed to Evangelicals and see them as marginal, maybe even as kind of nutty.'[69] Former Republican congressman, Randy Hultgren, was similarly sceptical, sharing his belief that in confrontations between the more secular populist wing around Steve Bannon and Stephen Miller and the Faith Advisory Board, 'my sense is that when came down to those two, the Steves won out most of the time'.[70] And well-connected Evangelical leader Michael Lindsay stated that

> I don't know too many committed Evangelicals who are in a high position in the present administration aside from Betsy DeVos, Mike Pompeo and the vice president. So, I think there is a decent amount of rhetoric that is propagated from Washington, but I don't see a lot of people who I would consider inner-circle Evangelicals at the table ... It feels largely symbolic.[71]

These views were echoed by Russell Moore who observed that,

> just as the sort of Chamber of Commerce wing of republicanism is not going completely away, but they're going away as being the hub of the Republican Party, I think the same thing is happening with [the] religious right in the party ... and this is frankly because the sort of angry, populist right constituency that one can tap into for mobilisation and money is increasingly coming form QAnnon and the related sort of groups, which are not only often not connected to churches, but exhibit a deep anti-clericalism.[72]

In sum, in spite of an abidingly religious composition of 'God's Own Party' in Congress, and the efforts of some members of the administration to moderate national populist elements, the Trump campaign appears to have gradually shifted the Republican Party away from civil religious language and religious culture wars towards a more secular right-wing identity politics. However, this shift in terms of policies and (lack of) public display of traditional Christian virtues notwithstanding, many of the former president's supporters still point to the third part of the cultural-ethical triangle to emphasise the administration's Christian credentials: its relationship with Christian leaders and the churches.

---

[69] Interview Schenck 2020.
[70] Interview Hultgren 2020.
[71] Interview Lindsay 2019.
[72] Interview R. Moore 2021.

14.3   Institutional Relations with the Church:
The End of American Civil Religion?

From the outset of his campaign, Trump's relationship with church leaders was highly ambiguous. Early on, his platform and rhetoric were opposed not only by Mainline Protestant and Catholic leaders, but also by significant parts of the Evangelical establishment. Thus, while many Catholic Bishops and Pope Francis himself repeatedly clashed with candidate Trump, openly declaring in 2016 that 'this man is not Christian',[73] several conservative Evangelical leaders and news outlets also opposed his campaign, with for example the Evangelical flagship magazine *Christianity Today* calling its readers to vote against Trump and ERLC president Russel Moore denouncing Trump's 'reckless, demagogic rhetoric' and 'us versus them identity politics'.[74] Moreover, during our interview, Moore stressed that 'early on there were many people in my [conservative Evangelical] world who opposed Trump publicly. Look for instance at the National Review issue against Trump where twenty-two of us gave essays to say why we were against Trump.'[75] Michael Lindsay echoed this assessment saying that he could 'not remember any main Evangelical leader being strong Donald Trump supporters early in the primary season'.[76] And NAE Vice President Galen Carey reported that

> In the fall of 2015 we surveyed our leaders … and asked which of the presidential candidates of either party they liked the most. The first choice was Marco Rubio, second was Ted Cruz, the third was John Kasich. Maybe 1 to 2 per cent named Trump, and in our meetings, I remember most leaders saying, 'I personally don't know anybody who's supporting him … that's not our person'.[77]

Even most members of the President's Faith Advisory Board I spoke to admitted their initial scepticism. To the question of whether Trump was his first choice during the primaries, Jay Strack for instance replied with a resounding 'heavens no, no, sir. He was not',[78] and Jim Garlow explained that 'there were sixteen candidates. Donald Trump was my seventeenth choice'.[79]

---

[73] Detrow 2016.
[74] Moore 2015; Crouch 2016; Alexander 2016.
[75] Interview R. Moore 2021.
[76] Interview Lindsay 2019.
[77] Interview Carey 2020; NAE 2015.
[78] Interview Strack 2020.
[79] Interview Garlow 2020.

However, the Trump campaign's effort to reach out to Christian constituencies after the Republican primaries seems to have been successful in shifting many Christian leaders' public stance. An important part of this initiative, which was repeatedly brought up during the interviews, was the invitation of Christian leaders to Trump Tower for discussions in June 2016, which at that time editor-in-chief of *Christianity Today*, Mark Galli, called 'the turning point' of Trump's relationship with Evangelical leaders.[80] Rob Schenck explained that when 'Trump called for the meeting with Evangelicals … many of my colleagues went and they came back supportive of him. One of them said to me "he's the only candidate who listened to us uninterrupted for forty-five minutes and then said: "I can deliver that for you." It was very transactional.'[81] This impression was echoed by religious freedom activist Carlson-Thies who was invited to one of these 'off-the-record discussions at Trump Tower, where … Trump seemed to have such a transactional view. … But I was also so surprised at the forty-five minutes he paid attention to the topic of religious freedom, and at how relatively deep his questions were.'[82] These meetings were soon to become the basis for the Trump Evangelical Faith Advisory Board, an unofficial group of (conservative Evangelical) faith leaders whom 'the White House occasionally will bring in to discuss different topics', as board member Robert Jeffress defined it.[83]

During our interviews many members of the board explicitly rationalised their joining of these meetings by emphasising that (unlike in countries like Germany where the official churches enjoyed a formalised access to the policy making process; see Chapter 4), in America's formally separationist mode, gaining personal favour with decision-makers was effectively the only way to influence the policymaking process.[84] Mark Galli, then editor-in-chief of *Christianity Today*, for instance, stressed that many of his Evangelical leaders 'who went on Trump's Faith Advisory Board and stopped publicly criticising, did so because they wanted a seat at the table to try to influence the president for instance on immigration policy, to help him become a little more liberal about it'.[85] Interviewed members of the White House Faith Advisory Board themselves often stressed their intention to use the board as a means to shape the administration's policies

---

[80] Interview Galli 2020.
[81] Interview Schenck 2020.
[82] Interview Carlson-Thies 2019.
[83] Interview Jeffress 2020.
[84] Cremer 2021b.
[85] Interview Galli 2020.

on issues like abortion and religious freedom, and to moderate alt-right and white nationalist tendencies. Jay Strack for instance explained that 'all of us have been able to express support to the president, but also to voice questions or express concerns, and the president has listened'.[86] Samuel Rodriguez similarly stressed that for him 'advising the president is really about being able to contribute in such a way that lives would be changed'.[87] Rodriguez and several of his fellow board members mentioned for instance issues such as the justice reform or the rights of dreamers (children of illegal immigrants born in the USA), in which members of the Faith Advisory Board have sought to influence government policy. However, they also noted that this approach came at the price of muting criticism in public. As one member of the White House Faith Advisory Board put it off the record, 'You got to praise and encourage publicly … all of us have been able to express a question or press concern or a warning, but you can only do this if you are in the room. … You want to be in the room … If you're not in the room, you don't have any influence.'

Most external observers, however, were doubtful about this strategy's effectiveness. Jonathan Burks for instance stated that 'the last time I thought about the Faith Advisory Board was the day it was announced. So, it may well be very influential within the building, but I've literally never heard anyone at the White House raise it in discussions or conversations.'[88] NAE vice president Galen Carey casted doubts on board members' ability to speak truth to power, saying that 'it becomes very difficult to be the prophet once you're in the palace'.[89] Other Evangelical leaders voiced concerns that 'the Evangelical Advisory Board has been more changed by Trump than it has changed him',[90] or that 'my friends, in their loyalty to a populist leader, Donald Trump, have changed more than they would ever admit'.[91] One Evangelical leader summarised his concerns off the record as follows:

> The main concern is how Evangelical support for Trump is changing us. I see virtually no evidence of Evangelical leaders standing up to him. They might be doing so in private but there are no policy changes. Instead, we see some of the most extreme policies on immigration unchallenged. And if people stand up to it, they can quickly lose their position, whereas Stephen Miller will still be there.

---

[86] Interview Strack 2020.
[87] Interview Rodriguez 2020.
[88] Interview Burks 2019.
[89] Interview Carey 2020.
[90] Interview Galli 2020.
[91] Interview Cizik 2019.

Furthermore, most religious leaders interviewed emphasised that regardless of whether the Faith Advisory Board had really shaped the administration's agenda or not, it was unrepresentative of American religion more broadly. The 'Evangelical' Faith Advisory Board, hence, broke with America's non-sectarian civil religious tradition by not including any Mainline Protestants, Catholics or Mormons, let alone representatives of other faiths. Indeed, religious leaders from these denominations reported significantly worse institutional relations with the government than under earlier administrations, thus partly confirming concerns that in America's system of formal separation, religious leaders who had publicly criticised President Trump or whose denominations had done so were left with few alternative ways of influencing the policymaking process. Executive director of the Interfaith Alliance, Rabbi Jack Moline, for instance, stated in 2020 that 'I haven't been in the White House since three days before Obama left',[92] while Catholic Bishop Paprocki explained that he was 'not aware of a lot of direct contact between the USCCB and the Trump administration. It's certainly less than in the past.'[93] NCC president Jim Winkler similarly stressed that 'under Presidents Obama, Bush and Clinton they frequently invited a cross-section of American faith groups to come to the White House for everything from celebrations to consultations, for conversations, for meals, for briefings', whereas under the Trump administration 'we have no access'.[94]

Even most Evangelical leaders interviewed contested the assumption that the Evangelical Faith Advisory Board was representative of their faith community. Evangelical leader and former Obama staffer Joshua Dubois, for instance, argued that the Faith Advisory Board consisted mainly of 'folks who are on the fringe of the Evangelical community, who would not be considered theological, pastoral or mainstream Evangelical leaders … the Advisory Board does not even comprise most prominent conservative Evangelicals'.[95] This view was echoed by NAE vice president Galen Carey who stressed that 'those people on the advisory council are not representative of our community. … [M]ost of our leaders had never heard of someone like Paula White [Trump's spiritual advisor].'[96]

---

[92] Interview Moline 2020.
[93] Interview Paprocki 2019.
[94] Interview Winkler 2019.
[95] Interview DuBois 2020.
[96] Interview Carey 2020. IRD president Mark Tooley hypothesised that members of the board 'often come from charismatic or Pentecostal Christianity, or to some extent the megachurch world, but not from traditional Evangelical elites, from denominations, from Christian colleges and seminaries or from Christian media outlets'. Yet, even Pentecostal bishop Tony Richie stressed that 'the Evangelical Advisory Board is not representative of the broader Evangelical opinion'; interview Richie 2019.

By contrast Carey stated that 'the Bush White House was much more friendly to Evangelicals … [W]e also had much more engagement under the Obama administration … We don't get that at all from this administration.'[97] Such impressions were confirmed by Republican senior operative Jonathan Burks who stressed that 'the formal engagement of religious groups in politics has actually declined. Things like the moral majority, that are explicitly organised around being Evangelical faith communities engaging politics, are much less important today than they have been in recent Republican administrations.'[98]

Taken together, the analysis of the Trump campaign and administration through the cultural-ethical triangle has yielded ambiguous results. On the one hand the Trump campaign closely catered to conservative Christians' policy demands on 'culture war' issues, sought an alliance with some Christian leaders and has prominently established an Evangelical Faith Advisory Board at the heart of the administration. Yet, on the other hand it has clashed with Christian doctrine on its identitarian core issues of immigration, race relations and Islam, and markedly differed from earlier administrations through its links to the secular alt-right and its embrace of an identitarian approach to Christianity. What is more, in its sectarian limitations and transactional approach to religious institutions the Trump administration has generated an important shift away from the tradition of American civil religion and earlier Republican administrations' focus on moral and religious issues in favour of secular white identity politics. Carlson-Thies took these developments to conclude that 'Trump is the epitome of the secularisation of the American right' and that his victory was 'not a return of the religious right, but the secularisation of what used to be the Christian right'.[99] The next chapter investigates this claim more closely by exploring Christian communities' relationship with Trumpism at the grassroots and the extent to which these demand-side reactions to Trumpism were shaped by supply-side actors, such as the Democratic Party and the behaviour of faith leaders.

---

[97] Interview Carey 2020.
[98] Interview Burks 2019.
[99] Interview Carlson-Thies 2019.

CHAPTER 15

A Faustian Bargain?
Understanding White Christian Support for Trump

Like the mighty eagle that is rising on the wind
Soaring t'ward our destiny
Hearts and voices blend
With a mighty melody oh let the song begin
And make America great again
Make America great again

> Excerpts from a hymn composed by a pastor of the
> First Baptist Church of Dallas and performed by its
> choir on 4 July 2017 in President Trump's presence

Political campaign slogans are not typically found in the devotional music of American Evangelicals, who historically emerged out of a non-conformist push against the politicisation of Christianity by the state in Europe.[1] However, this ode to President Trump's manifesto seemed representative not only of the attitudes within the First Baptist Church of Dallas, whose senior pastor Robert Jeffress also sat on Trump's Faith Advisory Board, but of American Christians' attitudes towards Trumpism more broadly.[2] With 81 per cent in 2016 and, according to some polls, up to 84 per cent in 2020, Donald Trump achieved a higher score among white Evangelicals than among any other demographic in both presidential elections.[3] White Evangelical support for Trump was also higher than that for his Republican predecessors Mitt Romney (74 per cent), John McCain (74 per cent) and even born-again Christian George W. Bush (78 per cent). Moreover, in 2016 Trump also won a record majority of white Catholics (60 per cent) and was only marginally topped by George W. Bush among Mainline Protestants in 2000 (58 per cent vs 59 per cent).[4]

---

[1] Kidd 2008; Hunter 1983.
[2] Hawkins 2017; Mooney 2019.
[3] Smith and Martinez 2016; Igielnik, Keeter and Hartig 2021.
[4] Smith and Martinez 2016.

Such data points seem to suggest that American Christians were not just unconcerned about the contradictions between Trumpism and traditional Christianity revealed in the previous chapter, but wholeheartedly supported Trump. Yet, at the same time there are also several indicators that point to a more complex relationship. For one, during the interviews political and religious leaders were unanimous in emphasising that Christian scepticism towards Trump had initially not been limited to leaders on the supply side but extended to Christian voters on the demand side. Conservative commentator Henry Olsen for instance observed that 'Trump's core supporters in the primary were not the most religious. Those people backed Ted Cruz',[5] and Bishop Paprocki noted that 'I don't think he [Trump] was the first choice for many Catholics.'[6] Former NAE vice president, Richard Cizik, stressed that even conservative Evangelicals' 'favourite candidates were Ted Cruz and Marco Rubio. They probably would have picked anybody but Trump initially',[7] and then ERLC president Russell Moore said that the one demographic 'where one did not see much support for Trump initially was amongst churchgoing Evangelicals and Evangelical leaders'.[8]

These assessments were confirmed by early polling data, showing that initially religiosity seemed to exercise a similar 'vaccinating effect' among American Christians against national populist appeals as among their Western European brethren. Pew Research found, for instance, that during the early GOP primaries, Trump's most solid supporters were religiously unaffiliated voters (57 per cent), whereas frequent churchgoers were the least supportive (29 per cent).[9] Research by AEI's Tim Carney similarly showed that 'the more frequently a Republican reported going to church, the less likely they were to vote for Trump in the early primaries'.[10] Indeed, Figure 15.1 reveals a strong negative correlation between church attendance and voting for Trump among GOP primary voters, with those who stated that they never attended church being almost twice as likely to vote for Trump than the most frequent churchgoers (62 per cent vs 32 per cent).

Yet, as the election outcome in November 2016 demonstrated, this 'religion gap' was only short lived.[11] Several surveys even indicate that over time, regular churchgoers became more supportive of the president than their

---

[5] Interview Olsen.
[6] Interview Paprocki 2019.
[7] Interview Cizik 2019.
[8] Interview R. Moore 2021.
[9] Doherty, Kiley and Johnson 2017.
[10] Carney 2019, 121.
[11] Smith 2017.

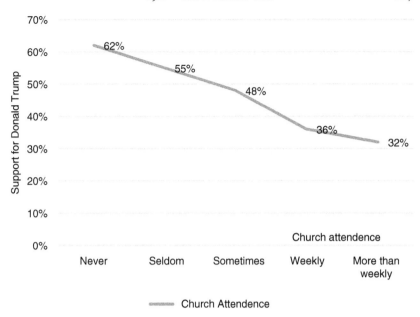

Figure 15.1   Church attendance and support for Donald Trump during the Republican primaries 2016. Source: Carney 2019, 121.

less devout neighbours.[12] This chapter explores this fundamental reversal of conservative Christian voters' attitudes towards Trumpism by looking at demand-side as well as political and religious supply-side factors.

15.1   The Demand Side: American Christians between Diversification and Secularisation

One of the most popular demand-side explanations for Christians' support for Trump posits that in spite of clashes between Trumpism and official church doctrine and leaders, Christians in the pews were closely aligned with Trump's national populist agenda due to the pervasive influence of white Christian nationalism.[13] This hypothesis builds on surveys showing that America's conservative Christians historically held more right-wing attitudes, especially on social issues such as abortion and gay marriage, but also on identitarian issues like immigration, race relations and national

---

[12] Nortey 2021; Schwadel and Smith 2019.
[13] Norris and Inglehart 2019; Ott and Téllez 2019; Whitehead and Perry 2020.

identity.[14] However, the findings from the interviews, combined with recent survey data suggest that, while this claim is generally true, new demographic trends had contributed to a certain reversal among *practising* Christians' views, many of whom had been pushed towards more cosmopolitan attitudes in the decade leading up to Donald Trump's election.

Melkonian-Hoover and Kellstedt, for instance, showed that between 2011 and 2018, just as anti-immigrant sentiment surged among Trump's base of secular conservatives, Evangelicals 'increased their support [for immigration] over time from 28% to 37% favouring citizenship for illegal immigrants'.[15] During our interview NAE vice president Galen Carey similarly reported that 'since 2011 up until about 2016 we've tracked a significant growth in pro-immigrant sentiment among our members'.[16] Moreover, in 2008 Knoll found that frequent religious practice was strongly correlated with more open views towards immigration among Catholics and Mainline Protestants.[17] This finding was confirmed and generalised by Emily Ekins, who showed that for American Christians of all denominations 'religious participation may have a moderating effect on politics, particularly on matters of race, immigration, and identity'.[18] This relative openness on identitarian issues was underlined by the essential (but often overlooked) finding of Whitehead and Perry that while Christian cultural identity correlates with Christian nationalist attitudes, religious practice often works in the opposite direction.[19]

Part of the reason behind such trends may be the broader shift towards internationalism in many Christian communities that began in the 1990s as a result of their global engagement and racial diversification.[20] American Catholicism for instance owes much of its relative numerical stability and vitality to the influx of non-white and Hispanic believers. John Carr, the Director of the Initiative on Catholic Social Thought and Public Life at Georgetown University, for instance, emphasised in our interview that 'what mitigates the nationalistic message in the Catholic community is that we worship together with the Latino community, we're part of the same family'.[21] Although less noted in the media and academic literature, similar

---

[14] Gorski 2020; Guth 2019; Whitehead and Perry 2020.
[15] Melkonian-Hoover and Kellstedt 2019, 58; Ekins 2018; McAlister 2018a.
[16] Interview Carey 2020.
[17] Knoll 2008.
[18] Ekins 2018, 25.
[19] Whitehead and Perry 2020, 87.
[20] Hoover 2019; Lindsay 2007; McAlister 2018a; Melkonian-Hoover and Kellstedt 2018.
[21] Interview Carr 2019. By 2017 the proportion of white Catholics had hence fallen to 55 per cent (from 87 per cent in 1992), while 52 per cent of Catholics under the age of 30 were Hispanic (see Jones and Cox 2017).

demographic trends have taken hold within America's Evangelical community.[22] A PRRI study hence found that by 2017 one in three self-identified Evangelicals were non-white, while a study from LifeWay Research put their share at 40 per cent.[23] Especially among younger Evangelicals, non-whites were often already a majority in congregations, and the majority of congregations in many theologically conservative denominations such as Pentecostal or Seventh-day Adventists were shown to be highly racially diverse.[24] On the elite level NAE president Galen Carey echoed these trends emphasising that

> we've been engaged internationally, we've been sending missionaries and humanitarian workers around the world for more than a hundred years, and, of course, the fastest-growing part of our churches are immigrant populations. And that's appreciated … [O]ur calling is certainly to be multicultural.[25]

Hispanic Evangelical leader Samuel Rodriguez similarly stressed the growing importance of Latinos within the Evangelical community, adding that 'our global presence is arguably now larger than our national presence'.[26] This demographic shift also manifested itself in leadership positions: in 2012 the largest Evangelical denomination, the Southern Baptist Convention, elected its first African American president, Fred Luter.[27] In 2019 the NAE followed suit, electing Walter Kim as its first Asian-American president and its first woman and first African American as Chair and deputy Chair.[28] The president of the Dietrich Bonhoeffer Institute Rob Schenck said that more diverse leaders 'will be the new voices of the movement'.[29] Rather than embracing white nationalism, many American faith leaders and churchgoers seemed to be influenced by new international connections and racial diversification leading them towards more cosmopolitan positions on identitarian core issues like immigration or race relations.

However, this trend among practising Christians was counterbalanced by the boom of another group, which held much more open attitudes

---

[22] Scholars have pointed out that the academic literature's focus on 'white Evangelicals' has often obscured not only the historic importance of black churches, but also the internationalisation and racial diversification of historically white Evangelical communities (Claiborne et al. 2018; Fea 2018; Gorski 2019a; Joustra 2019; Kidd 2019).
[23] Jones and Cox 2017; LifeWay 2017.
[24] LifeWay 2017.
[25] Interview Carey 2020.
[26] Interview Rodriguez 2020.
[27] Eckholm 2012.
[28] NAE 2019.
[29] Interview Schenck 2020.

towards right-wing populists' ethno-nationalist agenda: non-practising 'cultural Evangelicals'. Indeed, research shows that secularisation, which had fuelled communitarian and identitarian concerns among working-class whites more broadly, has also affected the Evangelical community. A LifeWay research survey found for instance that in 2017 'fewer than half of those who identified as Evangelicals (45%) strongly agreed with core Evangelical beliefs',[30] while Kidd noted that 'many self-identified Evangelicals rarely go to Church'.[31] Data gathered by political scientist Ryan Burge similarly showed that the share of Americans who embrace the Evangelical label but hardly attend church had risen steeply from 16 per cent in 2008 to 27 per cent in 2020.[32] Notably, these 'cultural Evangelicals' have not become more progressive but more politically conservative over the years. Thus, Burge found that whereas in 2008 about a third of evangelicals who never attend church self-identified as politically conservative, that number had risen to 50 per cent.[33] As a result, a Pew survey spoke of a growing divide between church-attending 'Sunday stalwarts' and 'God and Country Believers', who only have tenuous connections to congregations and a more culturalised approached to religion.[34] Although the emergence of 'cultural Evangelicals' is a relatively new development (as Galen Carey emphasised, historically 'if you're not actively involved, you're not really considered to be an Evangelical'),[35] studies show that they are becoming an increasingly important voter block, leading observers to speak of the 'secularisation of the Christian right'.[36]

This trend is amplified by the fact that the late twentieth-century association of Evangelicalism with Republican politics not only drove many practising but liberal Christians away from the term 'Evangelicalism', but also incited many secular conservatives to self-identify as Evangelicals even if they did not embrace Evangelicals' theological beliefs or practices.[37] A 2021 Pew Survey found, for instance, that from 2016 to 2020 more people adopted than shed the evangelical label, but also that this growth was almost entirely limited to supporters of Donald Trump, 16 per cent of whom newly adopted the Evangelical label during his presidency, compared to

---

[30] LifeWay 2017.
[31] Kidd 2019, 150.
[32] Burge 2020.
[33] Burge 2020.
[34] Morin et al. 2018.
[35] Interview Carey 2020.
[36] Beinart 2017; Carney 2019; Claiborne et al. 2018; Hochmann 2019; Joustra 2019; Kidd 2019.
[37] Campbell and Layman 2015; Claiborne et al. 2018; Margolis 2018.

1 per cent among non-Trump supporters.[38] Burge and others have interpreted this trend as a politicisation of the Evangelical label claiming that 'instead of theological affinity for Jesus Christ, millions of Americans are being drawn to the evangelical label because of its association with the GOP'.[39] This view was widely echoed among leaders interviewed for this study, many of whom claimed that 'Evangelical' had become a political, cultural and identitarian rather than religious label.[40] Barack Obama's former faith advisor, Michael Wear, for instance said that 'we have learned that if you are politically conservative – even if you're not a practising Evangelical – you might still identify as Evangelical. ... For these people it's a case of: "I don't care about the religious part as much as I care about what the cultural impact of religion should be."'[41] Former AEI president Arthur Brooks similarly stated that 'Evangelical Protestantism has become a cultural identity much like Judaism is often more of a cultural identity than a faith per se.'[42] Religious Freedom activist Carlson-Thies noted that 'Christianity and Evangelicalism are becoming markers of identity, just when many people are ending their practice of religion.'[43]

Like their culturally Catholic counterparts in France, America's non-practising cultural Evangelicals have proven not just more politically conservative but also significantly more sympathetic towards right-wing populist positions and candidates than their churchgoing brethren.[44] During the 2016 primaries political scientist Geoffrey Layman observed, for instance, that 'Trump does best among Evangelicals with one key trait: they don't really go to Church'.[45] Peter Beinart argued that this was because 'when cultural conservatives disengage from organised religion, they tend to redraw the boundaries of identity, de-emphasizing morality and religion and emphasising race and nation. Trump is both a beneficiary and a driver of that shift.'[46] During

---

[38] Smith 2021.

[39] Burge 2021.

[40] In 2017 a LifeWay survey found that only two-thirds (69 percent) of those who would be defined as Evangelicals by their expressed theological beliefs also self-identify with the term 'Evangelical' (LifeWay 2017). Indeed, while more and more scholars of Evangelicalism publish studies entitled 'Who Is an Evangelical?' (Kidd 2019), 'What Is an Evangelical?' (Joustra 2019) or 'Still Evangelical?' (Labberton 2018), during the interviews, former editor-in-chief of *Christianity Today*, Mark Galli, observed that '"Evangelical" is an increasingly contested term; if there's ten scholars in the room, you'll have twelve definitions of Evangelicals' (interview Galli 2020).

[41] Interview Wear 2020.

[42] Interview Brooks 2019.

[43] Interview Carlson-Thies 2019.

[44] Campbell and Putnam 2011; Ekins 2018; Ekins 2017; Knoll 2008.

[45] Layman 2016.

[46] Beinart 2017.

our interview, *Christianity Today*'s Mark Galli echoed such assessments, saying that 'we've known for some time that there is a behavioural difference between Evangelicals who go to church and those who don't … Evangelicals who don't go to church are very anti-immigration, whereas those who do go to church are much more open to it.'[47] And conservative commentator Henry Olsen observed that 'the people who identify as Christian but do not go to church are Trump's core group'.[48]

These findings suggest that sociological demand-side trends are crucial in understanding the make-up of the Trump base and the initial 'religion gap' among conservative voters. While growing racial diversification and internationalisation has pulled many faith leaders and churchgoers towards more cosmopolitan positions on identitarian issues, the emergence of 'cultural Evangelicalism' and subsequent secularisation of the Christian right has pushed many of their non-practising brethren towards communitarian and identitarian positions and Trump's national populist agenda. However, these demand-side explanations fail to explain why so many churchgoing Christians, who *initially* rejected Trump, subsequently changed course and joined their more secular brethren in voting for Trump during the 2016 and 2020 elections.[49] The following sections therefore turn to the political and religious supply sides to understand this development.

15.2 The Political Supply Side: A Lack of Alternatives and Negative Polarisation

When looking at political supply-side explanations, the two main factors to consider are party loyalty and the availability of political alternatives. The findings from the literature and interviews suggest that both factors significantly helped Donald Trump to attract and bind many initially sceptical Christian voters. A 2016 Pew study revealed for instance that among all Trump voters, white Evangelicals were the most likely group to say that they supported Trump, mainly because he was the Republican nominee (38 per cent of them gave this reason, compared to 28 per cent of GOP voters in general and 13 per cent of irreligious Trump supporters).[50]

---

[47] Interview Galli 2020.
[48] Interview Olsen 2020.
[49] This is so even though two years after the elections Trump voters who attended church regularly were still 'more likely than nonreligious Trump voters to have warm feelings toward racial and religious minorities, be more supportive of immigration and trade, and be more concerned about poverty' (Ekins 2018, 3).
[50] Smith 2016.

These numbers suggest that, just as Barber and Pope have shown, 'group loyalty is a stronger motivator of opinion than ideological principles',[51] as for many Christians, party loyalty may have superseded faith-based objections to Trump once he had become the Republican nominee in 2016.[52]

However, while party loyalty helps explain why many traditionally Republican faith voters fell in line during the general election, it is insufficient to account for the significant number of Christian voters who had voted Democrat only a few years earlier but changed sides in 2016. Indeed, more than 10 per cent of Mainline Protestants, one in five Catholics and one in three white Evangelicals who had voted for Obama in 2008 migrated to the Republican candidate in 2016.[53] For these voters, even more important than loyalty to the Republican Party (positive partisanship) seemed to have been their rejection of the Democratic alternative in 2016 (negative partisanship).[54] Indeed, a Pew survey in 2016 found that among Catholic, Evangelical and Mainline Protestant Trump voters Trump's single most attractive feature was that 'he is not Hillary Clinton', with 76 per cent of White Evangelicals citing this as a 'major reason' for supporting Trump.[55]

The role of 'negative partisanship' and a perceived lack of alternatives was also emphasised by interviewees. USCCB vice president, Archbishop Vigneron, argued that for Catholics, the decision to vote Trump was due to 'a lack of other choices, not wholehearted support',[56] while Francis Maier from the Archdiocese of Philadelphia explained that most Catholics were 'quite critical of Trump ... but ultimately he was just the lesser of two evils, because the Clinton campaign went out of its way to repudiate key concerns Catholic bishops and voters would have'.[57] Evangelical leaders such as Jackie Johns, from the Pentecostal Theological Seminary, concurred saying that 'for the majority of the congregation there was a lack of choice. They'd say we have to vote for Trump because we can't vote for Hillary Clinton.'[58] And even members of the president's own Evangelical Faith Advisory Board acknowledged that, as Robert Jeffress put it, 'for most Evangelicals, it came

[51] Barber and Pope 2019b, 38.
[52] During our interview Republican Congressman Francis Rooney perceived Evangelical support for Trump simply as a continuation of the Evangelicals' association with the Republican Party, noting that 'Lee Atwater did the outreach to Evangelicals to make them Republicans, they got them for Reagan, they got them for H. W. Bush, they got them for W. Bush and now they got them for Trump.'
[53] Smith and Martinez 2016.
[54] Abramowitz and McCoy 2019; Abramowitz and Webster 2018; Pew 2019b.
[55] Smith 2016.
[56] Interview Vigneron 2019.
[57] Interview Maier 2019.
[58] Interview Johns 2019.

down to a binary choice between Trump and Clinton. They really didn't know Donald Trump ... but knew they didn't want Hillary Clinton.'[59]

What was it about the Democratic platform and candidate in 2016 that gave many American Christians the impression of having no alternative to Trumpism? Some observers, such as former Democratic faith advisor Amy Sullivan, point to underlying sexism and personal animosity against Hillary Clinton who had 'been vilified by the right for almost thirty years ... and [the fact that] you still have a lot of religious traditionalists in the US, who hold the theological stance that women cannot be leaders.'[60] Others reiterated animosities towards minority candidates due to white Christian nationalism. These factors historically played an important role and certainly did so again in 2016 as well as in 2020.[61] However, a number of interviewees also pointed out that such explanations failed to fully account for why Donald Trump not only succeeded in attracting white democratic voters, but also significantly improved his performance among black Protestants or among Hispanic voters, 38 per cent of whom voted for Trump in 2020, the highest level of support among Hispanics for any Republican candidate since 2004.[62] Instead, several interviewees from both sides of the political divide suggested that the swing was also due to recent changes in the Democratic platform in response to the identity cleavage, and specifically Democrats' embrace of left-wing identity politics since the 2010s that had driven many faith voters – whites but also minorities – to Trump.

Such claims are notable, because in the 2000s and early 2010s Democrats had actually been remarkably successful in their attempts to narrow the historical God gap. DNC faith director Derrick Harkins for instance emphasised that throughout the 2000s the party had successfully begun 'to articulate a narrative around faith ... and to make it part of a visible party strategy, and we certainly capitalised on that in good ways'.[63] Eric Sapp, who advised hundreds of Democratic candidates on faith outreach, described how a strategy based on 'values outreach' and 'using religious values to bridge into these purple and red areas' allowed Democratic candidates using it to 'win everywhere and outperform other Democrats by fifteen points with Catholics and twenty points with white Protestants'.[64] These testimonies seemed to be borne out by empirical studies showing

---

[59] Interview Jeffress 2020.
[60] Interview Sullivan 2019.
[61] Silva 2019; Whitehead and Perry 2020.
[62] Igielnik, Keeter and Hartig 2021.
[63] Interview Harkins 2019.
[64] Interview Sapp 2019.

a gradual closing of the God gap throughout the 2000s as well as by the testimonies of Evangelical leaders like Gordon College president Michael Lindsay, who reported that 'many Evangelicals thought that Barack Obama's presidency would represent a new day'.[65]

Retrospectively, however, Lindsay lamented that 'things did not turn out that way', partly because of a shift in Democrats' attitudes towards religion in the early 2010s.[66] Insiders like Eric Sapp described how in 2012 'we were suddenly hearing from all these campaigns that we were working with that "if we do faith outreach any longer, we don't stand a chance of getting any money from the central party"'.[67] Instead he claimed that 'suddenly our candidates were being attacked by the leftists as 'Democrats in name only who argued that the party needed to get rid of them'.[68] Interviewees were adamant in stressing that this was not necessarily the doing of senior Democratic lawmakers or candidates themselves. Indeed, Obama, Clinton and Biden as well as numerous congressional leaders have been highly sensitive to faith questions and often outspoken about their personal faith during electoral campaigns. Instead, interviewees largely traced this shift back to a new generation of mid-level Democratic party operatives. Sapp for example argued that

> All these Ivy league educated white people came into the party [in the 2010s] and started to talk about people and use data only based on how people look. We as Democrats started thinking 'we know all we need to know about you … the moment you're born, if you are black, if you are brown or if you're a woman' … [I]n this narrative the churchgoers were suddenly the enemy.[69]

Former Obama White House official Michael Wear similarly observed that Obama's positive faith outreach 'ultimately failed', less because Obama was not willing to reach out nor because Christians were not receptive, but rather 'due to forces within the party that were completely against any sort of detente or plural view of Christianity and politics'.[70] Wear added that 'this anti-Evangelicalism was predominant among the elite, the strategy folks and staffers'.[71] His former colleague in the Obama campaign, Shaun Casey, echoed some of these observations, saying that 'the traditional Democratic

---

[65] Dickson 2012; Jones et al. 2010; Pew 2008; Sullivan 2008; Wear 2017.
[66] Interview Lindsay 2019.
[67] Interview Sapp 2019.
[68] Interview Sapp 2019.
[69] Interview Sapp 2019.
[70] Interview Wear 2020.
[71] Interview Wear 2020.

apparatchik is either secular or they have had a bad experience with religion
personally ... [T]hey just do not have the lived experience of actually talking and engaging with Christian religious leaders or religiously motivated
voters ... [T]here is an anti-religion virus and it's fear-based.'[72] Joe Biden's
deputy campaign director, John McCarthy, traced this development back
to two disconnects: first a generational 'disconnect between staffers and
officials. The average age of a house staffer is 26 ... they aren't going to
church on Sunday. Now, their bosses are often religious or culturally religious, but important religious issues might never get in front of them due
to this disconnect.'[73] The second disconnect mentioned was between many
white, highly educated and secular DNC operatives, and the very base of
minority communities that the Democrats' new identity politics intended to
empower. McCarthy hence noted that 'there's a lot of talk about the Obama
coalition and the importance of Latino voters, African American voters, etc.,
but ... these people actually tend to be significantly more religious, than
for instance the average white liberal'.[74] This assessment was confirmed by
Obama's former faith advisor, Joshua Dubois, who stressed that 'in terms of
those who are open to faith [in the Democratic party] I would say African
American Protestants are probably more open than others',[75] while Michael
Wear argued that the Democratic party is 'posturing greater diversity and
saying the backbone of our party is racial minority voters [but] when it
comes to faith, my party is more reflective of secular white liberals in a way
that creates tensions [with minorities]'.[76]

Certainly, election data show that Christian minority voters still feel
overwhelmingly welcome in the Democratic Party, especially when confronted with the alternative of Trump's white nationalist rhetoric that
became increasingly explicit in his response to the BLM movement.[77]
Yet, Democratic congressman Thomas Suozzi shared his concern that
Democrats increasingly struggle to connect to some faith voters and that
'if you win some Democratic primary races, candidates have to worry
about being too publicly religious'.[78] Meanwhile McCarthy lamented that
'we write faith voters off at our own peril',[79] and Wear stressed that in 2016

[72] Interview Casey 2019.
[73] Interview McCarthy 2019.
[74] Interview McCarthy 2019.
[75] Interview DuBois 2020.
[76] Interview Wear 2020.
[77] Doherty, Kiley and O'Hea 2018; Laird and White 2020.
[78] Interview Suozzi 2020.
[79] Interview McCarthy 2019.

'there were not insignificant numbers of Christians who would have liked to vote for anybody but Trump … but who were not given a real option to do so: they did not have a Democratic nominee who asked for their votes or was willing to speak to their concerns'.[80] In our interview, faith leaders NAE vice president Galen Carey confirmed this view and reported,

> going to one meeting with some of Hillary's campaign staff we told them: 'there are a lot of our members that are not very comfortable with the Republican candidate and you may have a better chance of reaching them if you would be more forthcoming about your approach to religion', but they really didn't do anything to reach out to Evangelicals. They basically wrote off our community. … So, it became more of a forced choice where many Evangelicals ended up voting for Donald Trump.[81]

Other Evangelical leaders like Michael Lindsay concurred, saying they were 'struck by how little Democratic leaders have made overtures to the Evangelical community in the last five years'.[82] And even progressive Mainline Protestant leaders like NCC president, Jim Winkler, lamented that recently 'the Democratic Party has much more of a secular orientation and sometimes has to be reminded that there are still many, many millions of Democrats who are people of faith'.[83]

While we have seen that this secularist image is not necessarily representative of Democratic leaders nor of the grassroots, but seems mainly limited to parts of the party apparatus, the impression it conveys has been successfully politicised by politicians like Trump in order to fuel pre-existing narratives of victimhood and fear of a secularist backlash in the Evangelical community.[84] *First Things* editor-in-chief Rusty Reno for instance argued that these developments directly played into Trump's hands as the perception of 'the Democratic Party's hostility towards Christians' and made it 'difficult for traditional Christians to vote for Democrats, because in doing so, they felt they would be voting for their own suicide'.[85] Faith leaders like Travis Wussow spoke of a 'sense of fear' among Evangelicals which 'causes us to defensively turn inward … and to be more susceptible to performative acts of faith from politicians',[86] and prominent conservative commentator Henry Olsen emphasised that 'the religious right twenty

---

[80] Interview Wear 2020.
[81] Interview Carey 2020.
[82] Interview Lindsay 2019.
[83] Interview Winkler 2019.
[84] Fea 2018; Kidd 2019.
[85] Interview Reno 2019.
[86] Interview Wussow 2020.

years ago thought it could win. Now it wants to set the terms of its defeat, but it fears that what it is asked for is unconditional surrender and the fear of unconditional surrender is what drives them to be Trump supporters.'[87]

Certainly, many interviewees also emphasised more recent efforts by Democratic leaders such as Pete Buttigieg, Amy Klobuchar, Nancy Pelosi and especially Joe Biden to rectify this impression by reaching out directly to Christian voters. Auburn Seminary president Katharine Henderson for instance said she was 'very interested in Pete Buttigieg and how he is experimenting with religious language'.[88] Amy Sullivan emphasised 'that somebody like Nancy Pelosi thinks faith outreach is of value'[89] and Joshua Dubois predicted that if Joe Biden 'ends up being the Democratic nominee he will continue to take faith issues very seriously. ... [H]is personal faith is very important.'[90] Indeed, the Biden campaign's faith engagement director Josh Dickson argued that 'what distinguished the Biden campaign from earlier Democratic campaigns was that it was much more proactive in appealing to faith voters' and that it 'sought to make people of faith feel valued and respected in the Democratic coalition and to show them that they are not seen as "deplorables" but as a central part of our platform'.[91] To this end the campaign made faith and morality a prominent part of Biden's platform; from campaign groups such as 'Believers for Biden', through TV advertisements targeting faith voters, to what Dickson described as the 'perhaps the most faith-driven Democratic convention in decades'.[92]

Dickson also acknowledged, however, that when the campaign reached out to faith voters, 'The two things we hear a lot from these voters are first that they are positively surprised that we reach out to them in the first place, and secondly that they are really concerned about the administration's rhetoric with regards to systematic racism.'[93] The latter observation suggests that faith voters might become a more accessible electoral potential for Democratic candidates as identitarian issues become more important. For instance, surveys showed that religious voters were disproportionately critical of Donald Trump's handling of the murder of George Floyd and the BLM protests with 40 per cent of Christians and even 33 per cent of Evangelicals calling it 'poor'.[94] However, the statement

[87] Interview Olsen 2020.
[88] Interview Katherine Rhodes Henderson 2019.
[89] Interview Sullivan 2019.
[90] Interview DuBois 2020.
[91] Interview Dickson 2020.
[92] Interview Dickson 2020.
[93] Interview Dickson 2020.
[94] Morning Consult 2020.

also shows the abiding barriers to realising this potential that remained, mainly due to the perception that the Democratic Party writ-large would be unfriendly to religion. Bishop Paprocki for example claimed that individual Democratic candidates' faith outreach would 'set them on a collision course with the rest of their own party, because many of its policies are contrary to traditional Christian values'.[95] This abiding scepticism remained visible in the 2020 elections, as although Biden campaign's faith outreach enabled the Democratic candidate to make decisive inroads in key battle states and to overcome some of the negative partisanship that had lost Hillary Clinton so many religious Obama voters, it did not succeed in fundamentally reversing faith voters' traditional alignment with the Republican Party.[96]

Overall, these findings suggest that developments on the political supply side significantly helped Trump to overcome initial opposition from churchgoing Christians. While his 'hostile takeover' of the Republican Party enabled him to tap into traditional party loyalties among Christian voters, a perceived secularist turn of parts of the Democratic Party intensified the sense of siege and victimhood among many Christians, which Trump skilfully catered to. Evangelical leader Rob Schenck even called Christian voters' turn to Trumpism a 'Faustian bargain', in which, driven by fear of marginalisation, 'we were trading our deeply held moral principles for political expediency'.[97] However, in the eyes of many Christians this 'Faustian bargain' seemed at least implicitly sanctified by the public behaviour of their religious leaders, as the analysis of the religious supply side shows.

15.3 The Religious Supply Side: A Faustian Bargain or a Lack of Christian Leadership?

Chapters 7 and 11 have highlighted the importance of church leaders' role in shaping Christian voters' attitudes towards national populist movements in Germany and France. Specifically, German and French church authorities appeared capable of creating and maintaining powerful social taboos within their flock against voting for the populist right. In the American context, we have seen that relations between the Trump campaign and faith leaders were initially also fraught with conflict and opposition and correlated with an early religion gap among churchgoing Republicans on

---

[95] Interview Paprocki 2019.
[96] Orr 2020; Wear 2020; Bond 2020.
[97] Interview Schenck 2020.

the demand side. However, the results from the interviews suggest that while most of America's religious establishment has often remained privately critical of Trump and his agenda, structural factors on the religious supply side have limited their willingness and ability to publicly communicate and bolster social taboos around the populist right, when compared to their European counterparts.

In terms of attitudes, the interviews revealed little evidence that would suggest a profound improvement of religious leaders' attitudes towards Trump's national populist agenda. Rather Catholic Archbishop Vigneron emphasised that 'many of the bishops are more critical of Trump ... and I think members of the active religious communities, like the Jesuits, the Mercy Sisters etc. are perhaps the most critical of the president'.[98] Mainline Protestant leaders like Auburn Seminary President Katharine Henderson stressed that 'Trump does not represent the Presbyterian Church at all',[99] while Rabbi Jack Moline, from the Interfaith Alliance, reported that among his colleagues 'they are all horrified by Steve Bannon in Christian communities, and in the Jewish community: I've been asked at least three times that we excommunicate Stephen Miller.'[100] Among Evangelical interviewees, Russell Moore, a prominent Trump critic, told me that he 'would have conversations, often with people in the administration or allies of Trump, who would spend a lot of time privately telling me that they agreed with me'.[101] Similarly, editor-in-chief of *Christianity Today*, Mark Galli, explained that 'all these leaders of what I would call establishment and mainstream Evangelical organisations are very much anti-Trump and those are the people that wrote me emails saying, thank you for finally speaking out against Trump.'[102] Indeed, Galli himself made international headlines only weeks prior to our interview by publishing an editorial in *Christianity Today* arguing that 'Trump should be removed from office'.[103] And the editorial was no isolated incident. Instead, Amy Sullivan emphasised that

---

[98] Interview Vigneron 2019.
[99] Interview Katherine Rhodes Henderson 2019.
[100] Interview Moline 2020.
[101] Interview R. Moore 2021.
[102] Interview Galli 2020.
[103] This not only triggered several angry responses from the president himself, who called Evangelicalism's largest news outlet 'a far-left magazine ...', which has been doing poorly', but also revealed abiding misgivings about the president among Christian leaders more broadly; see Galli 2019; Bogel-Burroughs 2020; Rupar 2019; Timmons and Lewis 2019.

from the very beginning, religious leaders were playing leading roles, showing up at airports to protest against the Muslim bans, and doing a lot of
the organised resistance around immigration policy ... I think it's not an
exaggeration to say that they have been the central organising point in a lot
of protests during the Trump age.[104]

Similarly, during the BLM demonstrations in the Summer of 2020,
faith leaders were at the forefront of the protests, and loudly criticised
President Trump for his reactions to the protests, especially his use of
religious symbols and buildings as photo-props. The Episcopal Bishop of
Washington, DC, Mariann Budde, hence publicly declared herself 'outraged' by President Trump's photo-shoot in front of St John's Episcopal
Church after forcefully removing protesters around it. She decried that
'the president just used a Bible, the most sacred text of the Judeo-Christian
tradition, and one of the churches of my diocese, without permission, as
a backdrop for a message antithetical to the teachings of Jesus'.[105] Even
staunch leaders of the Christian right like Pat Robertson publicly lamented
Trump's aggressive reaction to the protests saying that 'You just don't do
that, Mr President. It isn't cool!'[106]

However, whilst these actions have received some attention from individual scholars and journalists and were certainly keenly felt by right-
wing populist leaders themselves, they have often been overlooked in the
broader debate.[107] Part of the reason for this is that structural factors specific to America's religious landscape limit institutional churches' *ability
to be heard* over pro-Trump figures. Specifically, America's unregulated
and decentralised religious landscape, which evolved under the First
Amendment and created a religious marketplace full of diversity and vitality, also means that no single set of leaders could speak *ex officio* with a similar level of normative authority for American Christianity as for instance
an alliance of Protestant and Catholic bishops would be able to do in
Germany or France.[108] Instead, interviewees stressed that even though the
majority of America's religious 'establishment' had been initially critical of
Trump, and even though many of them spoke out against him, the historical lack of hierarchy between and within American churches meant that
their voices were often drowned out.

---

[104] Interview Sullivan 2019.
[105] Koran and Sullivan 2020.
[106] Teague 2020.
[107] Beyerlein and Ryan 2018; Gjelten 2019.
[108] Campbell and Putnam 2011; Stark 1999; Wuthnow 1988.

Instead, observers like Pete Wehner stressed that those who, like the members of the White House Faith Advisory Board, may lack institutional or denominational standing, but 'are often played up by the media ... and speak up constantly in support of Trump, as people of Christian faith' often drowned out denominational leaders and had an outsized influence on perceptions of Christians in the pews.[109] As a result, Evangelical leaders like Galli conceded it was 'obvious that since 2016, there is another group of leaders in the Evangelical world [the White House Faith Advisory Board] who are in another world altogether'.[110] Jim Garlow, a member of Trump's Faith Advisory Board, made the inherent challenge to Evangelical leaders' authority explicit when exclaiming that 'Evangelical never-Trumpers like *Christianity Today* – let it be known – they call themselves "elite". I find that obnoxious. ... condescending and inexcusable.'[111]

Gordon College president, Michael Lindsay, took such divisions as a cause to argue that the 'Trump presidency has brought the divide between Evangelical populists and Evangelical cosmopolitans more front and centre in the debate',[112] and Rusty Reno noted that

> perhaps 95 per cent of white Evangelical Christians with a PhD voted for someone other than Donald Trump, compared to 82 per cent of Evangelicals who voted for him. So, the churches have the same problem as the general culture, which is that the people who lead and the people whom they lead are increasingly out of sync.[113]

This challenge to denominational faith leaders' authority appears to be further exacerbated by the accelerating crisis of denominational hierarchies and institutions in America as secularisation progresses.[114] IRD president Mark Tooley hence explained that 'one of the explanations for Trump's success' was that, especially among Protestants, 'the big story in American religion is the collapse of the denominational traditions and the decentralisation of religion in America'.[115] Specifically, he argued that,

> Politically and socially, Mainline Protestants are now perceived to have almost no direct influence anymore, and when people talk about religion in public life, they primarily mean Evangelicals, followed by Catholics.

[109] Interview Wehner 2019.
[110] Interview Galli 2020.
[111] Interview Garlow 2020.
[112] Interview Lindsay 2019; Lindsay 2007.
[113] Interview Reno 2019.
[114] Bruce 2019; Campbell and Putnam 2011; Chaves 2011; Olson 2008.
[115] Interview Tooley 2020.

However, Evangelicals don't have a hierarchy; they usually don't have structures. They don't typically have singular leaders who speak for them.[116]

Former Republican co-host of the National Prayer Breakfast Randy Hultgren concurred, stressing that 'with regards to Evangelical faith leaders there really isn't a Billy Graham right now, so it's a little bit more diffused as to who the leaders of faith are',[117] while Pete Wehner observed that nobody knows 'who is the most prominent Mainline leader these days'.[118] Presbyterian leader Katherine Henderson added that even *within* Mainline denominations hierarchies are eroding and 'a lot of people would not be politically influenced by what their clergy say'.[119] Religious freedom activist Stanley Carlson-Thies argued that this lack of authority and deference was particularly strong in Protestant denominations, because 'we don't have the pope or somebody who can stand above it all'.[120] Yet, the fact that even interviewed representatives of America's Catholic Church emphasised that episcopal and papal authority were more limited in the US context and that, for instance, an 'Archbishop has very limited authority over local congregations unless it's a matter of faith or morals'[121] suggests that such dynamics are not just a result of Protestant theology in the USA, but a structural characteristic of America's religious landscape accelerated by trends of secularisation and deinstitutionalisation. As a result, whereas in Europe the traditional dominance of established churches seems to have significantly strengthened faith leaders' authority and ability to create social taboos, the American arrangement appears to have had the opposite effect, thus contributing to the erosion and even reversal of social taboos against right-wing populism among American Christians.[122]

Yet, even more important than these structural factors' impact on American faith leaders' *ability to be heard* may be their ramifications for leaders' *willingness to speak out* in the first place. Surveys have shown that half of American pastors felt limited in their ability to speak out on moral and social issues, and that only one in five (21 per cent) felt comfortable

---

[116] Interview Tooley 2020.
[117] Interview Hultgren 2020.
[118] Interview Wehner 2019.
[119] Republican operative Jon DeWitte similarly reported from congregations in his district that 'The Christian Reformed Church's leadership is reflective of what you see in *Christianity Today* … at the local level, we'll have them come in and talk about immigration issues and talk about social justice issues …. We'll listen kindly, but I know for a fact that they're not representing our constituency well and we will tell them that we're disappointed and report to our pastors that there's a disconnect.'
[120] Interview Carlson-Thies 2019.
[121] Interview Maier 2019.
[122] Cremer 2021b.

speaking out about specific political actors.[123] This hesitancy has significantly increased since 2014, as 'a number of pastors found that political remarks, which in previous years went mostly unnoticed, were suddenly received with some hostility'.[124] During our interviews, faith leaders confirmed that Trumpism was a particularly delicate topic, with Pete Wehner emphasising that 'in my experience, many pastors who are conservative politically are alarmed and worried about Trump, but they don't speak out'.[125] Then president of the Southern Baptist Convention's ERLC, Russell Moore, similarly reported that a lot of Evangelical leaders who were privately horrified by Trump but supportive publicly 'would tell me things along the lines of: "I'm just trying to keep the eye of Sauron off of me"'.[126]

Some interviewees traced this silence back to theological, historical and external factors. Carlson-Thies for instance stressed that the 'Presbyterian Church of America is facing a dilemma because ... the Church itself has a strong doctrine of not being political',[127] while NAE vice president Galen Carey emphasised that 'as a pastor I don't want people to come to my congregation and say, "Oh, this is a Republican or this is a Democrat so I must not belong here." We want it to be a place where people know that everyone is invited.'[128] Others emphasised the importance of the current abuse and financial scandals limiting Catholic leaders' willingness to engage politically. Former senior USCCB official, John Carr, for instance noted that 'most bishops are just trying to keep their head down, trying to do the best job they can in the middle of scandal, taking place in the middle of crisis, in the middle of bankruptcy'.[129]

However, most interviewees emphasised that the foremost reason for faith leaders' silence over Trumpism was structural and specifically linked to concerns about running into conflict with some of their own congregants or donors. Pete Wehner stressed that 'many leaders of Christian colleges are not weighing in because of their donors, who hate the people who hate Trump'.[130] IRD president Mark Tooley similarly explained that 'strong majorities of Mainline Protestant clergy tend to be more liberal, but they realise their congregations are often more conservative and so they

---

[123] Barna 2019.
[124] Barna 2019.
[125] Interview Wehner 2019.
[126] Interview R. Moore 2021.
[127] Interview Carlson-Thies 2019.
[128] Interview Carey 2020.
[129] Interview Carr 2019.
[130] Interview Wehner 2019.

tend to stay mostly non-political'.[131] And Evangelical leader Rob Schenck explained that in America's marketplace of religion 'it's very difficult for Evangelical clergy to speak up, particularly if you are compensated within these systems, if your livelihood depends on it. So, self-preservation is why these [anti-Trump] voices have quieted.'[132]

Several indicators suggest that such concerns are not unfounded. Russell Moore, for instance, ended up leaving his post at the ERLC in 2021 after being repeatedly confronted with – and even threatened to be sued over – allegations that his willingness to publicly condemn Trump may have cost the Southern Baptist Convention donations from Trump support-ers.[133] Interviewees emphasised that such developments on the national scale mirrored those on the local level. Jackie Johns from the Pentecostal Theological Seminary for instance reported that 'religious leaders in con-servative churches who opposed Trump were very quickly marginalised to the point that if they were pastors, many of them lost their churches, or if they kept their churches, they lost large portions of their congregation', making 'most conservative clergy who are opposed Trump so fearful of taking a stance against Trump that we don't know who they are'.[134]

Taken together these structural supply-side factors seem to have sig-nificantly reduced American faith leaders' ability and willingness to become the prophetic voice that had historically been so important in America's civil religious tradition. Instead of creating a social taboo around Trumpism this silence has often been read as an implicit legitimisation of Trump's identitarian references to religion. Jim Winkler emphasised for instance that, combined with the existence of a 'coterie of Christian lead-ers who surround president Trump and strikingly defend him, the silence from most Christian leaders at both the local and national levels has led many to believe the churches support President Trump, but that's not true'.[135] Mark Galli similarly stressed that the lack of criticism of Trump from America's Evangelical leaders 'basically legitimised the fact for many people that if you're an Evangelical, you can support this man'.[136] Put in the context of findings in the literature about the self-fulfilling spiral of populist-right mobilisation, in which the erosion of social taboos increases the populist right's vote share, which in turn further erodes social taboos,

[131] Interview Tooley 2020.
[132] Interview Schenck 2020.
[133] Smietana 2021; Blair 2018.
[134] Interview Johns 2019.
[135] Interview Winkler 2019.
[136] Interview Galli 2020.

the silence of American faith leaders can be seen as an important factor in accelerating many Christian voters' 'conversion' to Trumpism.[137]

15.4 Conclusion

In the light of these findings, we return to the questions guiding the US case study about the demand-side origins of the remaking of the American party landscape and of the rise of Trump, the nature of the Trump campaign's approach to religion on the supply side and the reactions of Christian communities. After the examination of the historical background, recent findings in the literature and the analysis of several dozen interviews with American political and faith leaders, four conclusions emerge. First, Chapter 12 has shown that America's civil religious tradition, which had been an important source of integration and prophetic criticism, has been profoundly challenged by the rise of a new secular identity cleavage that is increasingly superseding America's old religious culture wars. Second, in Chapter 13 we saw that the shift from culture wars to a more secular identity politics between liberal cosmopolitans and populist communitarians, appeared closely linked to the rapid decline of American Christianity, which along with globalisation, individualisation and rapid ethnic change had led to an identity crisis in parts of the white working class. Given the unresponsiveness of the traditional party system, Donald Trump succeeded to capitalise on this crisis of identity through a 'hostile takeover' of the GOP, and a gradual 'Europeanisation' of the American right, which shifted from a faith-based social conservatism to a more secular white identity politics. Third, Chapter 14 found that in the context of this identitarian turn, the Trump campaign still appealed to America's tradition of white Christian nationalism and forged an alliance with a subset of Christian leaders, but also departed from America's civil religious tradition, clashed with Christian doctrine on identitarian issues and adopted a more identitarian and transactional approach to Christian institutions, indicating the rise to prominence of a new 'post-religious right' in the USA. Finally, Chapter 15 found that although there appeared to be a 'religion gap' among American conservatives initially, religion's 'vaccination effect' against national populism has since diminished or even reversed in the USA. Christians' 'conversion' to Trump appears, however, to be less the result of a shift in their attitudes than of supply-side factors, and of a perceived lack of political alternatives as well as the inability and unwillingness of Christian leaders to publicly speak out against Trumpism.

[137] Kaufmann 2018.

The events of 6 January 2021 epitomised many of these developments. Specifically, the combination of religious symbols with radical populist rhetoric encapsulated the shift from a primarily faith-driven religious right to an increasingly race-driven post-religious right. Trump's calls to violence signalled the shift from civil religion to a revolutionary and identitarian populism. However, perhaps the most revealing feature of the Capitol riots was that its most iconic picture was neither one of fire-brand Evangelical preachers nor of sit-in prayers, but of a face-painted, bare-chested, spear-carrying, self-declared 'ordained shamanic practitioner', who, covered in tattoos and wearing animal skins and Viking-style animal horns, stood on the dais of the US Senate and shouted, 'Where's Pence? Show yourself.' This image illustrates how under Donald Trump's influence the GOP grassroots had become less characterised by 'suburban mothers' who organise themselves in church halls than by alt-right groups like the Proud Boys, and ill-defined conspiracy theories like QAnon, which are much more secular in outlook.

During the interviews several leaders have called many American Christians' alliance with this new populist right a 'Faustian bargain', driven more by fear from the secular left than by faith in Christ. In Johann Wolfgang von Goethe's masterwork *Faust*, the protagonist, driven by a desire for earthly gains and power, also enters a bargain with a bare-chested demonic creature wearing horns and animal skins that ends up costing him not his life but his soul. The QAnon shaman in the Capitol was certainly no Mephistopheles. Yet in light of this study's findings and of the deadly events at the Capitol, many American Christians may have started to wonder whether the bargain with the brand of post-religious far-right politics that the shaman came to represent might entail a similar cost.

PART V

Conclusion

This book set out to investigate the relationship between religion, populism and right-wing identity politics in Western democracies in the early twenty-first century. In particular, it has sought to explore the social and political drivers behind national populists' references to religion, the ways in which these references differ from traditional political appeals to religion, how religious communities have reacted to such appeals, and the consequences for the relationship between politics and religion in Western societies. Previous research has shown that right-wing populism and political references to religion have increased significantly in Western politics throughout the early twenty-first century.[1] Taking right-wing populists' increased uses of Christian symbols and language at face value, many observers have suggested that these two developments are related expressions of a reactionary backlash against the advance of liberal and secular society. However, national populists' poor performance among many practising Christians and public clashes with church leaders have cast doubt on such interpretations. Therefore, this book has investigated the relationship between national populism and religion systematically through the comparison of three in-depth case studies: Germany, France and the USA.

The preceding chapters have empirically analysed the dynamics between religion and national populism through the lens of a theoretical framework that distinguishes between the role of demand- and supply-side factors. On the political demand side, social science theory on social cleavages, individualisation and secularisation were employed to interpret new survey data and the findings from 116 elite interviews in order to understand how developments within the German, French and American electorates have driven the demand for both national populist politics and their references to religion. On the political supply side, conceptual tools such as

---

[1] Roy, McDonnell and Marzouki 2016; Kaltwasser et al. 2017a; Eatwell and Goodwin 2018.

the cultural-ethical triangle and the primary data from the elite interviews were used to understand how the AfD, RN and the Trump campaign have sought to harness this demand, and how other supply-side actors such as mainstream parties and the institutional churches have reacted. The findings reveal that while in Germany, France and the USA the rise of a new identity cleavage has created significant potential for national populists' right-wing identity politics, the latter's ability to harness this demand through references to religion depends on political and religious supply-side factors, specifically the existence of a 'Christian electoral alternative' and the behaviour of church leaders. These supply-side dynamics are in turn influenced by factors specific to each country, such as the historical and institutional settlement of church–state relations, the level of secularisation, the strength of traditional cleavages, the history and evolution of national populist movements, and the structure of the existing party system and of the institutional churches. It becomes clear that supply-side actors in general, and religious leaders in particular, play powerful roles in determining the success of right-wing populists' appeals to religion.

In the remainder of this conclusion section, I will bring the different strands from the empirical chapters together in more detail, assess common features and differences, distil general lessons and discuss their contribution to the existing literature. I will end with a short exploration of the findings' generalisability, their limitations and potential for new research.

CHAPTER 16

Squaring the Circle
Four Cornerstones of a General Theory of the Relationship between Right-Wing Populism and Religion in the West

The Introduction of this volume posed several key research questions: what are the social and demographic roots of national populism? How and why does religion feature in national populists' new brand of identity politics? How do Christian communities react to national populists' religiously laden rhetoric? And what is the role of mainstream parties and religious leaders in shaping the relationship between religion and right-wing populism? The empirical Parts II–IV explored these four questions in a case-by-case fashion. This chapter moves from the specifics to the general and seeks to assess the insights from each case study from a comparative perspective, discussing common and distinct patterns as we go through each of the research questions. It distils four conclusions that can serve as cornerstones for a more general theory for understanding the dynamics in each case study.

16.1 A Matter of Identity: The New Identity Cleavage and the Rise of Right-Wing Populism

The first major conclusion of this book is that the rise of right-wing populist movements and their identitarian references to religion are less the result of traditional social cleavages centred around economics and moral or religious issues, but rather the consequence of the emergence of a new identity cleavage between cosmopolitans and communitarians. This cleavage pits two visions of how to define identity (of the 'I', the 'us' and the 'other') against one another: on the cosmopolitan end of this divide stands a globalist vision of universalism, multiculturalism and diversity that is perceived to embrace group identities only for minorities, but to transcend traditional collective ties and identities for majority populations and replace them with individualist forms of identity. Opposed, on the communitarian end of the divide, stand those who favour clearly defined collective identities based on inherited group identity markers such as ethnicity, culture, history, institutions and language. In recent years, immigration, race relations and Islam have emerged as the core issues in this divide.[1]

The empirical sections on demand-side developments in Germany, France and the USA explored the rise of such a new cleavage in all three cases. Adding to recent scholarly debates about the reconfiguration of Western social cleavage systems, and specifically confirming the existence of new divides between 'communitarians and cosmopolitans' in Germany,[2] France[3] and the USA,[4] this book has distilled common features and differences between the national expressions of the identity divide in each case. It has shown how in all three case studies, the rise of the identity cleavage has involved a fundamental shift on the political demand side, which for most of the twentieth century was dominated by the two traditional economic and religious cleavages. 'Class struggles' and 'culture wars' had shaped not only all three political party systems, but also their post-war institutional settlement of church–state relations. While in Germany the emergence of Christian Democracy and a system of 'benevolent neutrality' helped to convert Germany's Christian churches to liberal democracy and pacify the old *Kulturkampf* between Catholicism and the state, in France the compromise of *Catho-laïcité* calmed tensions surrounding the centuries-old 'war of the two Frances' between *la France Catholique* and *la Republique laïque*. Meanwhile in the USA, the post-war heyday of American civil religion appeared to strike a balance between Christian nationalism and separationist interpretations of the First Amendment. In spite of continued tensions around culture-war issues, in particular in the USA, the interviews conducted for this book found that all three settlements were overwhelmingly accepted on both sides of the traditional divides, and thus relatively successful in creating common ground across the old cleavage system.

However, since the turn of the twenty-first century these traditional party systems and religious settlements have been fundamentally challenged by the rise of a new identity cleavage and of right-wing populist movements. This book has identified similar sources of the new identity cleavage in all three case studies. In line with recent findings in the literature, rapid ethnic change through immigration, the weakening of local, class and national ties through globalisation, international integration,

---

[1] Eatwell and Goodwin 2018; Fukuyama 2018; Kaufmann 2018; De Wilde et al. 2019; Sides, Tesler and Vavreck 2019.
[2] De Wilde et al. 2019.
[3] Fourquet 2018b.
[4] Hariri 2017.

individualisation, and the erosion of institutions are all key variables in understanding the rise of a new divide between cosmopolitan beneficiaries and communitarian losers of such shifts.[5]

The analysis of the demand side revealed, however, that one factor deserves particular attention in this context: the process of secularisation, which in all three countries has significantly accelerated since the turn of the millennium.[6] While in Germany the churches are losing members at a record pace, in France the erosion of society's underlying 'Catholic matrix' has undermined religious as well as social, territorial and even secularist sources of identity, making French society an increasingly disconnected social 'archipelago'.[7] In the USA the demise of religious institutions and communities has led to the looming collapse of one of the country's most important sources of social capital. In all three countries, the community that has been hardest hit by this development is the white working-class, among whom the process of secularisation is not only progressing most rapidly, but who historically have profited most from religion as a freely accessible but highly effective source of social capital.[8] Since scholars have emphasised that the white working-class is also particularly exposed to some of the downsides of the erosion of class identity, immigration and rapid ethnic change, it is unsurprising that demand for communitarian politics, which prioritises nationalism as a source of group identity and which opposes immigration, is particularly high within this group.[9]

As a result, this study found that secular white working-class voters have become the electoral backbone of the AfD in Germany, the RN and Éric Zemmour in France and of the Trump campaign in the USA, suggesting that these movements have successfully tapped into a representation gap of communitarian priorities on the political supply side. Indeed, the analysis of the traditional party systems' response to the new identity cleavage has shown a historical convergence of the mainstream right and left on the cosmopolitan end of identitarian wedge-issues like immigration and national identity.[10] Moreover, especially the French and American mainstream left's gradual abandonment of old working-class communitarian

---

[5] Goodhart 2017; Eatwell and Goodwin 2018; Fukuyama 2018; Kaufmann 2018; Sandel 2020.

[6] This is especially so in the case of France and the USA, where religious communities, faced with restrictions through the state, developed independent systems of social and civic institutions, and where an unprecedented acceleration of secularisation trends since the turn of the millennium have had enormous consequences for these countries' social fabric.

[7] Fourquet 2019.

[8] Campbell and Putnam 2011; Wilcox et al. 2012; Carney 2019; Fourquet 2019.

[9] Olsen 2017; Perrineau 2017; Eatwell and Goodwin 2018; Kaufmann 2018; Sobolewska and Ford 2020.

[10] Kriesi 2008; Bornschier 2010; Mudde and Kaltwasser 2012; Mudde and Kaltwasser 2017.

instincts in favour of meritocratic individualism, multiculturalism and left-wing identity politics has accelerated this development by giving their traditional constituency of white working-class voters the sense of being excluded from a new coalition of liberal college-educated elites and racial minorities. Notably, this research also found support for Bornschier's claim that the German SPD's comparative resistance to such a shift has helped hinder the success of national populist movements in Germany compared to other Western countries.[11]

However, by the late 2010s, national populist movements had tapped into the rising demand for communitarian politics even in Germany by completing an 'identitarian turn' and embracing a new form of white identity politics.[12] Mirroring but reversing the identity politics of the left, white identity promotes an ethno-pluralist and 'civilisationist' agenda, which uses the vocabulary of group rights and claims to defend the collective identity of the ethnic majority, rather than those of minorities.[13] Whilst the French FN/RN was one of the first champions of this 'identitarian turn' at the turn of the millennium, Germany's AfD, although initially conceived as a non-populist 'professors' party', followed the same trend after Germany's 'refugee crisis' in 2015, focusing increasingly on anti-immigration, national identity and opposition to Islam. In the USA the picture is more complicated. While the Republican Party as a whole cannot be defined as a right-wing populist party, the Trump campaign possesses all the characteristics of a right-wing populist movement and, under the leadership of Donald Trump and Steve Bannon, has also self-identified as such. Moreover, after what some interviewees described as a 'hostile takeover' of the Republican Party through the Trump campaign in 2016, the GOP broke with the 'compassionate conservatism' of earlier years and gradually adopted policies and rhetoric more reminiscent of national populist parties in Europe.

In the context of the AfD's and RN's identitarian turn, and the 'Europeanisation' of America's right, this study also observed a shift in these movements' attitudes to religion. Interviews with national populist leaders revealed that in order to leverage the new identity cleavage, the movements shifted from an ethnic to a civilisational discourse of 'othering', specifically identifying Islam as the 'external other'. Indeed, during the interviews almost all RN, Zemmour and AfD representatives referenced opposition to Islam as part of their definition of Christian identity,

---

[11] Bornschier 2012.
[12] Betz 1994; Fukuyama 2018; Jardina 2019.
[13] Fukuyama 2018; Kaufmann 2018; Lilla 2018; Haynes 2019; Sides, Tesler and Vavreck 2019.

whereas almost none of the interviewed clergy or mainstream politicians did. Through this re-politicisation of religion, national populists in
Germany, France and the USA have fundamentally challenged the old
institutional settlements of church–state relations.

The RN, Zemmour and AfD especially made the curtailing of Muslim
religious expression in the public sphere through a more secularist settlement of church–state relations and a re-politicisation of *laïcité* a top priority of their agendas. While such a secularist push against public religion is
not present in the USA, the Trump campaign made opposition to Islam
a more central piece of their agenda than earlier, traditionally more pro-
religious conservative movements in the USA. Moreover, while this study
found that traditional 'culture war' issues such as abortion, gay marriage
or religious freedom have become less prominent in these countries' politics in recent years, references to Christianity have surged in the public
debate. However, this is primarily a result of national populists' civilisational definition of the 'other' as Islam, in response to which Christianity
has become a civilisational identifier of the 'us'. A closer analysis of such
religious references hence showed that they are fundamentally different
from those of earlier conservative movements.

16.2 Godless Crusaders? Right-Wing Populists' 'Christian Credentials' Under Scrutiny

The second major conclusion of this volume is that while the AfD, the
RN, Éric Zemmour and the Trump campaign have explicitly employed
Christian symbols and language in their rhetoric as cultural identity markers, they have often remained distanced from Christian doctrine, ethics
and institutions. Based on the analysis of these movements' 'Christian
credentials' as viewed through the cultural-ethical triangle, which reviews
each group's policy alignment with Christian doctrine, public displays of
Christian ethics and relations with the institutional churches, this study
found empirical support for the claims of scholars like Roy, McDonnell,
Marzouki and Brubaker about national populists' 'hijacking' religion primarily as a secularised national identity marker.[14]

This dynamic was most apparent in the cases of the RN, Éric Zemmour
and the AfD. Although all three movements positioned themselves as
'defenders of the faith', referencing France's status as the 'first-born daughter of the church' and touting Germany's 'Judeo-Christian heritage', they

---

[14] Roy, McDonnell and Marzouki 2016; Brubaker 2017.

also embraced policy positions fundamentally in conflict with Christian doctrine. In-depth analysis of party manifestos and dozens of elite interviews revealed clashes between the universalist stances and pro-immigration positions of Germany's and France's churches and the policy proposals of the populist right on immigration, national identity and Islam. Moreover, this study uncovered evidence for largely overlooked conflicts on moral and societal issues as well as secularism. In France for instance, Marine Le Pen's RN has remained pointedly absent from demonstrations against gay marriage, embraced a liberal position on abortion, posed as the main defender of LGBTQ and women's rights against Islam, and advocated for a more radically secularist reading of *laïcité*. Meanwhile in Germany, after its 'identitarian turn', the AfD de-emphasised many of its earlier socially conservative positions in favour of secularist stances designed to curtail the public influence and visibility of religion at the expense of Germany's religion-friendly system of benevolent neutrality. Notably, the interviews also revealed profoundly different interpretations of 'Christian identity' itself between the churches and these far-right parties. Whereas during the interviews German and French clergy and mainstream politicians primarily emphasised aspects of Christian believing (such as Christian values, anthropology or theological concepts about sinfulness, the Trinity or the resurrection), AfD and RN officials focused overwhelmingly on Christianity as a form of national and cultural belonging (referencing history, architecture, music, traditions and territory), and as a contrast point against the Islamic 'other'. Éric Zemmour's public confirming that he was 'for the church but against Christ' encapsulates this identitarian logic in Europe.[15]

Right-wing populists' *ex negativo* focus on 'Christendom' as a form of civilisational 'belonging' and distinguishing feature against Islam, rather than on a positive embrace of Christian beliefs and values, was also prominent in the USA. Certainly, under Trump, the Republican Party still sought to balance clashes with America's churches on immigration and race relations through catering to the Christian right's policy priorities with regards to social and moral issues. However, the Trump campaign followed European right-wing populists' trajectory and broke with American conservative tradition on issues such as Islam and American civil religion writ large. Unlike earlier Republican leaders, who had sought to integrate Muslims as conservative 'people of faith' into America's civil religious tradition, Trump and Bannon embraced a more European-style discourse featuring Islam as the 'civilisational other'. They also openly

---

[15] Lindell 2022.

rejected traditional civil religious rhetoric, which had focused on shared religious values and beliefs, and instead reinterpreted Christian symbols (such as in 'the war on Christmas') as exclusivist ethno-cultural markers of belonging. Moreover, while Trump's personal lack of Christian piety has been discussed at length in the media and literature, the interviews with Republican insiders and faith leaders revealed that this shift away from Christian ethics extended to larger parts of the administration. For instance, interviewees confided that in spite of prominent groups such as the White House Faith Advisory Board, Christian voices within the Trump administration often clashed with and were sidelined by more secular national populist elements. This 'post-Christian right' does not yet appear to be as powerful within the GOP as within the AfD and RN, where some party leaders reported a targeted marginalisation of Christian voices through secularist or neo-pagan currents, and where the relationship with institutional churches is characterised by open hostility. Still, Trump's transactional (and at times openly antagonistic) relationship with America's faith leaders suggests that such tendencies might become more common as a result of the gradual secularisation and Europeanisation of the American right.

Such findings confirm claims about the gradual convergence of national populist politics on both sides of the Atlantic but challenge traditionally dominant interpretations in the literature, where national populists' Christian references are seen as a continuation of America's old religious culture wars and their spread to Europe.[16] Rather this research finds a reverse dynamic, with Europe's secular right-wing identity politics expanding to the USA, as the religious culture wars of the twentieth century are supplanted by the ethno-cultural identity politics of the twenty-first century.

16.3   Religious Immunity? Christian Voters' Reactions to Right-Wing Populism

The third conclusion of this book is that, on the demand side, national populists' identitarian references to religion are often most successful amongst irreligious voters and non-practising 'cultural Christians', whereas practising Christians often remain comparatively 'immune' to such appeals. Adding to the observations of earlier studies that identified a 'vaccination effect' of Christian religiosity against voting for national

---

[16] Bednarz 2018; Fourquet 2018a; Norris and Inglehart 2019; Eatwell and Goodwin 2018; Kaufmann 2018; Rose 2021.

populists in several Western European countries, this book found evidence for a similar 'religion gap' in Germany, France and – albeit in more complicated ways – even in the USA.[17]

This religion gap appeared to be most prominent in Europe. The German AfD, having initially been discussed as a potential 'Christian alternative' for disappointed CDU/CSU voters, has consistently underperformed among Protestants and Catholics compared to irreligious Germans in regional, national and European elections. Its electoral strongholds were found in the highly secularised regions of eastern Germany, while the party has underperformed in the more religious western and southern parts of the country. However, a closer analysis has revealed that Germany's 'religion gap' is not a mere replication of its historical East–West divide. Rather, the AfD has reliably performed significantly better among religiously unaffiliated Germans, compared to Catholics and Protestants in each German state, regardless of whether the state is located in the West or East. Similar dynamics have been observed in France, where sociologists have long identified Catholics as one of the most formidable bulwarks against the electoral progress of the FN.[18] Especially among churchgoing Catholics, the FN/RN has historically performed significantly worse than amongst most other parts of the population.[19] In the USA the picture is more complicated, as Trump performed extremely well with white Evangelical Christians in 2016 and 2020.[20] However, even in the USA an initial 'religion gap' was observed during the 2016 GOP primaries, when Donald Trump performed twice as well among those primary voters who never attended church, whereas frequent churchgoers were the least likely to be early supporters of his national populist agenda.

A review of the existing literature suggests that this 'religion gap' can partly be traced back to differences in social backgrounds and attitudes on the demand side. Specifically, national populists' core supporters and church-attending Christians were found to come from opposing ends of the socio-economic and demographic spectrum, with the RN, AfD and Trump campaign drawing most support from white working-class males, whereas church attendees increasingly tend to be well educated, upper middle class and more likely to be female.

---

[17] Arzheimer and Carter 2009; Immerzeel, Jaspers and Lubbers 2013; Montgomery and Winter 2015; Siegers and Jedinger 2021; Cremer 2021a.
[18] Perrineau 2014; Dargent 2016.
[19] Though as discussed in Chapter 11, this religion gap has been narrowing since 2017.
[20] Pew 2020.

Meanwhile, with regards to the issues of immigration, race relations and Islam, practising Christians in Germany, France and the USA are often shown to hold more 'cosmopolitan' attitudes than the general population, and supporters of national populist movements in particular. This finding supports some scholars' hypothesis of a growing schism amongst right-wing voters, between the traditional religious right and a new secular right electorate.[21] Broadly speaking, the former is composed of the churchgoing and more educated middle classes, committed to socially conservative church teachings but also to openness on immigration, and attached to conservative parties. By contrast, the latter typically consists of disenchanted working-class voters, who combine secular values with cultural nativism and authoritarian tendencies, have less allegiance to church teachings and look more favourably on right-wing populist policies. This volume finds support for this hypothesis, showing for instance that the participants in the French conservative Catholic *Manif pour Tous* movement against gay marriage, who were often portrayed in the media as being in cahoots with the RN, were conservative, but socially, politically and institutionally distinct from and often strongly opposed to the RN and its national populist agenda.[22] Even more important than demand-side differences between the Christian and national populists electorates, however, are factors that have emerged on the political and religious supply side.

16.4   A Faustian Bargain? The Ambiguous Responses of Christian Communities and the Importance of Christian Leadership

The fourth and final cornerstone of this book's findings is that national populists' ability to successfully employ religion as part of their ethnonationalist identity politics critically depends on the behaviour of other supply-side actors. Two sets of actors were found to be of particular importance: the representatives of mainstream parties and the leaders of Christian churches.

---

[21] De Koster and Van der Waal 2007; Achterberg 2009; Daenekindt, De Koster and Van Der Waal 2017; Ribberink, Achterberg and Houtman 2017.

[22] However, it exceeded the scope of this study to systematically test the relevance of demand-side explanations for the empirical 'religion gap' through primary quantitative research. Moreover, given that the review of the existing literature has only yielded inconclusive results and that, especially in France and the USA, the strength of the electoral 'religion gap' appeared to become increasingly volatile (in the USA even in terms of its direction) without a perceivable shift in Christian voters attitudes, the role played by supply-side actors in influencing the existence and strength of this religion gap emerged as the focus of our analysis.

On the political supply side, the empirical analysis in Chapters 7, 11 and 15 found evidence supporting Arzheimer and Carter's argument that a party that maintains ownership over the political expression of Christian values and identity 'vaccinates [Christian voters] against voting for a party of the radical right', by making them 'unavailable'.[23] Thus, this research's findings demonstrate that when such a Christian electoral alternative is available, for instance in the form of Germany's Christian Democrats, Christian voters are comparatively immune to national populists' identitarian and civilisational references to Christianity. By contrast, if such an alternative is lacking or is 'hijacked' by populist movements (like the GOP by Trumpism in the USA) the religion gap could break down.

One of the most instructive examples of this dynamic was found in France. Whereas historically French Catholic voters were closely bound to the centre-right, and therefore unavailable to the FN/RN, the former's gradual collapse since 2017 has significantly changed this dynamic. While the 'religion gap' proved to be sizable during the first round of the presidential election, when Catholics overwhelmingly supported the centre-right candidate François Fillon, it all but disappeared in the second round. With the centre-right option eliminated, Catholics were suddenly confronted with what one prominent Catholic interviewee described as the choice between the 'chaos' of a national populist RN and the 'decay' of Emmanuel Macron's socially liberal agenda. As especially non-practising 'cultural' Catholics felt politically 'homeless' and therefore became more open to the RN, the 'religion gap' was reduced to only the most frequent churchgoers, who still disproportionately supported Macron's LREM during the 2017 and subsequent elections. The interviews suggested, however, that even this reduced religion gap might be further undermined in the future by the LREM's increasingly libertarian positions on social and moral issues, which might intensify Catholics' perceived lack of alternatives to the RN and more recently to Éric Zemmour.

A similar dynamic was observed during the Republican primaries in the USA in 2016. During this contest most practising Evangelicals were among the least supportive constituencies for Trump, favouring traditional Republican competitors like Ted Cruz, Marco Rubio, Ben Carson or Jeb Bush. As one conservative faith leader pointedly phrased it (and as previously cited in Chapter 14), 'There were sixteen candidates in the Republican

---

[23] Arzheimer and Carter 2009, 1006. This aligns with the logic proposed in earlier studies, that due to their historical focus on the moral/religious cleavage many Christian voters are already bound to traditional conservative or specifically Christian Democratic parties, which combine a defence of Christian identity with policy proposals that are aligned with Christian values, beliefs and institutions.

primary and Donald Trump was my seventeenth choice.' However, most
practising Christians fell in line and voted for Trump during the general
election once the other Republican candidates were eliminated and the only
alternative to the national populist candidate was Hilary Clinton, who in
many Christians' view represented a pro-abortion and increasingly secularist Democratic platform. By contrast, in Germany interviewees suggested
that the abiding prominence of Angela Merkel's Christian Democrats, as
well as the behaviour of other mainstream parties such as the Greens and
the SPD, who have remained more open to religious voters than the French
or American centre-left, here played a crucial role in upholding a comparatively powerful and stable 'religion gap'.[24]

These findings about the importance of 'Christian electoral alternatives'
on the political supply side add to an ongoing rich debate within the political
science literature. By contrast, the role of the religious supply side has received
less scholarly attention. Based on the extensive primary research conducted,
this book addresses this lacuna, by showing that religious supply-side actors
such as church authorities and other faith leaders can have an outsized influence on national populists' willingness and ability to use Christian references
to appeal to voters. Specifically, this study found that by either challenging
or implicitly condoning national populists' identitarian references to religion,
faith leaders play a critical role in the creation and maintenance of social
taboos among their flock against voting for national populist movements.

In Germany, for instance, interviewees credited the churches' largely
unanimous, consistent and unambiguous public opposition to the AfD's
references to Christianity with having created a strong 'social firewall' in
religious communities against the AfD. Given church leaders' prominent
institutional positions in German public life, assured through the system
of benevolent neutrality, this effect seemed to expand well beyond frequent
churchgoers and may even have discouraged AfD leaders from employing Christian references in the first place. There were similar dynamics in
France, where scholars observed an 'institution' or 'Pope Francis effect'
shaping Catholics' attitudes vis-à-vis the RN.[25] However, although during
the interviews French church leaders were privately no less critical of the
populist right than their German counterparts, a reorientation towards a

---

[24] Specifically, the Christian Democrats' historical focus on the *christliche Menschenbild* (Christian
view of man) but rejection of national populist rhetoric, combined with the centre-left parties'
avoidance of combative identity politics and abstinence from secularist reactions of the AfD's
claims to defend Christianity, seemed critical in making Christian voters unavailable to the AfD.
See also Siegers and Jedinger 2021.
[25] Dargent 2016; Geisser 2018; More in Common 2018.

more inwardly focused and less politically involved church model significantly has more recently undermined their willingness to publicly uphold
the social taboo against the far right in the same way they had done in
earlier decades. Combined with a gradual radicalisation of *laïcité* and consequent sidelining of religious voices in the public debate, this shift seems
to have contributed to the RN's *dédiabolisation* and the rising popularity
of Éric Zemmour among many French Catholics. Nonetheless, at least
among frequent churchgoers the quiet but consistent internal church criticism of the far right through sermons and internal discussions still played
a significant role in upholding a religion gap in France.

By contrast, US faith leaders' inability or unwillingness to create a similar
social taboo around Trumpism appears to be a key variable in explaining
the erosion and reversion of America's religion gap. Thus, although results
from the interviews confirmed that members of America's religious 'establishment' (including many white Evangelical leaders) were strongly opposed
to Trumpism, this scepticism did not translate into the same social taboo
among their flock for two reasons. The first is that American faith leaders have been confronted with structural limitations affecting their *ability*
to 'speak for Christianity' in the way their French and German counterparts could do, due to the decentralised make-up of the American religious
landscape. Thus, whereas in Germany and France the Catholic Conference
of Bishops combined with the leaders of the largest national Protestant
church(es) would be largely uncontested in their authority on religious
issues, in the USA, the multiple and decentralised structures of denominations, as well as the prominence of non-denominational leaders, significantly
undermine the religious establishments' sway over voters. Second, American
faith leaders also appeared less *willing* to speak out against Trumpism, partly
because of concerns about being perceived as too political or even about
losing their jobs and followership in their congregations, and partly because
Trump's election to the presidency drove many leaders to mute their public
criticism and instead seek to influence government policy from the inside.

The findings of this research suggest that many of these concerns from
US church leaders are not unfounded. In Germany and France religious and
political leaders expressed worries that the churches' 'social firewall' against
national populism might lead to religious leaders' politicisation, undermine
their ability to bridge divides and thus further radicalise those outside the
firewall. In the USA such concerns played out in practice. Thus, American
faith leaders who openly spoke out against Trump lost almost all access to
the policymaking process as a result. However, this volume's findings also
cast significant doubt on the effectiveness of the alternative church strategy

of attempting to influence national populists from the inside, while refraining from public criticism. Thus, most political insiders expressed scepticism or even ridicule about faith leaders' ability to moderate national populist elements from within. Moreover, this study identified significant potential costs of church leaders' silence in the long run. In addition to undermining the religious vaccination effect and implicitly condoning national populists' identitarian reinterpretation of Christianity as a civilisational identity marker, failure to speak out might hence undermine the credibility and moral authority of Christian leaders. The 2020 BLM movement and Donald Trump's Bible photo-op in front of St John's Episcopal Church epitomise this risk. While Donald Trump sought to 'hijack' Christianity for his white identity politics through his photo-op at St John's Church, the lack of attention paid to Christian voices in the BLM movement compared to the role of religious leaders such as Martin Luther King Jr in the 1960s Civil Rights movement, demonstrates the crisis of America's civil religious prophetic tradition in fulfilling its historical role of bridging political, racial and social divides. In marked contrast, some interviewees suggested that Germany's churches' clear condemnation of national populist rhetoric and decisive involvement in the shouldering of the refugee crisis have helped restore some of the moral credibility lost during earlier abuse scandals.

Taken together, this book has established several cornerstones on which to build a more general theory of the dynamics between national populists' rise and their relationship with religion. It has explored the social and demographic origins of national populist movements in Germany, France and the USA, revealing their success as a response to a democratic lack of representation of the new identity cleavage. It investigated the AfD's, RN's and Trump campaign's strategies in responding to this demand, identifying their references to Christianity as part of a new white identity politics, in which Christianity serves as a civilisational marker of belonging, rather than source of religious believing. It studied Christian communities' responses to these movements, finding a potential 'vaccination' effect of religiosity against national populist appeals. Finally, this volume analysed the role of mainstream parties and faith leaders in combating or condoning national populist's co-optation of Christianity, showing that far from being helpless bystanders, their actions can play an immense role in shaping national populists' ability to redefine and re-politicise religion in German, French and American politics. Looking to other countries and into the future, the final question is to what extent such findings are generalisable, and what research might be necessary to develop them further.

CHAPTER 17

Democracy after God?
Faith, Populism and the Future of Liberal Democracy

Given the limitations of small-N qualitative studies, this volume does not claim that its conclusions are universally applicable to contexts beyond Germany, France, and the United States in the twenty-first century. However, it does provide the cornerstones of a solid theoretical framework of analysis and a number of empirically grounded and testable hypotheses, on the basis of which further research can be conducted.

17.1 Outlook and Avenues of Research

In terms of avenues of research we may note, for instance, exploring national populists' references to religion and the existence of empirical 'religion gaps' in other Western countries, such as the UK, the Netherlands, Italy or Denmark. This would be a critical step towards developing a general theory of the interaction between national populism and religion. Moreover, investigating similarities and differences between Western European right-wing populists' increasingly secular identity politics, and the more traditionally conservative right-wing populism seen in Eastern European countries could help to identify the extent to which such dynamics are dependent on each country's culture, national institutions and history.[1]

In addition to extending the geographic scope to test the viability of this study's conclusions in other countries, this volume's findings may also serve as a basis for new avenues of research when 'looking ahead'. For one, given current trends towards further secularisation, individualisation, deinstitutionalisation and the rise of left-wing identity politics challenging traditional group identities, the new identity cleavage appears likely to gain in salience, further dividing Western societies between cosmopolitans and communitarians, and increasing the demand for national populist politics. However, short-term consequences of the COVID-19 pandemic or Russia's invasion of Ukraine

---

[1] Alvis 2012; Pytlas 2015; Bozóki and Ádám 2016.

might slow down or even reverse some trends of globalisation and reduce the salience of national populists' core topics of Muslim immigration and anti-globalism.[2] Similarly, on the political supply side, trends such as Boris Johnson's attempts to transform the British Tory Party to appeal to white working-class voters, or hopes that the American Democratic party under a moderate like Joe Biden might be able to renew its appeals to working-class whites in the rustbelt and to moderate Christian voters, could change the opportunity structures for the populist right.[3] New quantitative research, using this book's demand-and-supply-side framework to study such dynamics, would therefore be highly auspicious. Similarly, qualitative analyses of whether, why and how supply-side actors in mainstream parties are shifting their policy platforms in response to the new identity cleavage and the rise of right-wing populism could build on this volume's findings to better understand the interaction between supply- and demand-side factors in general, and the corrective democratic potential of national populism in particular.

Another set of research questions arising from the findings of this book centres around how the process of secularisation might shape the role of religion in Western politics and national populism going forward. On the one hand, observations about how eroding religious group identities have contributed to the rise of the new identity cleavage would suggest that secularisation might continue to sharpen the identity divide, while gradually reducing the salience of the old 'culture wars' on both sides of the Atlantic. Moreover, given that secularisation also correlates with growing levels of religious illiteracy and an erosion of the institutional churches' voices in the public sphere, we might expect not only a continued rise of national populists' post-religious identity politics, but also that the identitarian redefinition and politicisation of Christian themes and their dissociation from Christian beliefs and institutions will become more prevalent.[4] On the other hand, secularisation may reduce the number of Christian voters so extensively that it would become less attractive for national populists to appeal to them. Secularisation could also strengthen the divide between an increasingly irreligious majority population, for whom Christian symbols might become irrelevant, and a small minority of practising Christians, who would assume a minority identity in Western societies, thus placing them on one side with other religious minority groups such as Jews and Muslims.[5] Future research could therefore further

---

[2] Cremer, Freston and Elcott 2020.
[3] Crines 2019; Baldini, Bressanelli and Gianfreda 2020; Rein 2020.
[4] Arato 2013; Davie and Dinham 2018; Roy 2019.
[5] Dreher 2017; Fourquet 2018a.

develop the findings of this volume by exploring how the secularisation of the political right may either make the movement more tolerant (as liberal political commentators traditionally hoped) or more nativist (as the findings of this volume suggest); how the shrinking of the Christian electorate might influence party leaders' willingness to reference Christianity; and how church leaders might deal with these developments in the future.

Finally, while this book focused on the interaction of demand-side developments and supply-side actors, it also showed that both are critically dependent on the specific institutional and constitutional framework in which they operate. Mainstream parties in France's or America's majoritarian system might for instance more easily be tempted to ignore national populist movements until they have reached a critical mass, whereas in Germany's proportional system parties are forced to address communitarian concerns much earlier. Additionally, this research found that the institutional settlement of church–state relations can have an immense impact on national populists' willingness and ability to make religion part of their identitarian appeal as well as on church leaders' willingness and ability to react to this. Future studies could build on these findings and explore which political systems might be better suited to adapt to a shifting social cleavage system, which institutional arrangements of church–state relations might be more likely to inhibit ethno-religious conflict in secularising and increasingly diverse societies, or how national populists' references to religion might lead to changes in current institutional settlements. Such research could make critical contributions, not only to the academic debate but also to the discussions within political parties and the churches themselves.

17.2   After Christendom: Religion, Populism and Right-Wing Identity Politics in the West

This book has sought to make its own small contribution to the debates above, and the overwhelmingly positive response and willingness to engage that I encountered among interviewees at the top echelons of the German, French and American political and religious landscapes make me optimistic about the potential impact of future research in this field. However, my research has also humbled me and exposed the limitations and potential biases of academic frameworks in evaluating and understanding the dynamics at play in today's modern and complex societies. After over six years 'in the field' in Germany, France and the USA, and hundreds of hours spent listening and trying to understand what drives and motivates the leaders of national populist movements, mainstream political parties and Christian communities alike, I for one now look at the episodes observed in the Introduction of this book in a different light.

To be sure, the PEGIDA demonstrators carrying crosses in Dresden may not have believed in the Christian doctrine, that the man who died on this cross did so for the sins of all humankind, including Muslim refugees. The RN protesters gathered around the statue of Joan of Arc in Paris might have had little love for the bishops and archbishops of the church that had made her a saint. And participants of the pro-Trump protests at the steps of the US Capitol might have been unbothered by their hero's public rejection of Christian public ethics and America's civil religious tradition. Yet, they all saw such Christian symbols as remnants of an identity, community and home that they had lost through the processes of secularisation, globalisation and individualisation. Worse still, in the eyes of these protesters, the 'liberal elite' (who are in many ways the winners of these processes) were perceived to delegitimise and ridicule their very yearning for community and group identity. National populists have recognised this problem and offered their own remedy: a godless crusade, in which Christianity is largely turned into a secularised 'Christianism' and a symbol of whiteness that is interchangeable with the Viking-veneer, the Confederate flag, neo-pagan symbols or even secularism.

Churches and mainstream parties might feel justified in rejecting this remedy and condemning the 'hijacking' of religion through the populist right. They might have good reason to turn off the lights of the church that PEGIDA demonstrators were gathering around, to condemn the RN's embrace of an anti-clerical version of *laïcité*, or to warn Christians of the risks involved in a 'Faustian bargain' with a national populist leader like Donald Trump. However, they will also need to recognise that in doing so they are only addressing the symptoms of a deeper democratic, social and spiritual crisis liberal democracies have been suffering from for several decades. Condemning right-wing populists' remedy is one thing. Coming up with alternative cures will be much harder. Still, the results of this book suggest that even at a moment of profound crisis, political and religious leaders in the West might yet have a powerful role to play, not only in challenging political uses of religious symbols, but also in bridging divides and offering sources of shared but inclusive forms of identity. As scenes like those seen in Dresden, Paris or Washington, DC are likely to become more common, and as the populists' godless crusade sweeps across the West, a new debate about the role of faith and identity for the future of liberal democracy has only just begun.

Appendix A
List of Interviewees

A.1 German Case Study

Name	Position	Date	Place
Dr Thomas Arnold	Director of the Catholic Academy Dresden-Meißen	26.06.2018	Dresden
Dr Liane Bednarz	Catholic Public Intellectual	10.08.2018	Hamburg
Bishop Dr Markus Dröge	Bishop of the Protestant Church of Berlin, Brandenburg Oberlausitz	13.08.2018	Berlin
Prälat Dr Martin Dutzmann	Representative of the Council of the Evangelical Church in Germany to the Federal Republic of Germany and the European Union	25.07.2018	Berlin
Katrin Göring-Eckardt,	Leader of the Alliance 90/The Greens in the Bundestag	31.07.2018	Berlin
Hermann Gröhe	Former General Secretary of the CDU and Former Minister of Health	14.08.2018	Berlin
Armin-Paulus Hampel	Member of the Federal Parliament for the AfD	11.09.2018	Berlin
Uwe Heimowski	Representative of the German Evangelical Alliance to the Federal Parliament and Government	28.08.2018	Berlin
Dr Michael Inacker	Protestant Public Intellectual and President of the International Martin Luther Foundation	27.07.2018	Berlin
Prälat Dr Karl Jüsten	President of the Catholic Office Berlin	29.08.2018	Berlin
Joachim Kuhs	Speaker of the Christians in the AfD	31.08.2018	Berlin
Dr Thomas Krüger	President of the Federal Agency for Civic Education	20.08.2018	Berlin
Cardinal Reinard Marx	Cardinal and President of the German Conference of Bishops	07.09.2018	Munich
Helmut Matthies	Former President of the Evangelical News Agency Idea and a representative of the Protestant Christian Conservatives	01.08.2018	Berlin

Name	Position	Date	Place
Christian Meißner	Director of the Protestant Association in the CDU/CSU	08.08.2018	Berlin
Prof. Dr Jörg Meuthen	President of the AfD	31.08.2018	Dresden
Volker Münz	Speaker for Religious Affairs of the AfD in the Bundestag	23.08.2018	Berlin
Marcus Pretzell	Former President of the AfD in NRW	22.08.2018	Düsseldorf
Dr Andreas Püttmann	Catholic Public Intellectual	09.08.2018	Bonn
Dr Stefanie Rentsch	Program Director of the German Protestant Church Day 2019	09.08.2018	Fulda
Annette Schultner	Former Speaker of the Christians in the AfD	22.08.2018	Düsseldorf
Dr Irmgard Schwätzer	President of the Synod of the Protestant Church	07.08.2018	Berlin
Dr Christian Staffa	Director of Studies for Democratic Culture and the Church at the Protestant Academy in Berlin	02.08.2018	Berlin
Stephan Steinlein	Chief of Staff of the German Federal President	25.07.2018	Berlin
Prof. Dr Thomas Sternberg	President of the Central Council of German Catholics	24.08.2018	Berlin
Wolfgang Thierse	Former Speaker of the Bundestag and prominent Christian in the SPD	27.07.2018	Berlin

A.2 French Case Study

Name	Position	Date	Place
Bernard Antony	Former Member of the Assemblée Nationale (FN)	25.04.2019	Paris
Nicolas Bay	Member of the European Parliament (RN) and Vice President of the ENL group in the European Parliament	26.04.2019	Paris
Jean-Louis Bianco	President of the Observatory of Laicité and former minister (PS)	27.03.2019	Paris
Christophe Billan	Former President of Sens Commun	17.04.2019	Paris
Xavier Breton	Member of the Assemblée Nationale (Les Republicains)	30.04.2019	Paris
Père Grégoire Catta	Director of the department of Family and Society at the French Bishops Conference	04.04.2019	Paris
François Clavairoly	President of the French Protestant Federation	30.04.2019	Paris
Gilbert Collard	Member of Parliament (Rassemblement National)	29.04.2019	Paris

Name	Position	Date	Place
Thibaud Collin	Member of the Academic Council of the ISSEP Lyon	11.04.2019	Paris
Jean-Pierre Delannoy	Chaplain/Deacon to the Assemblée nationale	02.04.2019	Paris
Francoise Dumas	Member of Assemblée National (La Republique en Marche) and of the 'Task Force Anti-FN'	27.03.2019	Paris
Père Jacques Enjalbert	Chaplain of Sciences Po Paris	18.04.2019	Paris
Père Francois Euvé	Editor-in-chief of the journal *Revue Etude*	21.03.2019	Paris
Bruno Gollnisch	Member of the European Parliament (RN) and of the executive committee of the RN	24.04.2019	Paris
Nino Galetti	Director of the KAS office in Paris	16.04.2019	Paris
Jacques de Guillebon	Editor-in-chief of *L'Incorrecte*	26.04.2019	Paris
Benjamin Harnwell	Director of the Trisulti Academy for the Judeo-Christian West	25.02.2019	Trisulti
Gerard Larcher	President of the Senate (Les Républicains)	26.06.2019	Paris
Erwan Le Morhedec	Catholic blogger and activist	21.03.2019	Paris
Jean-Marie Le Pen	Founder and former President of the RN (FN), Member of the European Parliament (RN)	26.04.2019	Paris
Marion Maréchal Le Pen	President of the ISSEP and former Member of the Assemblée Nationale (RN)	03.05.2019	Lyon
Mgr Dominique Lebrun	Bishop of Rouen	26.03.2019	Rouen
Stefan Lunte	General Secretary of Justice & Peace Europe of the Catholic Church in the European Union	25.03.2019	Paris
Amb. Nikolaus Mayer-Landrut	German Ambassador to France	27.06.2019	Paris
Jean-Fréderic Poisson	President of the Parti Democrate Chretienne (PDC)	12.04.2019	Phone call
Dominique Potier	Member of the Assemblée Nationale (PS)	30.04.2019	Paris
Dominique Quinio	President of the Semaine Sociales, former editor-in-chief of *La Croix* newspaper	20.03.2019	Paris
Mgr Dominique Rey	Bishop of Toulon	22.03.2019	Toulon
Mgr Matthieu Rougé	Bishop of Nanterre	13.04.2019	Nanterre
Lorrain de Saint Affrique	General Secretary of the Comités Jeanne	26.04.2019	Paris
Wallerand de Saint-Just	Treasurer of the Rassemblement National	02.04.2019	Paris

Name	Position	Date	Place
Emmaneulle Seyboldt	President of the United Protestant Church of France	27.03.2019	Paris
Laurent Schlumberger	Former President of the United Protestant Church of France	18.04.2019	Paris
Mgr Marc Stenger	Bishop of Troyes	29.03.2019	Paris
Jean-Richard Sulzer	Founder of Rassemblement national juif (RN)	29.04.2019	Paris
Najat Vallaud-Belkacem	Former minister of education (PS)	02.05.2019	Paris
Mgr Pascal Wintzer	Archbishop of Poitiers	23.04.2019	Poitiers

A.3 US Case Study

Name	Position	Date	Place
Rev. Barry Black	Chaplain of the United States Senate	12.02.2020	Phone call
Dr Arthur Brooks	President of the American Enterprise Institute (2008–2018)	16.12.2019	Phone call
Amb. Samuel Brownback	United States Ambassador at Large for International Religious Freedom (since February 2018); 46th Governor of Kansas (2011–18) (R)	05.02.2020	Washington, DC
Jonathan Burks	Former Chief of Staff, Speaker Paul Ryan; Former Deputy Policy Director, Romney–Ryan 2012	22.11.2020	Washington, DC
Rev. Galen Carey	Vice President of Government Relations for the National Association of Evangelicals (NAE)	04.02.2020	Washington, DC
Dr Stanley Carlson-Thies	Founder and Senior Director of the bipartisan Institutional Religious Freedom Alliance	04.12.2019	Washington, DC
John Carr	Director of the Initiative on Catholic Social Thought and Public Life at Georgetown University; Former Director of the Department of Justice, Peace and Human Development at the United States Conference of Catholic Bishops (USCCB)	06.12.2019	Washington, DC

Name	Position	Date	Place
Dr Shaun Casey	Director of Georgetown University's Berkley Center; US special representative for religion and global affairs and director of the US Department of State's Office of Religion and Global Affairs (2013–2017)	11.11.2019	Washington, DC
Rev. Richard Cizik	President of the New Evangelical Partnership for the Common Good; former Vice President for Governmental Affairs of the National Association of Evangelicals (NAE)	07.11.2019	Washington, DC
Rep. Doug Collins	Member of the US House of Representatives (R)	11.02.2020	Washington, DC
Fr. Patrick J. Conroy	Chaplain of the United States House of Representatives	12.11.2019	Washington, DC
Kim Daniels	Associate Director of the Initiative on Catholic Social Thought and Public Life at Georgetown University; Member of the Vatican Dicastery for Communication	06.12.2019	Washington, DC
Christopher DeMuth	President of the American Enterprise Institute (1986–2008); Organiser of the National Conservatism Conferences of 2019 and 2020	07.01.2020	Washington, DC
Jon DeWitte	Chief of Staff, Rep. Bill Huizenga at US House of Representatives (R)	08.01.2020	Washington, DC
Josh Dickson	National Faith Engagement Director at Biden for President 2020, Deputy Director to The White House Office of Faith-Based and Neighborhood Partnerships since 2021	10.10.2020	Phone call
Joshua DuBois	Head of the Office of Faith Based and Neighborhood Partnerships in the Executive Office of the President of the United States Barack Obama from 2009 to 2013	13.01.2020	Washington, DC
Mark Galli	Editor-in-chief of *Christianity Today*	13.02.2020	Wheaton, IL
Rev. Jim Garlow	Senior Pastor of Skyline Church, Member of President Donald Trump's White House Evangelical Faith Advisory Board	05.02.2020	Washington, DC

Name	Position	Date	Place
Tim Goeglein	Special assistant to US President George W. Bush and Deputy Director of the White House Office of Public Liaison (2001–2008)	10.02.2020	Phone call
Rev. Derrick Harkins	National Director of Interfaith Outreach for the Democratic National Committee; Senior Vice President at Union Seminary	18.11.2019	New York City
Rev. Katharine Rhodes Henderson	President of Auburn Seminary New York	19.11.2019	New York City
Rep. Randy Hultgren	Member of the US House of Representative (R) (2011 to 2019), Co-Host of the 2019 National Prayer Breakfast	05.02.2020	Washington, DC
Rev. Dr Robert Jeffress	Pastor of the First Baptist Church in Dallas, Texas; Member of President Donald Trump's White House Evangelical Faith Advisory Board	14.02.2020	Phone call
Prof. Dr Jackie Johns	Pentecostal Theological Seminary; Senior pastor of the Pentecostal New Covenant Church of God in Cleveland	05.02.2020	Phone call
Dr D. Michael Lindsay	President of Gordon College	09.11.2019	Phone call
Francis Maier	Special Assistant and Senior Adviser to the Archbishop of Philadelphia	08.11.2019	Philadelphia, PA
John McCarty	Deputy National Political Director – Biden for President 2020, National Director of Faith and Heritage Community Outreach – Hillary for America 2016	06.12.2019	Phone call
Mischaël Modrikamen	Managing director of 'The Movement' (a right-wing populist organisation founded by Steve Bannon to unite national right-wing populist movements in the US and Europe)	17.12.2019	Brussels, Belgium
Rabbi Jack Moline	Executive Director of Interfaith Alliance; Former director of the National Jewish Democratic Council	10.01.2020	Washington, DC

Name	Position	Date	Place
Rev. Johnnie Moore	Commissioner for the United States Commission on International Religious Freedom; Member of President Donald Trump's White House Evangelical Faith Advisory Board	04.11.2019	Washington, DC
Rev. Dr Russell Moore	President of the Southern Baptist Convention's Ethics & Religious Liberty Commission	12.02.2021	Phone call
Henry Olsen	Washington Post Columnist and Senior Fellow at the Ethics and Public Policy Center	21.01.2020	Washington, DC
Bishop Thomas Paprocki	Bishop of Springfield	06.11.2019	Chicago, IL
Pam Pryor	Senior adviser in the Office of Civilian Security, Democracy and Human Rights US State Department; Religious Outreach Director – Trump–Pence 2016	27.11.2019	Washington, DC
Russell Ronald, Reno	Editor of ecumenical and conservative religious journal *First Things* magazine	19.11.2019	New York City
Bishop Tony Richie	Bishop in the Church of God; adjunct Professor at the Pentecostal Theological Seminary Cleveland	16.10.2019	Phone call
Rev. Samuel Rodriguez	President of the National Hispanic Christian Leadership Conference, Member of President Donald Trump's White House Evangelical Faith Advisory Board	26.02.2020	Phone call
Rep. Francis Rooney	Member of the US House of Representatives (R); United States Ambassador to the Holy See (2005–2008)	08.01.2020	Washington, DC
Paul Ryan	54th Speaker of the United States House of Representatives	21.01.2020	Phone call
Eric Sapp	President of Public Democracy consulting firm that works with Democrats on religious outreach and communication	18.12.2019	Alexandria, VA
Rev. Rob Schenck	Founding President of The Dietrich Bonhoeffer Institute	27.11.2020	Alexandria, VA
Bishop Mark Seitz	Bishop of El Paso	23.02.2020	Phone call

Name	Position	Date	Place
Rev. Jay Strack	President and Founder of Student Leadership University; Member of President Donald Trump's White House Evangelical Faith Advisory Board	26.11.2020	Phone call
Amy Sullivan	Journalist and former religion editor of *TIME*, Yahoo, the *Washington Monthly* and *National Journal*	18.12.2019	Phone call
Rep. Thomas Suozzi	Member of the US House of Representatives (D); Co-Host of the National Prayer Breakfast 2020	10.01.2020	Washington, DC
Mark Tooley	President of the Institute on Religion and Democracy	08.01.2020	Washington, DC
Archbishop Allen Henry Vigneron	Archbishop of Detroit and Vice President of the United States Conference of Catholic Bishops	06.11.2019	Detroit, MI
Michael Wear	National Faith Vote Coordinator – Obama for President 2012	09.01.2020	Washington, DC
Pete Wehner	Contributing opinion writer for the New York Times; Deputy Director of Speechwriting to the US President George W. Bush; Head of the White House Office of Strategic Initiatives 2001–2008	14.11.2019	Washington, DC
Jim Winkler	President and General Secretary of the National Council of Churches	07.11.2019	Washington, DC
Travis Wussow	Vice President for Public Policy of Southern Baptist Convention's Ethics and Religious Liberty Commission	27.02.2020	Washington, DC

Appendix B
Sample Questionnaire (Religious Leaders)

Part 1:   Background

1. Could you briefly describe your position within your organisation and how in the context of your responsibilities you are confronted with the topic of right-wing populism?

Part 2:   Religion and Politics in Your Country

1. What does 'Christian identity' mean to you? How would you define it?
2. Do you think that Christianity is or should be part of your country's culture and national identity? Could you explain how this relationship manifests itself in practice? What about other religions such as Judaism and Islam?
3. How would you assess the role of religion in your country's politics? Has religion become more or less important in politics in recent years? Is this a positive or a negative development in your view?
4. What is your view on the current institutional settlement of church–state relations in your country? Is it applied in appropriate ways, given today's social and political circumstances?

Part 3:   Christianity and National Populism in Your Country

1. National populist movements often reference your country's Judeo-Christian heritage and identity in their rhetoric. How do you feel about such references? Are they a positive or a negative development? Why?
2. Many of your colleagues – and possibly yourself – are driven by their Christian faith in their professional lives. Many national populist politicians claim this, too. Can you understand their argumentation and is the common reference to faith a potential for 'common ground'?

3. Why do you think that national populist movements are making references to Christianity now while this was not necessarily the case with earlier right-wing populist parties?

Part 4: The Relationship between National Populism and the Institutional Church(es) in Your Country

1. National populists often present themselves as an electoral alternative for Christians, who no longer feel represented by the mainstream parties or the institutional church. Can you understand it when Christian voters turn towards national populist movements for religious reasons?
2. In recent years, many high-ranking church representatives and faith leaders have publicly criticised national populist movements and their references to religion. How do feel about this? When and why do you think that such interventions are legitimate and where do you see the limits of such a confrontation?
3. Is there much debate within your organisation/church about how to approach the question or national populism? Is the course of the church's leadership contested?
4. In your personal experience with various groups/factions/levels of authority within your organisation/church do you see any differences in their attitudes towards national populist movements? Which segments are the most critical, which the most accommodating? Why?

Part 5: Looking Ahead

1. Do you think that religion will become more or less important in your country's politics going forward? Do you think this is a positive or a negative development?
2. Do you think that relations between national populist movements and the institutional churches have recently improved or deteriorated in your country? Do you think this trend will continue? Why?
3. Which question have I forgotten? Is there anything else you think I should have asked or that you would like to share with me?
4. Whom else do you think I should talk to about this question either within your organisation or beyond?

References

20 Minutes société. 2017. 'Hommage à Johnny Hallyday: Pourquoi Emmanuel Macron n'a Pas Fait de Signe de Croix Devant Le Cercueil.' *20 Minutes Société*, 9 December. At www.20minutes.fr/societe/2184767-20171209-hommage-johnny-hallyday-pourquoi-emmanuel-macron-fait-signe-croix-devant-cercueil.

Abramowitz, Alan I. 2018. *The Great Alignment: Race, Party Transformation, and the Rise of Donald Trump*. New Haven, CT: Yale University Press.

Abramowitz, Alan I., and Jennifer McCoy. 2019. 'United States: Racial Resentment, Negative Partisanship, and Polarization in Trump's America.' *The ANNALS of the American Academy of Political and Social Science* 681, no. 1: 137–56.

Abramowitz, Alan I., and Steven W. Webster. 2018. 'Negative Partisanship: Why Americans Dislike Parties but Behave Like Rabid Partisans.' *Political Psychology* 39: 119–35.

Abromeit, J., B. Chesterton, G. Marotta and Y. Norman. 2015. *Transformations of Populism in Europe and the Americas: History and Recent Tendencies*. London: Bloomsbury Academic.

Acemoglu, D., E. Georgy and S. Konstantin. 2013. 'A Political Theory of Populism.' *The Quarterly Journal of Economics* 128, no. 2: 771–805.

Achterberg, P. 2009. 'A Christian Cancellation of the Secularist Truce? Waning Christian Religiosity and Waxing Religious Deprivatization in the West.' *Journal for the Scientific Study of Religion*: 48–4.

Addicott, Jeffrey F. 2018. 'Reshaping American Jurisprudence in the Trump Era – The Rise of Originalist Judges.' *California Western Law Review* 55: 341.

AfD. 2016. 'Programm für Deutschland: Grundsatzprogramme der Alternative für Deutschland.' *AfD*. At www.afd.de/wp-content/uploads/sites/111/2017/01/2016-06-27_afd-grundsatzprogramm_web-version.pdf.

　　2017. 'Wahlprogramm Bundestagswahl 2017.' *AfD*. At www.afd.de/wp-content/uploads/sites/111/2017/08/AfD_kurzprogramm_a4-quer_210717.pdf.

　　2018. *Bekenntnisse von Christen in der Alternative für Deutschland: Im Anhang: Grundsatzerklärung der Christen in der AfD. Das apostolische Glaubensbekenntnis*. Graz: AfD.

AfD Bayern. 2018. 'Bayern. Aber Sicher. Landtagswahlprogramm 2018.' *AfD*. At www.afdbayern.de/wahlen-2018/wahlprogramm-landtagswahl-2018/.

AfD Bundestagsfraktion. 2018. 'Antrag: Christenverfolgung Stoppen und Sanktionieren.' *Deutscher Bundestag.* At https://dip21.bundestag.de/dip21/btd/19/016/1901698.pdf.

AfD Heidelberg. 2018. 'Die Rücksichtslosigkeit Der Asylprofiteure.' *AfD.* At https://alternative-heidelberg.de/gruene-asyltraeume-auf-dem-ruecken-der-buerger/.

AfD Thüringen. 2019. 'Unheilige Allianz: Der Pakt Der Evangelischen Kirche Mit Dem Zeitgeist und Den Mächtigen.' *AfD Thüringen.* At https://afd-thl.de/wp-content/uploads/sites/20/2019/06/Kirchenpapier_Onlineversion.pdf.

Akkerman, A., C. Mudde, and A. Zaslove. 2015. 'How Populist Are the People? Measuring Populist Attitudes in Voters.' *Comparative Political* 47, no. 9: 1324–53.

Akkerman, T. 2005. 'Anti-Immigration Parties and the Defence of Liberal Values: The Exceptional Case of the List Pim Fortuyn.' *Journal of Political Ideologies* 10, no. 3: 337–54.

Alberta, Tim. 2017. 'Donald Trump and the Evangelical–Nationalist Alliance.' *Politico*, 14 October. At www.politico.com/magazine/story/2017/10/14/trump-evangelical-nationalist-alliance-215713.

2019. *American Carnage: On the Front Lines of the Republican Civil War and the Rise of President Trump.* New York: HarperCollins.

Albertazzi, D., and D. McDonnell. 2008. *Twenty-First Century Populism: The Spectre of Western European Democracy.* London: Palgrave Macmillan.

2015. *Populists in Power, Routledge Studies in Extremism and Democracy.* London: Routledge.

Albertini, Dominique. 2015. 'Pourquoi Le Front National Défile-t-Il Le 1er Mai?' *Liberation*, 1 May. At www.liberation.fr/france/2015/05/01/pourquoi-le-fn-defile-t-il-le-1er-mai_1272058.

Alexander, Claude. 2016. 'A Declaration by American Evangelicals concerning Donald Trump.' At www.change.org/p/donald-trump-a-declaration-by-american-evangelicals-concerning-donald-trump.

Algan, Yann, Elizabeth Beasley, Daniel Cohen and Martial Foucault. 2019. *Les Origines Du Populisme.* Paris: Le Seuil.

Algan, Yann, Elizabeth Beasley, Daniel Cohen, Martial Foucault and M. Péron. 2019. *Qui Sont Les Gilets Jaunes et Leurs Soutiens?* Paris: Technical report, CEPREMAP et CEVIPOF.

Aliot, Louis. 2019. 'Augmentation Des Actes de Malveillance Contre Les Églises.' *Rassemblement National.* At https://rassemblementnational.fr/interventions/augmentation-des-actes-de-malveillance-contre-les-eglises/.

Allensbach Institut. 2016. '"Zweitstimmen-Wahlabsicht", Allensbacher Archiv, IfD-Umfragen für die Frankfurter Allgemeine Zeitung.' *Frankfurter Allgemeine Zeitung.* At www.ifd-allensbach.de/studien-und-berichte/uebersicht.html.

Almeida, Dimitri. 2017. 'Exclusionary Secularism: The Front National and the Reinvention of Laïcité.' *Modern & Contemporary France* 25, no. 3: 249–63.

2019. 'Cultural Retaliation: The Cultural Policies of the "New" Front National.' *International Journal of Cultural Policy* 25, no. 3: 269–81.

Alvis, R. 2012. 'Faith and Fatherland: Catholicism, Modernity, and Poland.' *Nationalities Papers* 40, no. 1: 149–50.

Amann, M. 2017. *Angst für Deutschland: Die Wahrheit über die AfD: Wo sie herkommt, wer sie führt, wohin sie steuert.* München: Droemer.

Ankenbrand, H. 2013. 'Der Protestant.' *Frankfurter Allgemeine Zeitung*: 14 December. At www.faz.net/aktuell/wirtschaft/menschen-wirtschaft/bernd-lucke-der-protestant-12711334.html.

Appenzeller, Gerd. 2015. 'Wenn die Gottlosen für das christliche Abendland demonstrieren.' *Tagesspiegel.* At www.tagesspiegel.de/politik/pegida-und-das-christentum-wenn-die-gottlosen-fuer-das-christliche-abendland-demonstrieren/12345386.html.

Aprill, Ellen P. 2018. 'Amending the Johnson Amendment in the Age of Cheap Speech.' *University of Illinois Law Review On-Line*, Research Paper No. 2017-45: 1–18.

Arato, Andrew. 2013. 'Political Theology and Populism.' *Social Research: An International Quarterly* 80, no. 1: 143–72.

Araud, Gérard. 2016. 'The Future of Diplomacy Project Hosts French Ambassador Gérard Araud.' 15 September, Cambridge, MA. At www.belfercenter.org/publication/future-diplomacy-project-hosts-french-ambassador-gerard-araud.

Arendt, H. 1973. *The Origins of Totalitarianism.* Boston, MA: Houghton Mifflin Harcourt.

Art, D. 2006. *The Politics of the Nazi Past in Germany and Austria.* Cambridge: Cambridge University Press.

  2011. *Inside the Radical Right: The Development of Anti-Immigrant Parties in Western Europe.* Cambridge: Cambridge University Press.

Arzheimer, Kai. 2009. 'Contextual Factors and the Extreme Right Vote in Western Europe, 1980–2002.' *American Journal of Political Science* 53, no. 2: 259–75.

  2015. 'The AfD: Finally a Successful Right-Wing Populist Eurosceptic Party for Germany?' *West European Politics* 38, no. 3: 535–56.

Arzheimer, Kai, and Elisabeth Badinter. 2006. 'Political Opportunity Structures and Right-Wing Extremist Party Success.' *European Journal of Political* 45: 419–43.

Arzheimer, Kai, and Carl C. Berning. 2019. 'How the Alternative for Germany (AfD) and Their Voters Veered to the Radical Right, 2013–2017.' *Electoral Studies* 60: 1–10.

Arzheimer, Kai, and Elisabeth Carter. 2009. 'Christian Religiosity and Voting for West European Radical Right Parties.' *West European Politics* 32, no. 5: 985–1011.

Aslanidis, P. 2015. 'Is Populism an Ideology? A Refutation and a New Perspective.' *Political Studies.* Published online. https://journals.sagepub.com/doi/10.1111/1467-9248.12224.

Assheuer, T. 2017. 'Aufräumen im Miststall der Demokratie.' *Zeit Online* 27, no. 9. At www.zeit.de/2017/40/afd-weimarer-republik-rechte/komplettansicht.

Atkinson, W. 2007. 'Beck, Individualization and the Death of Class: A Critique.' *British Journal of Sociology* 58: 349–66.

Backes, U., and C. Mudde. 2000. 'Germany: Extremism without Successful Parties.' *Parliamentary* 53, no. 3: 457–68.

Badinter, Elisabeth. 2011. 'Elisabeth Badinter Déplore Qu'en Dehors de Marine Le Pen', plus Personne Ne Défende La Laïcité.' *Le Monde*, 29 September. At www.lemonde.fr/politique/article/2011/09/29/elisabeth-badinter-en-dehors-de-marine-le-pen-plus-personne-ne-defend-la-laicite_1580125_823448.html.

Bahr, P., M. Dutzmann, H. Falcke, J. Haberer, W. Huber and M. Welker. 2009. *Begründete Freiheit. Die Aktualität Der Barmer Theologischen Erklärung (Evangelische Impulse. Band 1).* Neukirchen–Vluyn: Neukirchener Verlag.

Baldini, Gianfranco, Edoardo Bressanelli and Stella Gianfreda. 2020. 'Taking Back Control? Brexit, Sovereignism and Populism in Westminster (2015–17).' *European Politics and Society* 21, no. 2: 219–34.

Bale, T., S. van Kessel and P. Taggart. 2011. 'Thrown around with Abandon? Popular Understandings of Populism as Conveyed by the Print Media: A UK Case Study.' *Acta Politica* 46, no. 2: 111–31.

Balent, Magali. 2013. 'The French National Front from Jean-Marie to Marine Le Pen: Between Change and Continuity.' *Exposing the Demagogues. Right-Wing and National Populist Parties in Europe. Joint Publication of CES and Konrad Adenauer Stiftung.* Belgium: Drukkerij Jo Vandenbulcke, 161–87.

Banon, P. 2016. *Marianne en péril: religions et laïcité: un défi français.* Paris: Presses de la Renaissance.

Barber, Michael, and Jeremy Pope. 2019a. 'Conservatism in the Era of Trump.' *Perspectives on Politics* 17, no. 3: 719–36.

———2019b. 'Does Party Trump Ideology? Disentangling Party and Ideology in America.' *American Political Science Review* 113, no. 1: 38–54.

Barbour, Henry, Sally Bradshaw, Ari Fleischer, Zori Fonalledas and Glenn McCall. 2013. 'Growth and Opportunity Project.' *The Republican National Committee.* At www.wsj.com/public/resources/documents/RNCreport03182013.pdf.

Barna, Group. 2019. 'Faith Leadership in a Divided Culture.' Barna Group. At www.barna.com/research/pastors-speaking-out/.

Bastié, Eugénie. 2016. 'Comment Marine Le Pen a Évolué Sur l'avortement.' *Le Figaro*, 12 December. At www.lefigaro.fr/politique/le-scan/2016/12/12/25001-20161212ARTFIG00210-comment-marine-le-pen-a-evolue-sur-l-avortement.php.

Baubérot, J. 2015. *Les 7 laïcités françaises.* Paris: Maison des Sciences de l'Homme.

Baubérot, Jean. 2005. *Histoire de La Laïcité En France.* Paris: Presses Universitaires de France.

Baubérot, Jean, Micheline Milot and Philippe Portier. 2014. *Laïcité, Laïcités: Reconfigurations et Nouveaux Défis.* Vol. 54. Paris: Maison des Sciences de l'Homme.

Baume, Maia De La, and Silvia Borellie. 2019. 'Steve Bannon's Stuttering European Adventure.' *Politico*, 3 May. At www.politico.eu/article/steve-bannon-european-parliament-the-movement-stuttering-european-adventure/.

Bayrische Staatszeitung. 2018. 'Kein religiöses Symbol?' At www.bayerische-staatszeitung.de/staatszeitung/politik/detailansicht-politik/artikel/kein-religioeses-symbol.html.

Beaumont, P. 1987. *The Decline of Trade Union Organisation*. London: Croom Helm.

Becher, P. 2016. *Der Aufstand des Abendlandes: AfD, Pegida & Co: vom Salon auf die Straße*. Köln: PapyRossa Verlag.

Beck, U. 2016. *Risikogesellschaft: Auf dem Weg in eine andere Moderne*. Berlin: Suhrkamp Verlag.

Beck, U., and E. Beck-Gernsheim. 2001. *Individualization: Institutionalized Individualism and Its Social and Political Consequences*. New York: SAGE.

Beck, U., and M. Ritter. 1992. *Risk Society: Towards a New Modernity*. London: Sage.

Beckwith, Ryan Teague. 2016. 'Read Donald Trump's Speech on the Orlando Shooting.' *Time*, June 13. At https://time.com/4367120/orlando-shooting-donald-trump-transcript/.

Bedford-Strohm, Heinrich. 2018. 'Bedford-Strohm: AfD-Spitze Im "Widerspruch Zum Christlichen Glauben."' *Evangelisch*, 23 December. At www.evangelisch.de/inhalte/154324/23-12-2018/bedford-strohm-afd-spitze-im-widerspruch-zum-christlichen-glauben.

Bednarz, L. 2018. *Die Angstprediger: Wie rechte Christen Gesellschaft und Kirchen unterwandern*. München: Droemer.

Beinart, Peter. 2017. 'Breaking Faith: The Culture War over Religious Morality Has Faded; in Its Place Is Something Much Worse.' *The Atlantic*, April. At www.theatlantic.com/magazine/archive/2017/04/breaking-faith/517785/.

Bélanger, Éric, and Bonnie M. Meguid. 2008. 'Issue Salience, Issue Ownership, and Issue-Based Vote Choice.' *Electoral Studies* 27, no. 3: 477–91.

Bellah, Robert N. 1967. 'Civil Religion in America.' *Daedalus* 96, no. 1: 1–21.

1975. *The Broken Covenant: American Civil Religion in Time of Trial*. Chicago: University of Chicago Press.

Bellon, Christophe. 2015. *La République Apaisée: Aristide Briand et Les Leçons Politiques de La Laïcité (1902–1919)*. Paris: Les éditions du Cerf.

Benen, Steve. 2015. 'Trump's Religious Talk Causes Unease among Social Conservatives.' *MSNBC*, 21 July. At www.msnbc.com/rachel-maddow-show/trumps-religious-talk-causes-unease-among-social-conservatives.

Benner, T. 2016. 'The End of German Populist Exceptionalism.' *GPPi*. At www.gppi.net/publications/peace-security/article/the-end-of-german-populist-exceptionalism/.

Bennett, Dalton, Sarah Cahlan, Aaron C. Davis and Joyce Lee. 2020. 'The Crackdown before Trump's Photo Op.' *Washington Post*, 8 June. At www.washingtonpost.com/investigations/2020/06/08/timeline-trump-church-photo-op/?arc404=true.

Béraud, Céline. 2014. 'Un Front Commun Des Religions Contre Le Mariage Pour Tous?' *Contemporary French Civilization* 39, no. 3: 335–49.

2015. *Prêtres, Diacres, Laïcs: Révolution Silencieuse Dans Le Catholicisme Français*. Paris: Presses universitaires de France.

Berbuir, N., M. Lewandowsky and J. Siri. 2015. 'The AfD and Its Sympathisers: Finally a Right-Wing Populist Movement in Germany?' *German Politics* 2, no. 154–78.

Berdah, Arthur. 2019. 'François-Xavier Bellamy (LR) Critiqué Pour Son Opposition "personnelle" à l'IVG.' Le Figaro, 20 January. At www.lefigaro .fr/politique/le-scan/2019/01/20/25001-20190120ARTFIG00142-francois-xavier-bellamy-lr-critique-pour-son-opposition-personnelle-a-l-ivg.php.

Berezin, Mabel. 2017. 'On the Construction Sites of History: Where Did Donald Trump Come From?' *American Journal of Cultural Sociology* 5, no. 3: 322–37.

Berg, C. 2014. 'Muslim Tea Party Movement Challenges Islamophobia on Home Turf.' *Illume*. At www.loonwatch.com/2012/12/illumemag-new-muslim-movement-challenges-islamophopbia-on-home-turf/.

Berger, P. 1990. *The Sacred Canopy: Elements of a Sociological Theory of Religion*. New York: Anchor Books.

1999. *The Desecularization of the World: Resurgent Religion and World Politics*. Grand Rapids, MI: Ethics and Public Policy Center Washington, DC/ Eerdmans.

Berry, Damon T. 2017. *Blood and Faith: Christianity in American White Nationalism*. Syracuse, NY: Syracuse University Press.

2018. 'Religion and Reactionary White Politics.' *Georgetwon University Berkley Center: Christianity and the Alt-Right in America*. At https://berkleycenter .georgetown.edu/posts/christianity-and-the-alt-right-in-america.

Bertelsmann Stiftung. 2016. 'Religionsmonitor 2013.' At www.bertelsmann-stiftung.de/fileadmin/files/BSt/Publikationen/GrauePublikationen/Studie_ Religionsmonitor_2013.pdf.

Besier, G. 1994. *Die evangelische Kirche in den Umbrüchen des 20. Jahrhunderts: gesammelte Aufsätze*. Neukirchen–Vluyn: Neukirchener Verlag.

Betz, Hans-Georg. 1994. *Radical Right-Wing Populism in Western Europe*. New York: St Martins Press.

2004. *Exclusionary Populism in Western Europe in the 1990s and Beyond*. United Nations Research Institute for Social Development.

2018a. 'The Radical Right and Populism.' In Jens Rydgren, ed. *The Oxford Handbook of the Radical Right*. Oxford: Oxford University Press.

2018b. 'The New Front National: Still a Master Case?' In John Erik Fossum, Riva Kastoryano and Birte Siim, eds. *Diversity and Contestations over Nationalism in Europe and Canada*. London: Palgrave MacMillan.

Betz, Hans-Georg, and S. Meret. 2009. 'Revisiting Lepanto: The Political Mobilization against Islam in Contemporary Western Europe.' *Patterns of Prejudice* 43, nos 3–4: 313–34.

Beyerlein, Kraig, and Peter Ryan. 2018. 'Religious Resistance to Trump: Progressive Faith and the Women's March on Chicago.' *Sociology of Religion* 79, no. 2: 196–219.

Bianco, J. L. 2016. *La France est-elle laïque?* Paris: Éditions de l'Atelier.

Bilici, Mucahit. 2008. 'Finding Mecca in America: American Muslims and Cultural Citizenship.' PhD Thesis, University of Michigan.

2011. 'Homeland Insecurity: How Immigrant Muslims Naturalize America in Islam.' *Comparative Studies in Society and History* 53, no. 3: 595–622.

Billington, Ray Allen. 1939. 'The Protestant Crusade, 1800–1860.' *Science and Society* 3, no. 3: 424–26.

Bizeul, Yves. 2018. 'Die Religiöse Dimension Im Denken und Handeln Der Französischen Rechtspopulisten.' *Zeitschrift Für Religion, Gesellschaft und Politik* 2, no. 2: 365–85.

Blair, Leonardo. 2018. 'Russell Moore-Led ERLC a Threat to SBC Funding, Unity Report Finds.' 3 April. At www.christianpost.com/news/russell-moore-led-erlc-a-threat-to-sbc-funding-report-finds.html.

Blokland, H. T. 1997. *Freedom and Culture in Western Society*. Hove: Psychology Press.

Bock, J. J. 2019. 'Negotiating Cultural Difference in Dresden's Pegida Movement and Berlin's Refugee Church.' In J. J. Bock and S. Macdonald, eds. *Refugees Welcome? Difference and Diversity in a Changing Germany*. New York: Berghahn Books, 2019.

Böckenförde, Ernst-Wolfgang. 1991. *Staat, Verfassung, Demokratie: Studien Zur Verfassungstheorie und Zum Verfassungsrecht*. Frankfurt am Main: Suhrkamp.

Bogel-Burroughs, Nicholas. 2020. 'Christianity Today Editor Laments 'Ethical Naïveté' of Trump Backers.' *New York Times*, 2 January. At www.nytimes.com/2020/01/02/us/christianity-today-mark-galli-evangelicals.html.

Bond, Paul. 2020. 'Evangelicals in Midwest Who Ditched Trump Cost Him the Election, Early Data Suggests.' *Newsweek*, 9 November. At www.newsweek.com/evangelicals-midwest-who-ditched-trump-cost-him-election-early-data-suggests-1545897?fbclid=IwAR3y53eQGv053lSEotRCG3dEqPNgXvpTVVfVBW5MyZ75PkflMVNWrM2-oVY.

Bonikowski, Bart. 2019. 'Trump's Populism.' In Kurt Weyland and Raúl L. Madrid, eds. *When Democracy Trumps Populism: European and Latin American Lessons for the United States*. Cambridge: Cambridge University Press.

Boorstein, Michelle, and Sarah Pulliam Bailey. 2017. 'Hate Saying "Merry Christmas" Now? Everyone Has Trump on the Brain.' *New York Times*, 22 December. At www.washingtonpost.com/news/acts-of-faith/wp/2017/12/22/hate-saying-merry-christmas-now-everyone-has-trump-on-the-brain/.

Bornschier, Simon. 2010. *Cleavage Politics and the Populist Right: The New Cultural Conflict in Western Europe*. Philadelphia: Temple University Press.

2012. 'Why a Right-Wing Populist Party Emerged in France but Not in Germany: Cleavages and Actors in the Formation of a New Cultural Divide.' *European Political Science Review* 4, no. 1: 121–45.

Boumediene, Anissa. 2014. 'L'extrême Droite Au Premier Rang de La Manif Pour Tous Ce Dimanche.' *20 Minutes Société*, 2 October. At www.20minutes.fr/societe/1453819-20141002-extreme-droite-premier-rang-manif-tous-dimanche.

Bourdin, B. 2018. 'République laïque et Église catholique. Proposition d'un pacte pour la cohésion nationale.' *Études*, CAIRN, 2018/6: 7-76.

Bourmaud, François-Xavier. 2019. 'Laïcité: Macron Tranche, LREM Poursuit Le Débat.' *Le Figaro*, 19 March. At www.lefigaro.fr/politique/2019/03/19/01002-20190319ARTFIG00175-laicite-macron-tranche-lrem-poursuit-le-debat.php.

Bouthors, Jean-François. 2016. 'Le Réveil Des Catholiques.' *L'Express*, 6 December. At www.lexpress.fr/actualite/societe/religion/plongee-chez-les-cathos-de-france_1857441.html.

Bozóki, András, and Zoltán Ádám. 2016. 'State and Faith: Right-Wing Populism and Nationalized Religion in Hungary.' *Intersections* 2, no. 1: 98–122.

Braunstein, Ruth. 2017. *Prophets and Patriots: Faith in Democracy across the Political Divide*. Berkeley: University of California Press.

Braunstein, Ruth, and Malaena Taylor. 2017. 'Is the Tea Party a "Religious" Movement? Religiosity in the Tea Party versus the Religious Right.' *Sociology of Religion* 78, no. 1: 33–59.

Bréchon, P. 2018. 'La religion explique-t-elle les attitudes politiques?' Paris. At https://halshs.archives-ouvertes.fr/halshs-01743004.

Brenan, Megan. 2021. 'Americans' Confidence in Major U.S. Institutions Dips.' Gallup. At https://news.gallup.com/poll/352316/americans-confidence-major-institutions-dips.aspx.

Breyton, Ricarda. 2017. '"Fast Schon Krank" – AfD Geißelt Käßmanns Nazi-Vergleich.' *Die Welt*, 29 May. At www.welt.de/politik/deutschland/article165057485/Fast-schon-krank-AfD-geisselt-Kaessmanns-Nazi-Vergleich.html.

Brink, C. 2012. 'Wo Wohnt Gott?' *Die Zeit* 23, no. 8. At www.zeit.de/2012/35/Glaube-Bibel-Religion.

Brocke, Manfred. 2004. 'Civil Religion, Fundamentalism, and the Politics and Policies of George W. Bush.' *Journal of Political Science* 32, no. 1: 95–124.

Brockschmidt, Annika. 2021. *Amerikas Gotteskrieger: Wie Die Religiöse Rechte Die Demokratie Gefährdet*. Hamburg: Rowohlt Polaris.

Brown, C. 2009. *The Death of Christian Britain Understanding Secularisation, 1800–2000*. Abingdon: Routledge.

Brubaker, R. 2017. 'Between Nationalism and Civilizationism: The European Populist Moment in Comparative Perspective.' *Ethnic and Racial Studies* 40, no. 8: 1191–1226.

Brubaker, Rogers. 2012. 'Religion and Nationalism: Four Approaches.' *Nations and Nationalism* 18, no. 1: 2–20.

Bruce, Steve. 2019. *A House Divided: Protestantism, Schism and Secularization*. Vol. 5 London: Routledge.

Brustier, G., and F. Escalona. 2015. 'La gauche et la droite face au Front National.' In S. Crépon, Nonna Mayer and A. Dézé, eds. *Les faux-semblants du Front national*. Paris: Presses de Sciences Po.

Bui, Doan, and David Le Bailly. 2018. 'Printemps Républicain: Enquête Sur Les Croisés de La Laïcité.' *Le Nouvel Observateur*, 21 April. At www.nouvelobs.com/societe/20180420.OBS5534/printemps-republicain-enquete-sur-les-croises-de-la-laicite.html.

Bump, Philip. 2018. 'Half of Evangelicals Support Israel Because They Believe It Is Important for Fulfilling End-Times Prophecy.' *Washington Post*, 14 May. At www.washingtonpost.com/news/politics/wp/2018/05/14/half-of-evangelicals-support-israel-because-they-believe-it-is-important-for-fulfilling-end-times-prophecy/.

Burge, Ryan. 2020. 'So, Why Is Evangelicalism Not Declining? Because Non-Attenders Are Taking On the Label.' *Religion in Public*, 10 December. At https://religioninpublic.blog/2020/12/10/so-why-is-evangelicalism-not-declining-because-non-attenders-are-taking-on-the-label/.

2021. 'Why "Evangelical" Is Becoming Another Word for "Republican".' New York Times, 26 October. At www.nytimes.com/2021/10/26/opinion/evangelical-republican.html?action=click&module=RelatedLinks&pgtype=Article.

Burghard, D. 2010. *Tea Party Nationalism: A Critical Examination of the Tea Party Movement and the Size, Scope and Focus of Its National Factions*. Kansas City: Institute for Research and Education on Human Rights.

Burnett, Erin. 2015. 'Trump: Drink My Little Wine, Have My Little Cracker.' *CNN*. At https://edition.cnn.com/videos/politics/2015/08/13/donald-trump-religion-serfaty-dnt-erin.cnn.

Busch, A., and P. Manow. 2001. 'The SPD and the Neue Mitte Germany. In New Labour.' In Stuart White, ed. *New Labour* London: Palgrave Macmillan.

Campbell, David E., and Geoffrey C. Layman. 2015. 'The Politics of Secularism in the United States.' In *Emerging Trends in the Social and Behavioral Sciences: An Interdisciplinary, Searchable, and Linkable Resource*. Wiley Online Library, 1–13.

Campbell, David E., Geoffrey C. Layman and John C. Green. 2020. *Secular Surge: A New Fault Line in American Politics*. Cambridge: Cambridge University Press.

Campbell, David E., Geoffrey C. Layman, John C. Green and Nathanael G. Sumaktoyo. 2018. 'Putting Politics First: The Impact of Politics on American Religious and Secular Orientations.' *American Journal of Political Science* 62, no. 3.: 551–65.

Campbell, David E., and Robert D. Putnam. 2011. 'America's Grace: How a Tolerant Nation Bridges Its Religious Divides.' *Political Science Quarterly* 126, no. 4: 611–40.

Camus, Jean-Yves. 1992. 'Political Cultures within the Front National: The Emergence of a Counter-Ideology on the French Far-Right.' *Patterns of Prejudice* 26, nos 1–2: 5–16.

2015. 'Le Front National et la nouvelle droite.' In S. Crépon, Nonna Mayer and A. Dézé, eds. *Les faux-semblants du Front national.* Paris: Presses de Sciences Po.

Camus, Renaud. 2011. *Le Grand Remplacement*. Paris: David Reinharc.

Carney, Timothy P. 2019. *Alienated America: Why Some Places Thrive While Others Collapse*. New York: HarperCollins.

Carstens, Peter. 2021. 'Thierse Erwägt SPD-Austritt.' *Frankfurter Allgemeine Zeitung*, 3 March. At www.faz.net/aktuell/politik/inland/wolfgang-thierse-erwaegt-spd-austritt-nach-streit-mit-parteifuehrung-17225186.html.

2022. 'Selbst Das C Ist Nicht Mehr Tabu.' *Frankfurter Allgemeine Zeitung*, January 26. At www.faz.net/aktuell/politik/wie-die-cdu-das-scheitern-bei-der-bundestagswahl-aufarbeitet-17753845.html?session.

Casanova, José. 1994. *Public Religions in the Modern World. Chicago*. London: University of Chicago Press.

2012a. 'The Politics of Nativism.' *Philosophy & Social Criticism* 38, nos 4–5: 485–95.

2012b. 'Rethinking Public Religions'. In *Rethinking Religion and World Affairs*. Oxford: Oxford University Press.

Case, Anne, and Angus Deaton. 2020. *Deaths of Despair and the Future of Capitalism*. Princeton, NJ: Princeton University Press.

Catta, G., B. M. Duffé, D. Fontaine, A. Nouis, D. Quinio, B. Saintôt and J. Vignon. 2016. 'Aux chrétiens tentés par le FN.' *Revue Projet* 5: 46–52.

CDU/CSU. 2017. 'Für Ein Deutschland, in Dem Wir Gut und Gerne Leben. Regierungsprogramm 2017–2021.' *CDU/CSU*. At www.cdu.de/system/tdf/media/dokumente/170703regierungsprogramm2017.pdf?file=1.

Cesari, Jocelyne. 2007. 'The Muslim Presence in France and the United States: Its Consequences for Secularism.' *French Politics, Culture & Society* 25, no. 2: 34–45.

Chadi, A., and M. Krapf. 2017. 'The Protestant Fiscal Ethic: Religious Confession and Euro Skepticism in Germany.' *Economic Inquiry* 55, no. 4: 1813–32.

Chappell, Bill. 2020. '"He Did Not Pray": Fallout Grows from Trump's Photo-Op at St. John's Church.' *NPR*, 2 June. At www.npr.org/2020/06/02/867705160/he-did-not-pray-fallout-grows-from-trump-s-photo-op-at-st-john-s-church?t=1592470201947.

Chaves, Mark. 2011. *American Religion Contemporary Trends*. Princeton, NJ: Princeton University Press.

Chazaud, Anne-Sophie. 2019. 'L'exclusion d'Agnès Thill Révèle Au Grand Jour l'intolérance Des Progressistes.' *Le Figaro*, 26 June. At www.lefigaro.fr/vox/politique/l-exclusion-d-agnes-thill-revele-au-grand-jour-l-intolerance-des-progressistes-20190626.

Chenu, Sébastien. 2019. 'Profanations d'églises, Silence on Saccage …' *Rassemblement National*. At https://rassemblementnational.fr/communiques/profanations-deglises-silence-on-saccage/.

Cherlin, Andrew. 2011. 'Between Poor and Prosperous: Do the Family Patterns of Moderately Educated Americans Deserve a Closer Look?' In Marcia Carlson and Paula England, eds. *Social Class and Changing Families in an Unequal America*. Palo Alto: Stanford University Press.

Cherlin, Andrew J. 2010. *The Marriage-Go-Round: The State of Marriage and the Family in America Today*. New York: Vintage.

Chevallier, Pierre. 2014. *La Séparation de l'église et de l'école: Jules Ferry et Léon XIII*. Paris: Fayard.

Chevènement, Jean-Pierre. 1997. 'Déclaration de M. Jean-Pierre Chevènement, Ministre de l'intérieur Chargé Des Cultes, Sur l'histoire Des Relations Entre l'Etat et Les Religions, l'attachement Au Maintien Du Régime Du

Concordat En Alsace Moselle et Sur Les Voies de l'intégration d'un Islam à La Françaisedu.' *Vie Publique*. At www.vie-publique.fr/discours/207645-declaration-de-m-jean-pierre-chevenement-ministre-de-l-interieur-charg.

Claassen, Ryan L. 2015. *Godless Democrats and Pious Republicans? Party Activists, Party Capture, and the 'God Gap'*. Cambridge: Cambridge University Press.

Claiborne, Shane, Jim Daly, Mark Galli, Lisa Sharon Harper, Tom Lin, Karen Swallow Prior, Soong-Chan Rah et al. 2018. *Still Evangelical? Insiders Reconsider Political, Social, and Theological Meaning*. Westmont, IL: InterVarsity Press.

Clarke, H., M. Goodwin, and P. Whiteley. 2017. 'Why Britain Voted for Brexit: An Individual-Level Analysis of the 2016 Referendum Vote.' *Parliamentary Affairs* 70, no. 3: 439–64.

Clift, Ben, and Sean McDaniel. 2017. 'Is This Crisis of French Socialism Different? Hollande, the Rise of Macron, and the Reconfiguration of the Left in the 2017 Presidential and Parliamentary Elections.' *Modern & Contemporary France* 25, no. 4: 403–15.

Combes, Émile. 1905. *Une Deuxième Campagne Laïque: Vers La Séparation*. Paris: Sociéte nouvelle de librairie et d'édition.

Comtat, Emmanuelle. 2009. *Les Pieds-Noirs et La Politique. Quarante Ans Après Le Retour*. Paris: Presses de Sciences Po.

Constitution de la IVe République. 1946. 'Constitution de 1946, IVe République.' *Conseil National*. At www.conseil-constitutionnel.fr/les-constitutions-dans-l-histoire/constitution-de-1946-ive-republique.

Cooperman, Alan, Gregory A. Smith and Katherine Ritchey. 2015. 'America's Changing Religious Landscape.' *Pew Research Center*. At www.pewforum.org/2015/05/12/americas-changing-religious-landscape/.

Coppins, McKay. 2015. *The Wilderness: Deep Inside the Republican Party's Combative, Contentious, Chaotic Quest to Take Back the White House*. London: Hachette UK.

Coq, Guy, Gaël Giraud, Véronique Margron, Olivier Mongin, Bernard Perret, Cécile Renouard and François Soulage. 2017. '"En Conscience, Au Nom de Notre Foi, Voter Front National, c'est Non" Par Des Catholiques Engagés et Leurs Amis, Contre Le FN.' *La Croix*, 28 April. At www.la-croix.com/Debats/Forum-et-debats/En-conscience-notre-voter-Front-National-cest-catholiques-engages-leurs-amis-sengagent-contre-FN-2017-04-28-1200843158.

Cornevin, Christophe. 2019. 'Les Églises, Victimes d'un Inquiétant Vandalisme.' *Le Figaro*, 28 March. At www.lefigaro.fr/actualite-france/2019/03/28/01016-20190328ARTFIG00098-les-eglises-victimes-d-un-inquietant-vandalisme.php.

Corre, Mikael. 2018. 'Emmanuel Macron A-t-Il La Foi?' *La Croix*, 25 June. At www.la-croix.com/Religion/Emmanuel-Macron-foi-2018-06-25-1200949964.

2019. 'Emmanuel Macron "ne Souhaite Pas Qu'on Change La Loi de 1905".' *La Croix*, 19 March. At www.la-croix.com/France/Politique/Emmanuel-Macron-souhaite-pas-quon-change-loi-1905-2019-03-19-1201009806.

Coury, David. 2016. 'A Clash of Civilizations? PEGIDA and the Rise of Cultural Nationalism.' *German Politics and Society* 34, no. 4: 54–67.

2021. 'The AfD, Pegida, and Ethnopluralism in Eastern Germany.' *German Studies Review* 44, no. 3: 565–80.

Cousins, Norman. 1958. *In God We Trust*. New York: Harper.

Cox, Gary W. 1997. *Making Votes Count: Strategic Coordination in the World's Electoral Systems*. Cambridge: Cambridge University Press.

Cremer, Tobias. 2018. 'The Religion Gap: Why Right-Wing Populists Underperform among Christian Voters and What This Means for the Role of the Church in Society.' *LSE: Populism and Religion Series*. At https://blogs .lse.ac.uk/religionglobalsociety/2018/12/the-religion-gap-why-right-wing-populists-underperform-among-christian-voters-and-what-this-means-for-the-role-of-the-church-in-society/.

2019. 'The Resistance of the Protestant Church in Nazi Germany and Its Relevance for Contemporary Politics.' *The Review of Faith & International Affairs* 17, no. 4: 36–47.

2021a. 'A Religious Vaccination? How Christian Communities React to Right-Wing Populism in Germany, France and the US.' *Government and Opposition*, published online: 1–21. At www.cambridge.org/core/journals/government-and-opposition/article/abs/religious-vaccination-how-christian-communities-react-to-rightwing-populism-in-germany-france-and-the-us/ D9024C99467049AD9B108ED1F9863E0C.

2021b. 'Nations under God: How Church–State Relations Shape Christian Responses to Right-Wing Populism in Germany and the United States.' *Religions* 12, no. 4. At www.mdpi.com/2077-1444/12/4/254.

2021c. 'The Rise of the Post-Religious Right: Christianism and Secularism in the French Rassemblement National.' *Party Politics*: Published online first: September 2021. At https://journals.sagepub.com/doi/full/10.1177/ 13540688211046859.

2021d. 'Civil Religion vs. White Nationalism: Which Role for Christianity in American Politics?' Berkley Forum, 22 January. At https://berkleycenter .georgetown.edu/responses/civil-religion-vs-white-nationalism-which-role-for-christianity-in-american-politics.

2021e. 'The Capitol Storming Epitomizes the Shift from a Religious to Post-Religious Right.' Providence Magazine, 27 January. At https:// providencemag.com/2021/01/us-capitol-storming-epitomizes-shift-religious-to-post-religious-right/.

Cremer, Tobias, Paul Freston and David Elcott. 2020. 'Will COVID-19 Spread Religious Nationalism?' *Centre for Geopolitics Cambridge: A Conversation on the Geopolitics of COVID-19*. At https://centreforgeopolitics.org/will-covid-19-spread-religious-nationalism/?fbclid=IwAR32cOYHsOYFjwurWRKYm BybixDBgRoaES4ErLfEtzjAdwq1ZIRsF4DvldA.

Crépon, S. 2015. 'La politique des mœurs au Front National.' In Sylvain Crépon, Nonna Mayer and A. Dézé, eds. *Les faux-semblants du Front national*. Paris: Presses de Sciences Po.

Crines, Andrew S. 2019. 'Boris Johnson and the Future of British Conservatism.' *Political Insight* 10, no. 3: 4–6.

Cristi, Marcela. 2006. *From Civil to Political Religion: The Intersection of Culture, Religion and Politics.* Waterloo: Wilfrid Laurier University Press.

Crouch, Andy. 2016. 'Speak Truth to Trump.' Christianity Today, 10 October. At www.christianitytoday.com/ct/2016/ariann-web-only/speak-truth-to-trump .html.

Crowley, Michael. 2017. 'The Man Who Wants to Unmake the West.' *Politico*, April. At www.politico.com/magazine/story/2017/03/trump-steve-bannon-destroy-eu-european-union-214889.

C-Span. 2015. 'User Clip: Trump Doesn't Ask God for Forgiveness.' *C-Span.* At www.c-span.org/video/?c4585899/user-clip-trump-god-forgiveness.

2020. 'National Prayer Breakfast.' *C-Span.* At www.c-span.org/video/?469058-1/ national-prayer-breakfast.

Czermak, Gerhard. 2019. 'Religions-und Weltanschauungsfreiheit in Deutschland und Ihre Juristische und Gesellschaftliche Gefährdung.' In *Wechselseitige Erwartungslosigkeit?* Berlin: De Gruyter.

Daenekindt, S., W. De Koster and J. Van Der Waal. 2017. 'How People Organise Cultural Attitudes: Cultural Belief Systems and the Populist Radical Right.' *West European Politics* 40, no. 4: 791–811.

Dargent, Claude. 2005. *Les Protestants En France Aujourd'hui.* La usanne: Payot. 2016. 'Les catholiques français et le Front national.' *Études* 12, no. 2016/12 Déc embre: 19–30.

Davie, G. 2000. *Religion in Modern Europe: A Memory Mutates.* Oxford: Oxford University Press.

2015. *Religion in Britain: A Persistent Paradox.* Second ed. London: Wiley.

Davie, Grace, and Adam Dinham. 2018. 'Religious Literacy in Modern Europe.' In Alberto Melloni and Francesca Cadeddu, eds. *Religious Literacy, Law and History: Perspectives on European Pluralist Societies.* London: Routledge.

Davies, P. 2010. 'The Front National and Catholicism: From Intégrisme to Joan of Arc and Clovis.' *Religion Compass* 4, no. 576–587.

De Cleen, B. 2017. *Populism and Nationalism.* Oxford: Oxford University Press.

de Jonge, Léonie. 2019. 'The Populist Radical Right and the Media in the Benelux: Friend or Foe?' *The International Journal of Press/Politics* 24, no. 2: 189–209.

De Koster, W., P. Achterberg, J. Van der Waal, Van Bohemen S. and R. Kemmers. 2014. 'Progressiveness and the New Right: The Electoral Relevance of Culturally Progressive Values in the Netherlands.' *West European Politics* 37, no. 3: 584–604.

De Koster, W., and Van der Waal J. 2007. 'Cultural Value Orientations and Christian Religiosity: On Moral Traditionalism, Authoritarianism, and Their Implications for Voting Behavior.' *International Political Science Review* 28, no. 4: 451–67.

De Wilde, Pieter, Ruud Koopmans, Wolfgang Merkel, Oliver Strijbis and Michael Zürn. 2019. *The Struggle Over Borders: Cosmopolitanism and Communitarianism.* Cambridge: Cambridge University Press.

Decker, F. 2002. 'Perspektiven des Rechtspopulismus in Deutschland am Beispiel der "Schill-Partei".' *Aus Politik und Zeitgeschichte* no. B 21: 22–31.

Decker, O., J. Kiess and Brähler, E. 2008. *Bewegung in der Mitte: Rechtsextreme Einstellungen in Deutschland 2008*. Gießen: Psychosozial-Verlag.

2012. *Die Mitte im Umbruch: Rechtsextreme Einstellungen in Deutschland*. Gießen: Psychosozial-Verlag.

2014. *Die stabilisierte Mitte. Rechtsextreme Einstellung in Deutschland*. Gießen: Psychosozial-Verlag.

2016. *Die enthemmte Mitte. Autoritäre und rechtsextreme Einstellung in Deutschland*. Gießen: Psychosozial-Verlag.

DeClair, E. 1999. *Politics on the Fringe: The People, Policies, and Organization of the French National Front*. Durh am, NC: Duke University Press.

Deharo, Ambre. 2016. 'Manif Pour Tous: Marion Maréchal-Le Pen et Le FN Prennent La Parole Pour La Première Fois.' Rtl.Fr, 16 October. At www.rtl .fr/actu/politique/manif-pour-tous-marion-marechal-le-pen-et-le-fn-prennent-la-parole-pour-la-premiere-fois-7785314817.

Denis, Tugdual. 2013. 'Marion Maréchal Le Pen Au Pèlerinage de Chartres.' *L'Express*, 13 June. At www.lexpress.fr/actualite/politique/marion-marechal-le-pen-au-pelerinage-de-chartres_1257089.html.

Denver, D. 2008. 'Another Reason to Support Marriage? Turnout and the Decline of Marriage in Britain.' *The British Journal of Politics and International Relations* 10, no. 4: 666–80.

Descamp, Henri. 1980. *La Démocratie Chrétienne et Le MRP de 1946 à 1959*. Paris: FeniXX.

Destal, Mathias. 2013. 'La Droite T oxique: Elle Joue La Politique Du Pire …' *Marianne*, 29 April. At www.marianne.net/politique/la-droite-toxique-elle-joue-la-politique-du-pire.

Detrow, Scot. 2016. 'Pope Says Trump "Is Not Christian".' NPR, 18 February. At www.npr.org/2016/02/18/467229313/pope-says-trump-is-not-christian?t= 1599642884978.

Deutsche Bischofskonferenz. 2016. 'Bischöfe: AfD nicht mit christlichem Glauben vereinbar.' *Deutsche Bischofskonferenz*. At www.faz.net/aktuell/politik/ inland/katholische-bischoefe-distanzieren-sich-von-der-afd-14917396.html.

Deutscher Bundestag. 2017. '*Datenhandbuch Deutscher Bundestag*.' Deutscher Bundestag.

Deutschlandfunk. 2018a. 'Die AfD und das Christentum.' *Deutschlandfunk*. At www.deutschlandfunk.de/religion-in-der-politik-die-afd-und-das-christentum .886.de.html.

2018b. 'Timo Versemann im Gespräch mit Anne Françoise Weber: "Hope Speech muss mehr sein als Friede, Freude, Eierkuchen" (Netzteufel).' *Deutschlandfunk*, 27 May. At www.deutschlandfunkkultur.de/evangelische-akademie-im-kampf-gegen-hassrede-hope-speech-100.html.

Dézé, A. 2015a. 'La construction médiatique de la 'nouveauté' du FN.' In Nonna Mayer, A. Dézé and Sylvain Crépon, eds. *Les Faux-semblants du Front National*. Paris: Presses de Sciences Po.

2015b. 'La Dédiabolisation: Une Nouvelle Stratégie.' In Sylvain Crépon, Nonna Mayer and A. Dézé, eds. *Les Faux-Semblant Du Front National.* Paris: Presses de Sciences Po.

Dickerson, John S. 2013. *The Great Evangelical Recession: 6 Factors That Will Crash the American Church … and How to Prepare.* Grand Rapids MI: Baker Publishing.

Dickson, Josh. 2012. 'MPP – Policy Analysis Exercise.' Master thesis, Harvard Kennedy School.

Die Linke. 2017. '"Sozial. Gerecht. Frieden. Für Alle." – Wahlprogramm Der Linke Zur Bundestagswahl 2017.' Die Linke. At www.bundestagswahl-bw .de/wahlprogramm-linke-btwahl2017.

Die Welt. 2013. 'Eurokritische AfD Bereitet Sich Auf Bundestagswahl Vor.' *Die Welt.* At www.welt.de/newsticker/news1/article115267251/Eurokritische-AfD-bereitet-sich-auf-Bundestagswahl-vor.html.

2016. 'AfD Wandelt Sich von Professoren- Zur Prekariats-Partei.' *Die Welt.* At www.welt.de/politik/deutschland/article153514296/AfD-wandelt-sich-von-Professoren-zur-Prekariats-Partei.html.

2017. 'Schulz Verurteilt AfD-Aufruf Zu Kirchenaustritt.' *Die Welt,* 25 April. At www.welt.de/politik/article163977128/Schulz-verurteilt-AfD-Aufruf-zu-Kirchenaustritt.html.

2015. 'Christliche Symbole bei Pegida-Demo "pervers".' *Die Welt.* At www .welt.de/regionales/nrw/article136026490/Christliche-Symbole-bei-Pegida-Demo-pervers.html.

Die Zeit. 2018a. 'AfD Erstmals Zweitstärkste Partei Nach Der Union.' *Die Zeit.* At www.zeit.de/politik/deutschland/2018–09/deutschlandtrend-wahl-afd-spd-union-grosse-koalition-umfrage-horst-seehofer.

2018b. 'Alexander Gauland Bezeichnet Übergriffe in Chemnitz Als Normal.' *Die Zeit,* 29 August. At www.zeit.de/gesellschaft/zeitgeschehen/2018-08/chemnitz-alexander-gauland-ausschreitungen.

2021. 'Katholiken Fordern Entschuldigung Für SPD-Werbespot.' *Die Zeit,* 12 August. At www.zeit.de/politik/deutschland/2021-08/spd-wahlkampf-wahlwerbespot-zdk-thomas-sternberg-olaf-scholz.

Dieckhoff, A., and Philippe Portier. 2017. *L'Enjeu mondial. Religion et politique.* Paris: Presses de Sciences Po.

Dilling, Matthias. 2018. 'Two of the Same Kind? The Rise of the AfD and Its Implications for the CDU/CSU.' *German Politics and Society* 36, no. 1: 84–104.

Dipper, Christof. 2019. '"… Daß Es Nicht Gelungen Ist, Dem Grundgesetz Eine Tiefere Religiöse Begründung Zu Geben': Die Konfessionen und Die Entstehung Des Grundgesetzes.' In H. J. Große Kracht and G. Schreiber, eds. Wechselseitige Erwartungslosigkeit? Berlin: De Gruyter.

Doherty, C, J. Kiley and B. Johnson. 2017. 'Political Typology Reveals Deep Fissures on the Right and Left: Conservative Republican Groups Divided on Immigration, "Openness."' *Pew Research Center.* At www.pewresearch.org/politics/2017/10/24/political-typology-reveals-deep-fissures-on-the-right-and-left/.

Doherty, Carroll, Jocelyn Kiley and Olivia O'Hea. 2018. 'Wide Gender Gap, Growing Educational Divide in Voters' Party Identification.' *Pew Research Center.* At www.people-press.org/2018/03/20/wide-gender-gap-growing-educational-divide-in-voters-party-identification/.

Domenach, Hugo. 2016. 'Pourquoi Marine Le Pen Déteste La Manif Pour Tous.' Le Point, 19 October. At www.lepoint.fr/presidentielle/pourquoi-marine-le-pen-deteste-la-manif-pour-tous-18-10-2016-2076802_3121.php.

Dosse, Françoise. 2017. *Le Philosophe et Le Président, Ricœur et Macron.* Paris: Stock.

Dostal, J. M. 2017. 'The German Federal Election of 2017: How the Wedge Issue of Refugees and Migration Took the Shine off Chancellor Merkel and Transformed the Party System.' *The Political Quarterly* 88, no. 4: 589–602.

Douglas, Mary. 2003. *Purity and Danger: An Analysis of Concepts of Pollution and Taboo.* London: Routledge.

Dreher, Rod. 2017. *The Benedict Option: A Strategy for Christians in a Post-Christian Nation.* London: Penguin.

Dreisbach, Daniel. 2002. *Thomas Jefferson and the Wall of Separation between Church and State.* New York: New York University Press.

Dröge, M. 2020. 'B. Z. Kolumne.' *Berliner Zeitung.* At www.ekbo.de/wir/bischof/bz-kolumne.html.

Du Cleuziou, Yann Raison. 2016a. 'Succès de François Fillon: Le Vote Ou Les Votes Catholiques?' *Esprit* November. At https://esprit.presse.fr/actualites/yann-raison-du-cleuziou/succes-de-francois-fillon-le-vote-ou-les-votes-catholiques-40172.

2016b. 'Dans le monde catholique, la relative banalisation du vote FN.' *La revue du Projet* 345. At: www.revue-projet.com/articles/2016-09-raison-du-cleuziou-chez-les-catholiques-la-relative-banalisation-du-vote-fn/8160.

2017. 'Définir le vote catholique légitime.' *Études* 7: 65–76.

2018. 'Sens commun: un combat conservateur entre deux fronts.' *Le Débat* 2 CAIRN: 105–14.

2019. *Une contre-révolution catholique: aux origines de la Manif pour tous.* Paris: Le Seuil.

Du Cleuziou, Yann Raison and Kévin Boucaud-Victoire. 2021. 'Droite Catho et Zemmour: "Le Sentiment de Minorité Menacée Légitime Un Glissement Xénophobe."' At www.marianne.net/agora/entretiens-et-debats/droite-catho-et-zemmour-le-sentiment-de-minorite-menacee-legitime-un-glissement-xenophobe.

Dubertret, Marianne. 1996. 'Et Pleurent Les Enfants de Quinze Ans Marseille Ne Mérite Pas Ça.' *La Vie*, 19 September. At www.lavie.fr/archives/1996/09/19/et-pleurent-les-enfants-de-quinze-ans-marseille-ne-merite-pas-ca,2136803.php.

Duchesne, Jean. 2016. *Le Catholicisme Minoritaire? Un Oxymore à La Mode.* Paris: Desclée de Brouwer.

Duyck, Alexandre, and Soazig Quéméner. 2017. *L'irrésistible Ascension. Les Dessous d'une Présidentielle Insensée: Macron, Le Pen, Fillon, Mélenchon, Hollande, Juppé, Sarkozy, Valls.* Paris: Flammarion.

Eatwell, Roger. 2003. 'Ten Theories of the Extreme Right.' In P. Merkl and L. Weinberg, eds. *Right-Wing Extremism in the Twenty-First Century.* London: Frank Cass.

Eatwell, Roger, and Matthew Goodwin. 2018. *National Populism: The Revolt against Liberal Democracy.* London: Penguin.

Eckholm, Erik. 2012. 'Southern Baptists Set for a Notable First.' *New York Times*, 17 June. At www.nytimes.com/2012/06/18/us/southern-baptists-set-to-elect-their-first-black-leader.html.

Economist. 2018. 'The Non-Trump Evangelicals.' *The Economist*, 18 April. At www.economist.com/united-states/2018/04/19/the-non-trump-evangelicals.

Economist Intelligence Unit. 2017. 'Democracy Index 2016: A Report from The Economist Intelligence Unit: Revenge of "Deplorables."' At www.eiu.com/public/topical_report.aspx?campaignid=DemocracyIndex2016.

Ehrhard, Thomas. 2016. 'Le Front National Face Aux Modes de Scrutin: Entre Victoire Sous Conditions et Influences Sur Le Système Partisan.' *Pouvoirs* 2: 85–103.

EKD. 1945. 'Stuttgarter Schuldbekenntnis.' Evangelische Kirche Deutschland. At www.ekd.de/Stuttgarter-Schulderklarung-11298.htm.

2015. 'Zur Aktuellen Situation Der Flüchtlinge.' *Evangelische Kirche Deutschland.* At http://static.evangelisch.de/get/?daid=CuHJjg3NFHgLFUAr_LoMIZo Hoo118099&dfid=download.

Ekins, Emily. 2017. 'The Five Types of Trump Voters: Who They Are and What They Believe.' *Democracy and Voter Study Group Washington, DC.* At www.voterstudygroup.org/publication/the-five-types-trump-voters.

2018. 'Religious Trump Voters. How Faith Moderates Attitudes about Immigration, Race, and Identity.' *Democracy and Voter Study Group Washington, DC.* At www.cato.org/publications/public-opinion-brief/religious-trump-voters-how-faith-moderates-attitudes-about.

Elcott, David, Tobias Cremer, Volker Haarmann and Colt Anderson. 2021. *Faith, Nationalism, and the Future of Liberal Democracy.* Notre Dame, IN: Notre Dame University Press.

Elff, Martin, and Sigrid Roßteutscher. 2017. 'Social Cleavages and Electoral Behaviour in Long-Term Perspective: Alignment without Mobilisation?' *German Politics* 26, no. 1: 12–34.

Elifson, Kirk W., and C. Kirk Hadaway. 1985. 'Prayer in Public Schools: When Church and State Collide.' *Public Opinion Quarterly* 49, no. 3: 317–29.

Ellinas, A. A. 2010. *The Media and the Far Right in Western Europe: Playing the Nationalist Card.* New York: Cambridge University Press.

Emelien, Ismaël, and David Amiel. 2019. *Le Progrès Ne Tombe Pas Du Ciel.* Paris: Fayard.

ERLC. 2020. 'Public Policy.' Ethics and Religious Liberty Commission of the Southern Baptist Convention. At https://erlc.com/about/public-policy.

Espejo, P. O. 2015. 'Power to Whom? The People between Procedure and Populism.' In C. Torre and A. Arato, eds. *The Promise and Perils of Populism: Global Perspectives.* Lexington: University Press of Kentucky.

Eurobarometer. 2017. 'Eurobarometer 79.' *Brussels: European Commission*. At https://ec.europa.eu/commfrontoffice/publicopinion/index.cfm.

2018. 'Eurobarometer 71–80.' *Brussels: European Commission* nos. 71–80. At https://ec.europa.eu/commfrontoffice/publicopinion/index.cfm.

Evangelisch.de. 2014. *AfD – die christliche Alternative für Deutschland?* At www.evangelisch.de/inhalte/93477/15-09-2014/afd-die-christliche-alternative-fuer-deutschland.

2018. 'Bedford-Strohm: AfD-Spitze im "Widerspruch zum christlichen Glauben."' At www.evangelisch.de/inhalte/154324/23-12-2018/bedford-strohm-afd-spitze-im-widerspruch-zum-christlichen-glauben.

Evans, G. A., ed. 1999. *The End of Class Politics? Class Voting in Comparative Context*. Oxford: Oxford University Press.

Ezrow, L. 2010. *European Consortium for Political Research*. Oxford: Oxford University Press.

Falter, Jürgen. 1991. *Hitlers Wähler*. München: Beck.

Favereau, Eric. 2018. 'Bioéthique: Macron Récupère Le Bébé.' *Liberation*, 25 September. At www.liberation.fr/france/2018/09/25/bioethique-macron-recupere-le-bebe_1681237.

F.A.Z. 2016a. 'AfD-Stellvertreter Gauland "Wir sind keine christliche Partei".' *Frankfurter Allgemeine Zeitung*. At www.faz.net/aktuell/politik/fluechtlingskrise/alexander-gauland-betrachtet-afd-nicht-als-christlich-14250064.html.

2016b. 'AfD attackiert Kirchen für Einsatz in der Flüchtlingskrise.' *Frankfurter Allgemeine Zeitung*. At www.faz.net/aktuell/politik/inland/kirchentag-afd-attackiert-kirchen-fuer-einsatz-in-der-fluechtlingskrise-14253596.html.

2017. 'Deutschen werden christliche Wurzeln wichtiger.' *Frankfurter Allgemeine Zeitung*. At www.faz.net/aktuell/politik/inland/christentum-wird-den-deutschen-immer-wichtiger-15350350.html.

2018a. 'Die Kirchen in Deutschland schrumpfen.' *Frankfurter Allgemeine Zeitung*. At www.faz.net/aktuell/politik/inland/austritte-aus-der-kirche-nimmt-in-deutschland-weiter-zu-15700450.html.

2018b. 'Evangelischer Kirchentag will keine AfD-Politiker als Redner.' *Frankfurter Allgemeine Zeitung*. At www.faz.net/aktuell/politik/inland/evangelischer-kirchentag-will-keine-afd-politiker-als-redner-15807904.html.

FDP. 2017. 'Wird denken neu: Das Programm der Freien Demokraten zur Bundestagswahl.' FDP. At www.fdp.de/sites/default/files/uploads/2017/08/07/20170807-wahlprogramm-wp-2017-v16.pdf.

Fea, John. 2018. *Believe Me: The Evangelical Road to Donald Trump*. Grand Rapids, MI: Eerdmans.

2019. 'Netflix Released a New Documentary on the Secretive Religious Group "The Family." Despite Its Flaws, It's a Must See.' Washington Post, 16 August. At www.washingtonpost.com/religion/2019/08/16/netflix-released-new-documentary-secretive-religious-group-family-despite-its-flaws-its-must-see/.

Feré, Vincent. 2017. 'Les Conséquences Des Élections Présidentielles.' *Commentaire* 1: 113–22.

Finchelstein, F. 2017. *From Fascism to Populism in History*. Berkeley: University of California Press.

Finchelstein, Gilles, Antoine Bristielle, Victoria Géraut, Tristan Guerra, Milo Lévy-Bruhl, Raphaël Llorca, Frédéric Potier, Mathieu Souquière and Brice Teinturier. 2021. *Le Dossier Zemmour: Idéologie, Image, Électorat*. Paris: Fondation Jean Jaurès.

Finger, B. 2017. 'The Rust Belt in Revolt.' *New Politics* 16, no. 2: 7–10.

Finke, Roger. 1990. 'Religious Deregulation: Origins and Consequences.' *Journal of Church & State* 32: 609–29.

Fligstein, N. 2008. *Euroclash the EU, European Identity, and the Future of Europe*. Oxford: Oxford University Press.

Focus. 2016. 'AfD-Politiker auf Katholikentag unerwünscht.' *Focus*. At www.focus.de/regional/leipzig/kirche-veranstalter-afd-politiker-auf-katholikentag-unerwuenscht_id_5566721.html.

　　2017. '"Rolle wie im Dritten Reich": AfD-Weidel erhebt schwere Vorwürfe gegen die Kirche.' *Focus*. At www.focus.de/politik/deutschland/alice-weidel-afd-fraktionschefin-erhebt-schwere-vorwuerfe-gegen-die-kirche_id_8036449.html.

Fondation Jean-Jaurès. 2019. 'Les Français, l'électorat Macroniste et Les Questions de La Laïcité.' *IFOP*. At www.ifop.com/wp-content/uploads/2019/03/116261_Présentation_Ifop_laicite_2019.03.22.pdf.

Forcari, Christophe. 2021. 'La "Reconquête" de Zemmour: L'extrême Référence Espagnole.' *Liberation*, 6 December. At www.liberation.fr/politique/elections/la-reconquete-de-zemmour-lextreme-reference-espagnole-20211206_OTSNYC4MJZANBHBGTHC2ASBNBA/.

Formisano, R. 2012. *The Tea Party: A Brief History*. Baltimore: Johns Hopkins University Press.

Forschungsgruppe Wahlen e.V. 2017. 'Bundestagswahl: eine Analyse der Wahl vom 24.09.2017.' *Mannheim*. At www.forschungsgruppe.de/Wahlen/Wahlanalysen/Newsl_Bund_170928.pdf.

Fourquet, Jérôme. 2015. 'Le vote Front National dans les électorats musulman et juif.' In Sylvain Crépon, Nonna Mayer and A. Dézé, eds. *Les faux-semblants du Front national*. Paris: Presses de Sciences Po.

　　2018a. *À la droite de Dieu: Le réveil identitaire des catholiques*. Paris: Les éditions du Cerf.

　　2018b. *Le nouveau clivage*. Paris: Les éditions du Cerf.

　　2019. *L'archipel français: Naissance d'une nation multiple et divisée*. Paris: Le Seuil.

Fourquet, Jérôme, and Hervé Le Bras. 2014. *La Religion Dévoilée: Nouvelle Cartographie Du Catholicisme*. Paris: Fondation Jean-Jaurès. At https://jean-jaures.org/nos-productions/la-religion-devoilee-une-nouvelle-geographie-du-catholicisme.

Fowler, Robert Booth. 2018. *Religion and Politics in America: Faith, Culture, and Strategic Choices*. London: Routledge.

François, Stéphane. 2007. 'Le néo-paganisme et la politique: une tentative de compréhension.' *Raisons politiques* 1: 127–42.

2008. *Les Néo-Paganismes et La Nouvelle Droite, 1980–2006: Pour Une Autre Approche*. Vol. 2. Milan: Archè.

Frank, T. 2005. *What's the Matter with Kansas? How Conservatives Won the Heart of America*. New York: Henry Holt.

Franklin, Mark N. 2010. 'Cleavage Research: A Critical Appraisal.' *West European Politics* 33, no. 3: 648–58.

Franzmann, Simon T. 2016. 'Calling the Ghost of Populism: The AfD's Strategic and Tactical Agendas until the EP Election 2014.' *German Politics* 25, no. 4: 457–79.

Freeden, M. 2003. *Ideology*. Oxford: Oxford University Press.

Freston, Paul. 2020. 'Bolsonaro, Populism and Evangelicals in Brazil.' Research paper presented at the Populism and Protestant Political Thought Conference in Cambridge 2020.

Friedrich, S. 2015. *Der Aufstieg der AfD. Neokonservative Mobilmachung in Deutschland*. Berlin: Bertz&Fischer.

Front National. 2017. 'Marine 2017: Engagements Présidentiels.' *Front National*. At https://rassemblementnational.fr/le-projet-de-marine-le-pen/.

Fukuyama, Francis. 2018. *Identity: The Demand for Dignity and the Politics of Resentment*. New York: Farrar, Straus and Giroux.

Galiero, Emmanuel. 2017. 'Sur France 2, Marine Le Pen Mise Sur Une Confrontation Entre "mondialistes et Patriote".' Le Figaro, 10 February. At www.lefigaro .fr/elections/presidentielles/2017/02/10/35003-20170210ARTFIG00001-marine-le-pen-deux-heures-pour-rassurer-les-electeurs.php.

Galli, Mark. 2019. 'Trump Should Be Removed from Office.' *Christianity Today*, 19 December. At www.christianitytoday.com/ct/2019/december-web-only/trump-should-be-removed-from-office.html.

García Bedolla, Lisa, and Kerry L. Haynie. 2013. 'The Obama Coalition and the Future of American Politics.' *Politics, Groups, and Identities* 1, no. 1: 128–33.

Gastaldi, L. 2018. 'Convergent or Unresponsive? The Effect of Austerity and Mainstream Party Positioning on the Electoral Success of Left-Wing Populist Parties in Western Europe.' Master thesis, University of Uppsala.

Gaston, Sophie, and Sacha Hilhorst. 2018. *At Home in One's Past: Nostalgia as a Cultural and Political Force in Britain, France and Germany*. N.p.: Demos.

Gebhardt, R. 2013. 'Eine "Partei neuen Typs"? Die "Alternative für Deutschland" (AfD) vor den Bundestagswahlen.' *Forschungsjournal Soziale Bewegungen* 26, no. 3: 86–91.

Geisser, Vincent. 2018. 'L'Église et Les Catholiques de France Face À La Question Migratoire: Le Grand Malentendu?' *Migrations Societe* 3: 3–13.

Gélie, Philippe. 2018. 'Marion Maréchal-Le Pen En Vedette Américaine à Washington.' Le Figaro, 22 February. At www.lefigaro.fr/politique/2018/02/22/01002-20180222ARTFIG00365-marion-marechal-le-pen-comme-vous-nous-voulons-reprendre-le-controle-de-notre-pays.php.

Gerson, Michael. 2020. 'Trump's Politicization of the National Prayer Breakfast Is Unholy and Immoral.' Washington Post, 7 February. At www .washingtonpost.com/opinions/trumps-politicization-of-the-national-prayer-breakfast-is-unholy-and-immoral/2020/02/06/529518e4-4931-11ea-bdbf-1dfb23249293_story.html.

Gerson, Michael, and Peter Wehner. 2010. *City of Man*. New York: HarperCollins.

GESIS Leibniz. 2017. 'European Values Study (EVS).' At www.europeanvaluesstudy.eu/page/survey-2008.html.

Giddens, A. 2013. *The Third Way and Its Critics*. Hoboken, NJ: John Wiley & Sons.

Givens, T. E. 2005. *Voting Radical Right in Western Europe*. New York: Cambridge University Press.

Gjelten, Tom. 2019. 'The Religious Left Is Finding Its Voice.' *NPR*, January 24. At www.npr.org/2019/01/24/684435743/provoked-by-trump-the-religious-left-is-finding-its-voice.

Goldberg, Andreas C. 2020. 'The Evolution of Cleavage Voting in Four Western Countries: Structural, Behavioural or Political Dealignment?' *European Journal of Political Research* 59, no. 1: 68–90.

Goodhart, D. 2017. *The Road to Somewhere: The Populist Revolt and the Future of Politics*. London: Penguin.

Goodheart, E. 2018. 'Trump's Cultural Populism.' *Society* 55, no. 1: 22–24.

Goodwin, Matthew, Henry Olsen and Josh Good. 2019. 'National Populism.' *Faith Angle*. At https://faithangle.org/podcasts/.

Gorce, Bernard. 2019. 'PMA, Le Pari Politique d'Emmanuel Macron.' *La Croix*, 25 July. At www.la-croix.com/Sciences-et-ethique/Ethique/PMA-pari-politique-dEmmanuel-Macron-2019-07-24-1201037337.

Gorski, Philip. 2019a. *American Covenant: A History of Civil Religion from the Puritans to the Present*. Princeton, NJ: Princeton University Press.

  2019b. 'Why Evangelicals Voted for Trump: A Critical Cultural Sociology.' *Politics of Meaning/Meaning of Politics*. New York: Springer.

  2020. *American Babylon: Christianity and Democracy before and after Trump*. London: Routledge.

Gorski, Philip, and Samuel L. Perry. 2022. *The Flag and the Cross: White Christian Nationalism and the Threat to American Democracy*. Oxford and New York: Oxford University Press.

Gougou, F. 2015. 'Les ouvriers et le vote Front National. Les logiques d'un réalignement électoral.' In Nonna Mayer, Sylvain Crépon and A. Dézé, eds. *Les faux-semblants du Front national*. Paris: Presses de Sciences Po.

Gourévitch, Jean-Paul. 2019. *Le Grand Remplacement, Réalité Ou Intox?* Paris: PG de Roux.

Graf, F. W. 2011. *Der Protestantismus. Geschichte und Gegenwart*. München: Beck.

Graham, David. 2021. 'A Sermon in America's Civic Religion.' The Atlantic, 20 January. At www.theatlantic.com/ideas/archive/2021/01/a-sermon-in-americas-civic-religion/617750/.

Green, Emma. 2021. 'A Christian Insurrection.' The Atlantic, 8 January. At www.theatlantic.com/politics/archive/2021/01/evangelicals-catholics-jericho-march-capitol/617591/.

Green, John C., James L. Guth, Corwin E. Smidt and Lyman A. 1996. *Religion and the Culture Wars: Dispatches from the Front*. Lanham, MD: Rowman & Littlefield.

Green, Joshua. 2017. *Devil's Bargain: Steve Bannon, Donald Trump, and the Storming of the Presidency.* London: Penguin.

Gregg, S. 2017. 'France's Catholic Moment.' *First Things* (February): 20–22. At www.firstthings.com/article/2017/02/frances-catholic-moment.

Gregory, Wilton D. 2020. 'Archbishop Wilton Gregory Issues Statement on Planned Presidential Visit.' *Archdiocese of Washington.* At https://adw.org/wp-content/uploads/sites/2/2020/06/060220-ADW-Press-Release.pdf.

Gruber, H. 2006. *Katholische Kirche und Nationalsozialismus 1930–1945.* Paderborn: Schöningh.

Grunberg, Gérard. 2019. 'Les "gilets Jaunes" et La Crise de La Démocratie Représentative.' *Le Debat* 2: 95–103.

Grundgesetz. 1949. 'Basic Law for the Federal Republic of Germany.' Bundesministerium der Justiz und für Verbraucherschutz. At www.gesetze-im-internet.de/englisch_gg/.

Grüne. 2017. 'Zukunft Wird Aus Mut Gemacht – Wahlprogramm 2017.' *Bündniss 90 Die Grünen.* At www.bundestagswahl-bw.de/wahlprogramm-gruene-btwahl2017.

The Guardian. 2017. 'Trump's Marriage to the Religious Right Reeks of Hypocrisy on Both Sides.' *The Guardian.* At www.theguardian.com/commentisfree/2017/oct/14/trumps-religious-right-hypocrisy-values-voter-summit.

Guardino, M., and D. Snyder. 2012. 'The Tea Party and the Crisis of Neoliberalism: Mainstreaming New Right Populism in the Corporate News Media.' *New Political Science* 34, no. 4: 527–48.

Guth, James L. 2019. 'Are White Evangelicals Populists? The View from the 2016 American National Election Study.' *The Review of Faith & International Affairs* 17, no. 3: 20–35.

Guth, James L, and Brent F. Nelsen. 2021. 'Party Choice in Europe: Social Cleavages and the Rise of Populist Parties.' *Party Politics* 27, no. 3: 453–64.

Habermas, J. 1985. *Die neue Unübersichtlichkeit.* Frankfurt am Main: Suhrkamp.

    2006. 'Religion in the Public Sphere,.' *European Journal of Philosophy* 14: 1–25.

Hacot, Valérie. 2016. 'FN: Marion Maréchal-Le Pen, l'égérie Des "tradis".' 15 October. At www.leparisien.fr/politique/marion-marechal-le-pen-l-egerie-des-tradis-15-10-2016-6210738.php.

Haidt, Jonathan. 2012. *The Righteous Mind: Why Good People Are Divided by Politics and Religion.* New York: Vintage.

Halikiopoulou, D., K. Nanou and S. Vasilopoulou. 2012. 'The Paradox of Nationalism: The Common Denominator of Radical Right and Radical Left Euroscepticism.' *European Journal of Political Research* 51, no. 4: 504–39.

Hambauer, V., and A. Mays. 2018. 'Wer wählt die AfD? – Ein Vergleich der Sozialstruktur, politischen Einstellungen und Einstellungen zu Flüchtlingen zwischen AfD-WählerInnen und der WählerInnen der anderen Parteien.' *Zeitschrift Für Vergleichende Politikwissenschaft* 12, no. 1: 133–54.

Hamburger, Philip. 2009. *Separation of Church and State.* Cambridge MA: Harvard University Press.

Hamid, Shadi. 2019. *The Role of Islam in European Populism: How Refugee Flows and Fear of Muslims Drive Right-Wing Support Shadi Hamid.* Washington, DC: Brookings Institution.

Hamid, Shadi, and Rashid Dar. 2017. 'The Rise of the "Westernists".' *The American Interest.* At www.the-american-interest.com/2017/11/16/the-rise-of-the-westernists/.

Handelsblatt. 2018. 'Die AfD im Dauerstreit mit den Kirchen.' *Handeslblatt.* At www.handelsblatt.com/politik/deutschland/nationalkonservative-und-christentum-die-afd-im-dauerstreit-mit-den-kirchen/21187370.html.

Hariri, Y. 2017. *Nationalism vs. Globalism: The New Political Divide.* TED Talk. At www.ted.com/talks/yuval_noah_harari_nationalism_vs_globalism_the_new_political_divide.

Harris Interactive. 2017. 'Le 1er tour de l'élection présidentielle 2017: Composition des différents électorats, motivations et éléments de structuration du vote.' Harris Interactive. At interactive.fr/wp-content/uploads/sites/6/2017/04/Rapport-Harris-Sondage-Jour-du-Vote-1er-tour-de-lelection-presidentielle-M6.pdf.

Hatch, Nathan O. 1989. *The Democratization of American Christianity.* London: Yale University Press.

Hauschild, Wolf D. 2008. 'Kontinuität Im Wandel. Die Evangelische Kirche in Deutschland und Die Sog. 68er Bewegung.' In B. Hey and V. Wittmütz, eds. *1968 und die Kirchen.* Münster: Verlag für Regionalgeschichte.

Haute, E. 2011. *Party Membership in Europe: Exploration into the Anthills of Party Politics.* Science Politique. Brussels: Editions de l'Université de Bruxelles.

Havertz, Ralf. 2020. 'Strategy of Ambivalence: AfD between Neoliberalism and Social Populism.' *Trames* 24, no. 4: 549–65.

2021. *Radical Right Populism in Germany: AfD, Pegida, and the Identitarian Movement.* Routledge.

Hawkins, Derek. 2017. 'Another "Make America Great Again" Song. This One, from Evangelicals, Is Trump-Approved.' *Washington Post,* 12 July. At www.washingtonpost.com/news/morning-mix/wp/2017/07/12/another-make-america-great-again-song-this-one-from-evangelicals-is-trump-approved/.

Hawkins, K. 2009. 'Is Chávez Populist? Measuring Populist Discourse in Comparative Perspective.' *Comparative Political Studies* 42, no. 8: 1040–67.

Hawkins, Kirk A, Ryan E. Carlin, Levente Littvay and Cristóbal Rovira Kaltwasser. 2018. *The Ideational Approach to Populism: Concept, Theory, and Analysis.* London: Routledge.

Hawley, George. 2017. *Making Sense of the Alt-Right.* New York: Columbia University Press.

Haynes, Jeffrey. 2017. 'Donald Trump, "Judeo-Christian Values", and the "Clash of Civilizations."' *The Review of Faith & International Affairs* 15, no. 3: 66–75.

2019. *From Huntington to Trump: Thirty Years of the Clash of Civilizations.* Lanham, MD: Rowman & Littlefield.

2020. 'Right-Wing Populism and Religion in Europe and the USA.' *Religions* 11, no. 10: 490–508.

Heath, A., J. K. Curtice and G. Elgenius. 2009. *Individualisation and the Decline of Class Identity: Identity in the 21st Century*. London: Palgrave McMillan.

Hehl, U., and C. v. Kösters. 1984. *Priester unter Hitlers Terror. Eine biographische und statistische Erhebung*. Paderborn: Schöningh.

Heimbach-Steins, Marianne, and Alexander Filipović. 2017. *Grundpositionen der Partei 'Alternative Für Deutschland' und der Katholischen Soziallehre im Vergleich*. Münster: WMU Münster.

Heinisch, R. 2017. *Political Populism: A Handbook*. Baden-Baden: Nomos.

Heinze, Anna-Sophie. 2018. 'Strategies of Mainstream Parties towards Their Right-Wing Populist Challengers: Denmark, Norway, Sweden and Finland in Comparison.' *West European Politics* 41, no. 2: 287–309.

Heredia, Luisa. 2011. 'From Prayer to Protest: The Immigrant Rights Movement and the Catholic Church.' *Rallying for Immigrant Rights*: 101–22.

Hermes, C. 2016. 'Kirchlich-politische Wachsamkeit.' In S. Orth and V. Riesing, eds. *AfD, Pegida & Co.: Angriff auf die Religion?* Freiburg: Herder Verlag.

Hermet, G. 2007. 'Populisme et Nationalisme.' In J. Rioux, ed. *Les Populismes*. Paris: Perrin.

Herreros, Romain. 2017. 'Hommage de Johnny Hallyday: Ce Moment Où Macron Était à Deux Doigts de Bénir Le Cercueil.' *Huffington Post*, 9 December. At www.huffingtonpost.fr/2017/12/09/hommage-de-johnny-hallyday-ce-moment-ou-macron-etait-a-deux-doigts-de-benir-le-cercueil_a_23302316/.

Heyes, C. 2002. *Identity politics*. *Online*. At https://plato.stanford.edu/entries/identity-politics/.

Höbelt, L. 2003. *Defiant Populist: Jörg Haider and the Politics of Austria*. Lafayette: West.

Hochmann, Nate. 2019. 'The Rise of the Post-Religious Right.' Aero, 12 November. At https://areomagazine.com/2019/11/12/the-rise-of-the-post-religious-right/.

Hochschild, Arlie Russell. 2018. *Strangers in Their Own Land: Anger and Mourning on the American Right*. New York: The New Press.

Hofmann, Kristina. 2019. 'Kritik an Evangelischer Kirche: AfD: Kirche Legt Sich Mit Mächtigen Ins Bett.', 11 June. At www.zdf.de/nachrichten/heute/afd-greift-kirchen-an-100.html.

Höhne, V., and P. Wensierski. 2017. 'Neue rechte Allianz: AfD auf dem Kreuzzug.' Spiegel, 29, no. 2017. At www.spiegel.de/spiegel/fromme-christen-und-rechte-waehler-verbuenden-sich-im-widerstand-a-1158077.html.

Holley, Peter. 2016. 'KKK's Official Newspaper Supports Donald Trump for President.' Washington Post, 2 November. At www.washingtonpost.com/news/post-politics/wp/2016/11/01/the-kkks-official-newspaper-has-endorsed-donald-trump-for-president/.

Holmes, S. 1995. *Die Anatomie des Antiliberalismus*. Hamburg: Rotbuch Verlag.

Hooghe, Liesbet, and Gary Marks. 2018. 'Cleavage Theory Meets Europe's Crises: Lipset, Rokkan, and the Transnational Cleavage.' *Journal of European Public Policy* 25, no. 1: 109–35.

Hoover, Dennis R. 2019. 'Populism and Internationalism, Evangelical Style: An Introduction to the Fall 2019 Issue.' *The Review of Faith & International Affairs* 17, no. 3.

Horowitz, Jason. 2018. 'Steve Bannon's "Movement" Enlists Italy's Most Powerful Politician.' *New York Times*, 7 September. At www.nytimes .com/2018/09/07/world/europe/italy-steve-bannon-matteo-salvini.html.

Human Development Index. 2017. 'United Nations Development Programme.' At http://hdr.undp.org/en/2016-report.

Hunter, James Davison. 1983. *American Evangelicalism: Conservative Religion and the Quandary of Modernity*. New Brunswick, NJ: Rutgers University Press.

   1992. *Culture Wars: The Struggle to Control the Family, Art, Education, Law, and Politics in America*. New York: Basic Books.

Huntington, Samuel P. 1996. *The Clash of Civilizations and the Remaking of World Order*. New York: Simon and Schuster.

   2004. *Who Are We? The Challenges to America's National Identity*. New York and London: Simon & Schuster.

Hurd, Elizabeth Shakman. 2009. *The Politics of Secularism in International Relations*. Vol. 112. Princeton, NJ: Princeton University Press.

Identity & Democracy Parliamentary Group. 2019. 'Statutes of the Identity and Demcocracy (ID) Group in the European Parliament.' *Identity & Democracy Parliamentary Group*. At https://d3n8a8pro7vhmx.cloudfront.net/kantodev/ pages/102/attachments/original/1582196570/EN_Statutes_of_the_ID_ Group.pdf?1582196570.

IFOP. 2010. 'Le Catholicisme En France.' *IFOP*. At www.ifop.com/publication/ catholicisme-en-france-en-2010/#.

   2017a. 'Le Vote Des Électorats Confessionnels Au Second Tour de l'élection Présidentielle.' *IFOP*. At www.ifop.com/publication/le-vote-des-electorats-confessionnels-au-second-tour-de-lelection-presidentielle/.

   2017b. 'L'adhésion à l'accueil Des Migrants Dans Différents Pays.' IFOP for Atlantico. At www.ifop.com/publication/ladhesion-a-laccueil-des-migrants-dans-differents-pays/.

   2019. 'Le Vote Des Électorats Confessionnels Aux Élections Européennes.' Ifop for La Croix Paris. At www.ifop.com/publication/le-vote-des-electorats-confessionnels-aux-elections-europeennes/.

   2022a. 'Le Vote Des Électorats Confessionnels Au Second Tour de l'élection Présidentielle.' Ifop for La Croix Paris. At www.ifop.com/wp-content/ uploads/2022/04/119119-Rapport.pdf.

   2022b. 'Le Vote Des Électorats Confessionnels Au 1er Tour de l'élection Présidentielle.' Ifop for La Croix Paris. At www.ifop.com/wp-content/ uploads/2022/04/119082-Rapport.pdf.

Igielnik, Ruth, Scott Keeter and Hannah Hartig. 2021. 'Behind Biden's 2020 Victory.' Pew Research Center. At www.pewresearch.org/politics/2021/06/30/ behind-bidens-2020-victory/.

Illouz, Eva. 2017. 'Le Populisme Émotionnel Menace La Démocratie.' *Le Monde*. At www.lemonde.fr/festival/article/2017/07/25/eva-illouz-le-populisme-emotionnel-menace-la-democratie_5164585_4415198.html.

Immerzeel, Tim, Eva Jaspers and Marcel Lubbers. 2013. 'Religion as Catalyst or Restraint of Radical Right Voting?' *West European Politics* 36, no. 5: 946–68.

Inacker, M. J. 1993. 'Die Evangelische Kirche in Deutschland zwischen SPD und SED: Anmerkungen zur Sozialdemokratisierung des Protestantismus.' *Kirchliche Zeitgeschichte* no. 1/1993: 235–49.

IPSOS. 2017. 'La Place de La Religion et de La Laïcité Dans l'élection Présidentielle 2017.' *France Télévision*. At www.ipsos.com/sites/default/files/files-fr-fr/doc_associe/religions_et_laicite_mars2017.pdf.

    2017. 'Sondage "Les protestants en France en 2017" (1): qui sont les protestants?' At www.reforme.net/actualite/societe/sondage-les-protestants-en-france-en-2017-1-qui-sont-les-protestants/.

Ivaldi, G. 2015. 'Du néolibéralisme au social-populisme?' In Sylvain Crépon, Nonna Mayer and A. Dézé, eds. *Les faux-semblants du Front national.* Paris: Presses de Sciences Po.

Jardina, Ashley. 2019. *White Identity Politics*. Cambridge: Cambridge University Press.

Jeanpierre, Lucette. 2017. 'Obsèques Johnny: Macron a Eu Raison de Ne Pas Faire Le Signe de Croix, Mais ...' *Riposte Laique*, 11 December. At https://ripostelaique.com/obseques-johnny-macron-a-eu-raison-de-ne-pas-faire-le-signe-de-croix-mais.html.

Jenkins, Samuel D. 2019. 'The Revenge of Dreyfus: Charles Maurras and His Influence on Right-Wing Political Discourse.' PhD thesis, Appalachian State University.

Johnson, Andre E. 2012. 'Avoiding Phony Religiosity: The Rhetorical Theology of Obama's 2012 National Prayer Breakfast Address.' *Journal of Contemporary Rhetoric* 2, no. 2: 44–53.

Joly, Laurent. 2015. *Naissance de l'Action Française: Maurice Barrès, Charles Maurras et l'extrême Droite Nationaliste Au Tournant Du Xxe Siècle.* Paris: Grasset.

Jones, Maldwyn Allen. 1992. *American Immigration*. Chicago: University of Chicago Press.

Jones, Paul Dafydd. 2018. 'Taking on the Alt-Right: Theological Considerations.' *Berkley Center for Religion, Peace and World Affairs. Berkley Forum: Christianity and the Alt-Right in America.* At https://berkleycenter.georgetown.edu/responses/taking-on-the-alt-right-theological-considerations.

Jones, Robert P, and D. Cox. 2010. 'Religion and the Tea Party in the 2010 Election.' *Public Religion Research Institute*. At www.prri.org/research/religion-tea-party-2010/.

Jones, Robert P, Rachel Laser, Nikki Yamashiro and Jim Kessler. 2010. 'Beyond the God Gap: A New Roadmap for Reaching Religious Americans on Public Policy Issues.' *Public Religion Research Institute*. At www.prri.org/wp-content/uploads/2011/06/Beyond-the-God-Gap-Religion-Cultural-Issues-Report.pdf.

Jones, Robert Patrick, and Daniel Cox. 2017. *America's Changing Religious Identity: Findings from the 2016 American Values Atlas*. Washington, DC: Public Religion Research Institute.

Jones, R. P. 2016. *The End of White Christian America*. New York: Simon & Schuster.

Joppke, C. 1999. *Immigration and the Nation-State: The United States Germany and Great Britain*. Oxford: Oxford University Press.

2017. 'Erst die Moral, dann das Fressen.' *Frankfurter Allgemeine Zeitung*. At www.faz.net/aktuell/politik/die-gegenwart/populismus-erst-die-moral-dann-das-fressen-15047823.html.

Jörgensen, P. 2017. 'Ein Missverständnis schreibt Geschichte. Warum Freikirchen mit 'evangelikal' falsch beschrieben sind.' In W. Thielmann, ed. *Alternative für Christen?: Die AfD und ihr gespaltenes Verhältnis zur Religion* Neukirchen-Vluyn: Neukirchener Verlag.

Journal du Dimanche. 2017. 'Guaino Critique Fillon: "Qui Imagine De Gaulle Dire 'Je Suis Le Candidat Catholique'?"' *Journal Du Dimanche*, 21 June. At www.lejdd.fr/Politique/Guaino-critique-Fillon-Qui-imagine-De-Gaulle-dire-je-suis-le-candidat-catholique-854762.

Joustra, Jessica. 2019. 'What Is an Evangelical? Examining the Politics, History, and Theology of a Contested Label.' *The Review of Faith & International Affairs* 17, no. 3: 7–19.

Judis, J. 2016. *The Populist Explosion: How the Great Recession Transformed American and European Politics*. New York: Columbia Open Reports.

Jung, C. 2016. 'The Trump Exception: Christian Morals and the Presidency.' *Harvard International Review, Summer* 2016, no. 37: 7–9.

Jungerstam-Mulders, S. 2003. 'Uneven Odds: The Electoral Success of the Freiheitliche Partei Österreichs, the Vlaams Blok, the Republikaner and the Centrumdemocraten under the Conditions Provided by the Political System in Austria, Belgium, Germany and the Netherlands.Helsinki.' Master thesis, Helsinki University.

Kaiser, W., and H. Wohnout. 2004. *Political Catholicism in Europe 1918–1945*. London: Routledge.

Kaltwasser, C. 2014. 'The Responses of Populism to Dahl's Democratic Dilemmas.' *Political Studies* 62, no. 3: 470–87.

Kaltwasser, C., P. Taggart, P. Espejo and P. Ostiguy, eds. 2017a. *The Oxford Handbook of Populism*. Oxford: Oxford University Press.

2017b. 'Populism: An Overview of the Concept and the State of the Art.' In C. Kaltwasser, P. Taggart, P. Espejo and P. Ostiguy, eds. *The Oxford Handbook of Populism*. Oxford: Oxford University Press.

Kalyvas, Stathis, and Kees Van Kersbergen. 2010. 'Christian Democracy.' *Annual Review of Political Science* 13, no. 1: 183–209.

Kampwirth, K. 2010. *Gender and Populism in Latin America: Passionate Politics*. University Park: Pennsylvania State University Press.

Karapin, R. 2002. *Far-Right Parties and the Construction of Immigration Issues in Germany. In Shadows over Europe*. New York: Palgrave Macmillan.

Karnitschnig, Matthew. 2021. 'Germany's Pivot from America.' Politico, 22 January. At www.politico.eu/article/germany-pivot-from-america/.

Katholisch.de. 2017. 'Das sagen die Parteien zur Religionspolitik.' *Katholisch.de*. At www.katholisch.de/aktuelles/aktuelle-artikel/bundestagswahl-wahlprogramme-parteien-zu-staat-und-kirche.

   2018. 'Breite Ablehnung für AfD-Antrag zur Christenverfolgung.' *Katholisch. de*. At www.katholisch.de/aktuelles/aktuelle-artikel/breite-ablehnung-fur-afd-antrag-zur-.

Kaufmann, Eric. 2017a. 'Immigration and White Identity in the West.' *Foreign Affairs.* At www.foreignaffairs.com/articles/united-states/2017-09-08/immigration-and-white-identity-west.

   2017b. 'Levels or Changes? Ethnic Context, Immigration and the UK Independence Party Vote.' *Electoral Studies* 48: 57–69.

   2018. *Whiteshift: Populism, Immigration and the Future of White Majorities.* London: Penguin.

Keohane, David. 2018. 'Marine Le Pen's Far-Right Party to Join Bannon Populist Project.' *Financial Times*, 18 September. At www.ft.com/content/57749590-bb3b-11e8-94b2-17176fbf93f5.

Kešić, Josip, and Jan Willem Duyvendak. 2019. 'The Nation under Threat: Secularist, Racial and Populist Nativism in the Netherlands.' *Patterns of Prejudice* 53, no. 5: 441–63.

Kidd, Thomas S. 2008. *The Great Awakening: The Roots of Evangelical Christianity in Colonial America.* New Haven, CT: Yale University Press.

   2019. *Who Is an Evangelical? The History of a Movement in Crisis.* New Haven, CT: Yale University Press.

Kissler, Alexander. 2021. 'Alles Sein, Bloss Nicht Unmodern: Warum Der Konservatismus in Deutschland so Schlechte Karten Hat.' *Neue Züricher Zeitung*, 29 December. At www.nzz.ch/international/alles-sein-bloss-nicht-unmodern-warum-der-konservatismus-in-deutschland-so-schlechte-karten-hat-ld.1661084?reduced=true.

Kitschelt, H. 1995. *The Transformation of European Social Democracy.* Cambridge: Cambridge Universty Press.

   2007. 'Growth and Persistence of the Radical Right in Postindustrial Democracies: Advances and Challenges in Comparative Research.' *West European Politics* 30, no. 5: 1176–1206.

Klose, J., and W. Patzelt. 2016. 'Was ist so schlimm am Rechtspopulismus?' In S. Orth and V. Resing, eds. *AfD, Pegida & Co.: Angriff auf die Religion?* Freiburg: Herder Verlag.

Knippenberg, Joseph M. 2010. 'The Personal (Is Not?) The Political: The Role of Religion in the Presidency of George W. Bush.' In Ronald Weed and John von Heyking, eds. *Civil Religion in Political Thought: Its Perennial Questions and Enduring Relevance in North America.* Washington, DC: Catholic University of America Press.

Knoll, Benjamin R. 2009. '"And Who Is My Neighbor?" Religion and Attitudes toward Immigration Policy.' *Journal for the Scientific Study of Religion* 48, no. 2: 313–331.

Konrad Adenauer Stiftung. 2021. 'Wahlanalysen.' *Konrad Adenauer Stiftung.* At www.kas.de/web/wahlen.kas.de/wahlanalysen.

Koran, Mario, and Helen Sullivan. 2020. 'Bishop "outraged" over Trump's Church Photo Op during George Floyd Protests.' *The Guardian*, 2 June. At www.theguardian.com/us-news/2020/jun/02/outrageous-christian-leaders-reject-trump-use-of-church-as-prop-during-george-floyd-protests.

Kriesi, H. 2008. *West European Politics in the Age of Globalization.* Cambridge: Cambridge University Press.

Kriesi, H., E. Grande, M. Dolezal, M. Helbling, D. Höglinger, S. Hutter and B. Wüest. 2012. *Political Conflict in Western Europe.* Cambridge: Cambridge University Press.

Kriesi, H., E. Grande, R. Lachat, M. Dolezal, S. Bornschier and T. Frey. 2006. 'Globalization and the Transformation of the National Political Space: Six European Countries Compared.' *European Journal of Political Research* 45, no. 6: 921–56.

Krug, François. 2016. 'Saint-Pie-X, l'école Où Marion Maréchal-Le Pen a Trouvé La Foi.' *Le Monde*, 20 April. At www.lemonde.fr/m-actu/article/2016/04/22/saint-pie-x-l-ecole-ou-marion-marechal-le-pen-a-trouve-la-foi_4907142_4497186.html.

Kuru, A. 2007. 'Passive and Assertive Secularism: Historical Conditions, Ideological Struggles, and State Policies toward Religion.' *World Politics* 59, no. 4: 568–94.

Kuzmany, Stefan. 2016. 'Mit Verachtung.' *Der Spiegel*, 28 April. At www.spiegel.de/kultur/tv/sandra-maischberger-ueber-populisten-nur-verachtung-uebrig-a-1089692.html.

La Croix. 2019. 'Agnès Thill Exclue de La République En Marche Pour Des Propos Sur La PMA.' 26 June. At www.la-croix.com/France/Politique/Agnes-Thill-exclue-Republique-marche-propos-PMA-2019-06-26-1201031575.

Labberton, Mark. 2018. *Still Evangelical? Insiders Reconsider Political, Social, and Theological Meaning.* Westmont: InterVarsity Press.

Lair, Noémie. 2022. 'Présidentielle: Éric Woerth Annonce Soutenir Emmanuel Macron et "Se Met En Congé" Des Républicains.' *France Inter*. At www.franceinter.fr/politique/presidentielle-eric-woerth-annonce-soutenir-emmanuel-macron-et-se-met-en-conge-des-republicains.

Laird, Chryl, and Ismail White. 2020. 'Why So Many Black Voters Are Democrats, Even When They Aren't Liberal.' *FiveThirtyEight*. At https://fivethirtyeight.com/features/why-so-many-black-voters-are-democrats-even-when-they-arent-liberal/.

Lambrecq, Maxence. 2019. 'Sur La PMA, Marine Le Pen Cherche La Bonne Formule.' *France Inter*, 9 September. At www.franceinter.fr/sur-la-pma-marine-le-pen-cherche-la-bonne-formule.

Landron, O. 2004. *Les Communautés nouvelles: nouveaux visages du catholicisme français.* Paris: Les éditions du Cerf.

Läsker, Kristina. 2021. 'Ein Mann Sieht Rot.' 29 September. At www.zeit.de/2021/40/spd-wahlkampagne-marketing-raphael-brinkert-olaf-scholz.

Lawrence, Paul. 2016. *Nationalism: History and Theory*. London: Taylor & Francis.

Layman, Geoffrey. 2016. 'Where Is Trump's Evangelical Base? Not in Church.' *Washington Post*, 29 March.

Le Bras, H., and E. Todd. 2013. *Le Mystère francais*. Paris: Le Seuil.

Le Normand, Xavier. 2022. 'Présidentielle 2022: Les Évêques s'adressent "à La Conscience et à La Liberté de Chacun".' *La Croix*, 13 April. At www.la-croix .com/Religion/Presidentielle-2022-eveques-sadressent-conscience-liberte-chacun-2022-04-13-1201210245.

Le Pen, Jean-Marie. 1958. '2e Séance Du 29 Janvier 1958, Assemblée Nationale.' *Débats Parlementaires – Assemblée Nationale*.

Le Pen, Marine. 2012. 'La Mondialisation va Profondément à l'encontre de La Nature Humaine.' *Le Point.Fr*. At www.lepoint.fr/presidentielle/marine-le-pen-la-mondialisation-va-profondement-a-l-encontre-de-la-nature-humaine-09-03-2012-1439416_3121.php.

Le Point. 2022. 'Présidentielle: Zemmour Évoque Marion Maréchal Comme Première Ministre.' Le Point, 17 February. At www.lepoint.fr/presidentielle/ presidentielle-zemmour-evoque-marion-marechal-comme-premier-minis-tre-17-02-2022-2465184_3121.php.

Lebourg, N. 2015. 'Le Front National et la galaxie des extrêmes droites radicales.' In Nonna Mayer, Sylvain Crépon and A. Dézé, eds. *Les faux-semblants du Front national*. Paris: Presses de Sciences Po.

Leclerc, Joseph. 1933. 'Le Roi de France, "fils Aîné de l'Église." Essai Historique.' *Études* 214: 21–36.

Lecoeur, E. 2003. *Un néo-populisme à la française: trente ans de Front national*. Paris: Éditions La Découverte.

Lees, David. 2017. 'A Controversial Campaign: François Fillon and the Decline of the Centre-Right in the 2017 Presidential Elections.' *Modern & Contemporary France* 25, no. 4: 391–402.

Leonard, Karen Isaksen. 2003. *Muslims in the United States: The State of Research*. New York: Russel Sage.

Leonardelli, Julien. 2019. 'Twitter Post from the 15th April 2019.' *Twitter*. At https://twitter.com/JLeonardelli_/status/1117864448067284992.

Lesegretain, Claire. 2017. 'En 2002, Les Évêques Appelaient à Ne Pas Voter Pour Le Front National Au Second Tour de La Présidentielle.' *La Croix*, 24 April. At www.la-croix.com/Religion/Catholicisme/France/En-2002-eveques-appelaient-voter-pour-Front-national-second-tour-presidentie lle-2017-04-24-1200841988.

Lesueur, Corentin. 2022. 'Les Catholiques, Nouvelle Ligne de Fracture Entre Marine Le Pen et Éric Zemmour.' La Croix, 6 February. At www.la-croix.com/France/ catholiques-nouvelle-ligne-fracture-entre-Marine-Le-Pen-Eric-Zemmour-2022-02-06-1201198835?utm_source=newsletter&utm_medium=email&utm_ campaign=NEWSLETTER__CRX_ESSENTIEL_MATIN_EDITO&utm_ content=20220207#edition=edition-matin-2022-02-07.

Leustean, L. N. 2008. 'Orthodoxy and Political Myths in Balkan National Identities.' *National Identities* 10, no. 4: 421–32.

Levillain, Philippe. 2010. *Rome n'est plus Dans Rome: Mgr Lefebvre et Son Église.* Paris: Perrin.

Levin, Yuval. 2020. *A Time to Build: From Family and Community to Congress and the Campus, How Recommitting to Our Institutions Can Revive the American Dream.* London: Hachette UK.

L'Express. 2015. 'Avec l'invitation de Marion Maréchal-Le Pen, l'évêque Du Var Brise Un Tabou.' L'Express, 27 August. At www.lexpress.fr/actualite/ politique/fn/avec-l-invitation-de-marion-marechal-le-pen-l-eveque-du-var- brise-un-tabou_1710222.html.

Lichterman, P. 2008. 'Religion and the Construction of Civic Identity.' *American Sociological Review* 73: 1–83.

Lienesch, Michael. 2019. '"In God We Trust": The US National Motto and the Contested Concept of Civil Religion.' *Religions* 10, no. 5. At www.mdpi .com/2077-1444/10/5/340.

LifeWay. 2017. 'Many Who Call Themselves Evangelical Don't Actually Hold Evangelical Beliefs.' LifeWay Research. At https://lifewayresearch .com/2017/12/06/many-evangelicals-dont-hold-evangelical-beliefs/.

Lijphart, A. 1971. 'Comparative Politics and the Comparative Method.' *American Political Science Review* 65, no. 3: 682–93.

Lilla, Mark. 2018. *The Once and Future Liberal: After Identity Politics.* Oxford: Oxford University Press.

Lindell, Henrik. 2022. 'Zemmour Réduit Le Christianisme à Un Instrument Contre l'islam.' 9 February. At www.lavie.fr/actualite/societe/iacopo- scaramuzzi-zemmour-reduit-le-christianisme-a-un-instrument-contre- lislam-80605.php.

Lindell, Henrik, Pierre Jova and Pascale Tournier. 2021. 'Mais Qui Sont Ces Catholiques Qui Suivent Éric Zemmour?' La Vie, 27 October. At www .lavie.fr/actualite/societe/mais-qui-sont-ces-catholiques-qui-suivent-eric- zemmour-78654.php.

Linden, I. 2009. *Global Catholicism: Diversity and Change since Vatican II.* El Paso, TX: Cinco Puntos Press.

Lindsay, D. Michael. 2007. *Faith in the Halls of Power: How Evangelicals Joined the American Elite.* Oxford: Oxford University Press.

2006. 'Is the National Prayer Breakfast Surrounded by a "Christian Mafia"? Religious Publicity and Secrecy within the Corridors of Power.' *Journal of the American Academy of Religion* 74, no. 2: 390–419.

Lipset, Seymour, and Stein Rokkan. 1990. *Cleavage Structures, Party Systems, and Voter Alignments: Cross National Perspectives.* New York: Springer.

Loi de 1905. 2019. 'Loi Du 9 Décembre 1905 Concernant La Séparation Des Eglises et de l'Etat.' *Legifrance.* At www.legifrance.gouv.fr/affichTexte.do?ci dTexte=JORFTEXT000000508749.

Loth, Wilfried, and Robert Picht. 1991. *De Gaulle, Deutschland und Europa.* Berlin: Springer.

Lubbers, M., and P. Scheepers. 2001. 'Explaining the Trend in Extreme Right-Wing Voting: Germany 1989–1998.' *European Sociological Review* 17, no. 4: 431–49.

MacWilliams, Matthew C. 2016. 'Who Decides When the Party Doesn't? Authoritarian Voters and the Rise of Donald Trump.' *PS: Political Science & Politics* 49, no. 4: 716–21.

Mandaville, P., and S. Silvestri. 2015. 'Integrating Religious Engagement into Diplomacy: Challenges and Opportunities.' *Issues in Governance Studies* 67. At www.brookings.edu/wp-content/uploads/2016/06/IssuesInGovStudiesMandavilleSilvestriefinal.pdf.

Manza, Jeff, and Clem Brooks. 1999. *Social Cleavages and Political Change: Voter Alignments and US Party Coalitions.* Oxford: Oxford University Press.

Margolis, Michele F. 2018. *From Politics to the Pews: How Partisanship and the Political Environment Shape Religious Identity.* Chicago: University of Chicago Press.

Marks, G., and C. Wilson. 2000. 'The Past in the Present: A Cleavage Theory of Party Response to European Integration.' *British Journal of Political Science* 30: 433–59.

Marks, Gary, David Attewell, Jan Rovny and Liesbet Hooghe. 2017. 'Dealignment Meets Cleavage Theory.' Paper presented at the American Political Science Association Meeting, San Francisco, CA.

Marsh, Charles. 2008. *The Beloved Community: How Faith Shapes Social Justice from the Civil Rights Movement to Today.* New York: Basic Books.

Martimort, Aimé Georges. 1973. *Le Gallicanisme.* Paris: Presses Universitaires de France.

Marzouki, Nadia. 2016. 'The Tea Party and Religion: Between Religious and Historical Fundamentalism.' In Olivier Roy, Duncan McDonnell and Nadia Marzouki, eds. *Saving the People: How Populist Hijack Religion.* London: Hurst & Company.

Matthews, Dylan. 2015. '"For Germans, Economics Is Still Part of Moral Philosophy": Why Germany Won't Help Greece.' *Vox*, 30 June. At www.vox.com/2015/6/30/8871981/germany-angela-merkel-greece.

Mayer, Nonna. 1999. *Ces Français qui votent FN.* Paris: Flammarion.

2013. 'From Jean-Marie to Marine Le Pen: Electoral Change on the Far Right.' *Parliamentary Affairs* 66, no. 1: 160–78.

2015a. 'Le plafond de verre électoral entamé, mais pas brisé.' In Sylvain Crépon, Nonna Mayer and A. Dézé, eds. *Les faux-semblants du Front national.* Paris: Presses de Sciences Po.

2015b. 'Le Mythe de La Dédiabolisation Du FN.' *La Vie Des Idées*, published online. At https://laviedesidees.fr/IMG/pdf/20151204_fn.pdf.

2016. 'Les constantes du vote FN.' *Revue Projet* 5: 11–14.

2017. 'Les électeurs du Front national (2012–2015).' In F. Gougou and V. Tiberj, eds. *La déconnexion électorale.* Paris: Fondation Jean-Jaurès.

Mayer, Nonna, Sylvain Crépon and A. Dézé, eds. 2015. *Les faux-semblants du Front national: Sociologie d'un parti politique (Fait politique).* Paris: Presses de Sciences Po.

Mayer, Nonna, and Pascal Perrineau. 1996. *Le Front National à Découvert.* Paris: Presses de Sciences Po.

McAlister, Melani. 2018a. *The Kingdom of God Has No Borders: A Global History of American Evangelicals.* Oxford: Oxford University Press.

    2018b. 'How Does Conservative Evangelicalism Engage Alt-Right Views?' *Berkley Center for Religion, Peace and World Affairs. Berkley Forum: Christianity and the Alt-Right in America.* At https://berkleycenter.georgetown.edu/responses/taking-on-the-alt-right-theological-considerations.

McCulloch, T. 2006. 'The Nouvelle Droite in the 1980s and 1990s: Ideology and Entryism, the Relationship with the Front National.' *French Politics* 4, no. 2: 158–78.

McDonnell, D. 2016. 'Populist Leaders and Coterie Charisma.' *Political Studies* 64, no. 3: 719–33.

McDougall, W. A. 1997. *Promised Land, Crusader State: The American Encounter with the World since 1776.* Boston, MA: Houghton Mifflin Harcourt.

    2017. 'Does Donald Trump Believe in American Civil Religion? If So, Which One?' *Foreign Policy Research Institute.* At www.fpri.org/article/2017/02/donald-trump-believe-american-civil-religion-one/.

McLoughlin, William G. 2013. *Revivals, Awakening and Reform.* Chicago: University of Chicago Press.

McQuarrie, Michael. 2016. 'Trump and the Revolt of the Rust Belt. USApp – LSE Blog.' *American Politics and Policy Blog.* At https://blogs.lse.ac.uk/usappblog/2016/11/11/23174/.

Meguid, Bonnie M. 2005. 'Competition between Unequals: The Role of Mainstream Party Strategy in Niche Party Success.' *American Political Science Review* 99, no. 3: 347–59.

Meier, Kurt. 1984. *Der evangelische Kirchenkampf, Vol. I–III.* Halle (Saale): VEB Niemeyer.

Melkonian-Hoover, Ruth M., and Lyman A. Kellstedt. 2018. *Evangelicals and Immigration: Fault Lines among the Faithful.* New York: Springer.

    2019. 'Populism, Evangelicalism, and the Polarized Politics of Immigration.' *The Review of Faith & International Affairs* 17, no. 3: 50–67.

Mény, Y., and Y. Surel. 2002. *Democracies and the Populist Challenge.* New York: Palgrave.

Menzel, Björn. 2014. 'Schwarz-Rot-Dumpf.' *Der Spiegel,* 22 December. At www.spiegel.de/politik/deutschland/anti-islam-demo-pegida-demonstranten-singen-stille-nacht-in-dresden-a-1010039.html.

Messiha, Jean. 2019. 'Twitter Post from the 15th April 2019.' *Twitter.* At https://twitter.com/jeanmessiha/status/1117889259862515713?lang=fr.

Mestre, A., and C. Monnot. 2015. 'Les Reseaux du Front National.' In S. Crépon, ed. *Les faux-semblants du Front National: Sociologie d'un parti politique.* Paris: Presses de Sciences Po.

Michelon, Vincent. 2018. 'Macron Veut 'Réparer Le Lien Entre l'Eglise et l'Etat' et Suscite de Très Vives Réactions.' *LCI,* 19 April. At www.lci.fr/politique/emmanuel-macron-veut-reparer-le-lien-entre-l-eglise-et-l-etat-et-suscite-de-vives-reactions-bernardins-eglise-catholique-2084090.html.

Milet, Jean-Philippe. 2014. 'L'extrême Droite Pour Tous.' *Lignes no.* 3: 43–56.

Mills, W. 1959. *The Sociological Imagination*. Oxford: Oxford University Press.

Modood, Tariq, ECPR London, and Erik Bleich. 2019. 'Essays on Secularism and Multiculturalism.' *Religion, State & Society* 47, nos. 4–5: 508–12.

Moffitt, B., and S. Tormey. 2014. 'Rethinking Populism: Politics, Mediatisation and Political Style.' *Political Studies* 62: 381–97.

Mongin, Olivier. 2018. 'Le Président Macron, l'Église et La Question Intranquille Du Salut.' *Commentaire* 2: 299–302.

Montgomery, Kathleen, and Ryan Winter. 2015. 'Explaining the Religion Gap in Support for Radical Right Parties in Europe.' *Politics and Religion* 8, no. 2: 379–403.

Mooney, Michael J. 2019. 'Trump's Apostle.' Texas Monthly, August. At www.texasmonthly.com/articles/donald-trump-defender-dallas-pastor-robert-jeffress/.

Moore, D. 2007. *Overcoming Religious Illiteracy: A Cultural Studies Approach to the Study of Religion in Secondary Education*. New York: Springer.

Moore, Russel. 2015. 'Russell Moore: Why Christians Must Speak out against Donald Trump's Muslim Remarks.' *Washington Post*, 8 December. At www.washingtonpost.com/news/acts-of-faith/wp/2015/12/07/russell-moore-people-who-care-an-iota-about-religious-liberty-should-denounce-donald-trump/.

Moran, Lee. 2019. 'Donald Trump Gets Stumped by Easy Bible Questions In Newly Resurfaced Video.' Huffington Post, 23 August. At www.huffingtonpost .co.uk/entry/donald-trump-bible-questions-old-video_n_5d5fc45be4b0b59d 25732db3?rii8n=true.

More in Common. 2017. 'Les Français et Leurs Perceptions de l'Immigration, Des Réfugiés et de l'Identité.' IFOP for More in Common. At www.ifop.com/ publication/les-francais-et-leurs-perceptions-de-limmigration-des-refugies-et-de-lidentite/.

2018. 'Perceptions et Attitudes Des Catholiques de France Vis-à-Vis Des Migrants.' IFOP for More in Common. At www.secours-catholique.org/ sites/scinternet/files/publications/rapport-mic-0606-bd_0.pdf.

Moreton, B. 2015. "Knute Gingrich, All American? White Evangelicals, U.S. Catholics, and the Religious Genealogy of Political Realignment.' In A. Preston, B. Schulman and J. Zelizer, eds. *Faithful Republic*. Philadelphia: University of Pennsylvania Press.

Morieson, N. 2017. 'Religion and Identity at the 2017 Dutch Elections.' *E-International Relations*. At www.e-ir.info/2017/03/26/ religion-and-identity-at-the-2017-dutch-elections/.

Morin, Rich, Becka A. Alper, Gregory A. Smith, Alan Cooperman and Anna Schiller. 2018. 'The Religious Typology: A New Way to Categorize Americans by Religion.' Pew Research Center. At www.pewforum.org/2018/08/29/ the-religious-typology/.

Morning Consult. 2020. 'National Tracking Poll.' Morning Consult. At https:// assets.morningconsult.com/wp-uploads/2020/06/01181629/2005131_ crosstabs_POLICE_RVs_FINAL_LM-1.pdf.

Moten, Abdul Rashid. 2018. 'US Embassy in Jerusalem: Reasons, Implications and Consequences.' *Intellectual Discourse* 26, no. 1: 5–22.

Mudde, Cas. 1996. 'The War of Words Defining the Extreme Right Party Family.' *West European Politics* 19, no. 2: 225–48.

2003. *'Die Republikaner': The Ideology of the Extreme Right.* Manchester: Manchester University Press.

2004. 'The Populist Zeitgeist.' *Government and Opposition* 39, no. 4: 541–63.

2007. *Populist Radical Right Parties in Europe.* Cambridge: Cambridge University Press.

2010. 'The Populist Radical Right: A Pathological Normalcy.' *West European Politics* 33, no. 6: 1167–86.

2014a. 'Populism and Political Leadership.' In P. Hart, C. Mudde, R. Kaltwasse and R. Rhodes, eds. *The Oxford Handbook of Political Leadership.* Oxford: Oxford University Press.

2014b. 'The European Parliament Elections Show the Increasingly Fragmented Nature of European Party Systems.' *LSE Blogs.* At http://eprints.lse .ac.uk/71922/1/blogs.lse.ac.uk-The%20European%20Parliament%20 elections%20show%20the%20increasingly%20fragmented%20nature%20 of%20European%20party%20systems.pdf.

2015. 'Conclusion: Some Further Thoughts on Populism.' In C. Torre and Andrew Arato, eds. *The Promise and Perils of Populism: Global Perspectives.* Lexington: University Press of Kentucky.

2016. 'The Study of Populist Radical Right Parties: Towards a Fourth Wave.' *C-Rex Working Paper Series* 1, no. 2016. 1–23.

2017. 'Populism: An Ideational Approach.' In Cristóbal Rovira Kaltwasser, Paul Taggart, Paulina Espejo and Pierre Ostiguy, eds. *The Oxford Handbook of Populism*, 1st ed. Oxford: Oxford University Press.

Mudde, Cas, and Cristóbal Rovira Kaltwasser. 2012. *Populism in Europe and the Americas: Threat or Corrective for Democracy?* Cambridge: Cambridge University Press.

2015. 'Vox Populi or Vox Masculini? Populism and Gender in Northern Europe and South America.' *Patterns of Prejudice* 49: 1–21.

2017. *Populism: A Very Short Introduction.* Oxford: Oxford University Press.

Müller, J. W. 2013. 'Towards a New History of Christian Democracy.' *Journal of Political Ideologies* 18, no. 2: 243–55.

2017. *What Is Populism?* London: Penguin.

2018a. 'Aus dem Zelt pissen' in Süddeutsche Zeitung. At www.sueddeutsche .de/kultur/europa-politik-aus-dem-zelt-pissen-1.4124979.

2018b. 'What Happens When an Autocrat's Conservative Enablers Finally Turn on Him?' The Atlantic 13, no. 9. At www.theatlantic.com/international/ archive/2018/09/orban-hungary-europe-populism-illiberalism/570136/.

Murphy, Andrew R. 2001. *Conscience and Community: Revisiting Toleration and Religious Dissent in Early Modern England and America.* Philadelphia: University of Pennsylvania Press.

NAE. 2015. 'Rubio Leads List for Evangelical Leaders; Many Undecided.' *National Association of Evangelicals.* At www.nae.net/rubio-leads-list-for-evangelical-leaders-many-undecided/.

2018. 'For the Health of the Nation: An Evangelical Call to Civic Responsibility.' National Association of Evangelcials. At www.nae.net/for-the-health-of-the-nation/.

2019. 'NAE Appoints Walter Kim as Next President.' National Association of Evangelicals, 17 October. At www.nae.net/nae-appoints-walter-kim-as-next-president/.

NCC. 2016. *National Council of the Churches of Christ in the U.S.A.* Nashville: Abingdon Press.

2020. 'Priorities.' *National Council of Churches.* At https://nationalcouncilofchurches.us/priorities/.

Nestler, C., and J. Rohgalf. 2017. 'Circling the Wagons: The Alternative Für Deutschland and the Rise of Eurosceptic Populism.' In C. Karner and M. Kapytowska, eds. *Germany in National Identity and Europe in Times of Crisis: Doing and Undoing Europe.* Bingley: Emerald Publishing Limited.

Neu, V. 2012. 'Religion, Kirchen und Gesellschaft.' Konrad Adenauer Stiftung. At www.kas.de/de/einzeltitel/-/content/-religion-kirchen-und-gesellschaft-online-publikation-.

Neuville, Heloïse de. 2021. 'Ces Catholiques Conservateurs Séduits Par Éric Zemmour.' *La Croix*, 1 December. At www.la-croix.com/France/catholiques-conservateurs-seduits-Eric-Zemmour-2021-12-01-1201187905.

Nicolet, S., and A. Tresch. 2009. 'Changing Religiosity, Changing Politics? The Influence of "Belonging" and "Believing" on Political Attitudes in Switzerland.' *Politics and Religion* 2, no. 1: 76–99.

Nilsson, Per-Erik. 2015. '"Secular Retaliation": A Case Study of Integralist Populism, Anti-Muslim Discourse, and (Il)Liberal Discourse on Secularism in Contemporary France.' *Politics, Religion & Ideology* 16, no. 1: 1–20.

Norris, Pippa, and Ronald Inglehart. 2011. *Sacred and Secular: Religion and Politics Worldwide.* Cambridge: Cambridge University Press.

2016. 'Trump, Brexit, and the Rise of Populism: Economic Have-Nots and Cultural Backlash.' Faculty Research Working Paper Series, Harvard Kennedy School.

2019. *Cultural Backlash: Trump, Brexit, and Authoritarian Populism.* Cambridge: Cambridge University Press.

Nortey, Justin. 2021. 'Most White Americans Who Regularly Attend Worship Services Voted for Trump in 2020.' Pew Research Center. At www.pewresearch.org/fact-tank/2021/08/30/most-white-americans-who-regularly-attend-worship-services-voted-for-trump-in-2020/.

Nouvel Observateur. 2016. 'Mariage Homo: Entre Le FN et La Manif Pour Tous, La Guerre Est Déclarée.' *Nouvel Observateur*, 14 April. At www.nouvelobs.com/politique/mariage-gay-lesbienne/20160414.OBS8516/mariage-homo-entre-le-fn-et-la-manif-pour-tous-la-guerre-est-declaree.html.

2022. 'Christine Lagarde, Citée Pour Devenir Sa Première Ministre, Décorée Par Emmanuel Macron.' Nouvel Observateur, 13 February. At www.nouvelobs .com/election-presidentielle-2022/20220213.OBS54412/christine-lagarde-citee-pour-devenir-sa-premiere-ministre-decoree-par-emmanuel-macron .html#modal-msg.

Nussbaum, Martha. 2008. *Liberty of Conscience: In Defense of America's Tradition of Religious Equality.* New York: Basic Books.

Observatoire de la Laïcité. 2019. 'État Des Lieux de La Laïcité En France.' *Viavoice Paris.* At www.gouvernement.fr/etat-des-lieux-de-la-laicite-en-france-2020-sondage-realise-par-viavoice-pour-l-observatoire-de-la.

Ohlert, M. 2014. *Zwischen 'Multikulturalismus' und 'Leitkultur': Integrationsleitbild und-politik der im 17. Deutschen Bundestag vertretenen Parteien.* Berlin: Springer.

Olsen, Henry. 2017. *The Working Class Republican: Ronald Reagan and the Return of Blue-Collar Conservatism.* New York: HarperCollins.

Olsen, Henry, and Dante Scala. 2016. *The Four Faces of the Republican Party and the Fight for the 2016 Presidential Nomination.* New York: Springer.

Olson, David T. 2008. *The American Church in Crisis: Groundbreaking Research Based on a National Database of over 200,000 Churches.* Grand Rapids: Zondervan.

Orr, Gaby. 2020. 'How Biden Swung the Religious Vote.' Politico, 11 November. At www.politico.com/news/2020/11/11/how-biden-swung-the-religious-vote-435954?fbclid=IwAR3PaDq8OuRAbkKxvL9Cxdkh u_b-ZXojhjiPjwZio_zEzz7L9b9WqadTU40.

Orth, S., and V. Resing. 2017. *AfD, Pegida & Co.: Angriff auf die Religion?* Freiburg: Herder Verlag.

Ott, Craig, and Juan Carlos Téllez. 2019. 'The Paradox of American Evangelical Views on Immigration: A Review of the Empirical Research.' *Missiology* 47, no. 3: 252–68.

Ozouf, Mona. 1992. *L'École, l'Église et La République: 1871–1914.* Vol. 165. Paris: Le Seuil.

Pacelle, Richard. 2019. *The Transformation of the Supreme Court's Agenda: From the New Deal to the Reagan Administration.* London: Routledge.

Pakulski, J., and M. Waters. 1996. *The Death of Class.* London: Sage.

Parrot, Clément. 2017. 'Le Front National Est-Il Vraiment Devenu "Gay Friendly"?' *France Info*, 12 March. At www.francetvinfo.fr/politique/marine-le-pen/le-front-national-est-il-vraiment-devenu-gay-friendly_2061745.html.

Pauwels, T. 2014. *Populism in Western Europe: Comparing Belgium, Germany and the Netherlands.* Abingdon: Routledge.

Pelletier, Denis, and Jean-Louis Schlegel. 2012. *À La Gauche Du Christ: Les Chrétiens de Gauche En France de 1945 à Nos Jours.* Paris: Le Seuil.

Perrineau, Pascal. 2014. *La France au Front.* Paris: Fayard.

2017. *Cette France de gauche qui vote FN.* Paris: Le Seuil.

Pestalozza, Christian. 1981. *Der Popularvorbehalt: direkte Demokratie in Deutschland.* Vol. 69. Berlin: Walter de Gruyter.

Pew Research Center. 2008. 'How the Faithful Voted.' Pew Research Center. At www.pewforum.org/2008/11/05/how-the-faithful-voted/.

2016a. 'Religious Landscape Study 2016.' Pew Research Center. At www .pewforum.org/religious-landscape-study/party-affiliation/.

2016b. 'For GOP Voters, a Winding Path to a Trump Nomination.' Pew Research Center. At www.people-press.org/2016/07/18/for-gop-voters-a-winding-path-to-a-trump-nomination/.

2017a. 'Support for Same-Sex Marriage Grows, Even Among Groups That Had Been Skeptical.' Pew Research Center. At www.people-press.org/2017/06/26/ support-for-same-sex-marriage-grows-even-among-groups-that-had-been-skeptical/.

2017b. 'Americans Express Increasingly Warm Feelings Toward Religious Groups.' Pew Research Center. At www.pewforum.org/2017/02/15/ americans-express-increasingly-warm-feelings-toward-religious-groups/.

2018. 'Being Christian in Western Europe.' Pew Research Center. At www .pewforum.org/2018/05/29/being-christian-in-western-europe/.

2019a. 'In U.S., Decline of Christianity Continues at Rapid Pace.' Pew Research Center. At www.pewforum.org/2019/10/17/in-u-s-decline-of-christianity-continues-at-rapid-pace/.

2019b. 'Partisan Antipathy: More Intense, More Personal.' Pew Research Center. At www.people-press.org/2019/10/10/partisan-antipathy-more-intense-more-personal/.

2020. 'White Evangelicals See Trump as Fighting for Their Beliefs, Though Many Have Mixed Feelings About His Personal Conduct.' Pew Research Center. At www.pewforum.org/2020/03/12/white-evangelicals-see-trump-as-fighting-for-their-beliefs-though-many-have-mixed-feelings-about-his-personal-conduct/.

Pfahl-Traughber, Armin. 2020. 'Die AfD Ist (Mittlerweile) Eine Rechtsextremistische Partei.' *Sozial Extra* 44, no. 2: 87–91.

Pickel, G. 2018. 'Religion als Ressource für Rechtspopulismus? Zwischen Wahlverwandtschaften und Fremdzuschreibungen.' *Zeitschrift Für Religion, Gesellschaft und Politik* 2, no. 2: 277–312.

Piketty, Thomas. 2015. *The Economics of Inequality.* Cambridge, MA: Harvard University Press.

2020. *Capital and Ideology.* Cambridge, MA: Harvard University Press.

Pokorny, S. 2018. 'Von A wie Angst bis Z wie Zuversicht: Eine repräsentative Untersuchung zu Emotionen und politischen Einstellungen in Deutschland nach der Bundestagswahl 2017.' *Analysen & Argumente.* At www.kas .de/de/analysen-und-argumente/detail/-/content/von-a-wie-angst-bis-z-wie-zuversicht1.

Pollack, Detlev, and Gergely Rosta. 2017. *Religion and Modernity: An International Comparison.* Oxford: Oxford University Press.

Portier, Philippe. 2011. 'Nouvelle modernite, nouvelle laicite. La republique francaise face au religieux (1880–2009).' *Estudos De Religiao* 25, no. 41: 43–56.

2016. *L'État et les religions en France: Une sociologie historique de la laïcité.* Rennes, France: Série.

Portier, Philippe, and Jean-Paul Willaime. 2012. 'Les mutations du religieux dans la France contemporaine.' *Social Compass* 59, no. 2: 193–207.
Poupard, Cardinal Paul. 1986. 'La France Fille Aînée de l'Église.' *Revue Des Deux Mondes*: 37–45.
Powers, Thomas F. 2010. 'Unsettling Faith: The Radicalization of the First Amendment and Its Consequences.' In Ronald Weed and John von Heyking, eds. *Civil Religion in Political Thought: Its Perennial Questions and Enduring Relevance in North America*. Washington, DC: Catholic University of America Press.
Preston, A. 2012. *Sword of the Spirit, Shield of Faith: Religion in American War and Diplomacy*. New York: Penguin.
Prévotat, Jacques, and René Rémond. 2001. *Les Catholiques et l'Action Française: Histoire d'une Condamnation, 1899–1939*. Vol. 744. Paris: Fayard.
Priol, Mélinée Le. 2019. 'Contre La Loi de Bioéthique, l'appel de Plusieurs Évêques.' *La Croix*, 25 September. At www.la-croix.com/Religion/Catholicisme/France/Contre-loi-bioethique-lappel-plusieurs-eveques-2019-09-25-1201049849.
Prissette, Nicolas. 2017. *Emmanuel Macron Le Président Inattendu*. Paris: First.
Projet Revue. 2016. 'Extrême Droite: Écouter, Comprendre, Agir.' *Eclairer l'avenir* 354. At www.revue-projet.com/questions-en-debat/extreme-droite-ecouter-comprendre-agir/320.
Pruvot, Samuel. 2016. *Le Mystère Sarkozy: Les Religions, Les Valeurs et Les Femmes*. Monaco: Editions du Rocher.
   2017. 'Christophe Billan: "Le Pen Ou Macron, c'est Le Choix Entre Le Chaos et Le Pourrissement".' *Famille Chrétienne*, 23 April. At www.famillechretienne.fr/politique-societe/presidentielle-2017/christophe-billan-le-pen-ou-macron-c-est-le-choix-entre-le-chaos-et-le-pourrissement-217073.
Putnam, R. D. 2000. *Bowling Alone: The Collapse and Revival of American Community*. New York and London: Simon & Schuster.
Putnam, Robert D. 2016. *Our Kids: The American Dream in Crisis*. New York: Simon & Schuster.
Putnam, Robert D., and David E. Campbell. 2012. *American Grace: How Religion Divides and Unites Us*. New York: Simon & Schuster.
Püttmann, A. 1994. *Ziviler Ungehorsam und christliche Bürgerloyalität: Konfession und Staatsgesinnung in der Demokratie des Grundgesetzes*. Paderborn: Schöningh.
   2016a. 'Was ist die AfD.' In V. Riesing and S. Orth, eds. *AfD, Pegida & Co.: Angriff auf die Religion?* Freiburg: Herder Verlag.
   2016b. 'Was ist die AfD – und wie mit ihr umgehen?' At www.stimmenderzeit.de/zeitschrift/ausgabe/details.
Pytlas, B. 2015. *Radical Right Parties in Central and Eastern Europe: Mainstream Party Competition and Electoral Fortune*. London: Routledge.
Rappeport, Alan, and Charlie Savage. 2016. 'Donald Trump Releases List of Possible Supreme Court Picks.' *New York Times*, 18 May. At www.nytimes.com/2016/05/19/us/politics/donald-trump-supreme-court-nominees.html?auth=login-email&login=email.

Raynaud, Philippe. 2019. 'L'état de La Droite.' *Commentaire* 3: 652–54.

2021. 'Le Cas Zemmour.' *Commentaire* 176, no. 4: 729–36.

Rebenstorf, H. 2018. '"Rechte" Christen? – Empirische Analysen zur Affinität christlich-religiöser und rechtspopulistischer Positionen.' *Zeitschrift Für Religion, Gesellschaft und Politik* 2, no. 2: 277–312.

Reckwitz, A. 2018. *Die Gesellschaft der Singularitäten: Zum Strukturwandel der Moderne*. Berlin: Suhrkamp.

Rein, Mildred. 2020. 'The End of Ideology, and the Choice for a Democratic Nominee for President.' *Challenge* 63, no. 4: 239–42.

Rémond, René. 2014. *Les Droites En France*. Paris: Aubier.

Rensmann, Lars. 2011. '"Against Globalism": Counter-Cosmopolitan Discontent and Antisemitism in Mobilizations of European Extreme Right Parties.' In L. Rensmann and J. Schoeps, eds. *Politics and Resentment*. Leiden: Brill.

Ribadeau Dumas, Olivier. 2017. 'Élections Présidentielles: L'Église Redit Son Rôle et Rappelle Ses Fondamentaux.' *Conférence Des Évêques de France*. At https://eglise.catholique.fr/espace-presse/communiques-de-presse/438036-elections-presidentielles-leglise-redit-son-role-et-rappelle-ses-fondamentaux/.

Ribberink, E., P. Achterberg and D. Houtman. 2017. 'Secular Tolerance? Anti-Muslim Sentiment in Western Europe.' *Journal for the Scientific Study of Religion* 56, no. 2: 259–76.

Ricard, Jean-Pierre. 2002. 'Discerner Les Valeurs Fondatrices de La Démocratie.' *Conférence Des Évêques de France*, 22 April. At https://eglise.catholique .fr/espace-presse/communiques-de-presse/368871-discerner-les-valeurs-fondatrices-de-la-democratie/.

Richard, Gilles. 2017. *Histoire Des Droites En France (1815–2017)*. Paris: Perrin.

Riehl, Katharina. 2021. 'Der Koalitionsvertrag Ist Eine Gesellschaftspolitische Wende.' Die Zeit, 26 November. At www.sueddeutsche.de/meinung/ampel-koalition-koalitionsvertrag-spd-gruene-fdp-cdu-1.5473011?reduced=true.

Ringshausen, Gerhard. 2014. 'Widerstand und Die Krichen.' In Philipp Thull, ed. *Christen Im Dritten Reich*. Darmstadt: Wissenschaft Buchgesellschaft.

Risse, Mathias. 2020. 'On American Values, Unalienable Rights, and Human Rights: Some Reflections on the Pompeo Commission.' *Ethics & International Affairs* 34, no. 1: 13–31.

Robien, Mathilde de. 2021. 'VG, PMA Pour Toutes, Peine de Mort … Ce Qu'en Pense Éric Zemmour.' *Aletia*, 10 December. At https://fr.aleteia.org/2021/12/10/ivg-pma-pour-toutes-peine-de-mort-ce-quen-pense-eric-zemmour/.

Rodrik, D. 2018. 'Populism and the Economics of Globalization.' *Journal of International Business Policy* 2018. At https://drodrik.scholar.harvard.edu/files/dani-rodrik/files/populism_and_the_economics_of_globalization.pdf.

Rose, Matthew. 2021. *A World After Liberalism: Philosophers of the Radical Right*. New Haven, CT: Yale University Press.

Rosenberg, Emma. 2021. 'Rally around the Steeple: Christian Democratic and Nativist Party Religious Rhetoric in Austria, Germany, and Switzerland.' Conference paper presented at the International Conference Celebrating 60 Years of Teaching and Researching International Relations in Slovenia.

Rothwell, J., and P. Diego-Rosell. 2016. 'Explaining Nationalist Political Views: The Case of Donald Trump.' Available at SSRN 2822059, http://dx.doi .org/10.2139/ssrn.2822059.

Rougé, Matthieu. 2018. 'Situation Politique Des Catholiques.' *Le Debat* 2: 78–87.

2019. 'Mgr Rougé: "Et La France Se Souvint Qu'elle Était Chrétienne".' *Le Figaro*, 17 April. At www.lefigaro.fr/vox/societe/mgr-rouge-et-la-france-se-souvint-qu-elle-etait-chretienne-20190417.

Roussel, Éric. 2002. *Charles de Gaulle*. Paris: Gallimard.

Roy, Olivier. 2008. *La Sainte Ignorance: Le temps de la religion sans culture*. Paris: Le Seuil.

2016. 'The French National Front: From Christian Identity to Laïcité.' In Nadia Marzouki, Duncan McDonnell and Olivier Roy, eds. *Saving the People: How Populists Hijack Religion*. London: Hurst.

2018. '"A Kitsch Christianity": Populists Gather Support While Traditional Religiosity Declines.' *LSE Blog: Religion & Global Society*. At http://blogs.lse .ac.uk/religionglobalsociety/2018/10/a-kitsch-christianity-populists-gather-support-while-traditional-religiosity-declines/.

2019. *L'Europe est-elle chrétienne*. Paris: Le Seuil.

Roy, Olivier, Duncan McDonnell and Nadia Marzouki, eds. 2016. *Saving the People: How Populists Hijack Religion*. London: Hurst & Company.

rtl.fr. 2014. 'Marine Le Pen Inquiète Des Persécutions Anti-Chrétiennes.' *Rtl.Fr*, 18 May. At www.rtl.fr/actu/politique/marine-le-pen-inquiete-des-persecutions-anti-chretiennes-7772088512.

Rupar, Aaron. 2019. '*Christianity Today* Made a Moral Case That Trump Needs to Go. He Responded by Proving Its Point.' *Vox*, 20 December. At www.vox.com/2019/12/20/21031611/christianity-today-trump-removal-editorial-response-mark-galli.

Rydgren, Jens. 2005. *Movements of Exclusion: Radical Right-Wing Populism in the Western World*. Hauppauge: Nova Publishers.

2008. 'France: The Front National, Ethnonationalism and Populism.' In D. Albertazzi and D. McDonnell, eds. *Twenty-First Century Populism: The Spectre of Western Democracy*. London: Palgrave MacMillan.

2010. 'Radical Right-Wing Populism in Denmark and Sweden: Explaining Party System Change and Stability.' *The SAIS Review of International Affairs* 30, no. 1: 57–71.

2018. *The Oxford Handbook of the Radical Right*. Oxford: Oxford University Press.

Saint Clair, Frédéric. 2017. 'François Fillon Le Catholique: Pourquoi Manuel Valls n'a Rien Compris.' Le Figaro, January 9. At www.lefigaro.fr/ vox/politique/2017/01/09/31001–20170109ARTFIG00261-francois-fillon-le-catholique-pourquoi-manuel-valls-n-a-rien-compris.php.

Samuel, Lieu. 2009. 'Manichaeism.' In David Hunter and Susan Ashbrook Harvey, eds. *The Oxford Handbook of Early Christian Studies*. Oxford: Oxford University Press.

Sandel, Michael. 2020. *The Tyranny of Merit: What's Become of the Common Good?* London: Allen Lane.

Sandstrom, Aleksandra. 2017. 'Faith on the Hill. The Religious Composition of the 115th Congress.' *Pew Research Center* 3. At www.pewforum.org/2019/01/03/faith-on-the-hill-116/.

2019. 'Faith on the Hill. The Religious Composition of the 116th Congress.' *Pew Research Center* 3. At www.pewforum.org/2019/01/03/faith-on-the-hill-116/.

Sapin, Charles. 2019. 'Jean-Marie Le Pen, Inattendu Soutien de La PMA.' *Le Figaro*, 24 July. At www.lefigaro.fr/politique/le-scan/jean-marie-le-pen-inattendu-soutien-de-la-pma-20190723.

2022. 'Présidentielle 2022: Marion Maréchal et Éric Zemmour, Les Coulisses d'un Ralliement Imminent.' *Le Figaro*, 2 March. At www.lefigaro.fr/elections/presidentielles/presidentielle-2022-marion-marechal-et-eric-zemmour-les-coulisses-d-un-ralliement-imminent-20220302.

Sargent, Greg. 2016. 'Donald Trump Is Running as Christianity's Savior. And It Might Work.' New York Times, 19 January. At www.washingtonpost.com/blogs/plum-line/wp/2016/01/19/donald-trump-is-running-as-christianitys-savior-and-it-might-work/.

Sautreuil, Pierre. 2019. 'Nathalie Loiseau Critiquée Pour Avoir Invité La Presse à La Messe.' *La Croix*, 16 April. At www.la-croix.com/France/Politique/Nathalie-Loiseau-critiquee-avoir-invite-presse-messe-2019-04-16-1201015965.

Scarbrough, E. 1984. *Political Ideology and Voting: An Exploratory Study.* Oxford: Clarendon.

Schain, M., A. Zolberg and P. Hossay. 2002. *Shadows over Europe: The Development and Impact of the Extreme Right in Western Europe.* New York: Palgrave.

Scheliha, Arnulf von. 2019. 'Der Deutsche Protestantismus Auf Dem Weg Zur Demokratie.' In H. J. Große Kracht and G. Schreiber, eds. *Wechselseitige Erwartungslosigkeit?* Berlin: De Gruyter.

Schlaich, K., and M. Heckel. 1997. *Gesammelte Aufsätze: Kirche und Staat von Der Reformation Bis Zum Grundgesetz.* Heidelberg: Mohr Siebeck.

Schlegel, J. L. 2015. 'Le front national tourmente l'église catholique.' *Esprit* 10: 114–19.

Schmitt, C. 1929. *Der Begriff des Politischen.* Berlin: Duncker & Humblot.

Schwadel, Philip, and Gregory A. Smith. 2019. 'Evangelical Approval of Trump Remains High, but Other Religious Groups Are Less Supportive.' *Pew Research Center*, 18 March. At www.pewresearch.org/fact-tank/2019/03/18/evangelical-approval-of-trump-remains-high-but-other-religious-groups-are-less-supportive/.

Schwengler, Bernard. 2005. 'Le Clivage Électoral Catholique–Protestant Revisité (France, Allemagne Fédérale, Suisse).' *Revue Française de Science Politique* 55, no. 3: 381–413.

Schwörer, Jakob, and Belén Fernández-García. 2021. 'Religion on the Rise Again? A Longitudinal Analysis of Religious Dimensions in Election Manifestos of Western European Parties.' *Party Politics* 27, no. 6: 1160–71.

Scott, Eugene. 2015. 'Trump Believes in God, but Hasn't Sought Forgiveness.' *CNN*, 19 July. At https://edition.cnn.com/2015/07/18/politics/trump-has-never-sought-forgiveness/index.html.

Seippel, Paul. 1905. *Les Deux Frances et Leurs Origines Historiques*. Lausanne: Payot.

Seiterich, T. 2016. 'Neuer Kampf um das Christliche.' *Katholisch.de* 28, no. 4. At www.katholisch.de/aktuelles/standpunkt/neuer-kampf-um-das-christliche.

Sénécat, Adrien. 2019. 'Intox Sur l'origine de l'incendie de Notre-Dame de Paris.' *Le Monde*, 16 April. At www.lemonde.fr/les-decodeurs/article/2019/04/16/intox-sur-l-origine-de-l-incendie-de-notre-dame-de-paris_5450914_4355770.html.

Sennett, Richard. 1987. 'A Republic of Souls: Puritanism and the American Presidency.' *Harper's Magazine* 275: 41–46.

Senneville, Loup Besmond de. 2015. 'Pendant Vingt Ans, Le FN Condamné sans Appel Par l'Église.' *La Croix*, 28 August. At www.la-croix.com/Religion/Actualite/Pendant-vingt-ans-le-FN-condamne-sans-appel-par-l-Eglise-2015-08-28-1349225.

Sharlet, Jeff. 2008. *The Family: The Secret Fundamentalism at the Heart of American Power*. New York: HarperCollins.

Shields, J. 2004. '"An Enigma Still": Poujadism Fifty Years On.' *French Politics, Culture and Society* 22, no. 1: 36–56.

Showalter, B. 2016. 'Did 81 Percent of Evangelicals Really Vote for Trump? Not So Fast, Some Say.' *Christian Post*. At www.christianpost.com/news/81-percent-evangelicals-vote-trump-eric-teetsel-joe-carter-171542/.

Sides, John. 2017. 'Race, Religion, and Immigration in 2016: How the Debate over American Identity Shaped the Election and What It Means for a Trump Presidency.' *Insights from the 2016 VOTER Survey*. At www.voterstudygroup.org/publication/race-religion-immigration-2016.

Sides, John, Michael Tesler and Lynn Vavreck. 2017. 'The 2016 US Election: How Trump Lost and Won.' *Journal of Democracy* 28, no. 2: 34–44.

2019. *Identity Crisis: The 2016 Presidential Campaign and the Battle for the Meaning of America*. Princeton NJ: Princeton University Press.

Siegers, P., S. Franzmann and M. Hassan. 2016. 'The Religious and Spiritual Underpinnings of Party Choice in Christian Europe.' *Electoral Studies* 44: 203–13.

Siegers, Pascal, and Alexander Jedinger. 2021. 'Religious Immunity to Populism: Christian Religiosity and Public Support for the Alternative for Germany.' *German Politics* 30(2): 149–169.

Sievert, Sara. 2021. 'Hinter Dem Roten Vorhang: Die Harmonie in Scholz' SPD Hängt Am Seidenen Faden.' *Focus*, 17 September. At www.focus.de/politik/portraet-lars-klingbeil-aus-der-tiefen-krise-zum-umfragehoch-ueber-den-mann-der-die-spd-zusammenhaelt_id_24219888.html.

Silva, Eric O. 2019. 'Donald Trump's Discursive Field: A Juncture of Stigma Contests over Race, Gender, Religion, and Democracy.' *Sociology Compass* 13, no. 12: e12757.

Silvestri, S. 2009. 'Islam and Religion in the EU Political System.' *West European Politics* 32, no. 6: 1212–39.

Skillen, James. 2020. 'Civil–Religious Nationalism in Protestant-Influenced Countries.' Research paper presented at the Nationalism, Populism and Protestant Political Thought Conference, Cambridge, UK, 15–17 April.

Smietana, Bob. 2021. 'SBC Report Calls Never-Trumper Russell Moore's Agency a "Significant Distraction."' Religion News Service, 1 February. At https://religionnews.com/2021/02/01/report-calls-agency-led-by-never-trumper-russell-moore-a-significant-distraction-for-southern-baptists/.

Smith, A. 2008. *The Cultural Foundations of Nations: Hierarchy, Covenant and Republic*. Malden, MA: Blackwell Publishing.

Smith, A. D. 1991. *National Identity*. London: Penguin.

Smith, Christian. 2014. *Disruptive Religion: The Force of Faith in Social Movement Activism*. London: Routledge.

Smith, Gregory A. 2016. 'Many Evangelicals Favor Trump Because He Is Not Clinton.' Pew Research Center. At www.pewresearch.org/fact-tank/2016/09/23/many-evangelicals-favor-trump-because-he-is-not-clinton/.

2017. 'Among White Evangelicals, Regular Churchgoers Are the Most Supportive of Trump.' Pew Research Center. At www.pewresearch.org/fact-tank/2017/04/26/among-white-evangelicals-regular-churchgoers-are-the-most-supportive-of-trump/.

2021. 'More White Americans Adopted than Shed Evangelical Label during Trump Presidency, Especially His Supporters.' Pew Research Center. At www.pewresearch.org/fact-tank/2021/09/15/more-white-americans-adopted-than-shed-evangelical-label-during-trump-presidency-especially-his-supporters/.

Smith, Gregory A., Claire Gecewicz, Anna Schiller and Haley Nolan. 2019. 'Americans Have Positive Views about Religion's Role in Society, but Want It out of Politics.' Pew Research Center. At www.pewforum.org/2019/11/15/americans-have-positive-views-about-religions-role-in-society-but-want-it-out-of-politics/.

Smith, Gregory A., and Jessica Martinez. 2016. 'How the Faithful Voted: A Preliminary 2016 Analysis.' Pew Research Center. At www.pewresearch.org/fact-tank/2016/11/09/how-the-faithful-voted-a-preliminary-2016-analysis/.

Smith, Jonathan Z. 1998. 'Religion, Religions, Religious.' In Mark Taylor, ed. *Critical Terms for Religious Studies*. Chicago: University of Chicago Press.

Smith, Tom W., Michael Davern, Jeremy Freese and Stephen L. Morgan. 2019. 'General Social Surveys, 1972–2018.' General AUSocial Survey. At www.norc.org/Research/Projects/Pages/general-social-survey.aspx.

Sobolewska, Maria, and Robert Ford. 2020. *Brexitland: Identity, Diversity and the Reshaping of British Politics*. Cambridge: Cambridge University Press.

Soper, J., K. Dulk and S. Monsma. 2017. *The Challenge of Pluralism: Church and State in Six Democracies*. Lanham, MD: Rowman & Littlefield Publishers.

Sorauf, Frank Joseph. 2015. *The Wall of Separation: The Constitutional Politics of Church and State*. Princeton, NJ: Princeton University Press.

SPD. 2017. 'Zeit Für Mehr Gerechtigkeit. Unser Regierungsprogramm Für Deutschland.' *SPD*. At www.spd.de/fileadmin/Dokumente/Bundesparteitag_2017/Es_ist_Zeit_fuer_mehr_Gerechtigkeit-Unser_Regierungsprogramm.pdf.

SPD, Bündnis 90/Die Grünen and FDP. 2021. 'Koalitionsvertrag 2021: Mehr Fortschritt Wagen – Bündnis Für Freiheit, Gerechtigkeit und Nachhaltigkeit.' At www.spd.de/fileadmin/Dokumente/Koalitionsvertrag/Koalitionsvertrag_2021–2025.pdf.

Spector, Stephen. 2009. *Evangelicals and Israel: The Story of American Christian Zionism.* Oxford and New York: Oxford University Press.

Spektorowski, A. 2000. 'The French New Right: Differentialism and the Idea of Ethnophilian Exclusionism.' *Polity* 33, no. 2: 283–303.

Der Spiegel. 2017. 'Kirchen Gegen AfD-Parteitag: "Unser Kreuz Hat Keine Haken."' 19 April. At www.spiegel.de/panorama/gesellschaft/afd-parteitag-kirchen-unser-kreuz-hat-keine-haken-a-1143900.html.

Spierings, N., M. Lubbers and A. Zaslove. 2017. '"Sexually Modern Nativist Voters": Do They Exist and Do They Vote for the Populist Radical Right?' *Gender and Education* 29, no. 2: 216–37.

Squiers, Anthony. 2018. *The Politics of the Sacred in America: The Role of Civil Religion in Political Practice.* New York: Springer.

Stanley, B. 2008. 'The Thin Ideology of Populism.' *Journal of Political Ideologies* 13, no. 1: 95–110.

2016. 'The Schmopulism Filter.' *Medium.* At https://medium.com/@BDStanley/the-schmopulism-filter-ba52042f379.

Stanley, Timothy. 2012. *The Crusader: The Life and Tumultuous Times of Pat Buchanan.* New York: Palgrave.

Stark, Rodney. 1999. 'Secularization, RIP.' *Sociology of Religion* 60, no. 3: 249–73.

Stark, Rodney, and Laurence R. Iannaccone. 1994. 'A Supply-Side Reinterpretation of the "Secularization" of Europe.' *Journal for the Scientific Study of Religion* 33, no. 3: 230–52.

Steppart, Timo, and Jens Giesel. 2018. 'Wahlanalyse Bayern: Spätentscheider Verhindern Das Schlimmste Für CSU.' *F.A.Z.* At www.faz.net/aktuell/politik/wahl-in-bayern/wahlanalyse-nach-der-landtagswahl-in-bayern-15829201.html.

Stille, Alexander. 2014. 'An Anti-Gay-Marriage Tea Party, French Style?' *The New Yorker.*[Online]. Available: Www. Newyorker. Com/News/News-Desk/an-Anti-Gay-Marriage-Tea-Party-French-Style.

Strauß, Harald. 2017. 'Comparatively Rich and Reactionary: Germany between "Welcome Culture" and Re-Established Racism.' *Critical Sociology* 1, no. 3–10.

Street. 2016. 'Evangelicals Rally to Trump, Religious "Nones" Back Clinton.' *Pew Research Center's Religion & Public Life Project.* At www.pewforum.org/2016/07/13/evangelicals-rally-to-trump-religious-nones-back-clinton/.

Strohm, Christoph. 2011. *Die Kirchen im Dritten Reich.* Nürnberg: Beck.

Strum, Philippa, and Danielle Tarantolo. 2003. *Muslims in the United States.* Washington, DC: Woodrow Wilson International Center for Scholars.

Stubager, R. 2008. 'Education Effects on Authoritarian-Libertarian Values: A Question of Socialization.' *British Journal of Sociology* 59, no. 2: 327–50.

Sugy, Paul. 2019. 'Dégradations Dans Des Églises: "Les Chrétiens Doivent Faire Entendre Leur Voix".' Le Figaro, 13 February. At www.lefigaro.fr/vox/religion/2019/02/13/31004-20190213ARTFIG00216-degradations-dans-des-eglises-les-chretiens-doivent-faire-entendre-leur-voix.php.

Sullivan, Amy. 2008. *The Party Faithful: How and Why Democrats Are Closing the God Gap.* New York: Simon & Schuster.

Sunar, L. 2017. 'The Long History of Islam as a Collective "Other" of the West and the Rise of Islamophobia in the U.S. after Trump.' *Insight Turkey* 19, no. 3: 35–51.

Tabard, Guillaume. 2015. 'L'Église et le Front national: pour en finir avec un faux débat.' *Le Figaro.* At www.lefigaro.fr/vox/societe/2015/08/29/31003-20150829ARTFIG00141-l-eglise-et-le-front-national-pour-en-finir-avec-un-faux-debat.php.

Tagesschau. 2014. 'Der Konformistische Rebell.' *Tagesschau.* At www.tagesschau.de/europawahl/koepfe/portraet-lucke100.html.

2017. 'Wählerwanderung Bundestagswahl 2017.' *Tagesschau.* At www.tagesschau.de/wahl/archiv/2017-09-24-BT-DE/analyse-wanderung.shtml.

Taggart, P. 1996. *The New Populism and the New Politics: New Protest Parties in Sweden in a Comparative Perspective.* Basingstoke: Macmillan.

2000. *Populism.* Buckingham: Open University Press.

2006. 'Populism and Representative Politics in Contemporary Europe.' *Journal of Political Ideologies* 9, no. 3: 269–88.

Taguieff, P. 2017. *L'islamisme et nous: Penser l'ennemi imprévu.* Paris: CNRS Editions.

Taguieff, Pierre-André. 2017. *Macron: Miracle Ou Mirage?* Paris: Éditions de l'Observatoire.

Tartakowsky, Danielle. 2005. *La Part Du Rêve: Histoire Du 1er Mai En France.* Paris: Hachette.

Taylor, C. 2007. *A Secular Age.* Cambridge, MA: Harvard University Press.

Taylor, Jessica. 2016. 'Citing "Two Corinthians," Trump Struggles to Make the Sale to Evangelicals.' *National Public Radio.* At www.npr.org/2016/01/18/463528847/citing-two-corinthians-trump-struggles-to-make-the-sale-to-evangelicals?t=1595773343206.

Teague, Matthew. 2020. 'Trump's Bible Photo Op Splits White Evangelical Loyalists into Two Camps.' *The Guardian,* 4 June. At www.theguardian.com/us-news/2020/jun/04/trumps-bible-photo-op-splits-white-evangelicals.

Teinturier, Brice, Jean-François Doridot and Federico Vacas. 2021. 'Enquête Électorale 2022: Vague 3.' Paris: IPSOS. At www.ipsos.com/sites/default/files/ct/news/documents/2021-12/Rapport%20Ipsos_CEVIPOF%20LEMONDE%20FJJ%20_Enquête%20électorale%202022%20vague%203%20-%20Décembre%202021%20.pdf.

Teixeira, Ruy. 2009. 'The Coming End of the Culture Wars.' *Center for American Progress.* At https://cdn.americanprogress.org/wp-content/uploads/issues/2009/07/pdf/culture_wars.pdf.

Terra Nova. 2011. 'Gauche: Quelle Majoirté Électorale Pour 2012.' *Projet 2012.* At https://tnova.fr/democratie/politique-institutions/gauche-quelle-majorite-electorale-pour-2012/.

Tevanian, Pierre. 2013. *La Haine de La Religion: Comment l'athéisme Est Devenu l'opium Du Peuple de Gauche.* Paris: La Découverte.

Thielmann, Wolfgang. 2017. *Alternative für Christen? Die AfD und ihr gespaltenes Verhältnis zur Religion.* Neukirchen–Vluyn: Neukirchener Verlag.

Thieme, Daniel, and Antonius Liedhegener. 2015. '"Linksaußen", politische Mitte oder doch ganz anders? Die Positionierung der Evangelischen Kirche in Deutschland (EKD) im parteipolitischen Spektrum der postsäkularen Gesellschaft.' *Politische Vierteljahresschrift* 56, no. 2: 240–77.

Thompson, P. 2000. 'Jörg Haider, Tony Blair und der Wirtschaftsliberalismus.' *Berliner Debatte INITIAL* 11, no. 4: 93–100.

Timmons, Heather, and Simon Lewis. 2019. 'Trump's Row with *Christianity Today* Exposes Deep Issues with White Evangelical America.' *The Independent*, 29 December. At www.independent.co.uk/news/world/americas/trump-christianity-today-impeachment-twitter-ct-editorial-white-evangelical-christian-a9263571.html.

Tincq, Henri. 2015. 'Catholiques et Front National: La Fin Du Cordon Sanitaire?' Slate, 31 August. At www.slate.fr/story/106203/catholiques-et-front-national-la-fin-du-veto.

2017. 'Aujourd'hui j'ai Honte d'être Catholique.' *Slate*, 28 April. At www.slate.fr/story/144646/aujourdhui-jai-honte-detre-catholique.

Tocqueville, Alexis de. 1990. *Democracy in America.* New York: Vintage.

Todd, E. 2008. *Après la démocratie.* Paris: Folio Actuel.

Torre, C. 2013. 'The People, Populism, and The Leader's Semi-Embodied Power.' *Rubrica Contemporanea* 2, no. 3: 5–20.

Torre, C., ed. 2018. *Routledge Handbook of Global Populism.* London: Routledge.

Torre, C., and A. Arato, eds. 2015. *The Promise and Perils of Populism: Global Perspectives.* Lexington: University Press of Kentucky.

Trump, Donald. 2016. 'Liberty University Commencement Address.' *C-Span.* At www.c-span.org/video/?428429-1/president-trump-delivers-liberty-university-commencement-address&live.

Turner, B. S. 2011. *Religion and Modern Society: Citizenship, Secularisation and the State.* Cambridge: Cambridge University Press.

Ueberschär, Gerd. 2006. *Für ein anderes Deutschland: Der deutsche Widerstand gegen den NS-Staat 1933–1945.* Frankfurt am Main: Fischer Taschenbuch Verlag.

Ulrich, Anne, Olaf Kramer and Dietmar Till. 2022. *Populism and the Rise of the AfD in Germany.*" In Kock, C.; Villadsen, L. eds. *Populist Rhetorics.* London: Palgrave Macmillan.

USCCB. 2020. 'Bishops' Statements.' *United States Conference of Catholic Bishops.* At www.usccb.org/about/migration-policy/bishops-statements/index.cfm.

Vaillant, Gauthier. 2017. 'Présidentielle: Les Paroles d'évêques de l'entre-Deux Tours.' *La Croix*, 5 May. At www.la-croix.com/Religion/Catholicisme/France/Presidentielle-paroles-deveques-lentre-deux-tours-2017-05-04-1200844627.

2019. 'Après l'incendie de Notre-Dame, l'espérance Du Président et La Prière de l'archevêque.' *La Croix*, 16 April. At www.la-croix.com/Religion/Catholicisme/lincendie-Notre-Dame-lesperance-president-priere-larcheveque-2019-04-16-1201015954.

Valeurs Actuelles. 2020. 'Immigration: Pour Eric Zemmour, "Le Pape François Est Un Ennemi de l'Europe."' Valeurs Actuelles, 6 October. At www.valeursactuelles.com/monde/video-immigration-pour-eric-zemmour-le-pape-francois-est-un-ennemi-de-leurope/.

van der Brug, W., M. Fennema and J. Tillie. 2005. 'Why Some Anti-Immigrant Parties Fail and Others Succeed: A Two-Step Model of Aggregate Electoral Support.' *Comparative Political Studies* 38, no. 5: 537–73.

Van Kessel, S. 2015. *Populist Parties in Europe: Agents of Discontent?* London: Palgrave Macmillan.

van Norden, G. 1979. *Der Deutsche Protestantismus Im Jahr Der Nationalsozialistischen Machtergreifung*. Gütersloh: Mohn.

Vannoni, M. 2014. 'What Are Case Studies Good For? Nesting Comparative Case Study Research into the Lakatosian Research Program.' *Cross-Cultural Research* 49, no. 4: 331–57.

Védrine, Hubert. 2017. 'François Mitterrand et La Religion.' L'Institut Mitterrand, October. At www.mitterrand.org/IMG/pdf/Lettre_17_02.pdf.

Voorhees, Josh. 2016. 'Donald Trump Tried to Tip Jesus.' Slate, 1 February. At https://slate.com/news-and-politics/2016/02/donald-trump-mistook-a-communion-plate-for-an-offering-plate.html.

Vovelle, Michel. 2002. *La Révolution Contre l'Eglise: De La Raison à l'être Suprême*. Vol. 130. Brussels: Editions Complexe.

Wajahat, A. 2011. 'Fear Inc.: The Roots of the Islamophobia Network in America.' *Center for American Progress*. At www.americanprogress.org/issues/religion/reports/2011/08/26/10165/fear-inc/.

Wald, Kenneth D, and Allison Calhoun-Brown. 2014. *Religion and Politics in the United States*. Lanham, MD: Rowman & Littlefield.

Waldhoff, Christian. 2013. *Was Bedeutet Religiös-Weltanschauliche Neutralität Des Staates Unter Dem Grundgesetz?* Religion Im Öffentlichen Raum. Paderborn: Ferdinand Schöningh.

Walzer, M. 2019. *Terrorism: A Critique of Excuses*. Problems of International Justice. London: Routledge.

Washington Post. 2015. 'Full Text: Donald Trump Announces a Presidential Bid.' *Washington Post*, 16 June. At www.washingtonpost.com/news/post-politics/wp/2015/06/16/full-text-donald-trump-announces-a-presidential-bid/?arc404=true.

2017. '"Demonic Activity Was Palpable" at Trump's Rally, Pastor Says.' At www.washingtonpost.com/news/acts-of-faith/wp/2017/02/22/demonic-activity-palpable-at-president-trumps-rally-pastor-says/.

Wattenberg, M. 1998. *The Decline of American Political Parties, 1952–1996*. Cambridge, MA: Harvard University Press.

Wear, Michael. 2020. 'The Faithful Voters Who Helped Put Biden Over the Top.' New York Times, November 11. At www.nytimes.com/2020/11/11/opinion/biden-evangelical-voters.html?fbclid=IwAR3QHoufNQi8TXUpZowxsl9h9dLYbQDBCyzycoI9guXzrBaDZqVzeyqdRzY&login=email&auth=login-email&login=email&auth=login-email.

Wear, Michael R. 2017. *Reclaiming Hope: Lessons Learned in the Obama White House about the Future of Faith in America.* Nashville, TN: Thomas Nelson.

Weed, Ronald and John von Heyking, eds. *Civil Religion in Political Thought: Its Perennial Questions and Enduring Relevance in North America.* Washington, DC: Catholic University of America Press.

Wehler, H. U. 1994. *Das Deutsche Kaiserreich, 1871–1918.* 9 Vols. Göttingen: Vandenhoeck & Ruprecht.

Weichert, Rune. 2022. 'Queer Beauftrager: Herr Lehmann, Braucht Man Im Jahr 2022 Überhaupt Einen Queer-Beauftragten?' Der Stern, 25 January. At www.stern.de/politik/deutschland/queer-beauftragter-sven-lehmann–deutschland-hinkt-bei-anti-diskriminierung-zurueck–31567312.html.

Weiss, V. 2017. *Die autoritäre Revolte: Die Neue Rechte und der Untergang des Abendlandes.* Stuttgart: Klett-Cotta.

Die Welt. 2015. 'Dresdner Frauenkirche macht wegen Pegida das Licht aus.' Vol. 21 3. At www.welt.de/regionales/sachsen/article137271051/Dresdner-Frauenkirche-macht-wegen-Pegida-das-Licht-aus.html.

Wetzel, Jakob, and Matthias Drobinski. 2018. 'Kardinal Marx Wirft Söder Spaltung Vor.' *Süddeutsche Zeitung*, 29 April. At www.sueddeutsche.de/bayern/kreuz-erlass-kardinal-marx-wirft-soeder-spaltung-vor-1.3962223.

The White House. 2001. 'President George W. Bush's Inaugural Address.' At https://georgewbush-whitehouse.archives.gov/news/inaugural-address.html.

2009. 'President Barack Obama's Inaugural Address.' At https://obamawhitehouse.archives.gov/blog/2009/01/21/president-barack-obamas-inaugural-address.

2017. 'President Donald J. Trump's Inaugural Address.' At www.whitehouse.gov/briefings-statements/the-inaugural-address/.

Whitehead, Andrew L., and Samuel L. Perry. 2020. *Taking America Back for God: Christian Nationalism in the United States.* Oxford: Oxford University Press.

Whitehead, Andrew L., Samuel L. Perry and Joseph O. Baker. 2018. 'Make America Christian Again: Christian Nationalism and Voting for Donald Trump in the 2016 Presidential Election.' *Sociology of Religion* 79, no. 2: 147–71.

Wiese, Rebekka. 2021. 'Gar Nicht so Wenig Revolution.' Die Zeit, 25 November. At www.zeit.de/politik/deutschland/2021-11/ampel-koalition-gesellschaftspolitik-schwangerschaftsabbruch-selbstbestimmungsgesetz?utm_referrer=https%3A%2F%2Fwww.google.com%2F.

Wilcox, Clyde. 2018. *Onward Christian Soldiers? The Religious Right in American Politics.* New York: Routledge.

Wilcox, W. Bradford, Andrew J. Cherlin, Jeremy E. Uecker and Matthew Messel. 2012. 'No Money, No Honey, No Church: The Deinstitutionalization of Religious Life among the White Working Class.' *Research in the Sociology of Work* 23, no. 1: 227–50.

Wiliarty, Sarah E. 2021. 'Germany: How the Christian Democrats Manage to Adapt to the Silent Counter-Revolution.' In Tim Bale and Cristóbal Rovira Kaltwasser, eds. *Riding the Populist Wave: Europe's Mainstream Right in Crisis.* Cambridge: Cambridge University Press.

Willaime, Jean-Paul. 2008. *Le Retour Du Religieux Dans La Sphère Publique, Vers Une Laïcité de Reconnaissance et de Dialogue.* Lyon: Editions Olivétan.

Willaime, Jean-Paul, Claude Langlois and Louis Chatellier. 2009. *Lumières, Religions, Laïcité.* Paris: Riveneuve.

Wills, Garry. 1990. *Under God: Religion and American Politics.* New York and London: Simon and Schuster.

Winock, Michel. 2015. *Nationalisme, Antisémitisme et Fascisme En France.* Paris: Le Seuil.

2016. *François Mitterrand.* Paris: Gallimard.

Wohlrab-Sahr, Monika. 2003. 'Politik und Religion: Diskretes Kulturchristentum Als Fluchtpunkt Europäischer Gegenbewegungen Gegen Einen Ostentativen Islam.' In Armin Nasehi and Markus Schroer, eds. *Soziale Welt. Sonderband.* Baden-Baden: Nomos.

Wolff, Michael. 2018. *Fire and Fury.* London: Hachette UK.

Woodward, Bob. 2019. *Fear: Trump in the White House.* New York: Simon & Schuster.

Wormser, Gérard. 2017. 'La Grande Transformation: L'élection Présidentielle Française de 2017.' *Sens Public.* At www.erudit.org/fr/revues/sp/2017-sp03802/1048838ar.pdf.

Wuthnow, Robert. 1988. *The Restructuring of American Religion: Society and Faith since World War II.* Princeton NJ: Princeton University Press.

Yendell, A., E. Brähler, D. P. A. Witt, J. M. Fegert, M. Allroggen and P. D. O. Decker. 2018. 'Die Parteien und das Wählerherz.' Leipzig: Abteilung für Medizinische Psychologie und Medizinische Soziologie der Universität Leipzig. At www.kredo.uni-leipzig.de/download/0/0/1905898900/6512eee07f32ded120940f37a09c662d89108c53/fileadmin/www.kredo.uni-leipzig.de/uploads/dokumente/Die_Parteien_und_das_Waehlerherz_2018_Yendell_et_al.pdf.

Zander, H. 1989. *Die Christen und die Friedensbewegungen in beiden deutschen Staaten: Beiträge zu einem Vergleich für die Jahre 1978–1987.* Beiträge zur politischen Wissenschaft 54. Berlin: Duncker & Humblot.

Zemmour, Éric. 2016. 'Débat Zemmour – Humbrecht: "Les Catholiques Doivent Sortir de La Culpabilité".' *Famille Chretienne.* At www.famillechretienne.fr/foi-chretienne/vivre-en-chretien/debat-zemmour-humbrecht-les-catholiques-doivent-sortir-de-la-culpabilite-204964.

2019. 'Éric Zemmour: "Quand Le Brasier de Notre-Dame Enflamme Les Mémoires".' *Le Figaro*, 19 April. At www.lefigaro.fr/vox/societe/eric-zemmour-quand-le-brasier-de-notre-dame-enflamme-les-memoires-20190419.

2021. 'Le Programme D'Éric Zemmour.' Reconquête. At https://programme .zemmour2022.fr/.

Zemmour, Éric, and Gérard Leclerc. 2018. 'Zemmour: "Je Suis Imprégné Du Christianisme".' *France Catholique*, 14 December. At www.france-catholique .fr/Zemmour-Je-suis-impregne-du-christianisme.html.

Zúquete, José Pedro. 2017. 'Populism and Religion.' In Cristóbal Rovira Kaltwasser, Paul Taggart and Paulina Espejo, eds. *The Oxford Handbook of Populism*. Oxford: Oxford University Press.

2018. *The Identitarians: The Movement against Globalism and Islam in Europe*. Notre Dame, IN: University of Notre Dame Press.

Index